P9-DDF-141

Betty Crocker's
NEW
INTERNATIONAL
COOKBOOK

Betty Crocker's
NEW INTERNATIONAL COOKBOOK

PRENTICE HALL

NEW YORK LONDON TORONTO SYDNEY TOKYO SINGAPORE

Prentice Hall
15 Columbus Circle
New York, New York 10023

Copyright © 1989, 1994 by General Mills, Inc., Minneapolis, Minnesota

All rights reserved, including the right of reproduction in whole or in part in any form.

Published simultaneously in Canada by Prentice Hall Canada Inc.

PRENTICE HALL is a registered trademark and colophon is a trademark of Prentice-Hall, Inc.

BETTY CROCKER is a registered trademark of General Mills, Inc.

Library of Congress Cataloging-in-Publication Data

Crocker, Betty.
Betty Crocker's new international cookbook.

Includes index.
1. Cookery, International.   I. Title.   II. Title:
New international cookbook.
TX725.A1C662   1989   641.59   88-32378
ISBN 0-671-88763-7

Manufactured in the United States of America

10   9   8   7   6   5   4   3   2   1

First Revised Edition

CREDITS

GENERAL MILLS, INC.
Editor: Diana Gulden
Test Kitchen Home Economist: Mary Jane Friedhoff
Copy Editor: Susan Meyers
Editorial Assistant: Phyllis Weinbender
Food Stylists: Cindy Lund, Katie McElroy, Mary Sethre
Photographer: Nanci E. Doonan
Photography Assistant: Carolyn Luxmoore
Director, Betty Crocker Food and Publications Center: Marcia Copeland
Assistant Manager, Publications: Lois Tlusty

Preceding pages (*from top left*): Prosciutto-stuffed Artichokes (page 235), Roasted Pepper Salad (page 220) and Green Rice (page 274)

CONTENTS

FOREWORD

America loves to travel, and *Betty Crocker's International Cookbook* opens up a wide world of delicious foods from foreign lands. From far-flung Java and Australia, around the globe and back home to neighboring Canada, our tour covers more than fifty countries. Of course you will find international classics here from well-traveled lands—favorites from France, Italy, Spain, Portugal and Germany. There are also delightful and tempting dishes from savory stews to sweet desserts, collected here for you from Finland, Cyprus, Tanzania, Russia and far beyond.

Betty Crocker's International Cookbook is a celebration of fabulous food, and more. We share with you the traditions and spirit of people who have tended their land, pulled their fish from the sea and made their way through the centuries. A good many of the recipes are honest country cooking, and wherever possible, we make the preparation of these authentic dishes simpler and easier. We've also included nutrition information for your reference, to give you a hand in planning your meals.

We introduce you to foods and techniques that may be unfamiliar in a handy reference: the International Food Terms and Ingredients (page 359). Have you longed for a once-tasted unforgettable Greek dish of lamb and melting eggplant, but can't imagine how to find it again without knowing its name? Our special Regional Index will help you find it, so you can re-create it along with countless favorites you thought would never be more than memories.

To help you imagine what a dish will be like, served in foreign fashion or made up of uncommon ingredients, we have filled this volume with full-page, gorgeous photographs that suggest a lot of presentation ideas, too. These photographs, designed especially for this book, give you a glimpse at the transforming magic of exotic cookery.

The most remote corners of the globe have never been closer, and here at your fingertips is a sure-footed guide for an unforgettable tour. With Betty Crocker recipes comes the confidence of delicious success time after time. We hope you enjoy your travels with us, on this journey from South American grasslands sweet with birdsong to the hushed peaks of African mountains.

THE BETTY CROCKER EDITORS

Dutch Fried Puffs (page 347) and Dutch Apricot Compote (page 318)

HOW TO USE NUTRITION INFORMATION

The nutrition information per serving or unit for each recipe includes the amounts for calories, protein, carbohydrate, fat, cholesterol and sodium. You will find this information at the end of each recipe.

- If ingredient choices are given, such as "⅓ cup plain yogurt or sour cream," the first ingredient listed was used to calculate the nutrition information.
- When a range is given for an ingredient, such as "¼ to ½ teaspoon salt," the first amount listed was used for nutrition calculation.
- Ingredients referred to as "optional" or "if desired" are not included in the nutrition calculations, whether mentioned in the ingredient listing or in the recipe text as a suggestion.
- For recipe testing and nutrition calculations, large eggs, 2% milk and regular stick margarine (not tub or whipped) were used. No low-fat or nonfat ingredients were used unless stated in the recipe.

Betty Crocker's
NEW
INTERNATIONAL
COOKBOOK

1
APPETIZERS

Appetizers, snacks, starters or hors d'oeuvres . . . call them what you will, they often play an important role in international kitchens and are always received with pleasure. This collection offers a tempting array of morsels and soups, to serve hot or cold, for formal and casual occasions alike.

If a spectacular opener is what you have in mind, look no further than Flaming Cheese, hot and tangy with Greek Kasseri. For a hearty start, succulent Chinese Barbecued Ribs served with a hot mustard sauce are quick and satisfying. These recipes represent some of the most tantalizing favorites from more than twenty-five countries, including Jamaica, Finland, Morocco, Afghanistan, Turkey, Italy and Spain. The ingredients, though, can be found easily in most American supermarkets and specialty groceries.

Appetizers are a splendid solution to entertaining woes. A varied selection makes for memorable party food. Select a few recipes that can be prepared in advance and you are on your way to hosting an international event you will enjoy as much as your guests will.

Clockwise from top: Chicken Kabobs with Peanut Sauce (page 30), Marinated Gingered Shrimp (page 32) and Crisp Wontons (page 16)

CLEAR JAPANESE SOUP

SUIMONO (soo-ee-moh-noh)

Simple garnishes for this soup are typical of traditional Japanese aesthetics. Select them with an eye for color and trim them neatly, into fanciful shapes if you like. If using lemon peel, pare only the yellow part of the peel, avoiding the bitter white pith.

3 cups water
1 tablespoon instant chicken bouillon
1 teaspoon soy sauce
Garnishes (below)

Heat water, bouillon and soy sauce to boiling, stirring occasionally. Serve in small bowls; top with 1 to 3 Garnishes.

GARNISHES   Thinly sliced mushrooms, green onion strips, celery leaves, thinly sliced lemon or lime, thinly sliced carrot, strips of lemon or lime peel.

4 servings (¾ cup each)

PER SERVING: Calories 10; Protein 1 g; Carbohydrate 1 g; Fat 0 g; Cholesterol 0 mg; Sodium 1040 mg

AVOCADO BROTH

This East African soup combines a clear, flavorful broth with smooth, rich avocado. Choose an avocado that is still somewhat firm, without any soft spots. Dip avocado slices into lemon juice if not adding them to the broth immediately; it will keep them from discoloring.

2 cans (10½ ounces each) condensed beef broth
2 broth cans water

3 to 4 drops red pepper sauce
2 tablespoons lemon juice
1 large ripe avocado, thinly sliced

Heat beef broth, water, red pepper sauce and lemon juice just to boiling. Add avocado.

10 servings (½ cup each)

PER SERVING: Calories 40; Protein 1 g; Carbohydrate 2 g; Fat 3 g; Cholesterol 0 mg; Sodium 90 mg

EGG DROP SOUP

TAN HUA T'ANG (don hwa tong)

Here is a Chinese classic that makes for a slightly mysterious first course, with its light threads of egg in golden broth. Serve it piping hot.

5 cups water
1 tablespoon plus 2 teaspoons instant chicken bouillon
½ teaspoon salt
3 tablespoons cold water
1 tablespoon plus 1½ teaspoons cornstarch
1 egg, slightly beaten
2 scallions or green onions (with tops), diagonally sliced

Heat 5 cups water, the bouillon and salt to boiling in 2-quart saucepan. Mix 3 tablespoons water and the cornstarch; stir gradually into broth. Boil and stir 1 minute. Slowly pour egg into broth, stirring constantly with fork, to form threads of egg. Remove from heat; stir slowly once or twice. Garnish each serving with scallions.

6 servings (about ¾ cup each)

PER SERVING: Calories 30; Protein 2 g; Carbohydrate 3 g; Fat 1 g; Cholesterol 35 mg; Sodium 1250 mg

TORTILLA SOUP

SOPA DE TORTILLA (<u>soh</u>-pah deh tohr-<u>tee</u>-yah)

This Mexican soup features a rich broth and a garnish of fried tortilla strips. Corn tortillas, with a fresh corn flavor and slight crunch, are widely available fresh, frozen and even canned.

6 six-inch corn tortillas
¼ cup vegetable oil
¼ cup water
1 medium tomato, cut into fourths
1 small onion, cut into fourths
1 clove garlic
2 cans (10¾ ounces each) condensed chicken
   broth
1 broth can water
¼ teaspoon ground coriander
¼ teaspoon salt
⅛ teaspoon pepper
1 sprig mint (optional)
1 cup shredded Monterey Jack or Cheddar
   cheese

Cut tortillas into ¼-inch strips. Heat oil in 10-inch skillet until hot. Fry ¼ of the tortilla strips at a time over medium heat, stirring occasionally, until crisp and brown, about 3 minutes; drain.

Place ¼ cup water, the tomato, onion and garlic in blender container. Cover and blend on high speed until smooth. Heat tomato mixture, chicken broth, 1 can water, the coriander, salt, pepper and mint sprig to boiling in 3-quart saucepan. Cook uncovered 3 minutes. Sprinkle each serving with cheese and tortilla strips.

8 servings (¾ cup each)

PER SERVING: Calories 155; Protein 5 g; Carbohydrate 9 g; Fat 12 g; Cholesterol 15 mg; Sodium 320 mg

EGG AND LEMON SOUP

SOUPA AVGOLEMENO (<u>soo</u>-pah ahv-ghoh-<u>leh</u>-meh-noh)

The Greeks are not the only ones who enjoy this savory lemon soup, thickened with rice and egg. It is popular in North Africa and the Middle East, where it is known by its Arabic name, *Bied bi Lamoun.*

1 can (46 ounces) chicken broth
⅓ cup uncooked regular rice
¼ teaspoon salt
2 eggs, beaten
3 tablespoons lemon juice
2 tablespoons snipped parsley, chives or mint

Heat chicken broth, rice and salt to boiling in 3-quart saucepan, stirring once or twice; reduce heat. Cover and simmer until rice is tender, about 14 minutes.

Mix eggs and lemon juice. Stir ¼ cup of the hot broth mixture into egg mixture; stir into broth mixture in saucepan. Cook and stir over low heat until slightly thickened, 2 to 3 minutes. (Do not boil or eggs will curdle.) Garnish each serving with parsley.

6 servings (about 1 cup each)

PER SERVING: Calories 95; Protein 7 g; Carbohydrate 10 g; Fat 3 g; Cholesterol 70 mg; Sodium 800 mg

Finnish Summer Vegetable Soup

FINNISH SUMMER VEGETABLE SOUP

KESÄKEITTO (<u>keh</u>-sah-<u>kay</u>-toh)

Serve this summer soup with freshly baked Finnish Rye Bread (page 290) and some cheese for a nice lunch.

2 cups water
2 small carrots, sliced
1 medium potato, cubed
¾ cup fresh or frozen green peas
1 cup cut fresh or frozen green beans
¼ small cauliflower, separated into flowerets
2 ounces fresh spinach, cut up (about 2 cups)
2 cups milk
2 tablespoons all-purpose flour
¼ cup whipping cream

1½ teaspoons salt
⅛ teaspoon pepper
Snipped dill weed or parsley (optional)

Heat water, carrots, potato, peas, beans and cauliflower to boiling in 3-quart saucepan; reduce heat. Cover and simmer until vegetables are almost tender, 10 to 15 minutes.

Add spinach; cook uncovered about 1 minute. Mix ¼ cup of the milk and the flour; stir gradually into vegetable mixture. Boil and stir 1 minute. Stir in remaining milk, the whipping cream, salt and pepper. Heat just until hot. Garnish each serving with dill weed.

10 servings (¾ cup each)

PER SERVING: Calories 85; Protein 3 g; Carbohydrate 11 g; Fat 3 g; Cholesterol 10 mg; Sodium 380 mg

ITALIAN VEGETABLE SOUP

MINESTRONE (mee-nes-<u>troh</u>-neh)

A scrumptious array of vegetables and herbs enhances this traditional chicken-based broth.

1 cup water
½ cup dried Great Northern, navy or kidney beans
4 cups chicken broth
2 small tomatoes, chopped
2 medium carrots, sliced
1 stalk celery, sliced
1 medium onion, chopped
1 clove garlic, chopped
½ cup uncooked macaroni
1 tablespoon snipped parsley
1 teaspoon salt
½ teaspoon dried basil leaves
⅛ teaspoon pepper
1 bay leaf
4 ounces green beans, cut into 1-inch pieces
   (about ¾ cup)
2 small zucchini, cut into 1-inch slices
Grated Parmesan cheese (optional)

Heat water and dried beans to boiling in Dutch oven; boil 2 minutes. Remove from heat. Cover and let stand 1 hour. Add enough water to cover beans if necessary. Heat to boiling; reduce heat. Cover and simmer until tender, 1 to 1½ hours (do not boil or beans will burst).

Add chicken broth, tomatoes, carrots, celery, onion, garlic, macaroni, parsley, salt, basil, pepper and bay leaf to beans. Heat to boiling; reduce heat. Cover and simmer 15 minutes. Add green beans and zucchini. Heat to boiling; reduce heat. Cover and simmer until macaroni and vegetables are tender, 10 to 15 minutes. Remove bay leaf. Serve with cheese.

5 servings (about 1¼ cups each)

PER SERVING: Calories 155; Protein 10 g; Carbohydrate 24 g; Fat 2 g; Cholesterol 5 mg; Sodium 1070 mg

SHREDDED CABBAGE SOUP

S'CHEE (shee)

Here is a hearty Russian soup, traditionally enriched with a dollop of sour cream just before serving. The vegetables used in *S'chee* may vary from one recipe to another, but cabbage always takes pride of place.

2 medium onions, thinly sliced
3 tablespoons bacon fat, margarine or butter
2 cans (10½ ounces each) condensed beef broth
2 broth cans water
1 small head green cabbage, coarsely shredded
   (5 cups)
2 medium carrots, sliced
2 medium potatoes, cubed
1 stalk celery (with leaves), sliced
2 medium tomatoes, coarsely chopped
1 teaspoon salt
Freshly ground pepper
Dairy sour cream
Dill weed or parsley

Cook and stir onions in bacon fat in Dutch oven until tender. Add beef broth, water, cabbage, carrots, potatoes and celery. Heat to boiling; reduce heat. Cover and simmer until vegetables are tender, about 20 minutes. Stir in tomatoes, salt and pepper. Simmer uncovered about 10 minutes. Top each serving with sour cream. Garnish with dill weed.

12 servings (about ¾ cup each)

PER SERVING: Calories 120; Protein 3 g; Carbohydrate 13 g; Fat 6 g; Cholesterol 20 mg; Sodium 360 mg

CREAM OF LETTUCE SOUP
POTAGE CRÈME DE LAITUE
(poh-tahzh krem duh leh-tew)

Make this fresh-flavored French soup when tender lettuces are in abundance at the market or threaten to take over the garden.

1 small onion, chopped
¼ cup margarine or butter
2 large heads Boston lettuce or 2 small bunches romaine, finely shredded (about 7 cups)
¼ cup all-purpose flour
3 cups water
1 tablespoon instant chicken bouillon
1 cup half-and-half
½ teaspoon salt
⅛ teaspoon pepper
Mint leaves or parsley

Cook and stir onion in margarine in 3-quart saucepan over low heat until tender. Reserve 1 cup lettuce; stir remaining lettuce into onion. Cover and cook over low heat until lettuce wilts, about 5 minutes. Stir in flour; cook and stir 1 minute. Add water and bouillon. Heat to boiling, stirring constantly. Boil and stir 1 minute.

Pour mixture into blender container. Cover and blend on high speed until smooth, about 30 seconds; pour into saucepan. Stir in reserved lettuce, the half-and-half, salt and pepper. Heat just to boiling. Garnish with mint.

6 servings (about ¾ cup each)

PER SERVING: Calories 165; Protein 3 g; Carbohydrate 9 g; Fat 13 g; Cholesterol 15 mg; Sodium 930 mg

COLD YOGURT–CUCUMBER SOUP
TARATOR (tahrr-ah-tor)

Nothing is more refreshing on a hot summer's day than this Middle Eastern favorite, a cool mixture of fresh cucumbers and tangy yogurt. It is the perfect make-ahead appetizer for sultry weather.

2 medium cucumbers
1½ cups plain yogurt
½ teaspoon salt
¼ teaspoon dried mint flakes
⅛ teaspoon white pepper

Cut 7 thin slices from 1 cucumber; reserve. Cut all remaining cucumber into ¾-inch chunks. Place half the cucumber chunks and ¼ cup of the yogurt in blender container. Cover and blend on high speed until smooth.

Add remaining cucumber chunks, the salt, mint and white pepper. Cover and blend until smooth. Add remaining yogurt; cover and blend on low speed until smooth. Cover and refrigerate at least 1 hour. Garnish with reserved cucumber slices.

7 servings (about ½ cup each)

PER SERVING: Calories 45; Protein 3 g; Carbohydrate 6 g; Fat 1 g; Cholesterol 5 mg; Sodium 190 mg

GAZPACHO

(gahs-<u>pah</u>-choh)

This cold vegetable soup is native to both Spain and Latin America. Not all *gazpachos* feature tomatoes or bread, and some recipes call for a smooth purée of vegetables rather than crisp chunks. If you like the flavor of olive oil, choose a good quality, fruity one to make this soup.

4 slices bread, torn into pieces
4 large ripe tomatoes, chopped
2 medium cucumbers, chopped
1 medium green pepper, chopped
1 medium onion, chopped
1 cup water
¼ cup olive or vegetable oil
⅓ cup red wine vinegar
2 cloves garlic, finely chopped
2 teaspoons salt
1 teaspoon ground cumin
⅛ teaspoon freshly ground pepper

Mix bread, ¾ of the tomatoes, ½ of the cucumbers, ¼ of the green pepper, ½ of the onion, the water and oil in large bowl. Cover and refrigerate 1 hour.

Place half the vegetable mixture in blender container. Cover and blend on high speed 8 seconds. Repeat with remaining mixture. Stir in vinegar, garlic, salt, cumin and pepper. Cover and refrigerate at least 2 hours.

Place remaining chopped vegetables in small bowls. Cover and refrigerate; serve as accompaniments.

6 servings (about ½ cup each)

PER SERVING: Calories 185; Protein 3 g; Carbohydrate 21 g; Fat 10 g; Cholesterol 0 mg; Sodium 810 mg

ITALIAN TOMATO AND BREAD SALAD

PANZANELLA (pahn-zah-<u>nel</u>-lah)

This recipe, at its best with bursting ripe tomatoes, is far more than a summery use for stale bread. Pungent basil and red tomatoes are the featured combination, with good olive oil and red wine vinegar soaking into the bread chunks.

4 cups 1-inch pieces stale Italian or French
    bread
2 medium tomatoes, cut into bite-size pieces
2 cloves garlic, finely chopped
1 medium green pepper, cut into bite-size pieces
⅓ cup snipped fresh basil leaves
2 tablespoons snipped parsley
⅓ cup olive oil
2 tablespoons red wine vinegar
½ teaspoon salt
⅛ teaspoon pepper

Mix bread, tomatoes, garlic, green pepper, basil and parsley. Shake remaining ingredients in tightly covered container. Pour over bread mixture; toss. Cover and refrigerate at least 1 hour. Garnish with Kalamata or Greek olives if desired.

6 servings (about 1 cup each)

PER SERVING: Calories 175; Protein 2 g; Carbohydrate 15 g; Fat 12 g; Cholesterol 0 mg; Sodium 300 mg

CELERY ROOT WITH HAZELNUT SAUCE

TARATORLU KEREVIZ (deh-reh-<u>toa</u>-luh keh-reh-<u>veez</u>)

The Turks dress celery root juliennes with a special vinaigrette, thickened with soft bread crumbs and flavored with rich hazelnuts. Allow at least an hour for this vegetable to marinate.

2 pounds celery root (celeriac)
½ cup hazelnuts (filberts)
2 cloves garlic, chopped
¼ cup soft bread crumbs
¼ cup vinegar
1 tablespoon water
½ teaspoon salt
½ cup olive or vegetable oil
Snipped parsley

Pare celery root; cut into ¼-inch strips. Place hazelnuts in blender container. Cover and blend on high speed until finely chopped, about 30 seconds. Add garlic, bread crumbs, vinegar, water and salt. Cover and blend on medium-high speed about 1 minute, stopping blender to scrape sides occasionally. With blender running, gradually pour in oil, blending until smooth.

Toss hazelnut mixture with celery root; cover and refrigerate at least 1 hour. Serve on lettuce-lined salad plates, and garnish with Greek olives if desired. Sprinkle with parsley.

12 servings (about ¾ cup each)

PER SERVING: Calories 145; Protein 1 g; Carbohydrate 6 g; Fat 13 g; Cholesterol 0 mg; Sodium 130 mg

Celery Root (Celeriac)

This root vegetable is variously known as celery knob and turnip-rooted celery, too. Celery root is making something of a comeback in the United States, where in the nineteenth century it was cooked and dressed in a creamy sauce. It is still far more popular abroad, where it is most often enjoyed raw. This knobby, rough-skinned root, untrimmed, will keep nicely in a cool place for about a week. To prepare celery root, pare away the skin. To keep the flesh from discoloring, sprinkle it with lemon juice or drop the pieces as they are cut into a bowl of acidulated water. Cut the flesh into juliennes, or shred it, to use for salads. Boil chunks and purée them. Celery root purée can be mixed with other purées (notably potato) for a combination with more body and deeper flavor.

Polish Salad with Pickled Eggs, *top* (page 12), and Celery Root with Hazelnut Sauce

BEAN AND TUNA SALAD
INSALATA DI FAGIOLI E TONNO
(een-sah-<u>lah</u>-tah dee fah-<u>joh</u>-lee eh <u>toh</u>-noh)

This is a straightforward Italian antipasto classic. Tender beans, with their gentle flavor, are a delicious background for tuna and thin rings of juicy onion. If you are in a hurry, canned beans make this appetizer even easier to assemble.

3 cups water
½ pound dried white kidney, Great Northern or navy beans*
⅓ cup olive or vegetable oil
3 tablespoons red wine vinegar
1 teaspoon salt
Freshly ground pepper
1 medium Spanish, Bermuda or red onion, thinly sliced
1 can (6½ ounces) tuna, drained
Snipped parsley

Heat water and beans to boiling; boil 2 minutes. Remove from heat; cover and let stand 1 hour. Add enough water to cover beans if necessary. Heat to boiling; reduce heat. Cover and simmer until tender, 1 to 1½ hours (do not boil or beans will burst). Drain and cool.

Mix oil, vinegar, salt and pepper; pour over beans and onion in shallow glass or plastic dish. Cover and refrigerate, stirring occasionally, at least 1 hour. Transfer bean mixture to serving platter with slotted spoon. Break tuna into chunks; arrange on bean mixture. Sprinkle with parsley.

12 servings (about ¾ cup each)

*2 cans (15 to 20 ounces each) cannellini or other white beans, drained, can be substituted for the cooked dried beans.

PER SERVING: Calories 140; Protein 8 g; Carbohydrate 11 g; Fat 7 g; Cholesterol 5 mg; Sodium 230 mg

POLISH SALAD WITH PICKLED EGGS
SALATKA Z PIKLOWANYMI JAJKAMI
(sah-<u>laht</u>-kah z'<u>peek</u>-loh-vah-<u>nee</u>-mee yaiy-<u>kah</u>-mee)

The kitchens of eastern Europe are famed for their hand with vinegars and the "warm" spices, among them cloves and allspice. This salad features pickled eggs, a striking magenta in color.

Pickled Eggs (below)
1 bunch leaf lettuce, torn into bite-size pieces
½ small red onion, thinly sliced and separated into rings
¼ cup olive or vegetable oil
2 tablespoons lemon juice
¼ teaspoon salt
Dash of pepper

Prepare Pickled Eggs. Toss lettuce and onion. Divide among 6 salad plates. Cut eggs into slices or fourths. Arrange 1 egg on top of each salad. Shake remaining ingredients in tightly covered container; drizzle over salads.

6 servings

PER SERVING: Calories 155; Protein 7 g; Carbohydrate 4 g; Fat 14 g; Cholesterol 210 mg; Sodium 240 mg

PICKLED EGGS

3 cups beet juice (cooking water from beets)
1 cup red wine vinegar
8 whole black peppercorns
4 whole allspice
4 whole cloves
1 bay leaf
6 hard-cooked eggs, peeled

Heat beet juice, vinegar, peppercorns, allspice, cloves and bay leaf to boiling; pour over eggs. Cover and refrigerate at least 24 hours.

DEEP-FRIED INDIAN PASTRIES

SAMOSAS (suh-<u>moh</u>-suss)

These golden brown turnovers are frequently served with mango chutney. Stir snipped coriander or parsley into plain yogurt for an easy additional sauce.

1 pound ground lamb or beef
1 medium onion, finely chopped
1 clove garlic, finely chopped
1 teaspoon salt
½ teaspoon ground coriander
¼ teaspoon ground cumin
¼ teaspoon ground ginger
¼ teaspoon pepper
Pastry (right)
Vegetable oil
Chutney (optional)

Cook and stir lamb, onion and garlic in 10-inch skillet until lamb is light brown; drain. Stir in salt, coriander, cumin, ginger and pepper. Cool.

Prepare Pastry; divide into fourths. Cover with damp towel to prevent drying. Roll one fourth into 12-inch circle (dough will be springy and may be slightly difficult to roll). Cut into 4-inch circles; cut circles into halves. Moisten edges with water. Place 1 teaspoon filling on each half circle. Fold pastry over filling to form triangle. Press edges to seal securely. Repeat with remaining pastry.

Heat oil (1 to 1½ inches) to 375°. Fry about 5 pastries at a time until light brown, turning 2 or 3 times, 3 to 4 minutes; drain. Keep warm in 200° oven. Serve warm with chutney.

About 60 pastries

PER PASTRY: Calories 45; Protein 1 g; Carbohydrate 3 g; Fat 3 g; Cholesterol 10 mg; Sodium 60 mg

PASTRY

2 tablespoons margarine or butter
1 tablespoon shortening
2 cups all-purpose flour
½ teaspoon salt
1 egg yolk
½ cup cold water

Cut margarine and shortening into flour and salt until mixture resembles fine crumbs; stir in egg yolk. Sprinkle in water, 1 tablespoon at a time, tossing with fork until all flour is moistened and pastry almost cleans side of bowl. Gather pastry into a ball; knead on lightly floured cloth-covered board until smooth, about 1 minute.

SOUTH-OF-THE-BORDER TURNOVERS

EMPANADITAS (ehm-pah-nah-<u>dee</u>-tahs)

Miniature *empanadas*—Mexican meat-stuffed turnovers—are versatile tidbits. Fill them with ham or chicken and serve them as party appetizers or as a sit-down first course, alone or with guacamole as an accompaniment.

⅔ cup shortening
2 tablespoons margarine or butter, softened
2 cups all-purpose flour
½ teaspoon salt
4 to 6 tablespoons cold water
Ham Filling or Chicken Filling (right)
1 egg, separated
1 tablespoon milk

Cut shortening and margarine into flour and salt until particles are size of small peas. Sprinkle in water, 1 tablespoon at a time, tossing with fork until all flour is moistened and pastry almost cleans side of bowl. Gather pastry into a ball; divide into halves. Shape one half into flattened round on lightly floured cloth-covered board. Roll pastry into rectangle, 13 × 10 inches; cut into 3-inch circles. Place on ungreased cookie sheet.

Prepare filling. Beat egg white slightly; brush on edges of pastry circles. Place 1 teaspoon filling on center of each circle. Fold pastry over filling; press edges with fork to seal securely. Repeat with remaining half pastry. Heat oven to 375°. Mix egg yolk and milk; brush turnovers with egg yolk mixture. Bake until light brown, 18 to 20 minutes.

About 24 turnovers

PER TURNOVER: Calories 110; Protein 2 g; Carbohydrate 8 g; Fat 8 g; Cholesterol 15 mg; Sodium 120 mg

HAM FILLING

1 can (4½ ounces) deviled ham
¼ cup grated Cheddar cheese
1 teaspoon prepared mustard
⅛ teaspoon pepper

Mix all ingredients.

CHICKEN FILLING

½ cup finely chopped cooked chicken
2 tablespoons taco or chili sauce
2 tablespoons chopped pimiento-stuffed olives
¼ teaspoon salt

Mix all ingredients.

DO-AHEAD TIP: After baking, turnovers can be covered and refrigerated several hours. Heat in 375° oven until hot, about 8 minutes.

CHEESE TRIANGLES

TIROPETES (tee-<u>roh</u>-peh-tes)

These are the famed Greek feta cheese triangles wrapped in phyllo dough. Fresh chives give the filling a hint of onion.

1 pound feta cheese*
2 eggs, slightly beaten
¼ cup finely chopped chives
¼ teaspoon white pepper
1 pound frozen phyllo leaves, thawed
¼ cup margarine or butter, melted

Crumble cheese in small bowl; mash with fork. Stir in eggs, chives and white pepper until well mixed. Cut phyllo leaves lengthwise into 3 strips. Cover with waxed paper, then with damp towel to prevent drying. Using 2 layers phyllo at a time, place 1 heaping teaspoon filling on end of 1 strip; fold end over end, in triangular shape, to opposite end. Place on greased cookie sheet. Repeat with remaining filling. (Puffs can be covered and refrigerated no longer than 24 hours at this point.)

Heat oven to 350°. Brush puffs with margarine. Bake until puffed and golden, about 20 minutes.

About 36 triangles

*Finely shredded Monterey Jack cheese can be substituted for the feta cheese.

PER TRIANGLE: Calories 85; Protein 3 g; Carbohydrate 9 g; Fat 4 g; Cholesterol 20 mg; Sodium 200 mg

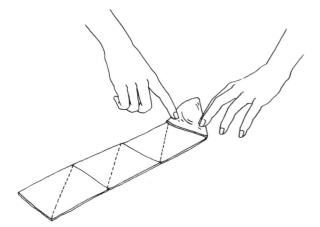

Place a heaping teaspoon filling on end of strip.

Fold end over end, in triangular shape, to opposite end.

CRISP WONTONS

CHA YUN T'UN (jah yuhn tuhn)

A mixture of pork and shrimp fills these crunchy appetizers. They are delicious with Chinese plum sauce, teriyaki sauce and Chinese barbecue sauces in addition to the sauces suggested here.

½ pound ground pork
1 can (4½ ounces) shrimp, drained and
  chopped
6 water chestnuts, finely chopped
2 green onions (with tops), chopped
1 tablespoon soy sauce
1 teaspoon cornstarch
½ teaspoon salt
1 pound wonton skins*
Vegetable oil
Sweet and Sour Sauce or Hot Mustard Sauce
  (right)

Stir-fry pork in wok or 10-inch skillet until brown; drain. Stir in shrimp, water chestnuts, green onions, soy sauce, cornstarch and salt. Stir-fry 1 minute.

Place 1 teaspoon filling on center of each wonton skin. Moisten edges with water. Fold each skin in half to form triangle; press edges to seal. Pull bottom corners of triangle down and overlap slightly. Moisten one corner with water; press to seal.

Heat oil (1 to 1½ inches) to 360°. Fry 6 to 8 wontons at a time until golden brown, turning occasionally, about 2 minutes; drain. Serve with Sweet and Sour Sauce.

About 48 wontons

*12 to 14 egg roll skins can be substituted for the wonton skins; cut each skin into fourths.

PER WONTON: Calories 65; Protein 2 g; Carbohydrate 7 g; Fat 3 g; Cholesterol 5 mg; Sodium 100 mg

SWEET AND SOUR SAUCE

¼ cup plum or grape jelly
¼ cup chili sauce

Heat jelly and chili sauce in small saucepan, stirring constantly, until jelly is melted.

HOT MUSTARD SAUCE

3 tablespoons dry mustard
2 tablespoons water
1 tablespoon soy sauce

Mix dry mustard, water and soy sauce until smooth.

Fold each wonton skin in half to form triangle; press edges to seal.

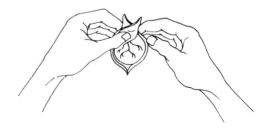

Fold one corner of egg roll skin over filling; overlap the two opposite corners

EGG ROLLS

CHI TAN CHUAN (jee don joo-ahn)

Serve these luscious pork rolls with two dipping sauces, one sweet and one hot. Egg roll skins are widely available, often in supermarkets.

1 pound ground pork
3 cups finely shredded green cabbage
1 can (8½ ounces) bamboo shoots, drained and chopped
½ cup chopped mushrooms
4 medium green onions, sliced
2 tablespoons soy sauce
1 teaspoon cornstarch
1 teaspoon five spice powder
1 teaspoon salt
½ teaspoon sugar
1 pound egg roll skins (16 to 18)
Vegetable oil
Sweet and Sour Sauce and Hot Mustard Sauce (page 16)

Stir-fry pork in wok or 10-inch skillet until brown. Remove pork from wok; drain, reserving 2 tablespoons fat. Stir-fry cabbage, bamboo shoots, mushrooms and green onions in reserved fat. Mix soy sauce, cornstarch, five spice powder, salt and sugar; pour over vegetable mixture. Stir-fry 1 minute; cool.

Mix pork and vegetables. Cover egg roll skins with damp towel to prevent drying. Place ¼ cup pork mixture on center of each egg roll skin. Fold one corner of egg roll skin over filling; overlap the two opposite corners. Moisten fourth corner with water; fold over to make into roll.

Heat oil (1½ to 1¾ inches) to 360°. Fry 3 to 5 egg rolls at a time until golden brown, turning once, about 3 minutes; drain. Serve hot with Sweet and Sour Sauce and Hot Mustard Sauce.

16 to 18 egg rolls

PER EGG ROLL: Calories 155; Protein 7 g; Carbohydrate 14 g; Fat 8 g; Cholesterol 25 mg; Sodium 320 mg

DO-AHEAD TIP: After frying, egg rolls can be covered and refrigerated no longer than 24 hours. Heat uncovered in 375° oven until hot, about 15 minutes.

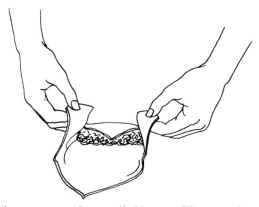

Fold one corner of egg roll skin over filling; overlap the two opposite corners.

Moisten fourth corner with water; fold over to make a roll.

Fried Squid

Cleaning Squid

Squid, or rather cleaning squid, has a reputation for being complicated. The idea of cleaning something when you can't even identify the head with any precision might seem daunting. It is easier than you might think. Grasp the tentacles in one hand and the conical body in the other, and give a good tug; this will pull the tentacle section out of the body, along with the head and some innards. Free the tentacles and discard the rest of that section. Pull the pen (a transparent bonelike structure) out of the body. Rinse the tentacles and the body, and the squid is ready to use.

FRIED SQUID

CALAMARES FRITOS (kah-lah-<u>mah</u>-rehs <u>free</u>-tohs)

This unusual appetizer is especially popular around the Mediterranean, particularly in Italy and Spain. There, a platter heaped with golden fried squid makes a sensational lunch or dinner, served with nothing more than a squeeze of lemon.

1 pound cleaned squid
Vegetable oil
½ cup all-purpose flour
2 eggs, slightly beaten
1 cup dry bread crumbs
Salt
Lemon wedges

Cut squid body cones into ½-inch slices; leave tentacles whole. Pat dry.

Heat oil (1 to 1½ inches) to 375°. Coat squid with flour. Dip into eggs; coat with bread crumbs. Fry a few squid pieces at a time until golden brown, 2 to 3 minutes. Drain; sprinkle with salt. Serve with lemon wedges.

8 servings

PER SERVING: Calories 210; Protein 13 g; Carbohydrate 17 g; Fat 10 g; Cholesterol 190 mg; Sodium 200 mg

GLAZED CHICKEN WINGS

Emphasize the Chinese flavor of these gently spiced chicken wings by serving them with Hot Mustard Sauce (page 16).

3 pounds chicken wings (about 15)
⅔ cup soy sauce
½ cup honey
2 tablespoons vegetable oil
2 teaspoons five spice powder
2 cloves garlic, crushed

Cut each chicken wing at joints to make three pieces; discard tips or save for use in making chicken broth. Place chicken wings in shallow glass or plastic dish. Mix remaining ingredients; pour over chicken. Cover and refrigerate, turning chicken occasionally, at least 1 hour.

Arrange chicken on rack in foil-lined broiler pan; reserve marinade. Brush chicken with reserved marinade. Cook in 375° oven 30 minutes. Turn chicken and cook, brushing occasionally with marinade, until done, about 30 minutes longer.

About 30 appetizers

PER APPETIZER: Calories 85; Protein 5 g; Carbohydrate 5 g; Fat 5 g; Cholesterol 15 mg; Sodium 380 mg

DO-AHEAD TIP: After cooking, chicken wings can be covered and refrigerated no longer than 24 hours. Heat uncovered in 375° oven until hot, about 15 minutes.

CHINESE BARBECUED RIBS

SHAO PI K'U (sha'ow bee koo)

Marinated ribs take on wonderful flavor. Choose velvety, intense hoisin sauce or spicy chili sauce as the primary note in the marinade below. Pass plenty of napkins when serving these delicious—and messy—ribs.

1½ to 2 pounds fresh pork spareribs, cut crosswise into 1½-inch pieces
¼ cup soy sauce
¼ cup hoisin sauce or chili sauce
2 tablespoons honey
2 tablespoons sake or dry sherry
1 small clove garlic, crushed

Place ribs in shallow glass or plastic dish. Mix remaining ingredients; spoon over ribs. Cover and refrigerate at least 2 hours.

Remove ribs from marinade, reserving marinade. Arrange ribs meaty sides up in single layer on rack in foil-lined broiler pan. Brush with reserved marinade. Cover and cook in 325° oven 1 hour. Brush ribs with marinade. Cook uncovered, brushing occasionally with marinade, until done, about 45 minutes longer.

About 30 appetizers

PER APPETIZER: Calories 30; Protein 1 g; Carbohydrate 2 g; Fat 2 g; Cholesterol 5 mg; Sodium 120 mg

SPICY HOT BEEF KABOBS

ANTICUCHOS (ahn-tee-<u>koo</u>-chohs)

In Peru, these peppery morsels are welcomed as casual appetizers, a festive first course or the main event itself. If offering *Anticuchos* as a main dish, serve them with mildly flavored foods since the kabobs are quite spicy themselves. Today *Anticuchos* are made with beef hearts; in the days before cattle were brought by the Spanish, some believe *Anticuchos* were probably made with the hearts of llamas.

3 calves' hearts (about 1 pound each), trimmed, or 2½ pounds beef boneless sirloin steak, 1 inch thick
3 large cloves garlic, finely chopped
1 small red jalapeño pepper, seeded and finely chopped
2 teaspoons ground cumin
1½ teaspoons salt
2 teaspoons water
15 whole black peppercorns
1 cup red wine vinegar
⅓ cup water
1 tablespoon annatto seed
¼ cup dried red chili peppers, seeded
1 tablespoon vegetable oil
1 teaspoon salt

Remove nerves and membranes from calves' hearts; cut hearts into 1-inch cubes. Place in large glass bowl. Mash garlic, jalapeño pepper, cumin, salt, 2 teaspoons water and the peppercorns to a smooth, thick paste, using the flat side of a wooden mallet on cutting surface. Toss garlic mixture with hearts, until thoroughly coated. Cover and let stand 10 minutes. Stir in vinegar and ⅓ cup water. Cover and refrigerate, stirring occasionally, 24 hours.

Cover annatto seed with boiling water. Let stand at least 12 hours.

Remove heart pieces, one at a time, from garlic mixture, using tongs and shaking off garlic and jalapeño pieces. Reserve garlic mixture.

Pour ½ cup boiling water over chili peppers. Let stand 30 minutes; drain. Drain annatto seed. Place chili peppers, annatto seed, oil, salt and ¾ cup reserved garlic mixture in blender container. Cover and blend on high speed, stopping blender to scrape sides occasionally, until smooth and well blended, about 3 minutes.

Thread heart cubes on six 11-inch skewers. Brush with annatto mixture. Set oven control to broil or 550°. Broil with tops about 4 inches from heat 5 minutes. Turn; brush with sauce. Broil until medium rare, 5 to 6 minutes longer. Heat remaining annatto mixture to boiling; serve with kabobs.

10 to 12 servings

PER SERVING: Calories 185; Protein 26 g; Carbohydrate 5 g; Fat 7 g; Cholesterol 170 mg; Sodium 590 mg

Spicy Hot Beef Kabobs and Plantain Chips (page 29)

CHEESE STRAW TWISTS

DIABLOTINS (d'yah-bloh-<u>tan</u>)

The French have more than one name for their cheese straws. The twists are *diablotins,* the flat ones are *paillettes* (from *paille,* meaning "straw"). This recipe takes advantage of frozen puff pastry, a very satisfactory solution to the time-consuming problem of making puff pastry.

1 package (17¼ ounces) frozen puff pastry
⅔ cup grated Parmesan cheese
1 tablespoon paprika
1 egg, slightly beaten

Thaw pastry as directed on package. Heat oven to 425°. Cover 2 cookie sheets with parchment or heavy brown paper. Mix cheese and paprika. Roll 1 sheet of pastry into rectangle, 10 × 12 inches, on lightly floured surface, using floured stockinet-covered rolling pin.

Brush pastry with egg; sprinkle with 3 tablespoons of the cheese mixture. Gently press cheese mixture into pastry. Turn pastry over; repeat with egg and cheese mixture. Fold pastry lengthwise into halves.

Cut pastry crosswise into ½-inch strips. Unfold strips; roll each end in opposite directions to twist. Place twists on cookie sheet. Bake until twists are puffed and golden brown, 7 to 8 minutes. Repeat with remaining sheet of pastry, egg and cheese mixture.

About 4 dozen twists

PER TWIST: Calories 55; Protein 1 g; Carbohydrate 3 g; Fat 4 g; Cholesterol 0 mg; Sodium 90 mg

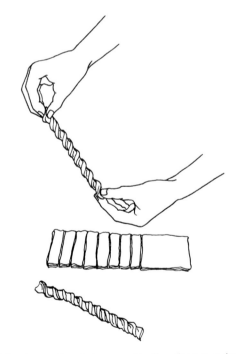

Fold pastry lengthwise in half.

Unfold strips; roll ends in opposite directions to twist.

Ingredients for Golden Potato Slices with Cilantro Chutney

GOLDEN POTATO SLICES WITH CILANTRO CHUTNEY

PAKAURA (pah-k'oh-rah)

Afghan batter-dipped potatoes are usually served with a chutney. Our choice: a fresh-tasting, ginger-sparked mixture from the same region, where it is known as *chutni gashneetch*.

4 medium potatoes (about 1½ pounds)
¾ cup all-purpose flour
½ cup water
½ teaspoon salt
¼ teaspoon ground turmeric
¼ teaspoon ground red pepper
1 egg
Vegetable oil
Salt
Cilantro Chutney (page 25)

Heat 1 inch salted water (½ teaspoon salt to 1 cup water) to boiling. Add potatoes. Heat to boiling; reduce heat. Cover and simmer until almost tender, about 10 minutes. Drain; cool.

Mix flour, ½ cup water, the salt, turmeric, red pepper and egg with fork until smooth. Cover and let stand 30 minutes.

Heat oil (1 to 1½ inches) to 375°. Cut potatoes into ¼-inch slices. Dip potato slices into batter, allowing excess batter to drip back into bowl. Fry a few potato slices at a time, turning occasionally, until golden brown, about 2 minutes. Remove with slotted spoon. Drain; sprinkle with salt. Serve with Cilantro Chutney.

8 servings

PER SERVING: Calories 175; Protein 3 g; Carbohydrate 23 g; Fat 8 g; Cholesterol 25 mg; Sodium 350 mg

CILANTRO CHUTNEY

1 cup snipped fresh cilantro
¼ cup lemon juice
2 tablespoons snipped fresh mint leaves or
 1½ teaspoons dried mint leaves
1 teaspoon chopped gingerroot
½ teaspoon salt
¼ teaspoon pepper
⅛ teaspoon ground red pepper
1 green jalapeño pepper, seeded and coarsely
 chopped
½ small onion, cut up

Place all ingredients in blender container or food processor. Cover and blend on high speed, stopping blender to scrape sides occasionally, until smooth, about 1 minute.

SPICY PEANUTS

CACAHUATES ENCHILADOS (kah-kah-<u>wah</u>-tehs ehn-chee-<u>lah</u>-dohs)

Dried ground chilies give peanuts dusky flavor and unmistakable fire when the two are stirred together briefly over medium heat.

2 teaspoons vegetable oil
2 cups dry roasted peanuts
1 to 1½ teaspoons ground dried chilies or
 ground red pepper

Heat oil in 10-inch skillet until hot. Cook and stir peanuts and dried chilies in oil over medium heat 2 minutes; cool.

2 cups peanuts

PER TABLESPOON: Calories 60; Protein 2 g; Carbohydrate 2 g; Fat 5 g; Cholesterol 0 mg; Sodium 40 mg

Golden Potato Slices with Cilantro Chutney (page 23)

AFRICAN RED DIP WITH SHRIMP

ATA SAUCE WITH SHRIMP

West African *ata* sauce is based on a homemade red pepper paste, complex with the flavors of many spices.

1 cup chili sauce
2 tablespoons Red Pepper Paste (below)
1 dozen chilled cooked shrimp

Mix chili sauce and Red Pepper Paste. Serve with chilled cooked shrimp.

6 servings

PER SERVING: Calories 20; Protein 0 g; Carbohydrate 5 g; Fat 0 g; Cholesterol 0 mg; Sodium 280 mg

RED PEPPER PASTE

¼ cup dry red wine
1 teaspoon ground red pepper
¾ teaspoon salt
¼ teaspoon ground ginger
⅛ teaspoon ground cardamom
⅛ teaspoon ground coriander
⅛ teaspoon ground nutmeg
⅛ teaspoon ground cloves
⅛ teaspoon ground cinnamon
⅛ teaspoon black pepper
⅛ of a medium onion
1 small clove garlic
¼ cup paprika

Place all ingredients except paprika in blender container. Cover and blend on high speed until smooth, scraping sides of blender frequently.

Heat paprika in 1-quart saucepan 1 minute. Add spice mixture gradually, stirring until smooth. Heat, stirring occasionally, until hot, about 3 minutes. Cool.

ONION TART

PISSALADIÈRE (pees-sah-lah-d'<u>yehr</u>)

This rustic French bread features the Provençal touch of olive oil and the wonderful anchovies and cured olives of the Mediterranean.

1 loaf (16 ounces) frozen bread dough
3 tablespoons olive or vegetable oil
3 large onions, thinly sliced
1 tablespoon snipped fresh basil or thyme
⅛ teaspoon white pepper
2 cans (2 ounces each) anchovy fillets, drained
10 oil-cured Greek olives, cut into halves and pitted

Arrange anchovies in lattice pattern on onions, then top with olives.

Thaw bread dough as directed on package. Heat oil in 10-inch skillet until hot. Stir in onions; reduce heat. Cover and cook, stirring occasionally, until onions are very tender, about 25 minutes. Stir in basil and white pepper.

Shape dough into flattened rectangle on lightly floured surface. Roll dough with floured rolling pin into rectangle, 14 × 11 inches. Place on lightly greased cookie sheet; let rest 15 minutes.

Spoon onion mixture evenly over dough to within 1 inch of edge. Arrange anchovies in lattice pattern on onions. Top with olives. Let tart rest 15 minutes.

Heat oven to 425°. Bake until crust is brown, 15 to 20 minutes.

8 to 10 servings

PER SERVING: Calories 380; Protein 13 g; Carbohydrate 59 g; Fat 10 g; Cholesterol 10 mg; Sodium 1000 mg

Preceding pages: Onion Tart, *left*, Herbed Liver Pâté (page 34) and Cheese Straw Twists (page 22)

STUFFED PRUNES WITH BACON

In the best British tradition, here all at once are dried fruit, nuts and deep-tasting port. These elements traditionally sound the last note of a well-rounded English dinner, when the dinner plates have been cleared from the table and the nutcracker and port decanter are set out. Wrapped in bacon, the stuffed prunes are broiled to make a savory hors d'oeuvre.

24 dried pitted prunes
24 walnut halves
½ cup ruby port
¼ cup water
12 slices bacon

Stuff each prune with walnut half. Mix port and water; pour over prunes in bowl. Let stand, stirring occasionally, until prunes are plump, about 2 hours.

Cut bacon slices into halves. Wrap bacon around prunes; secure with wooden picks. Arrange on rack in broiler pan. Set oven control to broil or 550°. Broil with tops about 4 inches from heat, turning once, until bacon is crisp, 10 to 12 minutes.

24 stuffed prunes

PER PRUNE: Calories 55; Protein 1 g; Carbohydrate 6 g; Fat 3 g; Cholesterol 5 mg; Sodium 50 mg

FLAMING CHEESE
SAGANAKI (sah-gah-nah-kee)

This middle Eastern appetizer is something of an attention-getter. Serve the melting-warm cheese with sesame crackers or wedges of pita bread, if preferred to rye bread.

½ pound Kasseri or Kefalotiri cheese*
1 tablespoon margarine or butter, melted
2 tablespoons brandy
½ lemon
Cocktail rye bread or assorted crackers (optional)

Cut cheese into 3 wedges; place in shallow heatproof serving dish. Brush cheese with margarine. Set oven control to broil or 550°. Broil cheese with top 4 to 6 inches from heat until bubbly and light brown, 5 to 6 minutes. Heat brandy until warm; pour over cheese.

Ignite immediately. Squeeze lemon over cheese. Cut wedges into halves. Serve with rye bread.

6 servings

*Mozzarella cheese can be substituted for the above cheeses.

PER SERVING: Calories 120; Protein 10 g; Carbohydrate 2 g; Fat 8 g; Cholesterol 20 mg; Sodium 220 mg

PLANTAIN CHIPS
PATACONES (pah-tah-kok-nehs)

Fried plantain slices are especially popular across Latin America.

3 large green plantains, pared and very thinly sliced
Vegetable oil
Salt

Cover plantain slices with iced water. Let stand 30 minutes; drain. Pat dry.

Heat oil (1 to 1½ inches) to 375°. Fry 12 to 14 plantain slices at a time, turning occasionally, until golden brown, about 2 minutes. Remove with slotted spoon. Drain; sprinkle with salt.

About 4½ cups

PER ½ CUP: Calories 205; Protein 1 g; Carbohydrate 32 g; Fat 8 g; Cholesterol 0 mg; Sodium 240 mg

---

Plantains

Plantains (*platanos*) can, at first glance, pass for bananas. On closer inspection, they are noticeably larger. A banana with a perfectly black peel is of interest to no one, but that is just what to look for in a thoroughly ripe—not overripe—plantain. Plantains taste like a cross between banana and winter squash. Less than ripe, the color of the skin may be deep yellow, reddish-yellow or green, depending on the variety and the degree of ripeness. To select a ripe plantain, test whether the black skin yields to gentle pressure. A fully ripe plantain can be stored, well wrapped in the refrigerator, for several days.

CHICKEN KABOBS WITH PEANUT SAUCE

SATÉ AJAM (sah-teh eye-<u>yem</u>)

Even in the most polite society, it seems acceptable to eat these small chicken kabobs directly from the bamboo skewer. This dish features the seductive Indonesian combination of spicy-hot and sweet.

2 large whole chicken breasts (about 2 pounds)
¼ cup soy sauce
1 tablespoon vegetable oil
1 teaspoon packed brown sugar
¼ teaspoon ground ginger
1 clove garlic, crushed
Peanut Sauce (right)

Remove bones and skin from chicken breasts. Cut chicken into ¾-inch pieces. (For ease in cutting, partially freeze chicken.) Mix chicken, soy sauce, oil, brown sugar, ginger and garlic in glass bowl. Cover and refrigerate, stirring occasionally, at least 2 hours.

Prepare Peanut Sauce. Remove chicken from marinade; reserve marinade. Thread 4 or 5 chicken pieces on each of 14 to 16 bamboo skewers. Brush chicken with reserved marinade. Set oven control to broil or 550°. Broil skewers with tops about 4 inches from heat 4 to 5 minutes; turn. Brush with marinade. Broil until chicken is done, 4 to 5 minutes longer. Serve with Peanut Sauce.

About 16 appetizers

PER APPETIZER: Calories 100; Protein 10 g; Carbohydrate 2 g; Fat 6 g; Cholesterol 20 mg; Sodium 300 mg

PEANUT SAUCE

1 small onion, finely chopped
1 tablespoon vegetable oil
⅓ cup peanut butter
⅓ cup water
1 tablespoon lemon juice
¼ teaspoon ground coriander
3 to 4 drops red pepper sauce

Cook and stir onion in oil in 1½-quart saucepan until tender. Remove from heat. Stir in remaining ingredients; heat over low heat just until blended (sauce will separate if overcooked).

CHEESE-STUFFED MUSHROOMS

FUNGHI ALLA PARMIGIANA
(<u>foon</u>-ghee ahl-lah par-mee-<u>jah</u>-nah)

Look for the prettiest mushrooms you can find, fresh and firm. When mushrooms are very fresh, their caps are closed and meet the top of the stem, hiding the gills. Serve these Italian mushrooms piping hot.

1 pound medium mushrooms (about 24)
¼ cup finely chopped green onions (with tops)
1 clove garlic, finely chopped
¼ cup margarine or butter
½ cup dry bread crumbs
¼ cup grated Parmesan cheese
2 tablespoons snipped parsley
½ teaspoon salt
½ teaspoon dried basil leaves
¼ teaspoon pepper

Remove stems from mushrooms; chop stems finely. Cook and stir mushroom stems, green onions and garlic in margarine over medium heat until tender, about 5 minutes. Remove from heat; stir in remaining ingredients.

Fill mushroom caps with stuffing mixture. Place mushrooms, filled sides up, in greased baking dish. Cook in 350° oven 15 minutes. Serve hot.

About 24 mushrooms

PER MUSHROOM: Calories 30; Protein 1 g; Carbohydrate 2 g; Fat 2 g; Cholesterol 0 mg; Sodium 100 mg

---

MUSHROOMS WITH GARLIC

CHAMPIÑONES AL AJILLO
(chahm-peen-yoh-nehs ahl ah-hee-yoh)

Sherry, olive oil and garlic underscore the Spanish origin of this mushroom dish. Avoid overcooking the mushrooms; that will make them less plump and juicy.

2 tablespoons olive or vegetable oil
4 cloves garlic, finely chopped
8 ounces medium mushrooms, cut into halves
2 tablespoons dry sherry
1 teaspoon lemon juice
¼ teaspoon salt
Dash of pepper
Snipped parsley

Heat oil in 10-inch skillet until hot. Cook and stir garlic over medium heat 1 minute; add mushrooms. Cook and stir 2 minutes; reduce heat. Stir in remaining ingredients except parsley. Cook and stir until hot, about 2 minutes. Sprinkle with parsley.

4 servings

PER SERVING: Calories 85; Protein 1 g; Carbohydrate 4 g; Fat 7 g; Cholesterol 0 mg; Sodium 140 mg

LITTLE LATIN MEATBALLS

ALBONDIGUITAS (ahl-bohn-dee-ghee-tahs)

These meatballs can be kept warm in their tomato salsa. Chop the jalapeño peppers finely and mix them thoroughly into the beef mixture.

2 jalapeño peppers
1 pound ground beef
1 egg
½ cup dry bread crumbs
¼ cup milk
¼ cup shredded Monterey Jack cheese
1 small onion, finely chopped
1 teaspoon salt
¼ teaspoon pepper
Salsa (below)

Remove stems, seeds and membranes from peppers; chop peppers. Mix peppers, beef, egg, bread crumbs, milk, cheese, onions, salt and pepper. Shape mixture into 1-inch balls. Place in ungreased pan, 13 × 9 × 2 inches. Cook uncovered in 400° oven until brown, 15 to 20 minutes. Serve with Salsa.

36 meatballs

PER MEATBALL: Calories 40; Protein 3 g; Carbohydrate 2 g; Fat 2 g; Cholesterol 15 mg; Sodium 130 mg

SALSA

1 can (8 ounces) tomato sauce
1 medium tomato, chopped
2 cloves garlic, finely chopped
2 tablespoons snipped parsley
1 tablespoon vinegar
⅛ teaspoon ground cumin
⅛ teaspoon salt

Heat all ingredients.

MARINATED GINGERED SHRIMP

This is a simple Japanese preparation that can be prettily arranged on a serving plate. Sweet sake is widely available, but the same quantity of sweet sherry may be substituted if sake is not to be found.

1½ pounds medium shrimp, cooked, peeled, and deveined
¼ cup soy sauce
3 ounces gingerroot, chopped
¼ cup vinegar
2 tablespoons sugar
2 tablespoons sweet sake
1½ teaspoons salt
2 to 3 tablespoons thinly sliced green onion

Arrange shrimp in single layer in glass or plastic container, 12 × 7 ½ ×2 inches. Heat soy sauce to boiling; add gingerroot. Reduce heat; simmer uncovered until most of the liquid is absorbed, about 5 minutes. Stir in vinegar, sugar, sake and salt; pour over shrimp. Cover and refrigerate at least 2 hours.

Remove shrimp from marinade with slotted spoon; arrange on serving plate. Garnish with green onion.

45 to 50 shrimp

PER SHRIMP: Calories 10; Protein 1 g; Carbohydrate 1 g; Fat 0 g; Cholesterol 10 mg; Sodium 130 mg

CHUNKY TUNA SALSA

ATUN CON PICO DE GALLO
(ah-toon kohn peek-oh deh gah-yoh)

Here is a wonderful use for that Mexican staple, *pico de gallo,* probably the best-known south-of-the-border salsa.

1 can (6½ ounces) tuna, well drained
¾ cup chopped red onion
1 large tomato, chopped
1 jalapeño pepper, seeded and chopped
1 tablespoon lemon juice
Snipped fresh cilantro
Tortilla chips

Break up tuna with fork. Gently mix tuna and remaining ingredients except cilantro and tortilla chips. Sprinkle with cilantro. Serve with tortilla chips.

About 2½ cups salsa

PER TABLESPOON: Calories 8; Protein 1 g; Carbohydrate 1 g; Fat 0 g; Cholesterol 0 mg; Sodium 15 mg

Chili and Pepper Safety

The flesh, ribs and seeds of chilis are rich in irritating, burning oils. When preparing chilis, always wash hands and utensils in soapy water. Be careful not to rub your face—eyes especially—until the oils have been thoroughly washed away. Some cooks who work with chilis for any extended length of time wear plastic gloves.

ANCHOVY-GARLIC DIP
BAGNA CAUDA (<u>bah</u>-n'yah kah-<u>oo</u>-dah)

Meaning "hot bath," *Bagna Cauda* is a versatile Italian dish. It was traditionally served steaming hot as a cold-weather meal, with lots of fresh bread for dipping.

2 cans (2 ounces each) anchovy fillets
½ cup margarine or butter, softened
2 cloves garlic, cut into halves
Snipped parsley
Vegetable Dippers (below) or Italian breadsticks
  (optional)

Drain anchovies, reserving 1 tablespoon oil. Place anchovies, reserved oil, the margarine and garlic in blender container. Cover and blend on medium speed, scraping sides of blender frequently, about 1 minute. Garnish with parsley. Serve at room temperature with Vegetable Dippers.

⅔ cup dip

PER TABLESPOON: Calories 90; Protein 2 g; Carbohydrate 0 g; Fat 9 g; Cholesterol 5 mg; Sodium 400 mg

VEGETABLE DIPPERS: Carrot sticks, cauliflower or broccoli flowerets, celery sticks, cucumber or zucchini sticks, green onion pieces, small whole mushrooms, red or green pepper strips, radishes with stems.

EGGPLANT DIP
BABA GHANNOOJ (<u>bah</u>-bah gah-<u>noosh</u>)

This is a popular Mediterranean dip made with roasted eggplant, which loses its bitter edge with long cooking.

1 medium eggplant (about 1 pound)
1 small onion, cut into fourths
1 clove garlic
¼ cup lemon juice
1 tablespoon olive or vegetable oil
1½ teaspoons salt
Vegetable Dippers (left) (optional)

Prick eggplant 3 or 4 times with fork. Cook in 400° oven until very soft, about 40 minutes. Cool. Pare eggplant; cut into cubes. Place eggplant, onion, garlic, lemon juice, oil and salt in blender container. Cover and blend on high speed until smooth. Serve with Vegetable Dippers.

About 2 cups dip

PER TABLESPOON: Calories 15; Protein 0 g; Carbohydrate 2 g; Fat 1 g; Cholesterol 0 mg; Sodium 100 mg

HERBED LIVER PÂTÉ

PÂTÉ PROVENÇAL (pah-teh proh-vahng-sahl)

This recipe calls for the special brandy made in the Cognac region of France. Like many pâtés, this one is delicious served with cornichons.

1 medium onion, chopped
2 tablespoons margarine or butter
1 pound chicken livers
½ teaspoon salt
½ teaspoon dried thyme leaves
½ teaspoon crushed dried rosemary leaves
½ teaspoon dried marjoram leaves
½ teaspoon ground sage
⅛ teaspoon pepper
2 tablespoons Cognac or Madeira
¼ cup whipping cream
French bread, thinly sliced and toasted (optional)

Cook and stir onion in margarine in 10-inch skillet over medium heat until tender. Add livers. Cook over medium-high heat, stirring occasionally, until livers are no longer pink inside, about 12 minutes. Reduce heat to low; stir in salt, thyme, rosemary, marjoram, sage and pepper. Cook and stir 1 minute.

Place liver mixture in food processor workbowl fitted with steel blade. Add Cognac to skillet; stir Cognac, and scrape drippings from skillet. Add to liver mixture. Cover and process with about 15 on/off motions until mixture is very finely chopped. Add whipping cream. Cover and process, adding 2 or 3 teaspoons whipping cream if necessary, until smooth and fluffy, about 15 seconds.

Pack liver mixture into small bowl or crock. Cover and refrigerate at least 6 hours. Let stand at room temperature about 30 minutes before serving. Serve with French bread. Garnish with cornichons and parsley if desired.

1½ cups pâté

PER TABLESPOON: Calories 35; Protein 3 g; Carbohydrate 1 g; Fat 2 g; Cholesterol 75 mg; Sodium 60 mg

Cornichons

A traditional accompaniment to all manner of pâtés, *cornichons* is the French name for tiny pickled gherkins. Cornichons are, as a rule, not sweet or even sweet-sour; they taste of spices and good, mellow vinegar. They are no thicker than an adult's little finger, and two or three of them, together with a few tiny pickled onions, would be the usual serving with a generous slice of pâté or terrine. Cornichons may be purchased in jars or in bulk.

RUSSIAN EGGPLANT SPREAD

BAKLAZHANNAIA IKRA (bah-klah-jhah-nay-ah ee-krah)

Enjoy this smooth, thick purée very cold. It tastes best with assertively flavored breads.

1 medium eggplant (about 1 pound)
1 medium green pepper
1 small onion, chopped
2 large cloves garlic, finely chopped
1 tablespoon vegetable oil
¼ cup tomato paste
1 tablespoon sugar
1 tablespoon lemon juice
½ teaspoon salt
⅛ teaspoon pepper
Cocktail pumpernickel rye bread or black bread
  (optional)

Prick eggplant 3 or 4 times with fork. Wrap green pepper in aluminum foil. Place eggplant and green pepper in shallow baking dish. Cook in 400° oven until eggplant is very soft, about 35 minutes; cool. Remove skin from eggplant and seeds from green pepper; chop eggplant and green pepper.

Cook and stir onion and garlic in oil in 10-inch skillet over medium heat until onion is tender. Stir in eggplant, green pepper and remaining ingredients except bread. Heat to boiling; reduce heat. Simmer uncovered, stirring occasionally, 5 minutes. Place mixture in blender container. Cover and blend on high speed, stopping blender occasionally to scrape sides, until smooth, about 1 minute. Cover and refrigerate until very cold, at least 4 hours. Serve with bread.

About 2 cups spread

PER TABLESPOON: Calories 15; Protein 0 g; Carbohydrate 2 g; Fat 1 g; Cholesterol 0 mg; Sodium 50 mg

BEAN AND SESAME SEED SPREAD

HUMMUS (hoo-muss)

This Middle Eastern spread is familiar to many Western cooks as *hummus bi tahini,* a name that acknowledges the contribution of the sesame seed, ground to a paste. Canned garbanzo beans make this recipe a snap to prepare.

1 can (15 ounces) garbanzo beans (chickpeas),
  drained (reserve liquid)
½ cup sesame seed
1 clove garlic, cut into halves
3 tablespoons lemon juice
1 teaspoon salt
Snipped parsley
Pocket Bread (page 293), Vegetable Dippers
  (page 33) or crackers (optional)

Place reserved bean liquid, the sesame seed and garlic in blender container. Cover and blend on high speed until mixed. Add beans, lemon juice and salt; cover and blend on high speed, stopping blender to scrape sides if necessary, until of uniform consistency. Garnish with parsley. Serve as spread or dip with wedges of Pocket Bread.

2 cups spread

PER TABLESPOON: Calories 35; Protein 1 g; Carbohydrate 3 g; Fat 2 g; Cholesterol 0 mg; Sodium 90 mg

YOGURT CHEESE

LABANEE or LABNEH (lah-bah-neh)

In the Middle East, this mild spread often makes an appearance as a breakfast cheese. The Syrians are particularly known for their fondness for Yogurt Cheese.

4 cups plain yogurt (without gelatin)
1 teaspoon salt
Pocket Bread (page 293), split, cut into wedges and toasted (optional)

Line a strainer with double-thickness cheesecloth. Place strainer over bowl. Mix yogurt and salt; pour into strainer. Cover and refrigerate at least 12 hours. Unmold onto plate. Garnish with snipped parsley, Moroccan Herbed Olives (below) or Greek olives if desired. Serve with Pocket Bread.

About 1½ cups

PER TABLESPOON: Calories 30; Protein 2 g; Carbohydrate 3 g; Fat 1 g; Cholesterol 5 mg; Sodium 120 mg

---

MOROCCAN HERBED OLIVES

Marinated olives are essential to a *mezze* or *mazza*, the Middle Eastern counterpart of an Italian *antipasto*. Moroccan market stalls are crowded with enormous ceramic jars filled with olives of all kinds. Moroccan Herbed Olives keep well tightly covered and refrigerated.

1 pound Kalamata or Greek olives
¼ cup olive or vegetable oil
2 tablespoons snipped parsley
2 tablespoons snipped fresh cilantro
1 tablespoon lemon juice
½ teaspoon crushed red pepper
2 cloves garlic, finely chopped

Rinse olives under running cold water; drain. Place in 1-quart jar with tight-fitting lid. Mix remaining ingredients; pour over olives. Cover tightly and refrigerate, turning jar upside down occasionally, 1 to 2 weeks. Serve at room temperature.

About 75 olives

PER OLIVE: Calories 10; Protein 0 g; Carbohydrate 0 g; Fat 1 g; Cholesterol 0 mg; Sodium 50 mg

Olives

Olives are loved the world over, but nowhere more than in the area around the Mediterranean. Green olives are just that: the unripe, green fruit of the olive tree. Unlike some fruits (the banana, for example), once an olive is picked it will not ripen any further. On the tree, olives progress from light green to brownish-green to brownish-purple to red-purple to deep purple and finally to black. Thus, what is meant by a "ripe olive" is a black olive. The curing or pickling of an olive is largely what determines its flavor.

Yogurt Cheese and Moroccan Herbed Olives

2

FISH AND SHELLFISH

L ook to these recipes for the exuberant accent of foreign lands: Brazilian Seafood Stew has a hint of coconut and peanut butter. Steamed Clams with Sausage is an irrepressibly festive and spicy stew from Portugal. Black Sea Bass with Fennel features one of Italy's most celebrated vegetables and combines it with a richly flavored fish for luscious results.

Today, fresh fish and seafood can be enjoyed almost anywhere in the United States, at almost any time of the year—thanks to improved cold storage techniques and the speed of air freight. In this chapter you will find a wide assortment of prize-winning fish and seafood entrées that are easy to prepare and take great advantage of this delicious, lower-calorie, lean resource.

Many of the recipes that follow are beautifully suited to entertaining, from such international classics as Fish with Green Grapes (the creamy *Poisson Véronique* of France) to new favorites like delicate Tempura from Japan, and Sweet and Sour Fish from China. Many recipes are kind to your budget as well and can be prepared with ingredients commonly on hand in your kitchen cupboard. Here, too, are recipes that make the most of traditionally expensive ingredients; Mussels in White Wine Sauce and Baked Crab with Port are based on ingredients that seem luxurious, and yet an economical amount of each goes a long way on flavor.

Clockwise from top left: Seafood Paella (page 40), Italian Focaccia (page 294) and Sliced Oranges in Syrup (page 318)

SEAFOOD PAELLA

(pah-<u>yeh</u>-ah)

A shallow, double-handled dish in which saffroned rice and a mélange of seafood are cooked together is known as a *paella*. Fresh-tasting peas, a sprinkling of pimientos and the squid so loved by the Spanish mark this as an Iberian specialty.

12 mussels
6 clams
¼ cup olive or vegetable oil
8 ounces raw shrimp, shelled and deveined
8 ounces scallops
8 ounces squid or octopus, cleaned and cut into
    ¼-inch rings
1 medium onion, chopped
2 cloves garlic, finely chopped
1 can (16 ounces) whole tomatoes (with liquid)
2 cups water
1 cup uncooked regular rice
1 teaspoon salt
½ teaspoon saffron or ground turmeric
¼ teaspoon pepper
½ cup frozen green peas
1 jar (2 ounces) sliced pimientos, drained

Clean clams and mussels as directed on pages 76–77. Discard any that are not tightly closed.

Heat oil in 14-inch metal paella pan or Dutch oven over medium heat until hot. Cook and stir shrimp in oil just until pink, about 2 minutes; remove with slotted spoon. Cook and stir scallops until slightly firm, 1 to 2 minutes; remove with slotted spoon. Cover and refrigerate shrimp and scallops. Cook and stir squid until rings begin to shrink, about 2 minutes; remove with slotted spoon.

Add more oil to pan if necessary. Cook and stir onion and garlic until onion is tender. Stir in squid and tomatoes; break up tomatoes with fork. Heat to boiling; reduce heat. Simmer uncovered, stirring occasionally, 20 minutes. Stir in shrimp, scallops, water, rice, salt, saffron and pepper. Heat to boiling; reduce heat. Simmer uncovered, stirring occasionally, 10 minutes.

Arrange mussels, clams and peas on top of rice mixture. Cover loosely with aluminum foil. Cook in 350° oven until liquid is absorbed, about 25 minutes in paella pan, 40 minutes in Dutch oven. Discard any unopened mussels or clams. Sprinkle with pimientos. Garnish with lemon wedges if desired.

6 servings

PER SERVING: Calories 390; Protein 32 g; Carbohydrate 38 g; Fat 12 g; Cholesterol 175 mg; Sodium 700 mg

Garam Masala

This Indian spice mixture is not a fixed combination of ingredients, but a formula that changes from cook to cook and from dish to dish. Some formulas result in a very fragrant *Garam Masala*, some in a hot and spicy one. The mixture usually contains cardamom, cinnamon and cloves, all "warm" spices. Then, depending on the recipe, it might go on to include coriander, cumin, nutmeg, mace or pepper. The spices are usually cooked briefly in hot fat before the principal ingredients of the dish are added; this heightens the flavor and aroma of the spices.

BROILED FISH WITH MANY SPICES

The fragrant brushing of spices called for here will add a piquant flavor redolent of Indian cooking to fish steaks, whether swordfish or halibut. Ghee doesn't burn as easily as unclarified butter does, and it keeps the fish moist under the intense heat of the broiler.

2 tablespoons lemon juice
2 tablespoons dry mustard
2 teaspoons ground cumin
1 teaspoon ground coriander
1 teaspoon salt
¼ teaspoon garam masala (optional)
4 swordfish or halibut steaks, 1 inch thick (about 2 pounds)
2 tablespoons Ghee (page 237) or melted margarine or butter

Mix all ingredients except fish and Ghee. Spread mixture evenly on both sides of fish. Place fish in shallow glass or plastic dish; cover and refrigerate at least 12 hours.

Set oven control to broil or 550°. Arrange fish on rack in broiler pan; drizzle with Ghee. Broil with tops about 4 inches from heat until light brown, about 7 minutes. Turn; drizzle with Ghee. Broil until fish flakes easily with fork, 5 to 7 minutes longer.

4 servings

PER SERVING: Calories 275; Protein 44 g; Carbohydrate 2 g; Fat 10 g; Cholesterol 120 mg; Sodium 790 mg

BAKED FISH, SPANISH STYLE

A squeeze of lemon and a dash of olive oil give your favorite fish the essence of Mediterranean cooking. A colorful array of bright vegetables and lemon slices make this simple dish distinctly Spanish.

1½ pounds fish steaks or fillets
1½ teaspoons salt
¼ teaspoon paprika
¼ teaspoon pepper
1 medium green pepper, cut into rings
1 medium tomato, sliced
1 small onion, sliced
2 tablespoons lemon juice
2 tablespoons olive or vegetable oil
1 clove garlic, finely chopped
Lemon wedges

If fish pieces are large, cut into serving pieces. Arrange fish in ungreased square baking dish, 8 × 8 × 2 inches; sprinkle with salt, paprika and pepper. Top with green pepper rings and tomato and onion slices. Mix lemon juice, oil and garlic; pour over fish. Cover and cook in 375° oven 15 minutes. Uncover and cook until fish flakes easily with fork, 10 to 15 minutes longer. Garnish with lemon wedges.

6 servings

PER SERVING: Calories 160; Protein 22 g; Carbohydrate 4 g; Fat 6 g; Cholesterol 60 mg; Sodium 630 mg

PERCH BAKED WITH SESAME SEED

SAMAK TAHINI (sah-mahk tah-hee-nee)

A subtle blend of sesame seed, red pepper, lemon and olive oil makes this a truly Middle Eastern dish. The sesame seed is toasted for a more pronounced flavor. Serve with Moroccan Herbed Olives (page 37), Pocket Bread (page 293) or hot cooked rice for a simple Middle Eastern meal.

1 medium red onion, sliced
1 tablespoon vegetable oil
⅓ cup sesame seed, toasted
¼ cup water
1 small clove garlic, finely chopped
½ teaspoon salt
2 tablespoons lemon juice
Dash of ground red pepper
Olive or vegetable oil
2 tablespoons dry bread crumbs
2 tablespoons snipped parsley
1 pound perch fillets
Parsley
Ripe olives (optional)

Cook and stir onion in 1 tablespoon oil until tender. Mix sesame seed, water, garlic, salt, lemon juice and red pepper. Lightly brush square baking dish, 8 × 8 × 2 inches, with oil; sprinkle with bread crumbs and 2 tablespoons parsley. Pat fish dry; arrange in baking dish. Pour sesame seed mixture over fish; top with onion. Cook uncovered in 400° oven until fish flakes easily with fork, 20 to 25 minutes. Garnish with parsley and ripe olives.

4 servings

PER SERVING: Calories 300; Protein 25 g; Carbohydrate 7 g; Fat 19 g; Cholesterol 60 mg; Sodium 390 mg

FISH BAKED WITH TOMATOES AND SPICES

MTUZI WA SAMAKI (m'too-zee wah sah-mah-kee)

The hallmark of much of African cooking is its hot and peppery nature. *Mtuzi wa Samaki,* a dish from Kenya, follows in that tradition.

1 large onion, sliced
2 cloves garlic, chopped
2 jalapeño peppers, seeded and chopped
2 tablespoons vegetable oil
1 can (16 ounces) whole tomatoes, drained and chopped
2 tablespoons vinegar
1¼ teaspoons ground cumin
¾ teaspoon ground coriander
½ teaspoon salt
4 halibut steaks, 1 inch thick (about 2 pounds)

Cook and stir onion, garlic and peppers in oil in 10-inch skillet over medium heat until onion is tender. Reduce heat; stir in remaining ingredients except fish. Cook uncovered over low heat, stirring occasionally, 5 minutes.

Arrange fish in ungreased oblong baking dish, 12 × 7½ × 2 inches. Spoon tomato mixture over fish. Cook uncovered in 350° oven until fish flakes easily with fork, 25 to 30 minutes. Sprinkle with snipped fresh cilantro if desired.

4 servings

PER SERVING: Calories 320; Protein 45 g; Carbohydrate 12 g; Fat 10 g; Cholesterol 120 mg; Sodium 640 mg

FISH FILLETS WITH SPINACH

FILETS DE POISSON FLORENTINE
(fee-leh duh pwa-sohng flaw-rawn-teen)

In French cuisine, the addition of spinach to a dish earns it the title *Florentine*. A pinch of nutmeg and of red pepper add a measure of piquancy to a dish blanketed by rich, homemade white sauce.

2 tablespoons margarine or butter
2 tablespoons all-purpose flour
1 teaspoon instant chicken bouillon
Dash of ground nutmeg
Dash of ground red pepper
Dash of white pepper
1 cup milk
⅔ cup shredded Swiss or Cheddar cheese
1 package (10 ounces) frozen chopped spinach, thawed and well drained
1 tablespoon lemon juice
1 pound fish fillets, cut into serving pieces
½ teaspoon salt
2 tablespoons grated Parmesan cheese
Paprika

Heat margarine over low heat until melted; stir in flour, bouillon, nutmeg, red pepper and white pepper. Cook over low heat, stirring constantly, until mixture is smooth and bubbly; remove from heat. Stir in milk. Heat to boiling, stirring constantly. Boil and stir 1 minute. Add Swiss cheese; cook, stirring constantly, just until cheese is melted.

Place spinach in ungreased oblong baking dish, 12 × 7½ × 2 inches, or square baking dish, 8 × 8 × 2 inches; sprinkle with lemon juice. Arrange fish on spinach; sprinkle with salt. Spread sauce over fish and spinach. Cook uncovered in 350° oven until fish flakes easily with fork, 20 to 25 minutes. Sprinkle with Parmesan cheese and paprika.

4 servings

PER SERVING: Calories 290; Protein 31 g; Carbohydrate 10 g; Fat 14 g; Cholesterol 85 mg; Sodium 910 mg

FISH WITH SOUR CREAM

BETYAR FOGAS (bet-yahr foh-gosh)

This creamy dish is rich and satisfying. In Hungary and Austria, *Betyar Fogas* is often accompanied by boiled russet potatoes.

1 pound fish fillets
4 ounces mushrooms, sliced
1 small onion, chopped
1 tablespoon margarine or butter
½ teaspoon salt
⅛ teaspoon pepper
½ cup dairy sour cream
3 tablespoons grated Parmesan cheese
2 tablespoons dry bread crumbs
Paprika
Snipped parsley

If fish fillets are large, cut into serving pieces. Pat fish dry; arrange in ungreased oblong baking dish, 12 × 7½ × 2 inches. Cook and stir mushrooms and onion in margarine until mushrooms are golden, about 3 minutes. Spoon mushroom mixture over fish; sprinkle with salt and pepper.

Mix sour cream and cheese; spread over mushroom mixture. Sprinkle with bread crumbs. Cook uncovered in 350° oven until fish flakes easily with fork, 25 to 30 minutes. Sprinkle with paprika and parsley.

4 to 6 servings

PER SERVING: Calories 225; Protein 25 g; Carbohydrate 6 g; Fat 11 g; Cholesterol 80 mg; Sodium 500 mg

FISH WITH GREEN GRAPES

POISSON VÉRONIQUE (pwah-<u>sohng</u> veh-raw-<u>neek</u>)

A hearty splash of wine and fresh green grapes distinguish this fish dish as *Véronique*. A hint of shallot and of lemon add to the subtlety of flavor that typifies French cuisine.

2 pounds fish fillets
1½ teaspoons salt
¼ teaspoon pepper
¾ cup dry white wine
1 cup water
2 tablespoons finely chopped shallots or green onion
1 tablespoon lemon juice
8 ounces (about 1⅓ cups) seedless green grapes
2 tablespoons margarine or butter
2 tablespoons all-purpose flour
½ cup whipping cream
2 tablespoons margarine or butter

Sprinkle fish with salt and pepper; fold in half. Place fish in 10-inch skillet; add wine, water, shallots and lemon juice. Heat to boiling; reduce heat. Cover and simmer until fish flakes easily with fork, 4 to 5 minutes. Remove with slotted spatula to heatproof platter; keep warm. Add grapes to liquid in skillet. Heat to boiling; reduce heat. Simmer uncovered 3 minutes. Remove grapes with slotted spoon.

Heat liquid in skillet to boiling; boil until reduced to 1 cup. Pour liquid into measuring cup; reserve. Heat 2 tablespoons margarine in skillet until melted; stir in flour. Cook and stir 1 minute; remove from heat. Stir in reserved liquid and the whipping cream. Heat to boiling, stirring constantly. Boil and stir 1 minute.

Add 2 tablespoons margarine; stir until melted. Drain excess liquid from fish; spoon sauce over fish. Set oven control to broil or 550°. Broil fish 4 inches from heat just until sauce is glazed, about 3 minutes. Garnish with grapes.

6 to 8 servings

PER SERVING: Calories 300; Protein 29 g; Carbohydrate 10 g; Fat 16 g; Cholesterol 100 mg; Sodium 760 mg

FISH WITH CUMIN PASTE

These piquant spices are typical of Middle Eastern and North African cooking. Snipped cilantro adds a fresh, distinctive fillip.

1½ pounds scrod or red snapper fillets
2 tablespoons ground cumin
2 tablespoons olive or vegetable oil
1 tablespoon lemon juice
½ teaspoon crushed red pepper
½ teaspoon paprika
¼ teaspoon salt
3 cloves garlic, cut into halves
3 tablespoons snipped fresh cilantro

If fish fillets are large, cut into serving pieces. Place fish in ungreased oblong baking dish, 13 × 9 × 2 inches.

Place remaining ingredients except cilantro in blender container. Cover and blend on high speed, scraping sides of blender occasionally, until smooth, about 30 seconds. Spread mixture evenly over fish. Cook uncovered in 350° oven until fish flakes easily with fork, 25 to 30 minutes. Sprinkle with cilantro; serve with lemon wedges if desired.

4 servings

PER SERVING: Calories 240; Protein 34 g; Carbohydrate 3 g; Fat 10 g; Cholesterol 95 mg; Sodium 290 mg

Clockwise from bottom: Fish with Cumin Paste, Orange Salad with Onion and Olives (page 234) and African Coriander Bread (page 289)

FRIED FISH IN PUNGENT SAUCE

ESCABECHE DE PESCADO FRITO
(ehs-kah-beh-che deh pehs-kah-doh free-toh)

Escabeche means "pickled" in Spanish, referring to the sweet and sour flavor that the combination of vinegar, brown sugar and ginger gives.

¼ cup olive or vegetable oil
1½ pounds fish fillets, cut into serving pieces
¾ cup water
2 medium carrots, thinly sliced
2 small onions, sliced
1 small green pepper, cut into rings
1 clove garlic, finely chopped
1 tablespoon packed brown sugar
½ teaspoon salt
¼ teaspoon ground ginger
⅓ cup vinegar
2 teaspoons cornstarch

Heat oil in skillet until hot. Pat fish dry. Cook over medium heat until fish flakes easily with fork, turning carefully, 8 to 10 minutes.

Heat water, carrots, onions, green pepper, garlic, brown sugar, salt and ginger to boiling in 1½-quart saucepan; reduce heat. Cover and simmer 5 minutes. Mix vinegar and cornstarch; stir into vegetables. Heat to boiling, stirring constantly. Boil and stir 1 minute. Pour vegetable mixture over fish.

8 servings

PER SERVING: Calories 165; Protein 16 g; Carbohydrate 7 g; Fat 8 g; Cholesterol 45 mg; Sodium 220 mg

SWEET AND SOUR FISH

TIEN SHUEN YU (dee-en shoo-wan you)

For added Oriental appearance, slice the carrots at an angle, starting from the tip of the carrot and working your way to the top. Serve with hot cooked rice and a pot of jasmine tea.

2 medium carrots, cut diagonally into thin slices
½ cup water
1½ pounds fish fillets, cut into 1-inch pieces
½ cup packed brown sugar
⅓ cup vinegar
2 tablespoons cornstarch
2 tablespoons soy sauce
1 can (15¼ ounces) pineapple chunks
1 medium green pepper, cut into 1-inch pieces
Vegetable oil
Batter (page 47)

Heat carrots and water to boiling. Cover and cook until crisp-tender, 8 to 10 minutes. Pat fish dry. Mix brown sugar, vinegar, cornstarch and soy sauce in 2-quart saucepan. Stir in carrots (with cooking liquid), pineapple (with syrup) and green pepper. Heat to boiling, stirring constantly. Boil and stir 1 minute. Keep warm.

Heat oil (1 to 1½ inches) to 360°. Prepare batter. Dip fish into batter with tongs. Allow excess batter to drip back into bowl. Fry 7 or 8 pieces at a time until golden brown, about 1 minute on each side; drain. Arrange on platter; pour sauce over fish.

6 servings

PER SERVING: Calories 370; Protein 23 g; Carbohydrate 45 g; Fat 11 g; Cholesterol 60 mg; Sodium 930 mg

BATTER

¾ cup water
⅔ cup all-purpose flour
1¼ teaspoons salt
½ teaspoon baking powder

Mix all ingredients.

SALT COD IN TOMATO SAUCE

BACALHAU COM TAMATADA
(bah-kahl-<u>yow</u> kohm toh-mah-<u>tah</u>-dah)

There are nearly as many ways of preparing salt cod as there are fish in the sea. In Portugal, this specially prepared fish is served with tomatoes, onion and a hint of garlic, and sprinkled with rings of ripe olives and hard-cooked eggs.

1½ pounds salt cod fillets
2 medium onions, sliced
1 tablespoon olive or vegetable oil
2 medium tomatoes, chopped
1 clove garlic, chopped
⅛ teaspoon pepper
2 hard-cooked eggs, peeled and sliced
¼ cup pitted ripe olives, sliced
Snipped parsley

If fish fillets are large, cut into serving pieces. Place fish in enamel or stainless steel pan or glass bowl. Cover with cold water; refrigerate 12 to 24 hours, changing water 3 or 4 times.

Cook and stir onions in oil until tender. Add tomatoes, garlic and pepper. Cover and simmer 5 minutes. Pour into ungreased oblong baking dish, 12 × 7½ × 2 inches.

Drain fish. Remove bones and skin if necessary; rinse fish in cold water. Arrange fish on tomato mixture. Cover and cook in 350° oven until fish flakes easily with fork, 20 to 30 minutes. Garnish with eggs, olives and snipped parsley.

8 servings

PER SERVING: Calories 140; Protein 22 g; Carbohydrate 4 g; Fat 4 g; Cholesterol 110 mg; Sodium 560 mg

---

Salt Cod

Cod harvested far from land was traditionally salted heavily as a preservative measure. Salt cod, the fillets sometimes literally stiff with salt, must be soaked in several changes of cold water before it can be cooked and eaten, whether creamed or with a spicy tomato sauce. The soaking time varies with the amount of salt in the fish and with the size of the fillet. Small, thin fillets take less soaking time than thick ones.

LEMON-BAKED COD

OVNSSTEKT TORSK MED SITRON
(ovn-stehkt toschk meh see-trohn)

Fresh codfish and lemon go hand in hand. Serve this simple Norwegian dish with crusty bread pulled warm from the oven or piping hot baked potatoes.

1 pound cod fillets
¼ cup margarine or butter, melted
2 tablespoons lemon juice
¼ cup all-purpose flour
½ teaspoon salt
⅛ teaspoon white pepper
Paprika

If fish fillets are large, cut into serving pieces. Mix margarine and lemon juice. In another bowl, mix flour, salt and white pepper. Dip fish into margarine mixture; coat fish with flour mixture. Place fish in ungreased square baking dish, 8 × 8 × 2 inches. Pour remaining margarine mixture over fish; sprinkle with paprika. Cook uncovered in 350° oven until fish flakes easily with fork, 25 to 30 minutes. Garnish with parsley sprigs and lemon slices if desired.

4 servings

PER SERVING: Calories 235; Protein 22 g; Carbohydrate 7 g; Fat 13 g; Cholesterol 60 mg; Sodium 490 mg

COD WITH VEGETABLES

KALAKASVISVUOKA (kuh-luh-kuhs-vees-voh-oo-kah)

Follow this Finnish favorite, with its lemony accent and crunchy topping, with a luscious dessert: Finnish Cranberry Whip (page 320).

2 pounds cod fillets
3 tablespoons lemon juice
1½ teaspoons salt
⅛ teaspoon pepper
2 medium carrots, coarsely shredded
1 large stalk celery, finely chopped
1 medium onion, chopped
5 slices bread (crusts removed), cubed
½ cup margarine or butter, melted
½ teaspoon salt
½ teaspoon ground sage
½ teaspoon ground thyme
3 tablespoons dry bread crumbs
2 tablespoons snipped parsley
½ teaspoon paprika

If fish fillets are large, cut into serving pieces. Arrange fish in ungreased oblong baking dish, 12 × 7½ × 2 inches, or square baking dish, 8 × 8 × 2 inches. Sprinkle with lemon juice, 1½ teaspoons salt and the pepper.

Mix carrots, celery, onion, bread cubes, margarine, ½ teaspoon salt, sage and thyme. Spread evenly over fish. Mix bread crumbs, parsley and paprika; sprinkle over vegetables. Cover and cook in 350° oven until fish flakes easily with fork, about 35 minutes.

6 servings

PER SERVING: Calories 360; Protein 31 g; Carbohydrate 18 g; Fat 18 g; Cholesterol 80 mg; Sodium 1170 mg

CODFISH PUDDING WITH DILL SAUCE

FISKEPUDDING (fee-sk′ poo-ding)

Fiskepudding is reputed to be served weekly in Norwegian homes. Though it is usually served hot, it can be served cold, spread on rye bread or crackers. It is important to make this pudding with fresh fish only; frozen fish loses the naturally gelatinous quality that gives this pudding body and a smooth texture.

1½ pounds fresh cod fillets*
1½ cups whipping cream
2 tablespoons cornstarch
1 teaspoon salt
Dash of ground red pepper
Dill Sauce (right)

Cut fish into 1-inch pieces. Place one third of the fish and ⅓ cup of the whipping cream in blender container. Cover and blend on high speed, stopping blender occasionally to scrape sides if necessary, until smooth and thick, about 1 minute. Pour mixture into large bowl. Repeat twice with remaining fish and ⅔ cup of the whipping cream. Shake remaining ½ cup whipping cream and the cornstarch in tightly covered jar. Stir cornstarch mixture, salt and red pepper into fish mixture. Beat vigorously with spoon until well blended and fluffy.

Spread fish mixture in oiled loaf pan, 8½ × 4½ × 2½ inches, or 6-cup mold; cover with aluminum foil. Place pan in oblong pan, 13 × 9 × 2 inches, on oven rack. Pour hot water into pan until almost full. Cook in 350° oven until knife inserted in center comes out clean, 60 to 70 minutes. Remove pan from water. Let stand, covered, 10 minutes. Carefully pour off any liquid around pudding. Unmold; serve with Dill Sauce.

8 servings

*Cod must be fresh, not frozen.

PER SERVING: Calories 365; Protein 19 g; Carbohydrate 9 g; Fat 28 g; Cholesterol 115 mg; Sodium 580 mg

DILL SAUCE

8 ounces mushrooms, sliced
¼ cup margarine or butter
3 tablespoons all-purpose flour
½ teaspoon salt
Dash of pepper
2 cups half-and-half
2 tablespoons snipped dill weed

Cook and stir mushrooms in margarine in 2-quart saucepan over medium heat 3 minutes; remove from heat. Stir in flour, salt and pepper. Gradually stir in half-and-half. Heat to boiling over medium heat, stirring constantly. Boil and stir 1 minute. Remove from heat; stir in dill weed.

Selecting Fish

Fish, whether fresh or frozen, should not have a strong smell. If it does, that is your first clue that the fish is "off." The eyes of very fresh fish are bright and clear, not sunken and opaque. Fresh fish is firm to the touch, with shiny scales and clearly pink gills. When buying frozen fish, look for fish that is tightly wrapped, frozen solid and has no evidence of discoloration.

JAMAICAN CODFISH FRITTERS

STAMP AND GO

These codfish fritters are a sample of early fast-food fish and chips—Jamaican style. Spicy and hot, they are delicious when topped with a squeeze of fresh lemon or lime.

8 ounces cod fillets
2 medium onions, chopped
2 tablespoons olive or vegetable oil
Vegetable oil
1 cup all-purpose flour
¾ cup milk
1 egg
1 teaspoon baking powder
1 teaspoon salt
1 teaspoon vegetable oil
¼ teaspoon ground red pepper

Heat fish and just enough water to cover to boiling; reduce heat. Cover and simmer until fish flakes easily with fork, 5 to 7 minutes; drain. Cool and flake. Cook and stir onions in 2 tablespoons oil until tender.

Heat oil (1 to 1½ inches) to 360°. Beat remaining ingredients with hand beater until smooth. Stir in fish and onions; drop by level table-spoonfuls into hot oil. Fry 5 or 6 at a time until golden brown, turning once, about 4 minutes; drain. Serve with tartar sauce and lemon wedges if desired.

About 36 fritters

PER FRITTER: Calories 45; Protein 2 g; Carbohydrate 3 g; Fat 3 g; Cholesterol 10 mg; Sodium 80 mg

SMOKED HADDOCK WITH WHITE SAUCE

FINNAN HADDIE WITH WHITE SAUCE

This traditional Scottish dish often is served as breakfast, but with potatoes it makes a substantial main meal. The name comes from Findon—a village renowned for the industry of curing fish. "Haddie" is a slang term for haddock.

1 pound smoked haddock or smoked cod
    fillets
2 tablespoons margarine or butter
1 small onion, chopped
¼ teaspoon salt
⅛ teaspoon pepper
¾ cup milk
2 teaspoons cornstarch

Cut fish into 1-inch pieces, removing any bones and skin. Heat margarine in skillet until melted; add fish and onion. Sprinkle with salt and pepper. Cook and stir 5 minutes.

Stir milk gradually into cornstarch in 1-quart saucepan; heat to boiling, stirring constantly. Boil and stir 1 minute. Pour over fish. Simmer uncovered until fish flakes easily with fork, 3 to 5 minutes. Serve with boiled or baked potatoes if desired.

4 servings

PER SERVING: Calories 210; Protein 30 g; Carbohydrate 5 g; Fat 8 g; Cholesterol 90 mg; Sodium 1090 mg

SMOKED HADDOCK WITH RICE

KEDGEREE (kech-uh-ree)

Kedgeree is originally an Indian dish that the British have adopted. The hint of red pepper called for here is all that remains of the spices in old Indian versions. This light dish can be served for brunch or dinner.

4 hard-cooked eggs
2 cups water
1 cup uncooked regular rice
1 teaspoon salt
1 pound smoked haddock or cod
1 large onion, chopped
¼ cup margarine or butter
¼ teaspoon salt
⅛ to ¼ teaspoon ground red pepper
Snipped parsley

Separate egg yolks from whites. Press yolks through sieve; chop whites. Heat water, rice and 1 teaspoon salt to boiling, stirring once or twice; reduce heat. Cover and simmer 14 minutes. (Do not lift cover or stir.) Remove from heat. Fluff rice lightly with fork; cover and let steam 5 to 10 minutes.

Cover fish with cold water. Heat to boiling; reduce heat. Cover and simmer 10 minutes; drain. Break fish into large flakes with fork, removing any bones and skin. Keep warm.

Cook and stir onion in margarine in 10-inch skillet until tender. Stir in chopped egg white, rice, ¼ teaspoon salt and the red pepper. Stir in flaked fish gently. Serve on heated platter; sprinkle with egg yolk and parsley.

8 servings

PER SERVING: Calories 245; Protein 19 g; Carbohydrate 22 g; Fat 9 g; Cholesterol 150 mg; Sodium 870 mg

RED SNAPPER, VERA CRUZ STYLE

HUACHINANGO A LA VERACRUZANA
(wa-chee-nahn-goh ah lah veh-rah-cru-zah-nah)

Lemon, tomatoes and pimiento-stuffed olives accent this entrée from Mexico's principal seaport.

2 pounds red snapper fillets
2 tablespoons capers
1 tablespoon lemon juice
1 jar (2 ounces) pimiento-stuffed green olives, drained
1 large onion, chopped
1 clove garlic, finely chopped
2 tablespoons vegetable oil
1 can (28 ounces) whole tomatoes, drained and chopped
½ teaspoon salt
⅛ teaspoon pepper

If fish fillets are large, cut into serving pieces. Arrange fish in lightly oiled oblong baking dish, 13 × 9 × 2 inches. Sprinkle with capers, lemon juice and olives.

Cook and stir onion and garlic in oil in 10-inch skillet over medium heat until onion is tender; add tomatoes, salt and pepper. Heat to boiling; reduce heat. Simmer uncovered, stirring occasionally, 5 minutes. Spoon tomato mixture evenly over fish. Cook uncovered in 350° oven until fish flakes easily with fork, 25 to 30 minutes. Serve with lemon wedges if desired.

6 servings

PER SERVING: Calories 225; Protein 30 g; Carbohydrate 8 g; Fat 8 g; Cholesterol 80 mg; Sodium 750 mg

BROILED GRAVLAX WITH MUSTARD SAUCE

GRAVLAX (g'<u>rahv</u>-lahx)

In many countries salmon was traditionally, cured by smoking and salting the fish. Another method, used in Scandinavia, involves sugar. The fresh pink fillets are weighted for two days in our version. Serve Gravlax with piquant, Dijon-style Mustard Sauce.

One 3-pound center-cut salmon fillet or two
   1½-pound salmon fillets
1 bunch dill weed
¼ cup sugar
2 tablespoons salt
½ teaspoon white peppercorns, crushed
Mustard Sauce (right)

If using 1 fillet, cut crosswise into halves. Place half of fish, skin side down, in ungreased oblong baking dish, 13 × 9 × 2 inches. Arrange dill weed on fish. Mix sugar, salt and peppercorns. Sprinkle evenly over dill weed. Top with other half of fish, skin side up. Cover dish loosely with aluminum foil. Weight fish with 2 or 3 unopened cans. Refrigerate, turning fish every 12 hours, 2 days. Pour off all liquid as it accumulates around fish.

Set oven control to broil or 550°. Remove dill weed; pat fish dry. Cut fish into serving pieces. Broil skin sides down with tops about 4 inches from heat until fish flakes easily with fork, 10 to 12 minutes. Serve with Mustard Sauce.

8 to 10 servings

PER SERVING: Calories 335; Protein 36 g; Carbohydrate 10 g; Fat 17 g; Cholesterol 65 mg; Sodium 1810 mg

Preceding pages: Broiled Gravlax with Mustard Sauce, shown before cooking

MUSTARD SAUCE

¼ cup Dijon-style mustard
¼ cup vegetable oil
2 tablespoons sugar
2 tablespoons vinegar
Dash of salt
2 tablespoons snipped dill weed

Beat all ingredients except dill weed with wire whisk. Stir in dill weed.

RUSSIAN SALMON LOAF

COULIBIAC (<u>coo</u>-l'yee-bee-ak)

Inside the light, flaky pastry of *Coulibiac* is a savory blend of poached salmon, rice, tender onions and mushrooms. In Russia, kasha is sometimes used instead of rice. A dollop of sour cream adds the final touch.

Pastry (page 55)
1 medium onion, sliced
1 bay leaf
5 black peppercorns
2 teaspoons salt
2 pounds salmon steaks,* about 1 inch thick
1 cup water
½ cup uncooked regular rice
1 teaspoon instant chicken bouillon
8 ounces mushrooms, thinly sliced
3 large onions, finely chopped
¼ cup margarine or butter
3 hard-cooked eggs, peeled and chopped
2 tablespoons snipped dill weed
1 teaspoon salt
1 egg yolk
1 tablespoon water
Dairy sour cream, melted margarine or butter
   (optional)

Prepare pastry. Heat 1½ inches water, 1 onion, the bay leaf, peppercorns and 2 teaspoons salt to boiling in 12-inch skillet; reduce heat. Arrange fish in single layer in skillet. Simmer uncovered until fish flakes easily with fork, 4 to 6 minutes. Drain and cool. Remove bones and skin from fish; flake fish.

Heat 1 cup water, the rice and bouillon to boiling in 1-quart saucepan, stirring once or twice; reduce heat. Cover and simmer 14 minutes. (Do not lift cover or stir.) Remove from heat. Fluff rice lightly with fork. Cook and stir mushrooms and 3 onions in ¼ cup margarine until onions are tender. Gently stir rice, mushrooms, onions, hard-cooked eggs, and dill weed into flaked salmon. Sprinkle with 1 teaspoon salt.

Heat oven to 400°. Shape one-half pastry into flattened rectangle on well-floured cloth-covered board. Roll pastry with floured stockinet-covered rolling pin into rectangle, 16 × 7 inches. Trim edges evenly. Place on ungreased cookie sheet. Mound salmon mixture over pastry to within 1 inch of edges. Roll other half pastry into rectangle, 18 × 9 inches. Moisten edges of pastry on cookie sheet with water. Carefully place second pastry half over filling. Press edges with fork or flute to seal. Leftover pastry can be cut into shapes to decorate top of pastry.

Cut 1-inch circle in center of top crust or cut slits so steam can escape. Mix egg yolk and 1 tablespoon water; brush pastry with egg yolk mixture. Bake until golden brown, 50 to 60 minutes. Serve with dairy sour cream.

8 to 10 servings

PER SERVING: Calories 825; Protein 36 g; Carbohydrate 64 g; Fat 47 g; Cholesterol 150 mg; Sodium 1370 mg

PASTRY

1 cup margarine or butter
⅓ cup shortening
4 cups all-purpose flour
1 teaspoon salt
10 to 12 tablespoons cold water

Cut margarine and shortening into flour and salt until particles are size of small peas. Sprinkle in water, 1 tablespoon at a time, tossing with fork until all flour is moistened and pastry almost cleans side of bowl. Gather pastry into a ball. Divide into halves; shape into 2 rounds. Cover and refrigerate until firm, about 3 hours.

*2 cans (16 ounces each) salmon, drained and flaked, can be substituted for the salmon steak; omit cooking step.

Mound salmon mixture on pastry to within 1 inch of edges.

Press edges with fork to seal.

GLAZED SALMON STEAKS WITH GREEN MAYONNAISE

CÔTELETTES DE SAUMON GLACÉES
(koh-t'let duh soh-mohng glah-seh)

Savory poached salmon steaks are coated in a white wine–based aspic and accompanied by dilled mayonnaise with fresh minced spinach and a sprinkling of chives. This would be refreshing fare for a scorching summer's day.

1½ cups dry white wine, plus additional wine
    as needed for poaching
1 cup water
1 small onion, sliced
1 stalk celery (with leaves), cut up
4 sprigs parsley
1 teaspoon salt
5 black peppercorns
1 bay leaf
¼ teaspoon dried thyme leaves
¼ teaspoon dried tarragon leaves
8 salmon steaks, 1 inch thick (about 4 pounds)
1 envelope unflavored gelatin
2 cups dry white wine
Pitted ripe olives
Pimiento
Green onion tops
Parsley sprigs
Green Mayonnaise (right)

Heat 1½ cups wine, the water, onion, celery, 4 sprigs parsley, the salt, peppercorns, bay leaf, thyme and tarragon leaves to boiling in 10-inch skillet; reduce heat. Cover and simmer 5 to 10 minutes. Place 4 of the salmon steaks in wine mixture; add enough water to cover steaks. Heat to boiling; reduce heat. Simmer uncovered until fish flakes easily with fork, 12 to 15 minutes.

Remove fish with slotted spatula; drain on wire rack. Remove skin and discard. Repeat with remaining fish; add equal parts wine and water to cover fish. Repeat. Place racks in shallow pan. Cover and refrigerate until cold.

Sprinkle gelatin on ½ cup wine in small bowl. Place bowl in pan of hot water over low heat until gelatin dissolves, about 5 minutes. Stir in remaining 1½ cups wine. Place bowl in pan of ice water, stirring occasionally, until mixture begins to thicken, 20 to 25 minutes. (Mixture should be consistency of unbeaten egg white.)

Cut olives lengthwise into fourths for flower decoration. Cut circles from pimiento; use green onion tops for stems. Spoon ⅔ of the glaze over salmon steaks until completely coated. Arrange decoration on glaze; spoon remaining glaze on decorations. (If glaze begins to thicken, place bowl in pan of hot water.) Refrigerate until glaze is firm. Remove salmon steaks from racks; place on serving plates. Garnish with parsley. Serve with Green Mayonnaise.

8 servings

PER SERVING: Calories 735; Protein 50 g; Carbohydrate 3 g; Fat 58 g; Cholesterol 120 mg; Sodium 660 mg

GREEN MAYONNAISE

2 cups mayonnaise or salad dressing
½ cup finely chopped fresh spinach
½ cup snipped parsley
2 to 3 teaspoons snipped fresh dill weed or 1
    tablespoon dried dill weed
1 tablespoon tarragon vinegar
1 tablespoon snipped chives

Place all ingredients in blender container. Cover and blend on high speed until smooth. Cover and refrigerate at least 2 hours.

TROUT FILLETS WITH ALMONDS

FILETS DE TRUITE AMANDINE
(fee-leh deh trweet ah-mawn-deen)

Sweet, tender trout is rendered even sweeter when poached in whole milk and butter and topped with toasted almonds. Serve with russet potatoes and butter and French-style beans, for a very French evening.

¼ cup all-purpose flour
½ teaspoon salt
⅛ teaspoon pepper
1 pound trout fillets, cut into serving pieces
¼ cup milk
Vegetable oil
¼ cup margarine or butter
¼ cup slivered almonds
Lemon wedges
Snipped parsley

Mix flour, salt and pepper. Dip trout in milk; coat with flour mixture. Heat oil (⅛ inch) in skillet until hot. Cook fish over medium heat until golden brown, turning carefully, about 5 minutes on each side. Remove trout to platter; keep warm.

Drain oil from skillet; add margarine and almonds. Cook over low heat until margarine starts to brown. Spoon over trout; garnish with lemon wedges and sprinkle with parsley.

4 servings

PER SERVING: Calories 395; Protein 26 g; Carbohydrate 8 g; Fat 29 g; Cholesterol 45 mg; Sodium 460 mg

TROUT WITH BACON

BRYTHYLL A CHIG MOCH (bruh-th'll ah chig mohnk)

It is said the Welsh love this dish for the smoky flavor bacon adds to the sweetness of trout.

12 slices bacon
6 drawn whole trout (about 5 ounces each)
2 tablespoons snipped parsley
1½ teaspoons salt
¼ teaspoon freshly ground pepper
Snipped parsley

Arrange bacon in single layer in broiler pan. Cook uncovered in 400° oven 10 minutes; drain.

Sprinkle inside of fish with 2 tablespoons parsley, the salt and pepper. Arrange fish in single layer on bacon in pan. Cover and cook until fish flakes easily with fork, about 20 minutes. Split fish down center along backbone; remove as many bones as possible. Serve each fish with 2 bacon slices. Garnish with parsley.

6 servings

PER SERVING: Calories 245; Protein 30 g; Carbohydrate 0 g; Fat 14 g; Cholesterol 60 mg; Sodium 790 mg

Black Sea Bass

The black sea bass lives up and down the Atlantic seaboard, but it is primarily fished from New York south to North Carolina. Black sea bass has snowy white meat and a delicate flavor; it is similar to the sea bream popular in Italy. This is by no means a large fish: at its heaviest, it weighs 5 pounds, but generally it weighs about 1½ to 3 pounds.

Ingredients for Black Sea Bass with Fennel

Black Sea Bass with Fennel

BLACK SEA BASS WITH FENNEL

IL PESCE CON FINOCCHI FRESCHI
(eel peh-sheh kohn fee-noh-kee frehs—kee)

Fresh fennel adds a gentle anise flavor while the bass poaches in a broth of dry white wine and lemon juice. Serve with pasta tossed with Parmesan cheese and freshly snipped parsley.

2 large fennel bulbs with green tops
¼ cup olive or vegetable oil
1 tablespoon lemon juice
¼ teaspoon salt
Dash of pepper
2 whole black sea bass (about 1½ pounds each), cleaned and scaled
Salt
Pepper
1 cup dry white wine

Cut green tops off fennel bulbs; reserve. Cut bulbs into ½-inch slices. Cook and stir fennel slices in oil in 10-inch skillet over medium heat until almost tender, 5 to 7 minutes. Arrange in ungreased oblong baking dish, 13 × 9 × 2 inches. Sprinkle with lemon juice, ¼ teaspoon salt and dash of pepper.

Sprinkle cavities of fish with salt and pepper. Arrange some of the reserved fennel greens in fish cavities. Place fish on fennel slices; pour wine over fish. Cook uncovered in 350° oven, spooning juices over fish occasionally, until fish flakes easily with fork, 25 to 30 minutes.

Carefully remove fish to serving platter. Remove fennel slices with slotted spoon; arrange around fish. Garnish with lemon wedges and reserved fennel greens if desired.

4 servings

PER SERVING: Calories 400; Protein 57 g; Carbohydrate 5 g; Fat 17 g; Cholesterol 160 mg; Sodium 560 mg

SEAFOOD AND VEGETABLES IN BROTH

YOSENABE (yoh-seh-nah-beh)

The name for this Japanese specialty means "a mixture of foods." The tender seafood morsels called for here, thin cellophane noodles steeped in a light chicken broth and an array of crisp, fresh vegetables all add up to a flavorful meal.

½ package (3¾-ounce size) cellophane noodles
4 cans (10¾ ounces each) condensed chicken broth
2 broth cans water
2 medium carrots, cut into ⅛-inch slices
1 pound raw shrimp, shelled and deveined
8 ounces cod or haddock fillets, cut into 1-inch pieces
4 ounces Chinese pea pods
1 tablespoon soy sauce
12 mushrooms, sliced
4 green onions (with tops), cut into 1½-inch pieces
Dipping Sauce (right)

Cover cellophane noodles with hot water. Let stand 10 minutes; drain. Cut into 2-inch lengths.

Heat chicken broth, water and carrots to boiling in Dutch oven; reduce heat. Simmer uncovered 5 minutes. Stir in noodles and remaining ingredients except Dipping Sauce. Cover and heat to boiling; reduce heat. Simmer until shrimp are pink and fish flakes easily with fork, 3 to 5 minutes. Serve with small dishes of Dipping Sauce.

6 servings

PER SERVING: Calories 210; Protein 29 g; Carbohydrate 15 g; Fat 4 g; Cholesterol 125 mg; Sodium 2920 mg

Tempura, *bottom* (page 71) and Seafood and Vegetables in Broth

DIPPING SAUCE

½ cup soy sauce
½ cup lemon juice
1 tablespoon thinly sliced green onion (with top)
Dash of red pepper flakes

Mix all ingredients.

CREAM OF SALMON SOUP

LOHIKEITTO (loh-ee-kay-toh)

In Finland this broth would be made using the head, tail and bones of the salmon. The recipe here requires only the skinless fillets. This thick and creamy soup is a filling meal in itself.

4 cups water
3 medium potatoes, pared and cut into ½-inch pieces
2 medium onions, chopped
1 teaspoon salt
¼ teaspoon white or black pepper
1 bay leaf
2 pounds skinless salmon fillets, cut into 1-inch pieces
1 cup whipping cream
Snipped dill weed (optional)

Heat water, potatoes, onions, salt, pepper and bay leaf to boiling in Dutch oven; reduce heat. Cover and simmer until potatoes are almost tender, about 10 minutes; stir in salmon. Cover and simmer until fish flakes easily with fork, about 5 minutes longer. Remove bay leaf.

Stir ½ cup of the soup liquid into whipping cream. Gently stir cream mixture into the soup; heat through. Sprinkle with dill weed.

6 servings

PER SERVING: Calories 395; Protein 34 g; Carbohydrate 17 g; Fat 21 g; Cholesterol 100 mg; Sodium 440 mg

FISH SOUP PROVENÇALE

BOURIDE (boo-<u>reed</u>)

This peasant's delight is flavored with wine, lemon and broth that has been thickened with mayonnaise. It is served with garlic-buttered French bread slices for a filling meal that one would find in the finest restaurants along the French Riviera.

1½ cups mayonnaise or salad dressing
3 cloves garlic, crushed
½ cup margarine or butter
12 slices French bread
1 clove garlic, cut into halves
1 pound fish fillets, cut into 1-inch pieces
1½ cups dry white wine
6 slices onion
3 slices lemon
5 sprigs parsley
1 bay leaf
1 teaspoon salt
Paprika

Mix mayonnaise and crushed garlic; cover and refrigerate. Heat ¼ cup of the margarine in 12-inch skillet until melted. Toast 6 of the bread slices in skillet over medium heat until brown on both sides; rub one side of bread with half clove garlic. Remove from skillet; keep warm. Repeat with remaining margarine, bread and garlic.

Place fish in single layer in skillet. Add wine, onion and lemon slices, parsley, bay leaf, salt and just enough water to cover. Heat to boiling; reduce heat. Simmer uncovered until fish flakes easily with fork, about 6 minutes. Remove fish with slotted spoon; keep warm.

Strain fish broth. Pour 1½ cups of the broth into 2-quart saucepan; gradually beat in may-onnaise mixture. Cook over low heat, stirring constantly, until slightly thickened. Place 2 slices of the French bread upright in each soup bowl; spoon fish between slices. Pour soup over fish; sprinkle with paprika.

6 servings

PER SERVING: Calories 745; Protein 20 g; Carbohydrate 31 g; Fat 60 g; Cholesterol 75 mg; Sodium 1210 mg

BRAZILIAN SEAFOOD STEW

VATAPA (vah-<u>tah</u>-pah)

This hot and spicy shrimp and codfish stew hails from Bahia, a coastal region, where tastes have been influenced by Africans who were brought to Brazil as slaves. Some recipes for *Vatapa* include palm oil; the recipe adapted here recalls the African heritage of the Bahian region with coconut milk and peanut butter.

1 package (5 ounces) dried shrimp (about 2 cups)
1 large onion, thinly sliced
3 to 5 Serrano chilies, seeded and finely chopped
2 cloves garlic, chopped
½ teaspoon paprika
½ teaspoon crushed red pepper
2 tablespoons olive or vegetable oil
3 cups Coconut Milk (page 72)
1 can (16 ounces) whole tomatoes, drained and chopped
1½ teaspoons salt
1 cup soft bread crumbs
1 cup natural peanut butter
3 tablespoons olive or vegetable oil
1 pound raw shrimp, shelled and deveined
1 pound cod fillets, cut into 1½-inch pieces
¼ cup snipped fresh cilantro

Cover dried shrimp with warm water. Let stand 15 minutes; drain. Finely chop shrimp; reserve.

Cook and stir onion, chilies, garlic, paprika and red pepper in 2 tablespoons oil in Dutch oven over medium heat until onion is tender. Stir in Coconut Milk, tomatoes, salt and reserved dried shrimp. Heat to boiling; reduce heat. Simmer uncovered 15 minutes. Stir in bread crumbs and peanut butter until well blended and mixture is consistency of thick sauce; keep warm over low heat.

Heat 3 tablespoons oil in 10-inch skillet until hot. Cook and stir raw shrimp in oil over medium heat until pink, about 3 minutes. Remove shrimp to sauce mixture with slotted spoon. Add more oil to skillet if necessary. Cook and stir fish until it flakes easily with fork, 3 to 4 minutes. Gently stir fish into sauce mixture. Sprinkle with cilantro; serve with salsa if desired.

8 servings

PER SERVING: Calories 655; Protein 36 g; Carbohydrate 24 g; Fat 46 g; Cholesterol 150 mg; Sodium 920 mg

---

Basmati Rice

This rice lives up to the word *exotic*. The grains are long and slender. Basmati rice is principally grown in the foothills of the Himalaya, but there are some small rice farms in the United States now that are producing this grain, which is known for its gentle, nutty aroma. The preferred basmati has been aged for a year, which heightens the fragrance.

AFGHAN-STYLE CATFISH STEW

MAHI LAQA (mah-hee lah-kah)

Catfish is common fare in Kabul during the winter months. This hearty stew, spiced with coriander and turmeric, is a warm and welcome treat in chilling weather. Serve it with hot cooked basmati rice for an authentic meal.

1 large onion, chopped
2 cloves garlic, finely chopped
¼ cup Ghee (page 237) or vegetable oil
1 cup water
1 can (28 ounces) whole tomatoes, drained and chopped
½ teaspoon salt
½ teaspoon ground turmeric
½ teaspoon ground coriander
⅛ teaspoon pepper
1½ pounds catfish fillets, cut into 2-inch pieces
Snipped chives
2 cups hot cooked basmati or regular rice

Cook and stir onion and garlic in Ghee in 10-inch skillet over medium heat until onion is tender and light brown. Stir in water, tomatoes, salt, turmeric, coriander and pepper. Heat to boiling; reduce heat. Simmer uncovered, stirring occasionally, 15 minutes.

Gently stir fish into vegetable mixture. Cover and cook over medium heat until fish flakes easily with fork, about 5 minutes. Sprinkle with chives. Serve with basmati rice.

4 servings

PER SERVING: Calories 510; Protein 39 g; Carbohydrate 41 g; Fat 21 g; Cholesterol 85 mg; Sodium 1080 mg

Ingredients for Stuffed Squid in Tomato Sauce

Stuffed Squid in Tomato Sauce

STUFFED SQUID IN TOMATO SAUCE

CALAMARI RIPIENI STUFATI AL VINO BIANCO
(kah-lah-mah-ree ree-p'yeh-nee stu-fa-tee ahl vee-noh
b'yahn-koh)

Tender squid is filled with soft bread crumbs,
parsley and piquant Parmesan cheese, then
sautéed and served with tangy tomato sauce.

12 squid, about 5 inches long, cleaned (about
   1½ pounds)
1 small onion, chopped
2 cloves garlic, chopped
2 tablespoons olive or vegetable oil
⅓ cup dry bread crumbs
¼ cup snipped parsley
2 tablespoons grated Parmesan cheese
1 tablespoon dry white wine
2 tablespoons olive or vegetable oil
1 can (14½ ounces) Italian plum tomatoes (with
   liquid)
¼ cup dry white wine
1 clove garlic, chopped
Snipped parsley

Wash body cones and tentacles of squid under
running cold water; pat dry. Finely chop
tentacles.

Cook and stir onion and 2 cloves garlic in 2
tablespoons oil in 10-inch skillet over medium
heat until onion is tender. Add tentacles; cook
and stir until hot, about 2 minutes. Remove
from heat; stir in bread crumbs, parsley, cheese
and 1 tablespoon wine. Loosely fill pockets
of cones with stuffing. Secure openings with
wooden picks.

Heat 2 tablespoons oil in Dutch oven until hot.
Cook squid over medium heat until light brown
on all sides. Mix tomatoes, ¼ cup wine and
1 clove garlic; break up tomatoes with fork. Pour
mixture over squid. Cover and simmer just until squid is tender when pierced with fork, about
30 minutes. Remove wooden picks. Garnish with
parsley. Serve with lemon wedges if desired.

4 servings

PER SERVING: Calories 355; Protein 31 g; Carbohydrate 19 g; Fat 17 g; Cholesterol 410 mg; Sodium 360 mg

FISH STEW WITH VEGETABLES

This spicy tomato-based African-style stew may be the predecessor of Louisiana's gumbos. Okra, a popular African and southern vegetable, is a common ingredient in gumbos; it is a delicious vegetable that acts as a thickening agent, too.

1 can (15 ounces) tomato sauce
4 cups water
1 cup uncooked regular rice
3 carrots, thinly sliced
1 onion, thinly sliced
1 tablespoon salt
½ teaspoon ground red pepper
1 package (10 ounces) frozen okra pods
1 package (10 ounces) frozen green beans
3 cups sliced cabbage
1½ pounds catfish, perch, bass or trout fillets, cut into serving pieces

Heat tomato sauce, water, rice, carrots, onion, salt and red pepper in Dutch oven to boiling; reduce heat. Cover and cook 10 minutes.

Rinse okra and green beans under running cold water to separate; drain. Cut okra lengthwise into halves. Add okra, green beans, cabbage and fish to Dutch oven. Heat to boiling; reduce heat. Cover and cook until fish flakes easily with fork and vegetables are tender, 10 to 12 minutes.

8 servings

PER SERVING: Calories 240; Protein 21 g; Carbohydrate 30 g; Fat 4 g; Cholesterol 45 mg; Sodium 1200 mg

RIVIERA SALAD BOWL
SALADE NIÇOISE (sah-lahd nee-swahz)

Traditional *Salade Niçoise* recipes call for the addition of cooked potatoes, but we offer a lighter version. Serve this refreshing salad with piping hot French bread for a reminder of Nice, the city on the Riviera that lends its name to this dish.

1 package (10 ounces) frozen French-style green beans
1 head Boston lettuce, torn into bite-size pieces
2 medium tomatoes, cut into sixths
2 hard-cooked eggs, peeled and cut into fourths
1 can (6½ ounces) tuna, drained
8 ripe olives
1 can (about 2 ounces) anchovy fillets, drained
Snipped parsley
Vinaigrette Dressing (below)

Cook beans as directed on package; drain. Cover and refrigerate at least 1 hour. Place lettuce in salad bowl; arrange beans, tomatoes and eggs around edge. Mound tuna in center. Garnish with olives, anchovies and parsley. Serve with Vinaigrette Dressing.

4 servings

PER SERVING: Calories 445; Protein 21 g; Carbohydrate 9 g; Fat 36 g; Cholesterol 125 mg; Sodium 1070 mg

VINAIGRETTE DRESSING

½ cup olive or vegetable oil
¼ cup white wine vinegar
½ teaspoon salt
½ teaspoon dried basil leaves
¼ teaspoon dry mustard
⅛ teaspoon pepper

Shake ingredients in covered jar; refrigerate.

HERRING SALAD

SILLSALLAD (sill-sah-lahd)

This herring salad calls for tart vinegar to off-set the sweetness of apples, sugar and beets. Serve this northern European favorite as an appetizer or as an unusual side dish.

1 jar (22 ounces) herring cutlets in wine sauce, drained
3 medium potatoes, cooked and cubed (2 cups)
1 jar (16 ounces) pickled beets, drained and cubed
2 small dill pickles, chopped
1 apple, cut up
1 small onion, chopped
¼ cup vinegar
2 tablespoons sugar
2 tablespoons water
⅛ teaspoon pepper
Dilled Sour Cream (below)

Place herring, potatoes, beets, pickles, apple and onion in glass or plastic bowl. Mix vinegar, sugar, water and pepper; pour over herring mixture. Toss lightly. Cover and refrigerate, stirring once or twice, at least 2 hours. Serve with Dilled Sour Cream. garnish with parsley and wedges of hard-cooked egg if desired.

6 to 8 servings

PER SERVING: Calories 415; Protein 13 g; Carbohydrate 43 g; Fat 21 g; Cholesterol 35 mg; Sodium 930 mg

DILLED SOUR CREAM

1 cup dairy sour cream
2 tablespoons milk
½ teaspoon dried dill weed

Mix all ingredients.

MARINATED SHRIMP SALAD

Aromatic bitters from Trinidad and lime juice give this recipe a flavor reminiscent of ceviche dishes, where fresh fish is marinated in citrus juice. Bits of fresh tomato and a dash of spicy red pepper give shrimp Caribbean flair.

4 cups water
1 tablespoon salt
1 pound raw shrimp, shelled and deveined
1 cup vegetable oil
⅓ cup lime juice
2 tablespoons snipped parsley
½ teaspoon salt
4 green onions (with tops), thinly sliced
2 medium tomatoes, seeded and chopped
2 cloves garlic, chopped
8 to 10 drops aromatic bitters
Dash of crushed red pepper
1 avocado, peeled and chopped
Lettuce leaves
Lime wedges

Heat water to boiling in 3-quart saucepan. Add 1 tablespoon salt and the shrimp. Cover and heat to boiling; reduce heat. Simmer until shrimp is pink, about 3 minutes; drain.

Mix oil, lime juice, parsley, ½ teaspoon salt, the green onions, tomatoes, garlic, bitters and red pepper in large bowl; stir in shrimp. Cover and refrigerate at least 6 hours. Just before serving, gently stir in avocado. Spoon shrimp mixture onto lettuce-lined plates with slotted spoon. Garnish with lime wedges. Serve with remaining marinade if desired.

4 servings

PER SERVING: Calories 280; Protein 18 g; Carbohydrate 5 g; Fat 21 g; Cholesterol 160 mg; Sodium 330 mg

SHRIMP WITH FETA CHEESE

GARIDES ME FETA (gah-ree-dehs meh feh-tah)

Here the rich taste of shrimp is enhanced by wine, lemon juice, olive oil and such fragrant herbs as basil and oregano. Crumbled feta cheese tops off this Greek delicacy, which can be served on a bed of hot cooked rice.

1 large onion, chopped
2 cloves garlic, chopped
3 tablespoons olive or vegetable oil
½ cup dry white wine
1 teaspoon dried basil leaves
1 teaspoon dried oregano leaves
½ teaspoon salt
Dash of ground red pepper
1 can (28 ounces) Italian plum tomatoes, drained and chopped
1 pound raw shrimp, shelled and deveined
2 tablespoons lemon juice
2 ounces feta cheese, crumbled
Snipped parsley

Cook and stir onion and garlic in oil in 10-inch skillet over medium heat until onion is tender. Stir in wine, basil, oregano, salt, red pepper and tomatoes. Heat to boiling; reduce heat. Simmer uncovered 20 minutes. Stir in shrimp and lemon juice. Cover and cook until shrimp is pink, 3 to 5 minutes. Sprinkle with cheese and parsley. Serve with hot cooked rice if desired.

4 servings

PER SERVING: Calories 265; Protein 21 g; Carbohydrate 12 g; Fat 15 g; Cholesterol 175 mg; Sodium 840 mg

Shrimp with Feta Cheese and Athenian Salad (page 222)

SHRIMP WITH LOBSTER SAUCE

TOU SHIH HSIA JEN (dough sher shee-ah ren)

This sweet Cantonese classic is served with a sauce made of soy sauce and fresh ginger, but it contains no hint of lobster. Lobster sauce is actually a combination of ingredients often used to accompany lobster.

2 cloves garlic, finely chopped
2 tablespoons soy sauce
1 tablespoon salted black beans, washed, drained and mashed
1 teaspoon finely chopped gingerroot
½ teaspoon sugar
½ teaspoon salt
2 tablespoons vegetable oil
1 pound raw shrimp, shelled and deveined
2 green onions (with tops), chopped (tops reserved)
½ cup hot water
1 tablespoon cold water
1 tablespoon cornstarch
2 eggs, slightly beaten
2 cups hot cooked rice

Mix garlic, soy sauce, beans, gingerroot, sugar and salt. Heat oil in 10-inch skillet until hot. Stir in shrimp, bean mixture and green onions. Cook and stir 1 minute. Stir in ½ cup water. Cover and cook until shrimp is pink, about 2 minutes.

Mix 1 tablespoon water and cornstarch; stir into shrimp mixture. Cook and stir until thickened. Add eggs; cook and stir just until eggs are set. Sprinkle with reserved green onion tops; serve with rice.

4 servings

PER SERVING: Calories 330; Protein 24 g; Carbohydrate 34 g; Fat 11 g; Cholesterol 270 mg; Sodium 1530 mg

SHRIMP CURRY, CARIBBEAN STYLE

The East Indies meets the West Indies in this fragrant and spicy dish that brings together such Indian spices as turmeric, ginger, cumin and coriander with red pepper, tomatoes and shrimp.

1 medium onion, chopped
2 tablespoons margarine or butter
4 medium tomatoes, chopped, or 2 cans (16 ounces each) tomatoes, drained and chopped
½ teaspoon salt
½ teaspoon ground coriander
½ teaspoon ground turmeric
¼ teaspoon ground ginger
¼ teaspoon ground cumin
⅛ teaspoon ground red pepper
2 cups cleaned cooked shrimp
3 cups hot cooked rice
Chutney (optional)

Cook and stir onion in margarine in 10-inch skillet until tender, about 3 minutes. Add tomatoes, salt, coriander, turmeric, ginger, cumin and red pepper. Heat to boiling; reduce heat. Cover and simmer 15 minutes. Stir in shrimp; heat until shrimp are hot, 3 to 5 minutes. Serve with rice and chutney.

6 servings

PER SERVING: Calories 235; Protein 13 g; Carbohydrate 35 g; Fat 5 g; Cholesterol 85 mg; Sodium 720 mg

INDONESIAN FRIED RICE
NASI GORENG (nah-<u>see</u> gohr-ring)

Indonesian fried rice differs from Chinese fried rice in many ways. One mark of distinction is the addition of such perfumed spices as curry powder, cumin and coriander.

2 medium onions, chopped
3 tablespoons vegetable oil
4 cups cooked rice
1 cup finely chopped fully cooked smoked ham
2 teaspoons curry powder
¼ teaspoon ground coriander
¼ teaspoon ground cumin
¼ teaspoon salt
1 can (5 ounces) tiny shrimp, drained
2 tablespoons snipped parsley

Cook and stir onions in oil in 12-inch skillet until tender. Add rice, ham, curry powder, coriander, cumin and salt. Cook and stir until rice is golden brown, 10 to 15 minutes. Stir in shrimp and parsley. Cover and cook 1 minute.

6 servings

PER SERVING: Calories 345; Protein 15 g; Carbohydrate 42 g; Fat 13 g; Cholesterol 70 mg; Sodium 680 mg

Cumin

This pungent spice is most strongly associated in American minds with Mexican cooking, but cumin is used with enthusiasm in China, Greece, India, Indonesia, Japan, Malaysia, Portugal, Sri Lanka, Spain, Thailand and many Arabic-speaking countries. The plant that gives us cumin seed is a relative of parsley. The seeds are used whole or ground, and though there are several varieties, the most common is a tawny brown.

TEMPURA

(tem-<u>poo</u>-rah)

Batter-dipped morsels of fresh seafood and tender vegetables, deep-fried to crisp, golden brown doneness, are what tempura-style cooking is all about. This Japanese favorite is served with a sweet soy-based sauce for dipping.

Shrimp with tails, shelled and deveined
Sea scallops, cut into halves
Fish fillets, cut into bite-size pieces
1 cup 1-inch pieces asparagus
1 cup ¼-inch slices carrots or celery
1½ cups cauliflowerets
1½ cups 2 × ¼-inch eggplant sticks
1 cup 2-inch pieces green beans, partially cooked
1 cup 2-inch pieces green onions
1 medium green pepper, cut into ¼-inch rings
1 medium onion, sliced and separated into rings
1 bunch parsley
1 cup pea pods
1 medium sweet potato, cut into ⅛-inch slices
Vegetable oil
Tempura Batter (right)
Tempura Sauce (right)

Choose 1 pound seafood (about 4 ounces per person). If serving shrimp, make several crosswise slits on undersides to prevent curling. Choose 3 or 4 vegetables from selection above. Pat seafood and vegetables dry; arrange attractively on platter. Cover and refrigerate until serving time, no longer than 2 hours.

Heat oil (1 to 1½ inches) in wok to 360° (see Note). Prepare Tempura Batter. Dip seafood and vegetables into batter with tongs, fork or chopsticks; allow excess batter to drip into bowl. Fry a few pieces at a time until golden brown, turning once, 2 to 3 minutes. Drain; keep warm. Serve with Tempura Sauce.

4 servings

PER SERVING: Calories 390; Protein 27 g; Carbohydrate 30 g; Fat 18 g; Cholesterol 180 mg; Sodium 1360 mg

TEMPURA BATTER

2 eggs, beaten
1 cup cold water
¾ cup all-purpose flour
1 tablespoon cornstarch
½ teaspoon baking powder
½ teaspoon salt

Mix all ingredients with fork just until blended. (Batter will be thin and slightly lumpy.)

TEMPURA SAUCE

¼ cup chicken broth
¼ cup water
¼ cup soy sauce
1 teaspoon sugar

Heat all ingredients until hot. Serve in small individual bowls.

NOTE: A wok is recommended for this recipe because of its large surface area and slanted sides, which protect against splattering.

SHRIMP IN SPICY SAUCE
SAMBAL GORENG UDANG (sahm-bahl gohr-ring oo-dung)

This sweet and spicy dish is served in Indonesia, accompanied by rice, peanuts and fresh, thinly sliced vegetables.

¼ cup vegetable oil
1 pound small raw shrimp, shelled and deveined
2 small onions, sliced
1 clove garlic, chopped
½ to ¾ teaspoon crushed red pepper
1 cup Coconut Milk (below)
1 medium tomato, coarsely chopped
1 medium green pepper, thinly sliced into rings
1 tablespoon packed brown sugar
½ teaspoon salt
Freshly ground pepper

Heat oil in 10-inch skillet until hot. Cook and stir shrimp, onions, garlic and red pepper until shrimp starts to turn pink, 2 to 3 minutes. Stir in remaining ingredients. Simmer uncovered until shrimp are tender, about 5 minutes. Serve in bowls.

4 servings

PER SERVING: Calories 370; Protein 19 g; Carbohydrate 11 g; Fat 28 g; Cholesterol 160 mg; Sodium 470 mg

COCONUT MILK

1 cup chopped fresh coconut*
1 cup hot water

Place coconut and hot water in blender container. Cover and blend on high speed until coconut is finely chopped. Strain through several layers of cheesecloth. Cover and refrigerate no longer than 48 hours.

*To open coconut, puncture eyes of coconut with ice pick; drain liquid. Bake coconut in 375° oven 12 to 15 minutes. Remove from oven. Tap shell with hammer to open. Cut meat out of shell. Pare brown skin from coconut meat.

BAKED CRAB WITH PORT
SANTOLA AO PORTO (sahn-toh-lah aoh pohr-toh)

The Portuguese *santola* is a hard-shelled crab with tender, sweet meat. Here, the meat is turned into a savory stuffing, sweetened with port wine and cooked in pretty baking shells. Dashes of capers and pimientos lend a slightly salty flavor, and a drop or two of red pepper sauce gives added zest. The crunchy, golden-brown topping is a final, elegant touch.

¼ cup mayonnaise or salad dressing
¼ cup whipping cream
2 tablespoons tawny port wine
1 tablespoon capers
1 tablespoon diced pimientos
½ teaspoon dry mustard
½ teaspoon salt
1 green onion (with top), sliced
6 drops red pepper sauce
1 pound lump crabmeat, cartilage removed
2 tablespoons dry bread crumbs
1 teaspoon margarine or butter, melted
Snipped parsley
Lemon wedges

Mix mayonnaise, whipping cream, wine, capers, pimientos, mustard, salt, green onion and pepper sauce in medium bowl. Gently stir in crabmeat. Divide mixture among 4 ungreased scallop baking shells or individual casseroles. Mix bread crumbs and margarine; sprinkle over crab mixture. Cook uncovered in 375° oven until mixture is bubbly and crumbs are golden brown, about 20 minutes. Sprinkle with parsley, and serve with lemon wedges.

4 servings

PER SERVING: Calories 285; Protein 23 g; Carbohydrate 5 g; Fat 19 g; Cholesterol 135 mg; Sodium 690 mg

Oysters

Oysters are prized the world over, so much so that for thousands of years men have actually cultivated them. Select fresh oysters with tightly closed shells that are free of cracks. Open fresh oysters with care, as they have a delicious liquor that adds immeasurably to an oyster stew or other seafood soup. Shuck a well-scrubbed oyster by chipping gently at the thin end of the shell with the handle of a heavy knife or with a hammer. Force the blade of a table knife (or use a shucking knife, if one is handy) into the chip, between the shells. Twist the knife, pulling the halves of the shell open over a strainer in a bowl.

OYSTER CASSEROLE
OSTIONES EN CAZUELA
(oh-stee-oh-nehs ehn kah-zweh-lah)

This Mexican dish features a hot and creamy tomato sauce, seasoned with ground cumin, allspice and spicy red pepper.

1 pint shucked select or large oysters, drained
2 medium tomatoes, chopped
½ cup half-and-half
2 cups cracker crumbs (about 20 crackers)
½ cup margarine or butter, melted
½ teaspoon salt
½ teaspoon ground cumin
¼ teaspoon ground allspice
⅛ teaspoon ground red pepper
Lemon or lime wedges

Mix oysters and tomatoes; arrange in ungreased oblong baking dish, 11 × 7 × 1½ inches. Pour ¼ cup of the half-and-half over mixture. Mix remaining ingredients except lemon wedges and remaining half-and-half; sprinkle over oysters and tomatoes. Pour remaining half-and-half over crumb mixture. Cook uncovered in 375° oven until light brown, about 30 minutes. Garnish with lemon wedges.

4 servings

PER SERVING: Calories 575; Protein 21 g; Carbohydrate 37 g; Fat 38 g; Cholesterol 140 mg; Sodium 1260 mg

Ingredients for Steamed Clams with Sausage

Steamed Clams with Sausage and Portuguese Sweet Bread (page 303)

STEAMED CLAMS WITH SAUSAGE

AMEIJOAS NA CATAPLANA
(ah-meh-jwas nah cah-tah-plah-nah)

Ameijoas na Cataplana is a centuries-old dish from Portugal. There are, understandably, many variations to this dish. The recipe here is a spicy, tomato-based soup flavored with garlic, paprika and red pepper.

2 pounds very small clams, about 1½ inches
1 large onion, thinly sliced
3 cloves garlic, chopped
1 small red or green pepper, cut into 1-inch
  pieces
½ teaspoon paprika
⅛ teaspoon crushed red pepper
2 tablespoons olive or vegetable oil
½ cup dry white wine
½ cup chopped fully cooked smoked ham

1 package (5 ounces) unsliced pepperoni,
  chopped
1 can (16 ounces) whole tomatoes (with liquid)
2 bay leaves

Clean clams as directed on page 76.

Cook and stir onion, garlic, pepper, paprika and crushed red pepper in oil in Dutch oven over medium heat until onion is tender. Stir in remaining ingredients; break up tomatoes with fork. Heat to boiling; reduce heat.

Simmer uncovered 15 minutes. Add clams to vegetable mixture. Cover and simmer 20 minutes. (Do not lift cover or stir.) Remove bay leaves and any unopened clams. Serve with French bread if desired.

4 servings

PER SERVING: Calories 360; Protein 19 g; Carbohydrate 13 g; Fat 26 g; Cholesterol 55 mg; Sodium 1110 mg

LINGUINE WITH WHITE CLAM SAUCE

LINGUINI CON VONGOLE BIANCO
(ling-gwee-nee kohn vahn-gho-lee b'yahn-koh)

Butter and Parmesan cheese lend a richness to this Northern Italian dish. Serve with a green salad tossed with a sharp vinaigrette dressing.

1 medium onion, chopped
1 clove garlic, finely chopped
3 tablespoons margarine or butter
1 tablespoon all-purpose flour
3 cans (6½ ounces each) minced clams (with liquid)
½ teaspoon salt
½ teaspoon dried basil leaves
⅛ teaspoon pepper
1 tablespoon salt
3 quarts water
8 ounces uncooked linguine
¼ cup snipped parsley
Grated Parmesan cheese (optional)

Cook and stir onion and garlic in margarine in 2-quart saucepan until onion is tender; stir in flour. Add clams, ½ teaspoon salt, the basil and pepper. Heat to boiling; reduce heat. Cover and simmer 5 minutes.

Add 1 tablespoon salt to rapidly boiling water in Dutch oven. Add linguine gradually so that water continues to boil. (If linguine strands are left whole, place one end in water; as they soften, gradually coil them into water.)

Boil uncovered, stirring occasionally, just until tender, 7 to 10 minutes. Test by cutting several strands with fork against side of Dutch oven. Drain quickly in colander or sieve. Add parsley to clam sauce. Serve sauce over hot linguine; sprinkle with cheese.

5 or 6 servings

PER SERVING: Calories 415; Protein 35 g; Carbohydrate 46 g; Fat 10 g; Cholesterol 75 mg; Sodium 600 mg

Clams

These rounded bivalves come in a range of sizes, and a general rule of thumb is that the smaller the clam, the more tender the meat. Smallest among the clams are steamers, followed by littlenecks, cherrystones and quahogs. Any clam much over three inches long is probably a better candidate for stewing than for steaming. Steamers are classified as soft-shell clams, and littlenecks, cherrystones and quahogs as hard-shell clams. Some clam species are quite spectacular, among them the razor clam and the geoduck (pronounced "gooeyduck"). Razor clams are narrow and long, named for their resemblance to old-fashioned barber's razors; they are sometimes featured in Chinese dishes, notably with a black bean sauce. Geoducks are huge, weighing on average three pounds, and are rarely eaten whole; they are hearty additions to chowders and stews.

To clean clams, scrub them thoroughly with a stiff brush under cold running water. Place the scrubbed clams in a large pot of cold water to which vinegar has been added (⅔ cup to each gallon water). Let the clams soak for 20 to 30 minutes, then change the water. This process will encourage the clams to disgorge sand and other impurities. Add a handful of cornmeal to the soaking water to purge the clams even more effectively. Discard any clams that have open, cracked or broken shells. Similarly, after cooking, discard any clams that have not opened.

MUSSELS IN WHITE WINE SAUCE

MEJILLONES A LA MARINERA
(meh-hee-lloh-nehs ah lah mah-ree-neh-rah)

Mejillones a la Marinera is just one of many Spanish *tapas*, the light snacks that one buys by the mouthful in tapas bars in Spain. There, these wonderful appetizers are served with drinks. Here, the fragrant mussels included in our recipe make a lovely course when served with hot sourdough or crusty bread.

2 pounds mussels
¼ cup finely chopped shallots or onion
2 cloves garlic, finely chopped
2 tablespoons olive or vegetable oil
1 cup dry white wine
Pinch of saffron or paprika
Snipped parsley

Clean mussels as directed (see box at right). Discard any that are not tightly closed.

Cook and stir shallots and garlic in oil in Dutch oven over medium heat until shallots are tender. Stir in wine and saffron. Heat wine mixture to boiling; add mussels. Cover and boil until mussels open, 3 to 5 minutes.

Remove mussels to bowl with slotted spoon; keep warm. Cook remaining liquid in pan over high heat until slightly thickened, about 5 minutes. Pour sauce over mussels. Sprinkle with parsley. Serve with French bread if desired.

2 servings

PER SERVING: Calories 295; Protein 27 g; Carbohydrate 11 g; Fat 16 g; Cholesterol 70 mg; Sodium 130 mg

Mussels

Mussels are generally sold by the pound, yielding about fifteen to twenty shells per pound. Sometimes they are sold by the quart, which equals about 1½ pounds. Mussels are prized in many countries. Sometimes they are stir-fried so briefly that they lose none of their plump, juicy quality. Often when they are steamed it is with garlic, wine and fresh herbs; the French feast on *moules* prepared this way.

As with any bivalve, discard mussels that have cracked or open shells or that are unusually light or heavy; when mussels have been cooked in their shells, discard those that do not open. Live mussels ingest sand, and the trick is to persuade them to spit it out before they are cooked. Scrub fresh mussels with a stiff brush under cold, running water, cleaning the shell thoroughly and pulling off the "beard." Place the mussels in a large pot of cold, fresh water and swish them around with your hands. Drain the mussels and repeat with fresh water until the water stays clear.

When mussels are steamed, it is easy to appreciate the amount of delicious "broth" or "liquor" they give up, a delicious addition to soups and wonderful for dipping when it has been seasoned.

IRISH SEAFOOD PIE

Savory pies of every description are hugely popular from one end of the British Isles to the other. This creamy scallop pie simmers and bubbles beneath a blanket of flaky crust. A hint of onion and dry white wine makes this pie especially delicious.

Pastry (right)
1 pound scallops
8 ounces mushrooms, sliced
½ cup chopped leek or green onions
½ cup margarine or butter
¼ cup all-purpose flour
¼ teaspoon salt
⅛ teaspoon dry mustard
Dash of pepper
1½ cups half-and-half
Dry white wine
1 egg yolk
1 tablespoon water

Prepare Pastry; wrap in plastic wrap. If scallops are large, cut into 1-inch pieces. Cook and stir mushrooms and leek in 2 tablespoons of the margarine in 10-inch skillet over medium heat until mushrooms are light brown and liquid is evaporated, about 5 minutes. Remove from skillet. Heat 2 tablespoons of the margarine in skillet until hot. Cook and stir scallops over medium heat until white, 4 to 5 minutes. Remove with slotted spoon. Drain liquid from skillet, reserving 2 tablespoons.

Heat remaining ¼ cup margarine in skillet over low heat until melted. Stir in flour, salt, mustard and pepper. Cook over low heat, stirring constantly, until smooth and bubbly. Remove from heat; stir in half-and-half. Add enough wine to reserved scallop liquid to measure ⅓ cup; stir into half-and-half mixture. Heat to boiling, stirring constantly; boil and stir 1 minute. Stir in mushroom mixture and scallops. Pour into ungreased shallow 1½-quart casserole.

Heat oven to 425°. Unwrap pastry and place on well-floured board. Roll dough 1 inch larger than top of casserole, using floured stockinet-covered rolling pin. Cut out designs with 1-inch cookie cutter. Place pastry over top of casserole; turn edges under and flute. Mix egg yolk and water; brush over pastry. Bake until golden brown, about 25 minutes. Serve with lemon wedges if desired.

4 servings

PER SERVING: Calories 815; Protein 34 g; Carbohydrate 42 g; Fat 57 g; Cholesterol 125 mg; Sodium 1010 mg

PASTRY

⅓ cup plus 1 tablespoon shortening
1 cup all-purpose flour
½ teaspoon salt
2 to 3 tablespoons cold water

Cut shortening into flour and salt until particles are size of small peas. Sprinkle in water, 1 tablespoon at a time, tossing with fork until all flour is moistened and pastry almost cleans sides of bowl. Gather pastry into a ball; shape into flattened round.

SCALLOPS AND MUSHROOMS IN WINE SAUCE

COQUILLES SAINT-JACQUES À LA PARISIENNE
(koh-kee-yuh sahng-zhahk ah lah pah-ree-zh'yen)

Coquille is the French word for "shell." *Coquilles Saint-Jacques* is the French name for scallops. In this classic French dish, the scallops are poached in white wine and then added to a rich, creamy sauce. They are topped with Swiss cheese and bread crumbs and then cooked in either porcelain or authentic scallop shells.

2 packages (12 ounces each) frozen scallops, thawed, or 1½ pounds fresh scallops
1 cup dry white wine
¼ cup snipped parsley
½ teaspoon salt
2 tablespoons margarine or butter
4 ounces mushrooms, sliced (about 2 cups)
2 shallots or green onions, chopped
3 tablespoons margarine or butter
3 tablespoons all-purpose flour
½ cup half-and-half
½ cup shredded Swiss cheese
1 cup soft bread crumbs
2 tablespoons margarine or butter, melted

If scallops are large, cut into 1-inch pieces. Place scallops, wine, parsley and salt in 3-quart saucepan. Add just enough water to cover scallops.

Heat to boiling; reduce heat. Simmer uncovered until scallops are tender, about 8 minutes. Remove scallops with slotted spoon; reserve liquid. Heat reserved liquid to boiling. Boil until reduced to 1 cup. Strain and reserve.

Heat 2 tablespoons margarine in 3-quart saucepan until melted. Cook and stir mushrooms and shallots in margarine until tender, 5 to 6 minutes. Remove from pan. Add 3 tablespoons margarine; heat until melted. Remove from heat; stir in flour. Cook over low heat, stirring constantly, until smooth and bubbly. Remove from heat; stir in reserved liquid. Cook and stir 1 minute. Stir in half-and-half, scallops, mushrooms, shallots and ¼ cup of the cheese; heat until hot.

Toss bread crumbs in melted margarine. Lightly brush 5 or 6 baking shells or ramekins with margarine. Divide scallop mixture among baking shells. Sprinkle with remaining cheese and the crumbs. Set oven control to broil or 550°. Broil 5 inches from heat until crumbs are toasted, 3 to 5 minutes.

6 servings

PER SERVING: Calories 415; Protein 33 g; Carbohydrate 24 g; Fat 21 g; Cholesterol 50 mg; Sodium 790 mg

3
POULTRY

Tender roast ducklings, succulent geese and golden brown chickens are relished the world over. In these pages you will find a dazzling Roast Goose with Apple Stuffing, a favorite Christmas tradition in Northern Europe and festive Turkey Mole from Mexico. From the Middle East and Asia we offer Honey-spiced Chicken with Orange Sauce (Israel), tandoori-style Roast Chicken with Spiced Yogurt (India) and Couscous (embraced by the French and lauded by Africans from Morocco to Algiers and Tunisia).

Spicy African Chicken and Rice Casserole is robust, practically a meal in itself, as is Russian Chicken Pie. Such Asian dishes as Lemon Chicken, Thai Chicken with Basil and Vietnam's Chicken with Lemon Grass feature the lively spark of citrus or mint. The unique spirit particular to each foreign kitchen comes through with bravado in poultry dishes, which depend on a skillful hand with seasoning for much of their character.

Exotic flavor gets top billing with the aromatic blend of Indian spices that make Mulligatawny Soup so piquant. Subtle seasoning characterizes Chicken and Leek Soup from Great Britain, while Chicken Soup with Tortellini is the most straightforward of all, for those occasions when only the truest essence of chicken will do. Fried chicken gets a zesty twist with lime and chili in our Mexican version, and such traditional favorites as Chicken Fricassee and Chicken Paprika with Dumplings are more richly satisfying than ever.

Clockwise from top right: Onion and Tomato Salad (page 230), Savory Green Beans with Coconut (page 237), Chicken Vindaloo (page 82) and Fried Bread Puffs (page 287)

CHICKEN VINDALOO
MURGH VINDALOO (murg veen-<u>dah</u>-loo)

Dishes prepared in the vindaloo style have mixed heritage—Indian and Portuguese. *Vindaloo* means "wine-garlic" and refers to a marinade of wine or vinegar and garlic. In our version, whole pieces of chicken are marinated in a spicy mixture of vinegar, molasses, jalapeño peppers and an assortment of exotic spices.

3 pounds chicken legs, thighs, and breast halves
¼ cup vinegar
2 tablespoons molasses
2 teaspoons ground turmeric
2 teaspoons ground coriander
1 teaspoon ground cumin
1 teaspoon chili powder
½ teaspoon dry mustard
2 cloves garlic, finely chopped
3 or 4 small jalapeño peppers, seeded and finely chopped
1 large onion, finely chopped
½ teaspoon crushed red pepper
2 tablespoons vegetable oil
2 large tomatoes, chopped
9 new potatoes (about 1 pound), cooked and cut into halves
Snipped fresh cilantro

Remove skin from chicken. Mix vinegar, molasses, turmeric, coriander, cumin, chili powder, mustard, garlic and jalapeño peppers. Pour into shallow glass dish. Add chicken; turn to coat all sides. Cover and refrigerate at least 12 hours.

Cook and stir onion and red pepper in oil in 12-inch skillet over medium heat until onion is light brown. Add tomatoes; cook and stir until tomatoes are very soft, 5 to 7 minutes. Add chicken and marinade; cook uncovered over high heat, turning chicken occasionally, 10 minutes. Reduce heat; cover and simmer 15 minutes. Add potatoes; cover and simmer until thickest pieces of chicken are done, 10 to 15 minutes longer. Sprinkle with cilantro.

6 servings

PER SERVING: Calories 370; Protein 33 g; Carbohydrate 32 g; Fat 12 g; Cholesterol 90 mg; Sodium 110 mg

ZESTY CHICKEN OREGANO
KOTOPOULO ME RIGANATES SKARAS
(koh-<u>toh</u>-puh-loh meh <u>rree</u>-gah-neh tees <u>skhah</u>-rahs)

Olive oil, garlic and lemon are flavors basic to many Greek foods, but this baked chicken spotlights their beloved oregano.

2½- to 3-pound broiler-fryer chicken, cut up
½ cup olive or vegetable oil
¼ cup lemon juice
2 teaspoons dried oregano leaves
1 teaspoon salt
½ teaspoon pepper
1 clove garlic, chopped
Lemon slices

Place chicken in ungreased oblong pan, 13 × 9 × 2 inches. Mix remaining ingredients except lemon slices; pour over chicken. Cook uncovered in 375° oven, spooning oil mixture over chicken occasionally, 30 minutes. Turn chicken; cook until thickest pieces are done, about 30 minutes longer. Garnish with lemon slices.

6 to 8 servings

PER SERVING: Calories 350; Protein 23 g; Carbohydrate 2 g; Fat 28 g; Cholesterol 70 mg; Sodium 420 mg

CHICKEN AND VEGETABLE STEW

SAUCOCHI DI GALLINJA (sow-oh-coh-chi dee gay-een-ha)

This flavorful Caribbean stew is spiced with hot chili and chock full of such tempting vegetables as sweet potatoes, sweet corn and winter squash. It is especially popular in the Dominican Republic.

2½- to 3-pound broiler-fryer chicken, cut up
6 cups water
2 tablespoons instant beef bouillon
2 medium tomatoes, chopped
2 medium onions, chopped
2 medium potatoes, cut into ½-inch slices
2 medium sweet potatoes or yams, cut into
    ½-inch slices
3 ears sweet corn, cut into 3 pieces
¼ pound winter squash, pared and cut into
    ½-inch pieces (about 1 cup)
½ cup fresh or frozen green peas
1 small hot chili, stemmed, seeded and sliced
2 teaspoons salt
¼ teaspoon pepper
Snipped chives

Heat chicken, water and bouillon to boiling in Dutch oven; reduce heat. Cover and simmer 30 minutes. Skim off fat. Add remaining ingredients except chives. Heat to boiling; reduce heat. Cover and simmer until thickest pieces of chicken are done and vegetables are tender, about 20 minutes. Garnish each serving with chives.

8 or 9 servings

PER SERVING: Calories 270; Protein 21 g; Carbohydrate 29 g; Fat 8 g; Cholesterol 50 mg; Sodium 1560 mg

AFRICAN CHICKEN AND RICE CASSEROLE

JOLLOF RICE GHANA (jaw-lawf rice gha-nah)

Jollof means that the rice is cooked with the other ingredients of the dish, rather than cooked separately. In our recipe for this Ghanan favorite, chicken and rice bake in a spicy tomato sauce with fresh green beans and cabbage.

2½- to 3-pound broiler-fryer chicken, cut up
2 cans (16 ounces each) stewed tomatoes (with
    liquid)
2 cups water
2 teaspoons salt
¼ teaspoon pepper
1 cup uncooked regular rice
¼ pound fully cooked smoked ham, cubed
    (¾ cup)
¼ teaspoon ground cinnamon
¼ to ½ teaspoon ground red pepper
3 cups coarsely shredded green cabbage
8 ounces green beans*
2 onions, cut into ½-inch slices
½ teaspoon salt

Heat chicken, tomatoes, water, 2 teaspoons salt and the pepper to boiling in 5-quart Dutch oven; reduce heat. Cover and simmer 30 minutes. Remove chicken. Stir in rice, ham, cinnamon and red pepper. Add chicken, cabbage, green beans and onions. Sprinkle with ½ teaspoon salt. Heat to boiling; reduce heat. Cover and simmer until thickest pieces of chicken are done, 20 to 30 minutes longer.

8 servings

*1 package (10 ounces) frozen French-style green beans, thawed, can be substituted for the green beans.

PER SERVING: Calories 300; Protein 23 g; Carbohydrate 30 g; Fat 10 g; Cholesterol 60 mg; Sodium 1030 mg

TARRAGON CHICKEN
POULET À L'ESTRAGON (poo-lay ah leh-strah-gawng)

The subtle anise flavor and fragrance of fresh tarragon makes this chicken dish a favorite in the Burgundy region of France.

2½- to 3-pound broiler-fryer chicken, cut up
1 cup chicken broth or bouillon
3 medium carrots, sliced
1 tablespoon snipped fresh tarragon or 1 teaspoon dried tarragon leaves
1½ teaspoons salt
⅛ teaspoon pepper
1 bay leaf
4 ounces mushrooms, sliced
2 stalks celery, sliced
1 medium onion, sliced
½ cup dry white wine
½ cup half-and-half
3 tablespoons all-purpose flour
1 egg yolk
Hot cooked noodles

Heat chicken, chicken broth, carrots, tarragon, salt, pepper and bay leaf to boiling in 12-inch skillet or Dutch oven; reduce heat. Cover and simmer 30 minutes. Add mushrooms, celery and onion. Heat to boiling; reduce heat. Cover and simmer until thickest pieces of chicken are done, about 15 minutes.

Remove chicken and vegetables to warm platter with slotted spoon; keep warm. Drain liquid from skillet; strain and reserve 1 cup. Pour reserved liquid and the wine into skillet. Mix half-and-half, flour and egg yolk until smooth; stir into wine mixture. Cook, stirring constantly, until thickened. Serve with chicken, vegetables and noodles.

6 to 8 servings

PER SERVING: Calories 370; Protein 30 g; Carbohydrate 31 g; Fat 14 g; Cholesterol 140 mg; Sodium 770 mg

CRUNCHY ALMOND CHICKEN

The silk road in Asia opened the door for more than trading in fine fabrics. It exposed traders from the West and the East to a world of spices as well. Pakistan lies at the heart of this ancient trade route, and the mélange of spices called for in this traditional dish reflects the centuries of trading at that crossroad.

1 cup blanched slivered almonds
1 clove garlic
1 thin slice gingerroot
1 teaspoon salt
1 teaspoon paprika
¼ teaspoon ground cumin
¼ teaspoon pepper
2½- to 3-pound broiler-fryer chicken, cut up
⅓ cup margarine or butter, melted

Place almonds, garlic and gingerroot in blender container; cover and blend until finely ground. Mix almond mixture, salt, paprika, cumin and pepper. Dip chicken into margarine; roll in almond mixture. Place chicken skin sides up in ungreased oblong pan, 13 × 9 × 2 inches. Cook uncovered in 375° oven until thickest pieces are done, 55 to 60 minutes.

6 to 8 servings

PER SERVING: Calories 400; Protein 27 g; Carbohydrate 5 g; Fat 30 g; Cholesterol 70 mg; Sodium 540 mg

CHICKEN FRICASSEE
FRICASSÉE DE POULET (free-kah-say duh poo-lay)

In classic French fashion, to make this fricassee the chicken is fried before it is stewed. White wine and chicken broth make a base for the sauce, enriched with eggs and cream. Serve this masterpiece over rice or buttered noodles.

2 medium carrots, sliced
1 medium onion, sliced
1 stalk celery, sliced
4 tablespoons margarine or butter
2½- to 3-pound broiler-fryer chicken, cut up
2 cups water
1 cup dry white wine
2 tablespoons instant chicken bouillon
½ teaspoon salt
2 Bouquets Garnis (right)
16 small white onions
2 tablespoons margarine or butter
8 ounces mushrooms, sliced
1 tablespoon lemon juice
2 egg yolks
½ cup whipping cream
2 tablespoons snipped parsley
3 to 4 cups hot cooked rice

Cook and stir carrots, sliced onion and the celery in 4 tablespoons margarine in 12-inch skillet or Dutch oven until onions are tender; push to side. Add chicken; cook uncovered until light brown, about 10 minutes.

Add water, ½ cup of the wine, the bouillon, salt and 1 Bouquet Garni. Heat to boiling; reduce heat. Cover and simmer until thickest pieces of chicken are done, about 40 minutes.

Heat 16 onions, 2 tablespoons margarine, remaining wine and Bouquet Garni to boiling; reduce heat. Cover and simmer until onions are tender, about 25 minutes. Remove chicken and onions to warm platter with slotted spoon. Strain bouillon and onion liquid together; discard Bouquets Garnis, carrots, onion and celery slices. Skim fat. Add mushrooms and lemon juice and heat to boiling; reduce heat. Simmer uncovered until reduced to 2½ cups.

Mix egg yolks and whipping cream. Beat 1 cup hot broth by tablespoonfuls into whipping cream mixture. Beat in remaining broth. Heat to boiling, stirring constantly. Boil and stir 1 minute; pour over chicken and onions. Sprinkle with parsley. Serve with rice.

6 to 8 servings

PER SERVING: Calories 605; Protein 31 g; Carbohydrate 53 g; Fat 30 g; Cholesterol 165 mg; Sodium 2080 mg

BOUQUETS GARNIS

4 sprigs parsley
1 bay leaf
¼ teaspoon dried rosemary leaves

For each Bouquet Garni, tie 2 sprigs parsley, ½ bay leaf and ⅛ teaspoon rosemary in cheesecloth bag or place in tea ball.

CHICKEN IN GROUNDNUT SAUCE

"Groundnut" is another name for the peanut. We recommend serving this African dish with raw peanuts, chutney, cucumber and green pepper.

1 can (1 ounce) anchovy fillets
2 tablespoons peanut or vegetable oil
2½- to 3-pound broiler-fryer chicken, cut up
1 cup hot water
2 tablespoons tomato paste
1 can (14½ ounces) whole tomatoes (with liquid)
1 medium onion, sliced
1 clove garlic, finely chopped
3 to 4 dried chilies, crumbled
1 tablespoon chopped candied ginger or ¼ teaspoon grated gingerroot
1½ teaspoons chili powder
½ teaspoon salt
1 to 1½ cups crunchy peanut butter
Accompaniments (right)
Whole chilies

Drain oil from anchovies into Dutch oven; add peanut oil. Heat until hot. Cook chicken over medium heat until brown on all sides, about 15 minutes. Remove chicken. Drain fat from Dutch oven. Heat anchovies, water, tomato paste, tomatoes, onion, garlic, dried chilies, ginger, chili powder and salt to boiling in Dutch oven; reduce heat. Cover and simmer 10 minutes. Add chicken; cover and simmer 45 minutes.

Stir some of the hot liquid into peanut butter; stir back into chicken mixture. Turn chicken to coat with sauce. Cover and cook until chicken is done, 10 to 15 minutes. Serve with a selection of Accompaniments; garnish with whole chilies.

8 servings

PER SERVING: Calories 395; Protein 26 g; Carbohydrate 12 g; Fat 27 g; Cholesterol 55 mg; Sodium 560 mg

ACCOMPANIMENTS: Fried sliced plantains, chopped raw peanuts, chutney, chopped tomatoes, diced green pepper, chopped onion, diced cucumber.

CHICKEN CURRY

The blend of spices used in Indian curries represents more than 2,000 years of tradition. Curry mixtures were used to preserve food as well as to add a mouthwatering aroma. The dish below is a shortcut to a classic, served with its own exotic Mango Chutney.

2 tablespoons vegetable oil
2½- to 3-pound broiler-fryer chicken, cut up
1 teaspoon salt
1 medium onion, chopped
2 tablespoons water
1 cup dairy sour cream
2 teaspoons curry powder
⅛ teaspoon ground ginger
⅛ teaspoon ground cumin
Mango Chutney (page 87)
3 to 4 cups hot cooked rice

Heat oil in 12-inch skillet or Dutch oven until hot. Cook chicken over medium heat until brown on all sides, about 15 minutes. Drain fat from skillet. Sprinkle chicken with salt, onion and water. Cover and simmer until thickest pieces of chicken are done, 30 to 40 minutes.

Remove chicken from skillet; keep warm. Pour liquid from skillet into bowl; skim fat. Return ¼ cup liquid to skillet; stir in sour cream, curry powder, ginger and cumin. Heat, stirring constantly, just until hot. Pour sauce over chicken. Serve chicken with Mango Chutney and rice.

6 to 8 servings

PER SERVING: Calories 770; Protein 29 g; Carbohydrate 112 g; Fat 23 g; Cholesterol 95 mg; Sodium 1210 mg

MANGO CHUTNEY

1 mango (about 1 pound), peeled and coarsely
    chopped
1 cup golden raisins
1 cup packed brown sugar
¾ cup vinegar
1 jar (2⅞ ounces) crystallized ginger, finely
    chopped
1 clove garlic, chopped
1 teaspoon salt

Heat all ingredients to boiling; reduce heat. Simmer uncovered until slightly thickened, about 45 minutes.

Mangoes

The exterior beauty of the tropical mango hints at the mouthwatering, perfumed fruit within. The smooth skin flushes from a vibrant green to apricot-gold to orange-red. The fruit of the mango is a creamy, bright apricot color; it is juicy and clings to a flat, oval central pit that runs the length of the mango. Because mangoes ripen after they are picked, they can be purchased quite green and set aside until the fruit yields to gentle pressure. Eaten by itself, this sweet beauty needs no sugar; mango is delicious in ice cream and sorbets, mousses and refreshing, yogurt-based drinks.

FIVE SPICE CHICKEN
WU HSIANG CHI (woo shee-ong jee)

The five spices used in our recipe are similar to the traditional spices called for in Chinese dishes. Five spice powders may contain, in addition to the spices below, fennel seed, Szechuan peppers or star anise. The Chinese use five spice powder sparingly.

2½- to 3-pound broiler-fryer chicken, cut up
⅓ cup soy sauce
2 tablespoons vegetable oil
1 small onion, chopped
1 clove garlic, finely chopped
½ teaspoon ground ginger
¼ teaspoon ground cinnamon
¼ teaspoon crushed anise seed
⅛ teaspoon ground nutmeg
⅛ teaspoon ground cloves

Place chicken in shallow glass or plastic dish. Mix remaining ingredients; pour over chicken. Cover and refrigerate, spooning marinade over chicken occasionally, at least 1 hour.

Remove chicken from marinade; reserve marinade. Place chicken in ungreased oblong baking dish, 12 × 7½ × 2 inches. Brush marinade on chicken. Cook uncovered in 350° oven, brushing once or twice with marinade, until thickest pieces of chicken are done, about 1 hour.

6 to 8 servings

PER SERVING: Calories 230; Protein 23 g; Carbohydrate 23 g; Fat 14 g; Cholesterol 70 mg; Sodium 970 mg

MOROCCAN CHICKEN WITH OLIVES

TAJINE B'ZEETOON (tah-<u>jheen</u> b'zee-toon)

Traditionally Kalamata olives (light-colored black olives) garnish this Moroccan dish to add a slightly salty flavor. Preserved lemons are an authentic ingredient; using fresh lemon instead holds the kitchen time to a minimum.

¼ cup snipped fresh cilantro
1 tablespoon paprika
2 teaspoons ground cumin
½ teaspoon salt
½ teaspoon ground turmeric
½ teaspoon ground ginger
2 cloves garlic, finely chopped
3- to 3½-pound broiler-fryer chicken, cut up
⅓ cup all-purpose flour
½ cup water
¼ cup lemon juice
1 teaspoon instant chicken bouillon
½ cup Kalamata or Greek olives
1 lemon, sliced

Mix cilantro, paprika, cumin, salt, turmeric, ginger and garlic. Rub mixture on all sides of chicken; coat with flour. Place chicken in ungreased oblong baking dish, 13 × 9 × 2 inches. Mix water, lemon juice and bouillon; pour over chicken. Add olives and lemon slices. Cook uncovered in 350° oven, spooning juices over chicken occasionally, until thickest pieces of chicken are done, about 1 hour. Serve with couscous or rice if desired.

6 servings

PER SERVING: Calories 265; Protein 28 g; Carbohydrate 9 g; Fat 13 g; Cholesterol 85 mg; Sodium 370 mg

Moroccan Chicken with Olives, *bottom,* and Tomato and Green Pepper Salad (page 230)

MEXICAN ORANGE-PINEAPPLE CHICKEN

POLLO CON JUGO DE NARANJA
(<u>poy</u>-yoh kohn <u>hoo</u>-goh deh nah-<u>rahn</u>-hah)

This Mexican fried chicken is served in a sauce sweetened with orange juice, raisins and pineapple, spiced with cinnamon and clove and spiked with rum. Toasted slivered almonds are an elegant topping.

½ cup all-purpose flour
1 teaspoon salt
½ teaspoon pepper
3- to 3½-pound broiler-fryer chicken, cut up
3 tablespoons vegetable oil
¾ cup orange juice
½ cup raisins
¼ cup dark rum
¼ teaspoon ground cinnamon
⅛ teaspoon ground cloves
1 can (8 ounces) crushed pineapple, undrained
¼ cup toasted slivered almonds

Mix flour, salt and pepper. Coat chicken with flour mixture. Heat oil in 12-inch skillet until hot. Cook chicken over medium heat until brown on all sides, about 15 minutes. Place chicken in ungreased oblong baking dish, 13 × 9 × 2 inches.

Mix remaining ingredients except almonds; pour over chicken. Cook uncovered in 350° oven, spooning juices over chicken occasionally, until thickest pieces of chicken are done, 40 to 50 minutes. Sprinkle with almonds.

6 servings

PER SERVING: Calories 425; Protein 29 g; Carbohydrate 28 g; Fat 22 g; Cholesterol 80 mg; Sodium 480 mg

HONEY-SPICED CHICKEN WITH ORANGE SAUCE

In Israel, as in much of the Middle East, honey is an ingredient used to signal festive occasions, to celebrate the sweetness of life or of a new year. Honey, lemon and orange juice, ginger and nutmeg flavor this golden brown chicken and provide a sweet sauce, too. Serve with Couscous (page 91) or Jewish Egg Braid (page 296).

2 tablespoons vegetable oil or chicken fat
2½- to 3-pound broiler-fryer chicken, cut up
2 medium onions, sliced
1 teaspoon salt
1 teaspoon paprika
⅛ teaspoon pepper
1 cup orange juice
¼ cup honey
2 tablespoons lemon juice
½ teaspoon ground ginger
¼ teaspoon ground nutmeg
½ cup pitted ripe olives
1 tablespoon cold water
2 teaspoons cornstarch
Orange slices (optional)

Heat oil in skillet until hot. Cook chicken over medium heat until brown on all sides, about 15 minutes. Place chicken in ungreased oblong baking dish, 11 × 7 × 1½ inches; top with onions. Sprinkle with salt, paprika and pepper. Mix orange juice, honey, lemon juice, ginger and nutmeg; pour over chicken. Add olives. Cover and cook in 350° oven until thickest pieces of chicken are done, 45 to 60 minutes.

Arrange chicken, onions, and olives on platter. Pour pan juices into saucepan; heat to boiling.

Mix water and cornstarch; stir into juices. Cook and stir until slightly thickened, 1 to 2 minutes. Garnish chicken with orange slices; serve with orange sauce.

6 to 8 servings

PER SERVING: Calories 320; Protein 23 g; Carbohydrate 21 g; Fat 16 g; Cholesterol 70 mg; Sodium 690 mg

COUSCOUS WITH CHICKEN

(koos-koos)

Couscous is popular in Morocco, Algiers and Tunisia. With the colonization of North Africa, the French have embraced couscous in their cuisine, too. *Couscous* grains are traditionally steamed in a *couscousière,* set on a rack over a bubbling stew of chicken, vegetables or meat.

2 tablespoons olive or vegetable oil
2½- to 3-pound broiler-fryer chicken, cut up
4 small carrots, cut into 2-inch pieces
2 medium onions, sliced
2 medium turnips or small rutabaga, cut into fourths
2 cloves garlic, finely chopped
2 teaspoons ground coriander
1½ teaspoons salt
1 teaspoon instant chicken bouillon
¼ teaspoon ground red pepper
1 cup water
3 zucchini, cut into ¼-inch slices
1 can (15 ounces) garbanzo beans, drained
Couscous (page 91)

Heat oil in Dutch oven until hot. Cook chicken in oil until brown on all sides, about 15 minutes. Drain fat from Dutch oven. Add carrots, onions, turnips, garlic, coriander, salt, bouillon and red pepper. Pour water over vegetables. Heat to boiling; reduce heat. Cover and simmer 30 minutes.

Add zucchini to chicken mixture. Cover and cook until thickest pieces of chicken are done and vegetables are tender, about 10 minutes. Add beans; heat 5 minutes.

Prepare Couscous. Mound on center of heated platter; arrange chicken and vegetables around Couscous.

8 servings

PER SERVING: Calories 385; Protein 24 g; Carbohydrate 38 g; Fat 15 g; Cholesterol 50 mg; Sodium 830 mg

COUSCOUS

1⅓ cups couscous (wheat-grain semolina)
¾ cup raisins
½ teaspoon salt
1 cup boiling water
½ cup margarine or butter
½ teaspoon ground turmeric

Mix couscous, raisins and salt in 2-quart bowl; stir in boiling water. Let stand until all water is absorbed, 2 to 3 minutes. Heat margarine in 10-inch skillet until melted; stir in couscous and ground turmeric. Cook and stir 4 minutes.

MEXICAN FRIED CHICKEN

Many Mexican recipes are based on fresh lime marinades. Here, chicken steeps in a piquant mixture of garlic and lime juice, then is coated with chili-flecked flour and fried until golden brown and crisp.

1 clove garlic
½ teaspoon salt
2½- to 3-pound broiler-fryer chicken, cut up
¼ cup lime juice
1 small onion, finely chopped
Vegetable oil
½ cup all-purpose flour
1 teaspoon salt
1 teaspoon chili powder

Mash garlic and ½ teaspoon salt to a paste. Rub chicken with garlic mixture. Arrange chicken in shallow glass or plastic dish. Sprinkle with lime juice and onion. Cover and refrigerate, turning occasionally, at least 3 hours. Remove chicken from marinade; pat dry.

Heat oil (¼ inch) in skillet until hot. Decrease heat to medium. Mix flour, 1 teaspoon salt and the chili powder. Coat chicken with flour mixture. Place chicken in skillet skin sides down. Cover and cook 5 minutes. Uncover and cook 15 minutes. Turn chicken. Cover and cook 5 minutes longer. Uncover and cook until thickest pieces are done, 10 to 15 minutes; drain.

6 to 8 servings

PER SERVING: Calories 305; Protein 23 g; Carbohydrate 10 g; Fat 19 g; Cholesterol 70 mg; Sodium 600 mg

CHICKEN WITH GOLDEN PILAF
KABULI PELAU (kah-boo-lee puh-low)

Curried rice pilaf with sweet raisins and almond slivers accompanies our recipe for a traditional Afghan fried chicken.

2 tablespoons vegetable oil
2½- to 3-pound broiler-fryer chicken, cut up
1 teaspoon salt
2 medium carrots
1 medium onion, chopped
¼ cup margarine or butter
2¼ cups water
1 cup uncooked regular rice
½ cup raisins
1 tablespoon instant chicken bouillon
½ teaspoon curry powder
¼ teaspoon salt
¼ teaspoon dried thyme leaves
¼ cup toasted slivered almonds

Heat oil in 12-inch skillet or Dutch oven until hot. Cook chicken over medium heat until brown on all sides, about 15 minutes; reduce heat. Sprinkle with 1 teaspoon salt. Cover and cook over low heat until thickest pieces are done, 30 to 40 minutes. (Add water if necessary.) Uncover during last 5 minutes of cooking to crisp chicken.

Cut carrots lengthwise into ¼-inch strips; cut into 1-inch pieces. Cook and stir onion in margarine in 2-quart saucepan until tender. Add carrots, water, rice, raisins, bouillon, curry powder, ¼ teaspoon salt and the thyme. Heat to boiling, stirring once or twice; reduce heat. Cover and simmer 14 minutes. (Do not lift cover or stir.)

Remove from heat. Fluff rice lightly with fork; cover and let steam 5 to 10 minutes. Serve chicken with rice; top with almonds.

6 to 8 servings

PER SERVING: Calories 500; Protein 27 g; Carbohydrate 42 g; Fat 25 g; Cholesterol 70 mg; Sodium 1250 mg

CHICKEN WITH DILL SAUCE
KURCZETA Z SOSEM KOPERKOWYM
(koorr-cheh-tah z sohs-ehm koh-perr-koh-veem)

This Polish favorite pairs the light flavor of chicken with a zesty sauce of lemon and dill weed.

3- to 3½-pound broiler-fryer chicken, cut up
1½ cups water
1 teaspoon salt
¼ teaspoon white pepper
1 cup half-and-half
3 tablespoons all-purpose flour
1 tablespoon snipped dill weed
1 teaspoon lemon juice

Heat chicken, water, salt and white pepper to boiling in 10-inch skillet; reduce heat. Cover and simmer until thickest pieces of chicken are done, 45 to 50 minutes. Remove chicken; keep warm. Shake half-and-half and flour in tightly covered jar. Stir half-and-half mixture, dill weed and lemon juice into pan juices. Heat to boiling, stirring constantly; boil and stir 1 minute. Pour some of the sauce over chicken; serve with remaining sauce and with Little German Noodle Dumplings (page 283) or cooked cauliflower, if desired.

6 servings

PER SERVING: Calories 275; Protein 28 g; Carbohydrate 5 g; Fat 16 g; Cholesterol 100 mg; Sodium 450 mg

CHICKEN PAPRIKA WITH DUMPLINGS

CSIRKE PAPRIKAS (<u>cheer</u>-kah <u>pah</u>-pree-kosh)

There are many varieties of Hungarian paprika. We recommend using sweet Hungarian paprika in this dish. Moist chicken and chewy dumplings are pure luxury in this velvety sauce.

2 tablespoons vegetable oil
2½- to 3-pound broiler-fryer chicken, cut up
2 medium onions, chopped
1 clove garlic, chopped
1 medium tomato, chopped
½ cup water
½ teaspoon instant chicken bouillon
2 tablespoons paprika
1 teaspoon salt
¼ teaspoon pepper
1 medium green pepper, cut into ½-inch strips
Dumplings (right)
1 cup dairy sour cream

Heat oil in 12-inch skillet until hot. Cook chicken over medium heat until brown on all sides, about 15 minutes. Remove chicken. Cook and stir onions and garlic in oil until onions are tender; drain fat from skillet. Stir in tomato, water, bouillon, paprika, salt and pepper; loosen brown particles from bottom of skillet. Add chicken. Heat to boiling; reduce heat. Cover and simmer 20 minutes. Add green pepper; cover and cook until thickest pieces of chicken are done, 10 to 15 minutes longer. Prepare Dumplings.

Remove chicken to heated platter; keep warm. Skim fat from skillet. Stir sour cream into liquid in skillet; add Dumplings. Heat just until hot. Serve chicken with Dumplings and sour cream sauce.

6 to 8 servings

PER SERVING: Calories 515; Protein 32 g; Carbohydrate 40 g; Fat 25 g; Cholesterol 200 mg; Sodium 1540 mg

DUMPLINGS

8 cups water
1 teaspoon salt
3 eggs, well beaten
½ cup water
2 cups all-purpose flour
2 teaspoons salt

Heat 8 cups water and 1 teaspoon salt to boiling in Dutch oven. Mix eggs, ½ cup water, the flour and 2 teaspoons salt; drop dough by teaspoonfuls into boiling water. Cook uncovered, stirring occasionally, 10 minutes. Drain. (Dumplings will be chewy.)

CHICKEN WITH PINEAPPLE

POLLO EN PIÑA (<u>poy</u>-yoh ehn <u>peen</u>-yah)

Our *Pollo en Piña* closely follows the Guatemalan preparation. Chicken is stewed in a broth of dry sherry, vinegar and fresh tomatoes. Cinnamon and clove add their fragrance and flavor; pineapple adds its juicy sweetness. Hot cooked rice accompanies this tempting stew.

2 tablespoons olive or vegetable oil
3- to 3½-pound broiler-fryer chicken, cut up
1 medium onion, chopped
2 cloves garlic, chopped
1 pineapple, pared and cut into 1-inch pieces, or 1 can (20 ounces) unsweetened pineapple chunks, drained
½ cup dry sherry
2 tablespoons vinegar
1 teaspoon salt
¼ teaspoon ground cinnamon
¼ teaspoon ground cloves
⅛ teaspoon pepper
2 medium tomatoes, coarsely chopped
3 cups hot cooked rice

Heat oil in 12-inch skillet until hot. Cook chicken over medium heat until brown on all sides, about 15 minutes. Remove chicken. Cook and stir onion and garlic in oil until onion is tender.

Return chicken to skillet. Mix remaining ingredients except tomatoes and rice; pour over chicken. Heat to boiling; reduce heat. Cover and simmer 20 minutes. Add tomatoes; simmer uncovered until thickest pieces of chicken are done, about 20 minutes longer. Serve with rice.

6 servings

PER SERVING: Calories 455; Protein 30 g; Carbohydrate 45 g; Fat 17 g; Cholesterol 85 mg; Sodium 830 mg

CHICKEN WITH RED PEPPERS

POLLO A LA CHILINDRON
(<u>poy</u>-yoh ah lah chee-leen-<u>drohn</u>)

Fresh red peppers and prosciutto flavor this lightly fried chicken. In Spain both ripe and green olives are served as an accompaniment.

2 tablespoons vegetable oil
3- to 3½-pound broiler-fryer chicken, cut up
1 medium onion, chopped
1 clove garlic, chopped
3 medium red peppers, cut into thin strips
2 medium tomatoes, chopped
½ cup chopped prosciutto (about 2 ounces)
1 teaspoon salt
¼ teaspoon pepper

Heat oil in 12-inch skillet until hot. Cook chicken over medium heat until brown on all sides, about 15 minutes; remove chicken. Cook and stir onion and garlic in oil until onion is tender. Stir in remaining ingredients. Heat to boiling; reduce heat.

Return chicken to skillet. Simmer uncovered, turning chicken pieces occasionally, until thickest pieces of chicken are done, about 40 minutes. Remove chicken to warm platter; keep warm. Cook and stir sauce over medium heat until very thick, about 5 minutes; serve over chicken. Garnish with ripe or Kalamata olives if desired.

6 servings

PER SERVING: Calories 305; Protein 30 g; Carbohydrate 6 g; Fat 18 g; Cholesterol 90 mg; Sodium 550 mg

Chicken with Red Peppers and Lemon and Celery Pilaf (page 274)

SZECHWAN CHICKEN WITH CASHEWS

GAI DING (guy ding)

Much of Szechwan cooking is hot and spicy. Our recipe for chicken and cashews follows in that vein. Gingerroot, chili pepper paste and hoisin sauce fire this dish. Serve with hot cooked rice, a cooling respite from the heat.

2 whole chicken breasts (about 1½ pounds)
1 egg white
1 teaspoon cornstarch
1 teaspoon salt
1 teaspoon finely chopped gingerroot
1 teaspoon soy sauce
Dash of pepper
1 tablespoon vegetable oil
1 cup raw cashews
½ teaspoon salt
4 tablespoons vegetable oil
6 green onions (with tops), chopped (reserve 2 tablespoons tops)
1 large green pepper, cut into ½-inch squares
1 can (4 ounces) button mushrooms, drained (reserve liquid)
1 tablespoon hoisin sauce
2 teaspoons chili pepper paste*
½ cup chicken broth
1 tablespoon cold water
1 tablespoon cornstarch
1 tablespoon soy sauce

Remove bones and skin from chicken breasts; cut chicken into ½-inch pieces. (For ease in cutting, partially freeze chicken about 1 hour.) Mix egg white, 1 teaspoon cornstarch, 1 teaspoon salt, the gingerroot, 1 teaspoon soy sauce and the pepper in 2-quart glass bowl; stir in chicken. Cover and refrigerate at least 30 minutes.

Heat 1 tablespoon oil in wok or 10-inch skillet until hot. Stir-fry cashews until light brown, about 1 minute; drain. Sprinkle with ½ teaspoon salt. Heat 2 tablespoons of the oil until hot. Add chicken; stir-fry until chicken turns white, about 3 minutes. Remove chicken. Heat remaining 1 tablespoon oil until hot. Add green onions, green pepper, mushrooms, hoisin sauce and chili pepper paste. Stir-fry about 1 minute. Add chicken, chicken broth and reserved mushroom liquid; heat to boiling. Mix the water, 1 tablespoon cornstarch and 1 tablespoon soy sauce; stir into chicken mixture. Cook and stir until thickened, about 1 minute. Stir in cashews; garnish with reserved green onion tops.

6 servings

*1 teaspoon crushed red pepper flakes can be substituted for the chili pepper paste.

PER SERVING: Calories 400; Protein 30 g; Carbohydrate 12 g; Fat 26 g; Cholesterol 60 mg; Sodium 1090 mg

LEMON CHICKEN, HUNAN STYLE

Hunan Province is the home of the sweet and sour sauce. These batter-dipped chicken morsels are deep-fried to a golden brown, then are served with a honey-sweetened Lemon Sauce.

3 large whole chicken breasts (about 2½ pounds)
Vegetable oil
¼ cup all-purpose flour
¼ cup water
1 egg
2 tablespoons cornstarch
2 tablespoons vegetable oil
1 teaspoon salt
1 teaspoon soy sauce
¼ teaspoon baking soda
Lemon Sauce (right)
½ lemon, thinly sliced

Remove bones and skin from chicken breasts; cut chicken into halves. Heat oil (1 to 1½ inches) to 360°. Beat remaining ingredients except Lemon Sauce and lemon slices with hand beater until smooth. Dip chicken pieces one at a time into batter. Fry 2 pieces at a time until golden brown, turning once, about 7 minutes; drain. Repeat with remaining chicken.

Cut chicken crosswise into ½-inch slices; arrange in single layer on heated platter. Keep warm. Prepare Lemon Sauce; pour over chicken. Garnish with lemon slices.

6 servings

PER SERVING: Calories 430; Protein 42 g; Carbohydrate 21 g; Fat 20 g; Cholesterol 140 mg; Sodium 870 mg

LEMON SAUCE

½ cup water
½ teaspoon grated lemon peel
¼ cup lemon juice
¼ cup honey
1 tablespoon catsup
½ teaspoon instant chicken bouillon
½ teaspoon salt
1 clove garlic, finely chopped
1 tablespoon cold water
1 tablespoon cornstarch

Heat ½ cup water, the lemon peel, lemon juice, honey, catsup, bouillon, salt and garlic to boiling. Mix 1 tablespoon water and cornstarch; stir into sauce. Cook and stir until thickened, about 30 seconds.

DO-AHEAD TIP: After frying chicken, cover and refrigerate no longer than 24 hours. Heat chicken on ungreased cookie sheet in 400° oven until hot, 10 to 12 minutes. Cut crosswise into ½-inch slices.

TUSCAN CHICKEN ROLLS WITH PORK STUFFING

ROLLATINI DI POLLO (rohl-lah-<u>tee</u>-nee dee <u>pohl</u>-loh)

These savory rolls are filled with soft, garlic-flavored bread crumbs and then poached in a dry white wine and broth. The recipe is inspired by the chicken dishes of Tuscany, the region over which Florence reigns.

3 large whole chicken breasts (about 2½ pounds)
½ pound ground pork
1 small onion, finely chopped
1 clove garlic, chopped
1 egg, beaten
½ cup soft bread crumbs
½ teaspoon salt
¼ teaspoon ground savory
¼ teaspoon pepper
2 tablespoons margarine or butter, melted
½ teaspoon salt
½ cup dry white wine
½ cup cold water
2 teaspoons cornstarch
½ teaspoon instant chicken bouillon
Snipped parsley

Remove bones and skin from chicken breasts; cut chicken into halves. Place between 2 pieces plastic wrap; pound until ¼ inch thick, being careful not to tear the meat.

Cook and stir pork, onion and garlic over medium heat until pork is brown. Drain fat. Stir in egg, bread crumbs, ½ teaspoon salt, the savory and pepper. Place about ⅓ cup pork mixture on each chicken breast half. Roll up; secure with wooden picks. Place rolls in greased oblong baking dish, 11 × 7 × 1½ inches. Brush rolls with margarine; pour any remaining margarine over rolls. Sprinkle with ½ teaspoon salt. Add wine.

Cook uncovered in 400° oven until chicken is done, 35 to 40 minutes.

Remove chicken to warm platter; remove wooden picks. Keep warm. Pour liquid from baking dish into 1-quart saucepan. Stir water into cornstarch; pour into liquid. Stir in bouillon. Heat to boiling over medium heat, stirring constantly. Boil and stir 1 minute. Pour gravy on chicken. Top with parsley.

6 servings

PER SERVING: Calories 390; Protein 50 g; Carbohydrate 9 g; Fat 17 g; Cholesterol 160 mg; Sodium 690 mg

JAVANESE-STYLE CHICKEN

AYAM GORENG (eye-<u>yahm</u> goh-<u>reng</u>)

"Hot and tangy" describes this Javanese chicken recipe with tamarind.

¾ cup water
1 tablespoon tamarind pulp or powder, or 2 tablespoons lemon juice
2 teaspoons ground coriander
1½ teaspoons salt
¼ teaspoon ground turmeric
6 blanched whole almonds
1 small onion, cut into fourths
1 clove garlic, cut into fourths
2 small jalapeño peppers, cut into halves and seeded
1 stalk lemon grass, cut lengthwise into halves, or 3 thin strips lemon peel
2 large whole chicken breasts, cut into fourths
3 tablespoons vegetable oil
3 cups hot cooked rice

Place water, tamarind, coriander, salt, turmeric, almonds, onion, garlic and peppers in blender container. Cover and blend on high speed until ingredients are chopped and mixture is well blended, about 1 minute.

Heat water mixture, lemon grass and chicken in 12-inch skillet to boiling; reduce heat. Simmer uncovered over medium heat, turning chicken occasionally, until sauce is very thick and begins to stick to skillet, about 25 minutes. Remove chicken; discard lemon grass. Scrape sauce from skillet; reserve.

Heat oil in skillet until hot. Cook chicken over medium heat until brown on all sides and thickest pieces of chicken are done, 15 to 20 minutes. Mix reserved sauce with rice; serve with chicken.

4 servings

PER SERVING: Calories 545; Protein 37 g; Carbohydrate 48 g; Fat 23 g; Cholesterol 90 mg; Sodium 1470 mg

---

Tamarind

It is tamarind that gives Worcestershire sauce its curiously sour edge. Tamarind is a legume, the long brown pods containing seeds cushioned in pulp. It is the pulp that is used in cooking, but first it must be freed of the pod, sticky fibers and seeds. Another name for tamarind is "Indian date," and like dates, tamarind is sometimes sold in compressed, sticky bricks. Tamarind is also sold in powder form and, easiest of all to use, as a cooked-down paste.

THAI CHICKEN WITH BASIL

Fresh basil and fresh mint are essential to this dish. They are gentle counterparts to the fiery peppers and salty fish sauce. This simple, elegant dish calls for hot cooked rice.

4 boneless, skinless chicken breast halves (about 12 ounces)
2 tablespoons vegetable oil
3 cloves garlic, finely chopped
2 red jalapeño peppers, seeded and finely chopped
1 tablespoon fish sauce
1 teaspoon sugar
¼ cup snipped fresh basil
1 tablespoon snipped fresh mint leaves
1 tablespoon chopped unsalted roasted peanuts

Cut each breast half into 4 pieces.

Heat oil in wok or 12-inch skillet until hot. Cook and stir garlic and peppers over medium-high heat until garlic is golden brown. Add chicken; stir-fry until chicken is done, 8 to 10 minutes. Stir in fish sauce and sugar. Sprinkle with remaining ingredients. Garnish with lemon wedges if desired.

4 servings

PER SERVING: Calories 195; Protein 20 g; Carbohydrate 6 g; Fat 10 g; Cholesterol 45 mg; Sodium 60 mg

GREEK CHICKEN WITH ARTICHOKES

KOTTOPOULO ME ANGINARES
(koh-toh-poo-loh meh ahn-jee-nah-rehs)

Avgolemeno is how the Greeks describe one of their best-loved sauces, made with chicken broth and lemon and enriched with golden egg yolks.

4 large chicken breast halves (about 2 pounds)
2 tablespoons vegetable oil
½ teaspoon salt
⅛ teaspoon pepper
1 clove garlic, chopped
1 cup water
1 teaspoon instant chicken bouillon
1 can (14 ounces) small artichoke hearts, drained
2 tablespoons lemon juice
1 teaspoon cornstarch
2 eggs

Remove bones and skin from chicken breast halves. Heat oil in 10-inch skillet until hot. Cook chicken over medium heat until brown on both sides, about 15 minutes; drain fat. Sprinkle chicken with salt, pepper and garlic. Add water and bouillon. Heat to boiling; reduce heat. Cover and simmer 10 minutes. Add artichoke hearts. Cover and simmer until chicken is done and artichoke hearts are hot, about 5 minutes.

Remove chicken and artichoke hearts to warm platter with slotted spoon; keep warm. Beat lemon juice, cornstarch and egg in small bowl until smooth, using fork.

Add enough water to pan juices to measure 1 cup. Beat into egg mixture, using fork. Return mixture to skillet. Heat to boiling over medium heat; boil and stir 1 minute. Pour sauce over chicken and artichokes. Sprinkle with snipped parsley if desired.

4 servings

PER SERVING: Calories 420; Protein 55 g; Carbohydrate 10 g; Fat 18 g; Cholesterol 230 mg; Sodium 940 mg

CHICKEN WITH SPICY WALNUT SAUCE

SATSIVI (saht-see-vee)

The tart walnut sauce (*Satsivi*) used here is a traditional element of meat, fish, or poultry dishes from the Georgian Republic. Pomegranates may be juiced at home, but take care that the cranberry-red juice does not spatter onto clothing, as it will stain.

6 large chicken breast halves (about 2½ pounds)
2 tablespoons vegetable oil
1 large onion, chopped
¾ cup finely chopped walnuts
¾ cup unsweetened pomegranate juice
¼ cup water
1 teaspoon ground cinnamon
½ teaspoon salt
¼ teaspoon ground coriander
⅛ teaspoon ground allspice
⅛ teaspoon pepper

Remove bones and skin from chicken breast halves. Heat oil in 12-inch skillet until hot. Cook chicken over medium heat until brown on both sides, about 10 minutes. Remove chicken.

Cook and stir onion in oil until tender. Stir in remaining ingredients. Add chicken. Heat to boiling; reduce heat. Cover and simmer until chicken is done, about 10 minutes.

Remove chicken to warm platter with slotted spoon; keep warm. Heat walnut mixture to boiling; reduce heat. Simmer uncovered, stirring occasionally, until thickened, about 5 minutes. Spoon sauce over chicken. Serve with Cracked Wheat Pilaf (page 269) if desired.

6 servings

PER SERVING: Calories 380; Protein 43 g; Carbohydrate 9 g; Fat 19 g; Cholesterol 105 mg; Sodium 280 mg

CHICKEN WITH SAUERKRAUT

Pungent caraway seed gives this German dish its unique flavor. Serve with Little German Noodle Dumplings (page 283).

2 tablespoons vegetable oil
6 large chicken breast halves (about 2½ pounds)
1 can (16 ounces) sliced potatoes, drained
1 can (16 ounces) sauerkraut, drained
½ teaspoon caraway seed
¼ teaspoon crushed red pepper
⅓ cup dairy sour cream

Heat oil in 12-inch skillet until hot. Cook chicken over medium heat until brown on both sides, about 15 minutes; drain fat. Add potatoes to skillet.

Mix sauerkraut, caraway seed and red pepper; spoon over potatoes. Cover and cook over low heat until chicken is done, 35 to 40 minutes. Serve with sour cream.

6 servings

PER SERVING: Calories 315; Protein 42 g; Carbohydrate 10 g; Fat 12 g; Cholesterol 110 mg; Sodium 590 mg

Pomegranate Juice

The juice can be extracted from pomegranate halves with the aid of a citrus juicer. Alternatively, remove the little seeds from the membrane and squeeze them in a cheesecloth bag. Pomegranate juice is a little work to obtain fresh. Fortunately, it can be purchased in health-food stores, Middle Eastern specialty markets and some larger supermarkets. The fresh juice can be kept, tightly covered and refrigerated, for about four or five days.

SCANDINAVIAN CHICKEN WITH APRICOTS

A sweet assortment of apricots and currants graces this savory winter dish. Lemon and apricot brandy, along with a topping of toasted, slivered almonds, add finesse.

6 large chicken breast halves (about 2½ pounds)
½ cup water
¼ cup apricot brandy
1 package (6 ounces) dried apricots (about 1¼ cups)
2 tablespoons currants
2 tablespoons vegetable oil
1 teaspoon salt
½ teaspoon dried thyme leaves
¼ teaspoon pepper
1 lemon, thinly sliced
⅓ cup toasted slivered almonds (optional)

Remove skin from chicken breasts. Mix water, brandy, apricots and currants; let stand 15 minutes.

Heat oil in 12-inch skillet until hot. Cook chicken over medium heat until brown on both sides, about 15 minutes; drain fat. Sprinkle chicken with salt, thyme and pepper. Add apricot mixture and lemon slices. Heat to boiling; reduce heat. Cover and cook, spooning pan juices over chicken occasionally, until chicken is done, 35 to 40 minutes. Sprinkle with almonds.

6 servings

PER SERVING: Calories 350; Protein 42 g; Carbohydrate 23 g; Fat 10 g; Cholesterol 105 mg; Sodium 450 mg

Following pages: Scandinavian Chicken with Apricots, Danish Pickled Cucumbers (page 246), Sugar-browned Potatoes (page 261) and Fried Potato Bread (page 286)

JAPANESE CHICKEN OVER RICE

YAKITORI DOMBURI (yah-kee-<u>toh</u>-ree dohm-<u>boo</u>-ree)

Yakitori is a lean dish that is long on flavor. Although the sauce used here is similar to that used for *teriyaki, yakitori* is usually made with poultry and requires no marinating time. *Domburi* signifies that the dish is served over rice.

6 large chicken breast halves (about 2½ pounds)
½ cup soy sauce
½ cup mirin (sweet Japanese cooking wine) or sake
1 teaspoon finely chopped gingerroot
1 clove garlic, finely chopped
2 tablespoons vegetable oil
2 cups water
2 tablespoons sugar
2 green onions (with tops), cut diagonally into ¼-inch slices
3 cups hot cooked rice

Remove bones and skin from chicken breast halves. Mix soy sauce, mirin, gingerroot and garlic in medium glass or plastic bowl. Place chicken in soy mixture. Cover and refrigerate 1 hour.

Drain chicken, reserving soy mixture. Heat oil in 12-inch skillet until hot. Cook chicken over medium heat until brown on both sides and done, about 15 minutes.

Heat water, sugar and reserved soy mixture to boiling in 3-quart saucepan; boil and stir 2 minutes. Stir in green onions. Cut each chicken breast half into 6 diagonal slices; place 6 slices on rice in soup bowl. Spoon hot liquid over chicken.

6 servings

PER SERVING: Calories 420; Protein 45 g; Carbohydrate 38 g; Fat 10 g; Cholesterol 105 mg; Sodium 1860 mg

Holding the knife or cleaver at a 45-degree angle to the cutting surface, cut each chicken breast half into 6 diagonal slices.

CHICKEN WITH LEMON GRASS

THIT GA XAO DAM GUNG SA
(teet gah djow dahm guhng sah)

The exotic sauce of this Vietnamese dish is fragrant and satisfying—sweet, sour, tart and faintly salty, all at once. Skinned and boned, the meat cooks quickly and remains succulent.

6 chicken thighs (about 2 pounds)
1 stalk lemon grass, chopped, or 3 thin strips
    lemon peel
1 tablespoon fish sauce
3 tablespoons vegetable oil
1 medium onion, sliced
2 cloves garlic, chopped
3 green onions (with tops), cut into 1-inch pieces
2 tablespoons vinegar
1 tablespoon finely chopped gingerroot
¼ cup water
1 tablespoon fish sauce
1 teaspoon cornstarch
1 teaspoon sugar
¼ teaspoon crushed red pepper
2 cups hot cooked rice

Remove bones and skin from chicken thighs; cut chicken into 1-inch pieces. Mix lemon grass and 1 tablespoon fish sauce in glass or plastic bowl; stir in chicken. Cover and refrigerate at least 1 hour.

Heat oil in wok or 10-inch skillet until hot. Add sliced onion and garlic; stir-fry 1 minute. Add chicken and green onions; stir-fry 5 minutes.

Reduce heat; cover and cook, stirring occasionally, 2 minutes.

Mix vinegar and gingerroot; reserve. Mix remaining ingredients except rice; stir into chicken mixture. Stir in reserved vinegar mixture. Heat to boiling, stirring constantly; cook and stir until thickened, about 1 minute. Serve with rice.

4 servings

PER SERVING: Calories 405; Protein 26 g; Carbohydrate 35 g; Fat 18 g; Cholesterol 80 mg; Sodium 490 mg

Lemon Grass

This is indeed a grass, a tall-growing tropical grass that looks something like a vastly overgrown scallion with a woody base. Lemon grass, used extensively in Burmese, Indian, Indonesian, Laotian, Malaysian, Thai and Vietnamese cookery, is also known by the name of "citronella root." It is a seasoning that, like the bay leaf, is not meant to be eaten; for safety's sake, it is usually removed from a dish before it is served. Until recently, few American specialty markets carried fresh lemon grass. In dried form, lemon grass is usually soaked before it is added to food. It is often recommended, for both fresh and dried lemon grass, that the pieces be given a hearty smack with a heavy pot or hammer to fan the woody fibers out a bit; the herb gives up more of its exotic, citrus flavor when it has been "bruised."

Thai Chicken Salad   Ingredients for Thai Chicken Salad

THAI CHICKEN SALAD

After handling the chili, wash your hands thoroughly with soap and water to remove every trace of its intensely irritating oil.

4 small dried cloud ears or 2 pieces of dried
  black fungus
½ package (3¾ ounces) cellophane noodles
2 green onions (with tops), thinly sliced
1 small whole chicken breast, cooked, skinned
  and shredded
4 ounces medium shrimp (about 6), cooked and
  coarsely chopped
½ cup shredded fresh spinach
¼ cup coarsely chopped peanuts
1 tablespoon snipped mint leaves
Romaine or leaf lettuce leaves
Snipped fresh cilantro
Dressing (right)

Cover cloud ears with hot water. Let stand 20 minutes; drain. Cut into thin slices. Cover cellophane noodles with cold water. Let stand 10 minutes; drain. Cook noodles in boiling water until tender, about 10 minutes; drain. Cut noodles to shorten strands; cool.

Mix green onions, chicken, shrimp, spinach, peanuts and mint. Line a small platter with romaine leaves; arrange cellophane noodles on top. Spoon chicken mixture over noodles. Sprinkle with cilantro and cloud ears. Serve with Dressing.

4 servings

PER SERVING: Calories 230; Protein 18 g; Carbohydrate 22 g; Fat 8 g; Cholesterol 60 mg; Sodium 140 mg

DRESSING

¼ cup lemon juice
3 tablespoons fish sauce
2 teaspoons sugar
1 serrano chili, seeded and chopped

Mix all ingredients.

Cloud Ears

Cooked in liquid, these dried Chinese mushrooms expand five or six times in size. There are dark and light cloud ears. Most recipes intend the use of the dark ones, which are more common and less expensive than the "albino" variety. They may be large and thick (meaty, when cooked) or small and delicate (more prized, thus more expensive). Cloud ears are popular not only with the Japanese and the Chinese but with the Thais, Malaysians and Indonesians, too. This fungus is readily available in Oriental markets, gourmet shops and some large supermarkets.

CHICKEN IN RED WINE

COQ AU VIN ROUGE (kohk oh vahng <u>roozh</u>)

Red wine is the dominant flavor for the sauce in this classic French dish. This is a true fricassee —the meat is browned before it is stewed—and it is as elegant a dish as any. Serve *Coq au Vin Rouge* over noodles or, as tradition dictates, with parsleyed potatoes.

6 slices bacon
½ cup all-purpose flour
1 teaspoon salt
¼ teaspoon pepper
3- to 3½-pound broiler-fryer chicken, cut up
1 pound mushrooms
½ pound tiny pearl onions
8 baby carrots
2½ cups dry red wine
1½ cups chicken broth
2 cloves garlic, finely chopped
1 teaspoon salt
Bouquet Garni (right)
Snipped parsley

Fry bacon in Dutch oven until crisp; remove bacon. Mix flour, 1 teaspoon salt and the pepper. Coat chicken with flour mixture. Cook chicken in hot bacon fat over medium heat until light brown on all sides, 15 to 20 minutes. Remove chicken. Cook mushrooms, onions and carrots until light brown. Drain fat.

Return chicken to Dutch oven; crumble bacon over chicken and vegetables. Stir in wine, chicken broth, garlic, 1 teaspoon salt and the Bouquet Garni. Heat to boiling; reduce heat. Cover and simmer until thickest pieces of chicken are done, 35 to 40 minutes. Skim fat; remove Bouquet Garni. Sprinkle with parsley; serve in soup bowls.

6 to 8 servings

PER SERVING: Calories 350; Protein 33 g; Carbohydrate 19 g; Fat 16 g; Cholesterol 90 mg; Sodium 1110 mg

BOUQUET GARNI

4 sprigs parsley
2 bay leaves
1 teaspoon dried thyme leaves

Tie parsley, bay leaves and thyme leaves in cheesecloth bag or place in tea ball.

MULLIGATAWNY SOUP

(moo-lee-guh-<u>taw</u>-nee)

Mulligatawny is an Indian spice-filled soup adapted to British tastes in the days of colonial strength.

2½- to 3-pound broiler-fryer chicken, cut up
4 cups water
1½ teaspoons salt
1 teaspoon curry powder
1 teaspoon lemon juice
⅛ teaspoon ground cloves
⅛ teaspoon ground mace
1 medium onion, chopped
2 tablespoons margarine or butter
2 tablespoons all-purpose flour
1 medium carrot, thinly sliced
1 apple, chopped
1 medium green pepper, cut into ½-inch pieces
2 medium tomatoes, chopped
Parsley

Heat chicken, water, salt, curry powder, lemon juice, cloves and mace to boiling in Dutch oven; reduce heat. Cover and simmer until thickest pieces of chicken are done, about 45 minutes. Remove chicken and broth; skim fat from broth if necessary. Add enough water to broth if necessary to measure 4 cups. Remove bones and skin from chicken; cut chicken into pieces.

Cook and stir onion in margarine in Dutch oven until tender. Remove from heat; stir in flour. Gradually stir in broth. Add chicken, carrot, apple, green pepper and tomatoes. Heat to boiling; reduce heat. Cover and simmer until carrot is tender, about 10 minutes. Serve in shallow soup bowls; garnish with parsley.

6 servings (about 1¼ cups each)

PER SERVING: Calories 195; Protein 20 g; Carbohydrate 11 g; Fat 8 g; Cholesterol 55 mg; Sodium 640 mg

CHICKEN AND LEEK SOUP

COCK-A-LEEKIE

This chicken soup is enhanced with the flavor of leeks, the national symbol of Wales, though the soup is of Scottish origin. Cock-a-leekie is a rustic dish, honest country fare that dates to the days of Shakespeare.

2½ pound broiler-fryer chicken, cut up
4 cups water
1 medium carrot, sliced
1 medium stalk celery, sliced
½ cup barley
2 teaspoons instant chicken bouillon
2 teaspoons salt
¼ teaspoon pepper
1 bay leaf
1½ cups sliced leeks (with tops)

Heat all ingredients except leeks to boiling in Dutch oven; reduce heat. Cover and simmer 30 minutes. Add leeks. Heat to boiling; reduce heat. Cover and simmer until thickest pieces of chicken are done, about 15 minutes. Remove chicken from broth; cool slightly. Remove chicken from bones and skin; cut chicken into 1-inch pieces. Skim fat from broth; remove bay leaf. Add chicken to broth; heat until hot, about 5 minutes.

7 servings (about 1 cup each)

PER SERVING: Calories 245; Protein 32 g; Carbohydrate 14 g; Fat 7 g; Cholesterol 85 mg; Sodium 710 mg

CHICKEN SOUP WITH TORTELLINI

POLLO IN BRODO CON TORTELLINI
(pohl-loh een broh-doh kohn tor-teh-lee-nee)

Chicken-filled Italian dumplings grace a chicken stock that has long been favored in Piedmont, in northern Italy. Serve it as an elegant and satisfying supper with a glass of Italian wine. With homemade *tortellini*, this soup makes a sensational first course.

3- to 4-pound broiler-fryer chicken, cut up
6 cups water
1 stalk celery (with leaves), cut into 1-inch pieces
1 medium carrot, cut into 1-inch pieces
1 medium onion, cut into fourths
2 sprigs parsley
1 bay leaf
2½ teaspoons salt
1 teaspoon black peppercorns
Tortellini (right), or 1 package commercial fresh tortellini
2 cups water
Snipped parsley
Grated Parmesan cheese (optional)

Heat chicken, 6 cups water, the celery, carrot, onion, 2 sprigs parsley, the bay leaf, salt and peppercorns to boiling in Dutch oven; reduce heat. Cover and simmer until thickest pieces of chicken are done, about 45 minutes. Remove chicken from broth; strain broth. Refrigerate chicken and broth separately until cool.

Remove chicken from bones and skin. If making Tortellini, finely chop enough dark meat to measure ¾ cup; cover and refrigerate. Cut remaining chicken into bite-size pieces; add to broth. Cover and refrigerate. Prepare Tortellini; if using commercial tortellini, do not precook.

Skim fat from broth. Heat broth and 2 cups water to boiling. Add Tortellini. Heat to boiling; reduce heat. Cover and simmer until Tortellini are tender, about 30 minutes. Sprinkle each serving with snipped parsley. Serve with cheese.

8 servings (about 1¼ cups each)

PER SERVING: Calories 230; Protein 22 g; Carbohydrate 20 g; Fat 7 g; Cholesterol 105 mg; Sodium 1060 mg

TORTELLINI

1½ cups all-purpose flour
1 egg
1 egg, separated
2 tablespoons water
1 tablespoon olive or vegetable oil
1 teaspoon salt
Reserved ¾ cup finely chopped chicken
2 tablespoons grated Parmesan cheese
⅛ teaspoon grated lemon peel
⅛ teaspoon salt
Dash of ground mace
Dash of pepper

Make a well in center of flour; add 1 egg, 1 egg white, the water, oil and 1 teaspoon salt. Stir with fork until mixed; gather dough into a ball. (Sprinkle with a few drops water if dry.) Knead dough on lightly floured board until smooth and elastic, about 5 minutes. Cover and let rest 10 minutes.

Mix reserved ¾ cup chicken, the egg yolk, cheese, lemon peel, ⅛ teaspoon salt, the mace and pepper. Divide dough into halves. Roll one half on lightly floured board into 12-inch square. Cut into twenty 2-inch circles. Place ¼ teaspoon filling on center of each circle.

Moisten edge of each circle with water. Fold circle in half; press edge with fork to seal. Shape into rings by stretching tips of each half circle slightly; wrap ring around index finger. Moisten one tip with water; gently press tips together. Repeat with remaining dough. Place on tray; cover and refrigerate no longer than 24 hours.

DO-AHEAD TIP: Freeze broth and Tortellini separately no longer than 2 weeks. To serve, heat broth and 2 cups water to boiling; continue as directed except simmer 40 minutes.

Shape half circle into a ring by stretching tips slightly; wrap ring around index finger, then press tips together.

CARIBBEAN CHICKEN AND RICE

ASOPAO DE POLLO (ah-sah-<u>pow</u> deh <u>poh</u>-l'yoh)

Asopao means "souplike," in Spanish, but this version is more of a casserole. Smoked ham, capers and green olives add a slightly salty flavor to this Puerto Rican specialty that begins with a zesty *sofrito* of tomatoes with onion and garlic.

2½- to 3-pound broiler-fryer chicken, cut up
2 teaspoons salt
1 teaspoon dried oregano leaves
½ teaspoon ground coriander
¼ teaspoon pepper
2 cups water
1 can (16 ounces) stewed tomatoes (with liquid)
1 medium onion, chopped
1 clove garlic, crushed
1 cup uncooked regular rice
1 package (10 ounces) frozen green peas
1 medium green pepper, chopped
½ cup cubed fully cooked smoked ham (about 2 ounces)
⅓ cup pitted small green olives
1 tablespoon capers
Grated Parmesan cheese (optional)

Place chicken in 12-inch skillet or Dutch oven. Sprinkle with salt, oregano, coriander and pepper. Add water, tomatoes, onion and garlic. Heat to boiling; reduce heat. Cover and simmer 30 minutes.

Stir rice into liquid. Cover and simmer until thickest pieces of chicken are done, about 20 minutes. Rinse frozen peas under running cold water to separate; drain. Add peas, green pepper, ham, olives, capers and 1 tablespoon caper liquid to chicken. Cover and simmer 5 minutes. Serve with cheese.

8 servings

PER SERVING: Calories 325; Protein 23 g; Carbohydrate 33 g; Fat 11 g; Cholesterol 60 mg; Sodium 970 mg

RUSSIAN CHICKEN PIE

KURNIK (<u>koorr</u>-nek)

Rich and lemony, this Russian recipe folds chicken into a creamy sauce and tops it with a flaky crust. Here again is that lively East European favorite, fresh dill weed.

Pastry (right)
2 cups water
1 cup uncooked regular rice
2 teaspoons instant chicken bouillon
2 large onions, thinly sliced
8 ounces mushrooms, sliced
2 tablespoons margarine or butter
1 cup half-and-half
2 teaspoons cornstarch
1 cup chicken broth
3 cups cut-up cooked chicken
2 tablespoons snipped parsley
2 teaspoons lemon juice
1 teaspoon salt
½ teaspoon ground nutmeg
⅛ teaspoon pepper
4 hard-cooked eggs, peeled and finely chopped
1 tablespoon snipped dill weed
1 egg yolk
1 tablespoon water

Prepare Pastry; wrap in plastic wrap. Heat water, rice and bouillon to boiling, stirring once or twice; reduce heat. Cover and simmer 14 minutes. (Do not lift cover or stir.) Remove from heat. Fluff rice lightly with fork; cover and let steam 5 to 10 minutes.

Cook and stir onions and mushrooms in margarine in 10-inch skillet over medium heat until onions are light brown. Mix half-and-half and cornstarch; stir into onion mixture. Stir in chicken broth. Heat to boiling, stirring constantly; boil and stir 1 minute. Stir in chicken, parsley, lemon juice, salt, nutmeg and pepper. Mix chopped eggs and dill weed.

Spread one-third of the rice mixture in bottom of ungreased oblong baking dish, 12 × 7½ × 2 inches. Layer with half of the chicken mixture and half of the egg mixture. Repeat the layers; top with remaining rice mixture.

Heat oven to 400°. Unwrap Pastry; place on well-floured cloth-covered board. Roll into rectangle, 13 × 8 inches, with floured stockinet-covered rolling pin. Cut a 1-inch circle in center of pastry. Place Pastry over top of dish; turn edges under and flute. Mix egg yolk and water; brush over pastry. Bake until golden brown, about 30 minutes.

8 servings

PER SERVING: Calories 510; Protein 26 g; Carbohydrate 43 g; Fat 26 g; Cholesterol 190 mg; Sodium 940 mg

PASTRY

¼ cup firm margarine or butter
¼ cup shortening
1⅓ cups all-purpose flour
¼ teaspoon salt
3 to 4 tablespoons cold water

Cut margarine and shortening into flour and salt until particles are the size of small peas. Sprinkle in water, 1 tablespoon at a time, tossing with fork until all flour is moistened and pastry almost cleans side of bowl. Gather pastry into ball; shape into flattened rectangle.

Russian Chicken Pie

ROAST CHICKEN WITH SPICED YOGURT

TANDOORI MURGHI (tahn-<u>door</u>-ee <u>mur</u>-ghee)

In India and Pakistan, *tandoori* dishes flourish. A traditional *tandoor* (clay) oven maintains an even heat that keeps the chicken succulent and allows the aromatic spices to flavor each piece. Serve with hot cooked rice and *Puris* (page 287).

3- to 4-pound broiler-fryer chicken
½ teaspoon water
¼ teaspoon dry mustard
1 cup plain yogurt
¼ cup lemon juice
1 clove garlic, chopped
1½ teaspoons salt
½ teaspoon ground cardamom
¼ teaspoon ground ginger
¼ teaspoon ground cumin
¼ teaspoon crushed red pepper
¼ teaspoon pepper
¼ cup water

Place chicken in large glass or plastic bowl. Mix ½ teaspoon water and the mustard in 1-quart bowl; stir in yogurt, lemon juice, garlic, salt, cardamom, ginger, cumin, red pepper and pepper. Pour over chicken; turn to coat well with marinade. Cover and refrigerate 12 to 24 hours.

Place chicken on rack in shallow roasting pan, reserving marinade. Roast uncovered in 375° oven, spooning reserved marinade over chicken during last 30 minutes of roasting, until thickest pieces are done, 1¾ to 2¼ hours. (Place a tent of aluminum foil loosely over chicken during last 30 minutes to prevent excessive browning.)

Remove chicken from pan; stir ¼ cup water into pan juices. Heat just until hot. Serve sauce with chicken.

8 to 10 servings

PER SERVING: Calories 180; Protein 22 g; Carbohydrate 3 g; Fat 9 g; Cholesterol 65 mg; Sodium 480 mg

SCOTTISH-STYLE ROAST CHICKEN

HOWTOWDIE

This roast chicken is a traditional Scottish preparation that usually is served with "skirlie," a stuffing of oats and onion, seasoned with nutmeg, coriander and ground black pepper.

Oat Stuffing (page 115)
3- to 4-pound broiler-fryer chicken
6 medium onions, cut into halves
¼ cup margarine or butter, melted

Prepare Oat Stuffing. Fill wishbone area of chicken with stuffing. Fasten neck skin to back with skewer. Fold wings across back with tips touching. Fill body cavity lightly. (Do not pack; stuffing will expand during cooking.) Tie or skewer drumsticks to tail.

Place chicken, breast side up, in shallow roasting pan. Arrange onions around chicken. Brush chicken and onions with margarine. Roast uncovered in 375° oven, brushing chicken and onions several times with remaining margarine, until chicken and onions are done, about 1½ hours.

6 servings

PER SERVING: Calories 460; Protein 31 g; Carbohydrate 21 g; Fat 28 g; Cholesterol 80 mg; Sodium 430 mg

Scottish-style Roast Chicken

OAT STUFFING

1 large onion, finely chopped
¼ cup margarine or butter
1 cup regular oats
½ teaspoon salt
½ teaspoon ground coriander
¼ teaspoon pepper
⅛ teaspoon ground nutmeg

Cook and stir onion in margarine in 10-inch skillet over medium heat until light brown. Stir in remaining ingredients. Cook and stir until oats are golden brown and crisp, 3 to 4 minutes.

ROAST GOOSE WITH APPLE STUFFING

GÄNSEBRATEN MIT APFELFÜLLUNG
(<u>gens</u>-eh-brah-t'n mitt <u>ahp</u>-f'l-fuh-loong)

Succulent roast goose is a marvelous Christmas feast. In Germany goose is baked to a crisp golden brown and served with giblet gravy and a sweet apple stuffing.

1 goose (8 to 10 pounds), giblets reserved
2 cups water
1 small onion, sliced
1¼ teaspoons salt
6 cups soft bread crumbs
3 tart apples, chopped
2 stalks celery (with leaves), chopped
1 medium onion, chopped
¼ cup margarine or butter, melted
2 teaspoons salt
1 teaspoon ground sage
½ teaspoon ground thyme
¼ teaspoon pepper
1 teaspoon salt
¼ cup all-purpose flour

Trim excess fat from goose. Heat giblets, water, sliced onion and 1¼ teaspoons salt to boiling; reduce heat. Cover and simmer until giblets are done, about 1 hour. Strain broth; cover and refrigerate. Chop giblets; toss with remaining ingredients except 1 teaspoon salt and the flour.

Rub cavity of goose with 1 teaspoon salt. Fold wings across back with tips touching. Fill neck and body cavities of goose lightly with stuffing. (Do not pack; stuffing will expand during cooking). Fasten neck skin of goose to back with skewers. Fasten opening with skewers; lace with string. Tie drumsticks to tail. Prick skin all over with fork. Place goose, breast side up, on rack in shallow roasting pan.

Roast uncovered in 350° oven until done, 3 to 3½ hours, removing excess fat from pan occasionally. Place a tent of aluminum foil loosely over goose during last hour to prevent excessive browning. Goose is done when drumstick meat feels very soft. Place goose on heated platter. Let stand 15 minutes for easier carving.

Pour off all but ¼ cup drippings from pan. Stir in flour. Cook over low heat, stirring constantly, until smooth and bubbly. Remove from heat. Add enough water to reserved broth if necessary to measure 2 cups. Stir into flour mixture. Heat to boiling, stirring constantly. Boil and stir 1 minute. Serve goose with apple stuffing and gravy.

8 servings

PER SERVING: Calories 1040; Protein 64 g; Carbohydrate 68 g; Fat 57 g; Cholesterol 200 mg; Sodium 1910 mg

Carving a Goose

Geese are anatomically different from other poultry. The wings have little or no meat, and some people like to remove them in the kitchen rather than at the table. When a roast goose is placed, breast up, on a platter, the legs are farther down on the bird and hard to reach. For this reason, consider removing the legs in the kitchen as well. With the wings and legs removed, cut away the two sections of breast meat, each as a single piece; it is easier to slice these portions off the bird than on.

DUCKLING WITH ORANGE SAUCE

CANETON À L'ORANGE (kah-neh-tawng ah loh-rawnjh)

A tangy sauce is served with this tender, succulent bird. The rich flavor of duck is just right for an autumn evening.

1 duckling (4 to 5 pounds)
2 teaspoons grated orange peel
½ cup orange juice
¼ cup currant jelly
1 tablespoon lemon juice
⅛ teaspoon dry mustard
⅛ teaspoon salt
1 tablespoon cold water
1½ teaspoons cornstarch
1 orange, peeled and sectioned
1 tablespoon orange-flavored liqueur (optional)

Fasten neck skin of duckling to back with skewers. Lift wing tips up and over back for natural brace. Place duckling, breast side up, on rack in shallow roasting pan. Prick skin with fork. Roast covered in 325° oven until done, about 2½ hours, removing excess fat from pan occasionally. (If duckling becomes too brown, place piece of aluminum foil lightly over breast.) Duckling is done when drumstick meat feels very soft. Let stand 10 minutes for easier carving.

Heat orange peel, orange juice, jelly, lemon juice, mustard and salt to boiling. Mix water and cornstarch; stir into sauce. Cook over medium heat, stirring constantly, until mixture thickens and boils. Boil and stir 1 minute. Stir in orange sections and liqueur. Brush duckling with some of the orange sauce; serve with remaining sauce.

4 servings

PER SERVING: Calories 670; Protein 34 g; Carbohydrate 21 g; Fat 50 g; Cholesterol 150 mg; Sodium 180 mg

DANISH STUFFED DUCKLING

STEGT AND (steak ond)

A sweet measure of prunes and apple flavors this hearty rye bread stuffing. Roast duck makes a handsome presentation, perfect for entertaining.

1 duckling (4 to 5 pounds)
3 cups rye bread crumbs
1 apple, chopped
1 small onion, chopped
½ cup cut-up prunes or raisins
1 teaspoon salt
½ teaspoon dried marjoram leaves
1 egg, beaten

Fasten neck skin of duckling to back with skewers. Lift wing tips up and over back for natural brace. Mix remaining ingredients. Fill body cavity of duckling lightly with stuffing. (Do not pack; stuffing will expand during cooking.) Fasten opening with skewers. Place remaining stuffing in small greased baking dish. Cover and refrigerate; place in oven with duckling during last 30 minutes of roasting. Place duckling, breast side up, on rack in shallow roasting pan. Prick skin with fork.

Roast duckling uncovered in 350° oven until done, about 3 hours, removing excess fat from pan occasionally. (If duckling becomes too brown, place piece of aluminum foil lightly over breast.) Duckling is done when drumstick meat feels very soft. Place duckling on heated platter. Let stand 10 minutes for easier carving. Serve with stuffing.

4 servings

PER SERVING: Calories 985; Protein 45 g; Carbohydrate 77 g; Fat 55 g; Cholesterol 205 mg; Sodium 1210 mg

SOUTH AMERICAN ROAST TURKEY

PAVITA RELLENA A LA CRIOLLA
(pah-vee-tah reh-yeh-nah ah lah kree-oh-lah)

Tangy Spanish olives, spicy pork sausage and fresh, sweet peaches cook to moist perfection inside this bird. A creamy giblet gravy adds an elegant touch to our South American specialty.

1 medium onion, chopped
1 pound bulk sweet Italian sausage
2 eggs
4 cups soft bread crumbs
¼ cup chopped pimiento-stuffed olives
2 large peaches, peeled and coarsely chopped, or 1 package (16 ounces) frozen unsweetened peach slices, thawed and coarsely chopped
1 teaspoon dried oregano leaves
½ teaspoon salt
¼ teaspoon pepper
12-pound turkey, giblets and neck reserved
Olive oil
Gravy (right)

Cook and stir onion and sausage in 10-inch skillet over medium heat until sausage is brown; drain. Beat eggs with fork in 2½-quart bowl. Add sausage mixture, bread crumbs, olives, peaches, oregano, salt and pepper; toss.

Remove giblets and neck from turkey; prepare for Gravy. Fill wishbone area of turkey with stuffing. Fasten neck skin to back with skewer. Fold wings across back with tips touching. Fill body cavity lightly. (Do not pack; stuffing will expand during cooking.) Tuck drumsticks under band of skin at tail, or tie or skewer to tail.

Place turkey, breast side up, on rack in shallow roasting pan. Insert meat thermometer so tip is in thickest part of inside thigh muscle or thickest part of breast meat and does not touch bone. Brush with oil. Roast in 325° oven, brushing with pan juices every 45 minutes, until meat thermometer registers 185°, 3½ to 4 hours. Let turkey stand 20 minutes before carving. Prepare Gravy; serve with turkey.

12 to 14 servings

PER SERVING: Calories 798; Protein 67 g; Carbohydrate 30 g; Fat 43 g; Cholesterol 233 mg; Sodium 907 mg

GRAVY

Giblets and neck of turkey
2 cups water
½ teaspoon salt
⅔ cup turkey drippings (fat and juices)
⅔ cup all-purpose flour
½ cup half-and-half
Salt and pepper to taste

Heat giblets, neck, water and ½ teaspoon salt to boiling; reduce heat. Cover and simmer 30 minutes. Remove giblets and neck; chop giblets and discard neck. Reserve broth for gravy. (Cover and refrigerate giblets and broth if not using immediately.)

Pour and scrape all drippings from roasting pan. Pour ⅔ cup drippings into 3-quart saucepan; stir in flour. Cook over low heat, stirring constantly, until mixture is thick and bubbly; remove from heat. Stir in reserved broth, the half-and-half and chopped giblets. Heat to boiling, stirring constantly; boil and stir 1 minute. Stir in salt and pepper.

TURKEY MOLE

PAVO EN MOLE POBLANO
(pah-voh ehn moh-leh poh-blah-noh)

The dark pumpkin seed– and chocolate-spiked chili sauce that keeps the turkey so moist is an ancient Aztec combination. The flavor of chocolate is undetectable here, but it adds a deep note of mystery to the *mole*.

8- to 10-pound turkey, cut up
2 medium onions, chopped
3 cloves garlic, finely chopped
¼ cup margarine or butter
4 six-inch tortillas, torn into pieces and dried
  (see Note)
4 squares unsweetened chocolate, chopped
⅓ cup slivered almonds
⅓ cup peanuts
⅓ cup shelled pumpkin seeds or sunflower nuts
¼ cup toasted sesame seed
½ to ¾ cup chili powder
2 to 3 tablespoons sugar
2 teaspoons ground cumin
1 teaspoon salt
¼ teaspoon anise seed
1 two-inch stick cinnamon, broken

Heat turkey and enough salted water to cover (1 tablespoon salt to 1 quart water) to boiling; reduce heat. Cover and simmer until thickest pieces are done, about 1½ hours. Drain; reserve 4 cups broth. Place turkey in 2 ungreased baking dishes.

Cook and stir onions and garlic in margarine until onions are tender. Place 1 cup of the reserved broth, the tortilla pieces and onion mixture in blender container. Cover and blend on high speed until smooth. Pour into large bowl. Place 1½ cups of the turkey broth, the chocolate, almonds, peanuts, pumpkin and sesame seeds in blender container. Cover and blend until smooth. Add to onion mixture in bowl.

Place remaining 1½ cups turkey broth, the chili powder, sugar, cumin, salt, anise seed and cinnamon in blender container. Cover and blend until smooth. Add to onion mixture in bowl. Mix all ingredients thoroughly. (Mixture will be consistency of chocolate sauce.) Pour sauce over turkey. Heat, uncovered, in 300° oven until hot, 30 to 40 minutes.

10 servings

PER SERVING: Calories 790; Protein 86 g; Carbohydrate 24 g; Fat 39 g; Cholesterol 225 mg; Sodium 660 mg

NOTE: To dry tortillas, let pieces stand at room temperature until dry and brittle, 1 to 2 hours.

DO-AHEAD TIP: After pouring sauce over turkey, cover and refrigerate no longer than 24 hours.

RABBIT STEWED IN STOUT

The alcohol in the Irish stout evaporates while the fullness of its flavor remains. Serve this hearty bacon-scented stew with parsleyed potatoes or egg noodles. Serve stout or, if preferred, red wine.

4 slices bacon
½ cup all-purpose flour
1 teaspoon salt
¼ teaspoon pepper
¼ teaspoon paprika
3- to 3½-pound rabbit, cut up
8 ounces mushrooms, cut into halves
1 jar (16 ounces) whole onions, drained
½ teaspoon dried thyme leaves
1 bay leaf
1 bottle (12 ounces) Irish stout or dark beer
2 tablespoons cold water
1 tablespoon cornstarch
Snipped parsley

Fry bacon in Dutch oven until crisp. Remove bacon and reserve. Reserve fat in Dutch oven.

Mix flour, salt, pepper and paprika. Coat rabbit pieces with flour mixture. Heat bacon fat until hot. Cook rabbit over medium heat until brown on all sides, about 15 minutes. Add mushrooms, onions, thyme and bay leaf. Pour stout over rabbit and vegetables. Crumble reserved bacon over mixture. Heat to boiling; reduce heat. Cover and simmer until thickest pieces of rabbit are done, about 1 hour.

Remove rabbit and vegetables to warm platter; keep warm. Remove bay leaf. Heat stout mixture to boiling. Mix water and cornstarch; stir into stout mixture. Boil and stir 1 minute. Pour sauce over rabbit and vegetables. Sprinkle with parsley.

6 servings

PER SERVING: Calories 370; Protein 39 g; Carbohydrate 26 g; Fat 12 g; Cholesterol 105 mg; Sodium 610 mg

Rabbit Stewed in Stout, Mashed Potatoes with Cabbage (page 263) and Irish Soda Bread (page 281)

4

MEATS

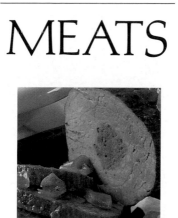

There is a great deal more to the world of meats than the simple beef roast so popular in America. Meat does not play a large role in every culture but, wherever it appears, the preparation is inspired and thoughtful. For many people of the world, meat is a luxury. And for that reason, delicious recipes that make the most of inexpensive cuts abound.

Here are dishes that run the gamut from streamlined family fare to festive food for entertaining. The preparations go beyond simple grilling or sautéing, and their hallmark is ingenuity. From faraway Burma comes saucy Burmese Curried Pork. Ghana's renowned Squash and Bean Soup features stewing beef at its succulent best. Here are stalwart English Steak and Kidney Pie and tangy Serbian Skillet Pork with Feta Cheese. Ground meats, stewing cuts, chops, sausages, filets and pot roasts—all are as practical as they are delectable.

The following pages bring you more than eighty sensational tastes from fifty foreign lands. They are filled with delicious suggestions perfect for every pocketbook, for every season, for any occasion.

Clockwise from top: Hearts of Palm in Tomato Sauce (page 251), Chorizo-stuffed Beef Roast (page 124), Rice with Chayote (page 271) and Baked Plantains (page 254)

CHORIZO-STUFFED BEEF ROAST

BOLA (<u>boh</u>-lah)

This is a succulent roast stuffed with spicy sausage and braised in a savory tomato sauce: a classic from Latin America. Chorizo is a chili-spiked favorite in the Dominican Republic.

3-pound beef boneless eye of round roast or
    rolled rump roast
½ pound bulk chorizo or Italian sausage
2 tablespoons olive or vegetable oil
1 medium onion, chopped
3 cloves garlic, finely chopped
1 large green pepper, coarsely chopped
1 teaspoon dried oregano leaves
1 teaspoon salt
¼ teaspoon pepper
2 bay leaves
1 can (8 ounces) tomato sauce

Cut a narrow (1-inch) X shape all the way through beef roast with long, thin sharp knife. Fill X cuts with sausage. Heat oil in Dutch oven until hot. Cook beef over medium heat until brown on all sides, about 15 minutes; drain fat.

Add remaining ingredients. Heat to boiling; reduce heat. Cover and simmer until beef is tender, 2 to 2½ hours.

Remove bay leaves. Slice beef; arrange on platter. Skim fat from sauce. Pour some of the sauce over beef. Serve beef with remaining sauce and hot cooked black beans or rice if desired.

8 to 10 servings

PER SERVING: Calories 510; Protein 56 g; Carbohydrate 5 g; Fat 30 g; Cholesterol 155 mg; Sodium 900 mg

Using a long, thin knife, cut a 1-inch "X" all the way through roast.

Chorizo

Latin American cooking dotes on chorizo, a highly seasoned sausage made from smoked pork. The spices most often used in making chorizo are ground red pepper (cayenne), pimiento, robust paprika and more than a touch of garlic. This sausage usually is purchased in links, about the same size but a bit narrower than sweet Italian sausage. Chorizo is a favored ingredient in Spain as well.

FRENCH BOILED DINNER
POT AU FEU (poh-toh-<u>fuh</u>)

Pot au Feu literally means "pot in the fire." In traditional recipes, a beef roast or poultry is stewed in its own broth with herbs, spices and a healthy crop of vegetables. When done, the beef and vegetables are served separately from the broth, which is served steaming hot as a first course.

1½-pound beef boneless chuck roast
1 marrow bone (optional)
8 black peppercorns
1 teaspoon salt
¼ teaspoon dried thyme leaves
1 bay leaf
4 cups water
1½ pounds chicken drumsticks
10 to 12 small carrots
10 to 12 small onions or 3 large onions, cut into
    fourths
3 medium turnips, cut into fourths
4 stalks celery, cut into 1-inch pieces
¾ teaspoon salt
⅛ teaspoon pepper

Place beef, marrow bone, peppercorns, 1 teaspoon salt, the thyme and bay leaf in Dutch oven. Add water. Heat to boiling; reduce heat. Cover and simmer 1 hour. Add chicken; cover and simmer 1 hour longer.

Add carrots, onions, turnips and celery; sprinkle with ¾ teaspoon salt and the pepper. Cover and simmer until beef and vegetables are tender, about 45 minutes. Remove chicken and vegetables to warm platter; slice beef. Strain broth; serve in soup bowls as a first course.

10 to 12 servings

PER SERVING: Calories 275; Protein 31 g; Carbohydrate 14 g; Fat 12 g; Cholesterol 85 mg; Sodium 510 mg

DUTCH BOILED DINNER
HUTSPOT MET KLAPSTUK (<u>heut</u>-spot meht <u>klahp</u>-stuhk)

This beef and potato stew is a national dish in Holland, first served to honor the victory of the Netherlands over Spain in 1574.

2-pound beef brisket
1½ cups water
1 teaspoon salt
4 medium potatoes, pared and cut into fourths
4 medium carrots, sliced
3 medium onions, chopped
1½ teaspoons salt
¼ teaspoon pepper
Snipped parsley
Prepared mustard or horseradish

Heat beef, water and 1 teaspoon salt to boiling in Dutch oven; reduce heat. Cover and simmer 1½ hours. Add potatoes, carrots and onions; sprinkle with 1½ teaspoons salt and the pepper. Cover and simmer until beef and vegetables are tender, about 45 minutes.

Drain meat and vegetables, reserving broth. Mash vegetables or purée in food mill; mound on heated platter. Cut beef across grain into thin slices; arrange around vegetables. Garnish with parsley; serve with reserved broth and the mustard.

6 to 8 servings

PER SERVING: Calories 455; Protein 28 g; Carbohydrate 26 g; Fat 28 g; Cholesterol 90 mg; Sodium 990 mg

RUSSIAN POT ROAST

Rich sour cream, lemon and fresh dill weed are what gives this pot roast Russian flair. To satisfy a ravenous crowd, toss hot egg noodles with butter and serve them with the pot roast.

5 medium potatoes, cut into 1-inch pieces
2 medium onions, sliced
3 tablespoons vegetable oil
3- to 4-pound beef boneless rump roast, chuck eye roast or bottom round roast
1 teaspoon instant beef bouillon
¼ teaspoon pepper
1 cup dairy sour cream
¼ cup water
1 tablespoon all-purpose flour
¼ cup snipped dill weed
1 teaspoon lemon juice

Cook and stir potatoes and onions in oil in Dutch oven over medium heat until onions are tender, about 10 minutes. Remove potatoes and onions with slotted spoon. Cook beef in remaining oil, turning occasionally, until brown on all sides, about 15 minutes; drain.

Add potatoes and onions to beef in Dutch oven; sprinkle with bouillon and pepper. Mix sour cream, water and flour with fork until smooth; pour over potato mixture. Heat to boiling; reduce heat. Cover and simmer 1½ hours.

Stir in dill weed and lemon juice. Cover and simmer until beef is tender, about 30 minutes longer. Garnish with fresh dill if desired.

8 to 10 servings

PER SERVING: Calories 525; Protein 51 g; Carbohydrate 21 g; Fat 27 g; Cholesterol 150 mg; Sodium 290 mg

MARINATED POT ROAST WITH POTATO DUMPLINGS
SAUERBRATEN MIT KARTOFFELKLÖSSEN
(zow-er-brah-t'n mett kahr-tohf-f'l-kluh-sen)

Marinades have long been used to tenderize and flavor meats. For *sauerbraten*, tart wine vinegar and piquant cloves marinate the beef for several days, allowing for a high flavor to develop. Then, crumbled ginger snaps lend their sweet-spicy flavor to the dish. A healthy helping of potato dumplings completes this German classic.

3- to 4-pound beef rolled rump roast, boneless chuck eye roast or bottom round roast
2 cups water
1 cup red wine vinegar
1 medium onion, sliced
6 whole cloves
4 black peppercorns, crushed
1½ teaspoons salt
1 bay leaf
3 tablespoons vegetable oil
½ cup water
Potato Dumplings (page 127)
8 gingersnaps, crushed (about ⅓ cup)
2 tablespoons packed brown sugar
⅓ cup water
3 tablespoons all-purpose flour

Prick beef roast thoroughly with fork. Place beef in 4-quart glass bowl or earthenware crock. Mix 2 cups water, the vinegar, onion, cloves, peppercorns, salt and bay leaf; pour over beef. Cover and refrigerate, turning several times each day, 2 to 3 days.

Remove beef from marinade; pat dry. Strain marinade; reserve. Heat oil in Dutch oven until hot. Cook beef in hot oil, turning occasionally, until brown, about 10 minutes. Remove beef; pour off fat. Heat 2 cups of the reserved marinade and ½ cup water to boiling in Dutch oven (reserve remaining marinade). Return beef to Dutch oven; reduce heat. Cover and simmer until beef is tender, about 2 hours.

Prepare Potato Dumplings. Remove beef to heated platter; keep warm. Pour liquid from Dutch oven into large measuring cup; skim fat from liquid. Add enough reserved marinade to measure 2½ cups if necessary. Return to Dutch oven. (If liquid measures more than 2½ cups, boil rapidly to reduce to 2½ cups.)

Stir in gingersnap crumbs and brown sugar. Mix ⅓ cup water and the flour; stir gradually into liquid. Heat to boiling, stirring constantly. Boil and stir 1 minute. Strain gravy; serve with beef and Potato Dumplings.

12 servings

PER SERVING: Calories 450; Protein 36 g; Carbohydrate 32 g; Fat 20 g; Cholesterol 120 mg; Sodium 820 mg

POTATO DUMPLINGS

2 tablespoons margarine or butter
2 slices white bread (crusts removed), cubed
3½ cups riced, cooked potatoes (5 medium)
1 cup all-purpose flour
1½ teaspoons salt
⅛ teaspoon nutmeg
⅛ teaspoon white pepper

2 eggs, beaten
4 quarts water
2 teaspoons salt
2 teaspoons margarine or butter
2 tablespoons dry bread crumbs

Heat 2 tablespoons margarine in 8-inch skillet until melted. Cook bread cubes in margarine over medium heat, stirring frequently, until golden brown.

Mix potatoes, flour, 1½ teaspoons salt, the nutmeg and white pepper. Stir in eggs; beat until dough holds its shape. Flour hands lightly. Shape about 2 tablespoons dough into ball. Press hole in center with fingertip; drop 4 bread cubes into hole. Seal by shaping into ball again. Repeat with remaining dough and bread cubes.

Heat water and 2 teaspoons salt to boiling in 6- to 8-quart Dutch oven. Heat 2 teaspoons margarine in skillet until melted. Cook and stir bread crumbs in margarine until margarine is absorbed; reserve.

Drop dumplings into boiling water; stir once or twice. Reduce heat. Simmer uncovered until dumplings are done, 12 to 15 minutes. Remove with slotted spoon. Sprinkle dumplings with reserved bread crumbs.

BRAISED BEEF WITH ASPIC AND MARINATED VEGETABLES

BOEUF À LA MODE EN GELÉE
(buhf ah lah mohd awn jheh-leh)

Our version of this popular French entrée uses a wine-based aspic to glaze beef that has been roasted, then cooled. Saucy marinated vegetables serve as an accompaniment. *Boeuf à la Mode en Gelée* would be a very appropriate main course for a summer brunch or buffet.

2 tablespoons vegetable oil
3-pound beef rolled rump roast
½ cup water
1 teaspoon salt
¼ teaspoon pepper
1 envelope unflavored gelatin
2 tablespoons cold water
1 teaspoon instant beef bouillon
1 cup dry red wine
Marinated Vegetables (right)

Heat oil in Dutch oven until hot. Cook beef over medium heat until brown on all sides; drain. Add ½ cup water; sprinkle beef with salt and pepper. Cover and cook in 325° oven until tender, about 1½ hours. Cool slightly. Cover and refrigerate beef and broth separately at least 8 hours.

Sprinkle gelatin over 2 tablespoons water in saucepan; stir in bouillon and wine. Cook over medium heat, stirring constantly, until gelatin is dissolved. Remove from heat. Skim fat from broth; add enough cold water to broth to measure 1 cup. Stir into gelatin mixture. Place pan with gelatin mixture in bowl of ice and water; stir until mixture begins to thicken, 5 to 10 minutes.

Remove string from beef; trim fat. Cut beef into very thin slices; arrange on large platter. Coat entire surface of beef with small amount of gelatin mixture. Pour any remaining mixture into loaf dish, 9 × 5 × 3 inches. Cover and refrigerate beef and gelatin mixture no longer than 24 hours. Prepare Marinated Vegetables.

Arrange vegetables around beef. Cut aspic in loaf dish into small diamonds or squares; arrange around beef or serve separately.

10 to 12 servings

PER SERVING: Calories 335; Protein 45 g; Carbohydrate 13 g; Fat 13 g; Cholesterol 115 mg; Sodium 560 mg

MARINATED VEGETABLES

8 medium carrots (about 1¼ pounds)
1 pound green beans
1 can (16 ounces) whole onions, drained
⅔ cup olive or vegetable oil
⅓ cup red wine vinegar
2 cloves garlic, finely chopped
2 teaspoons salt
⅛ teaspoon pepper

Cut carrots into 2-inch pieces, rounding the edges so they resemble baby carrots if desired. Cover and cook carrots and beans in 1 inch boiling salted water (½ teaspoon salt to 1 cup water) in separate saucepans until tender; beans 15 to 20 minutes, carrots 20 to 25 minutes. Drain.

Arrange cooked vegetables and the onions in separate sections in shallow glass dish. Shake remaining ingredients in tightly covered jar; pour over vegetables. Cover and refrigerate, spooning marinade over vegetables occasionally, at least 2 hours.

SWEDISH POT ROAST WITH ANCHOVIES

SLOTTSSTEK (slot-steek)

This pot roast is braised to succulence in a brandy-molasses sauce. Allspice and anchovy add a hint of the exotic. In Sweden, the sauce is usually thickened for gravy and the roast served with buttered peas and carrots.

2 tablespoons vegetable oil
3- to 4-pound beef boneless rump roast, chuck eye roast or bottom round roast
1 teaspoon ground allspice
½ teaspoon salt
½ teaspoon pepper
⅓ cup hot water
2 tablespoons brandy
2 tablespoons molasses
2 tablespoons vinegar
½ teaspoon instant beef bouillon
2 to 4 anchovy fillets, chopped
1 bay leaf

Heat oil in Dutch oven until hot. Cook beef in oil over medium heat, turning occasionally, until brown on all sides, about 15 minutes; drain. Sprinkle beef with allspice, salt and pepper. Add remaining ingredients. Heat to boiling; reduce heat. Cover and simmer, turning beef occasionally, until tender, 1½ to 2 hours.

Remove beef to serving platter; keep warm. Skim fat from cooking liquid. Heat liquid to boiling; reduce heat. Simmer uncovered until reduced to 1 cup, about 10 minutes. Serve sauce with beef. Serve with buttered peas and carrots if desired.

8 to 10 servings

PER SERVING: Calories 390; Protein 49 g; Carbohydrate 4 g; Fat 20 g; Cholesterol 130 mg; Sodium 370 mg

STEAK WITH BLUE CHEESE SAUCE

ENTRECOTE AL QUESO CABRALES
(ehn-tray-koh-tay ahl kay-soh kah-brah-lehs)

In Spain, a strong, leaf-wrapped blue cheese called *queso cabrales* would be used to flavor a rich sauce for these steaks. We find that Roquefort or another blue cheese works quite nicely.

8 ounces blue cheese, crumbled
1 clove garlic, finely chopped
2 tablespoons dry white wine
Dash of ground red pepper
2 tablespoons margarine or butter
4 small New York strip or rib eye steaks, 1 inch thick (about 2 pounds)
Freshly ground pepper
¼ cup water
Snipped parsley

Cook and stir cheese, garlic, wine and red pepper over low heat, stirring frequently, until cheese is melted; keep warm.

Heat margarine in 12-inch skillet until hot. Cook beef steaks over medium-high heat, turning once, until medium doneness, about 5 minutes on each side. Sprinkle with pepper. Remove from skillet; keep warm. Add water to skillet. Heat to boiling, stirring constantly to loosen browned bits; boil 2 minutes. Stir pan juices into cheese mixture. Pour over steaks. Sprinkle with parsley.

4 servings

PER SERVING: Calories 710; Protein 54 g; Carbohydrate 2 g; Fat 54 g; Cholesterol 170 mg; Sodium 960 mg

FRIED STEAK WITH BEER SAUCE

HOLLANDSCHE BIEFSTUK (hoh-lahnd-sheh beef-stuk)

Marinated beef served with a lightly sweet beer-based sauce speaks of the lowlands. For this Flemish version of a Dutch dish, the marinated beef is pan-fried. Buttered potatoes with parsley are a traditional side dish to this Flemish and Dutch favorite.

1½-pound beef boneless sirloin steak, 1 inch thick
2 tablespoons red wine vinegar
½ teaspoon salt
¼ teaspoon coarsely ground pepper
1 tablespoon margarine or butter
2 teaspoons all-purpose flour
¼ cup beer
¼ cup water
1 teaspoon packed brown sugar
⅛ teaspoon salt
⅛ teaspoon coarsely ground pepper
⅛ teaspoon dried rosemary leaves, crushed
Sliced green onions (with tops)

Slash outer edge of fat on beef diagonally at 1-inch intervals to prevent curling (do not cut into lean). Place beef in shallow glass or plastic dish. Mix vinegar, ½ teaspoon salt and ¼ teaspoon pepper; spoon over both sides of beef. Cover and refrigerate, turning occasionally, at least 1 hour.

Heat margarine over medium-high heat in 10-inch skillet until hot. Add beef and cook until desired doneness, about 7 minutes on each side for medium. Remove from heat; remove beef to warm platter.

Stir flour into pan drippings. Stir in beer, water, brown sugar, ⅛ teaspoon salt, ⅛ teaspoon pepper and the rosemary. Heat to boiling; reduce heat. Cook and stir 1 minute. Pour sauce over beef; sprinkle with green onions.

4 or 5 servings

PER SERVING: Calories 300; Protein 28 g; Carbohydrate 4 g; Fat 19 g; Cholesterol 85 mg; Sodium 440 mg

---

SPICY GRILLED STEAK

SHAWAYUH (sh'why-yuh)

In much of the Middle East, meat is a hard-to-come-by commodity that is reserved for special occasions. When it is served, as in the case of this Yemenite specialty, it is spiced with a mixture of fragrant spices like the turmeric, caraway and cardamom called for here, then grilled over an open flame. Hot cooked rice or Pocket Bread (page 293) would be served as well.

2-pound beef boneless sirloin steak, 1½ inches thick
1½ teaspoons coarsely ground pepper
¾ teaspoon caraway seed
¾ teaspoon ground turmeric
¼ teaspoon cardamom seed, crushed

Slash outer edge of fat on beef steak diagonally at 1-inch intervals to prevent curling (do not cut into lean). Mix remaining ingredients. Sprinkle on both sides of beef; lightly press into beef. Cover and refrigerate at least 1 hour.

Grill beef 4 to 5 inches from medium coals, turning 2 or 3 times, until of desired doneness, 25 to 35 minutes for medium. Cut into serving pieces.

6 servings

PER SERVING: Calories 225; Protein 25 g; Carbohydrate 0 g; Fat 14 g; Cholesterol 75 mg; Sodium 60 mg

FLANK STEAK WITH CHIMICHURRI SAUCE

Chimichurri sauce marinates much of what is grilled by the Argentine gauchos on an open barbecue in the pampas. Flank steak becomes tender with the help of a marinade and is quickly cooked.

1½-pound beef flank steak
4 cloves garlic, finely chopped
1 cup vegetable oil
½ cup white wine vinegar
½ cup lemon juice
¼ cup snipped parsley
1 teaspoon crushed red pepper

Cut diamond pattern ⅛ inch deep into both sides of beef. Place beef in shallow glass or plastic dish. Shake remaining ingredients in tightly covered jar. Pour 1 cup of the sauce over beef. Cover remaining sauce. Cover and refrigerate beef, turning occasionally, at least 4 hours.

Remove beef from sauce. Grill beef 4 or 5 inches from medium coals, turning and brushing with sauce once, until desired doneness, 6 to 8 minutes on each side for medium. Cut beef diagonally across the grain into thin slices. Serve with reserved sauce.

4 to 5 servings

PER SERVING: Calories 755; Protein 35 g; Carbohydrate 5 g; Fat 66 g; Cholesterol 95 mg; Sodium 90 mg

BEEF AND LIVER KABOBS
KYINKYINGA (chih-<u>ching</u>-gah)

These piquant African kabobs are rendered hot and spicy with small doses of ginger and red pepper. A squeeze of fresh lemon juice makes them tangy, too. Serve over hot cooked rice to catch all the delicious juices.

1 pound high-quality beef chuck, tip or round,
    1 inch thick
½ pound beef liver, 1 inch thick
¼ cup lemon juice
3 tablespoons vegetable oil
1 clove garlic, chopped
1½ teaspoons onion salt
¼ teaspoon ground ginger
⅛ teaspoon crushed red pepper

Cut beef and liver into 1-inch cubes. (For ease in cutting, partially freeze meat about 1½ hours.) Place meat in glass bowl. Mix remaining ingredients; pour over meat. Cover and refrigerate, stirring occasionally, at least 6 hours.

Thread beef and liver cubes on each of 6 skewers. Brush with marinade. Set oven control to broil or 550°. Broil kabobs with tops 4 inches from heat 5 to 6 minutes; turn. Brush with marinade; broil 5 to 6 minutes longer.

6 servings

PER SERVING: Calories 305; Protein 24 g; Carbohydrate 1 g; Fat 23 g; Cholesterol 165 mg; Sodium 160 mg

Ingredients for Mango-marinated Beef Kabobs

Mango-marinated Beef Kabobs and Curried Peas and Rice (page 253)

MANGO-MARINATED BEEF KABOBS

These morsels of beef marinate in a sweet and tangy Caribbean sauce of minced mango, brown sugar, vinegar and other spices, then are grilled to tender doneness on skewers with juicy pineapple and creamy banana.

1 small ripe mango
1 medium onion, chopped
1 clove garlic, finely chopped
2 tablespoons vegetable oil
2 tablespoons packed brown sugar
1 tablespoon curry powder
2 tablespoons vinegar
½ teaspoon salt
6 drops red pepper sauce
1 pound beef boneless sirloin steak, cut into
   1½-inch cubes
2 large firm bananas, each cut into 6 pieces
12 pieces (1½ inches each) fresh pineapple

Pare and remove seed from mango; place mango in blender container. Cover and blend on low speed until smooth, about 30 seconds.

Cook and stir onion and garlic in oil until onion is tender. Mix onion mixture, mango, brown sugar, curry powder, vinegar, salt and pepper sauce in glass or plastic bowl; stir in beef. Cover and refrigerate at least 24 hours.

Remove beef from marinade; reserve marinade. Alternate beef, banana and pineapple pieces on each of four 14-inch metal skewers. Brush marinade over all sides of fruit. Set oven control to broil or 550°. Broil kabobs with tops about 4 inches from heat 7 to 8 minutes. Turn; brush with marinade. Broil until beef is of medium doneness and fruit is brown, 7 to 8 minutes longer. Heat remaining marinade to boiling. Serve kabobs with marinade and hot cooked rice, if desired.

4 servings

PER SERVING: Calories 395; Protein 20 g; Carbohydrate 42 g; Fat 18 g; Cholesterol 55 mg; Sodium 320 mg

STUFFED ROLLED STEAK

CARNE RELLENA (<u>kahr</u>-nay ray-<u>yay</u>-nah)

This Latin American favorite is known as *matambre* ("hunger killer") in Argentina. In this hearty version, a thin slice of boneless round steak is topped with smoked ham, mild chilies, fresh chopped tomatoes, tender onion, garlic and crunchy bread crumbs, then rolled and braised.

1½-pound beef boneless round steak, ½ inch thick
1½ teaspoons salt
½ teaspoon dried oregano leaves
¼ teaspoon pepper
4 ounces thinly sliced fully cooked smoked ham
2 medium tomatoes, chopped
1 can (4 ounces) mild green chilies, drained and chopped
1 medium onion, chopped
1 clove garlic, finely chopped
¼ cup dry bread crumbs
1 medium carrot
1 hard-cooked egg, peeled and cut lengthwise into fourths
½ teaspoon salt
2 tablespoons vegetable oil
¾ cup water
1 teaspoon vinegar
1 teaspoon Worcestershire sauce
1 bay leaf

Trim fat from beef. Pound until about ¼ inch thick. Sprinkle beef with 1½ teaspoons salt, the oregano and pepper. Arrange ham evenly on beef. Sprinkle tomatoes, chilies, onion, garlic and bread crumbs on ham.

Cut carrot lengthwise into halves; cut halves lengthwise into 3 strips. Arrange on ham. Place egg pieces down center of ham. Sprinkle with ½ teaspoon salt. Carefully roll up beef. Fasten with metal skewers or tie with string. (If beef separates when rolled, fasten with wooden picks.)

Heat oil in Dutch oven until hot. Carefully transfer beef roll to Dutch oven; cook over medium heat until brown on all sides. Drain fat. Add water, vinegar, Worcestershire sauce and bay leaf. Cover and cook in 325° oven until beef is tender, about 1½ hours. Remove skewers. Cut beef into 1-inch slices. Remove bay leaf from cooking liquid; serve beef with cooking liquid.

8 servings

PER SERVING: Calories 190; Protein 19 g; Carbohydrate 7 g; Fat 10 g; Cholesterol 75 mg; Sodium 990 mg

Arrange a row of egg pieces across ham; roll up beef.

BRAISED STUFFED BEEF ROLLS

RINDERROULADEN (<u>ren</u>-der-rroo-lah-den)

Rinderrouladen is a sturdy German dish, often served with boiled potatoes. Bacon bastes the beef rolls from the inside out.

2-pound beef boneless round steak, ½ inch
thick
Salt and pepper
2 tablespoons prepared mustard
3 slices bacon, cut into halves
1 medium onion, chopped
¼ cup snipped parsley
3 dill pickles, cut into halves
2 tablespoons vegetable oil
1¼ cups water
½ teaspoon salt
¼ teaspoon pepper
2 tablespoons cold water
1 tablespoon all-purpose flour

Pound beef until ¼ inch thick. Cut into pieces, about 7 × 4 inches. Lightly sprinkle with salt and pepper. Spread each piece with 1 teaspoon mustard. Place ½ strip bacon down center of each piece. Sprinkle with onion and snipped parsley. Place pickle half on narrow end of each; roll up. Fasten with wooden picks.

Heat oil in 10-inch skillet until hot. Cook rolls over medium heat until brown. Add 1¼ cups water, ½ teaspoon salt and ¼ teaspoon pepper. Heat to boiling; reduce heat. Cover and simmer until beef is tender, about 1 hour.

Remove rolls to warm platter; keep warm. Add enough water to liquid in skillet if necessary to measure 1 cup. Shake 2 tablespoons water and the flour in tightly covered container; stir gradually into cooking liquid. Heat to boiling, stirring constantly. Boil and stir 1 minute. (Add water if necessary.) Serve gravy with rolls.

6 servings

PER SERVING: Calories 235; Protein 30 g; Carbohydrate 5 g; Fat 11 g; Cholesterol 75 mg; Sodium 940 mg

AFRICAN BEEF AND RICE
MOUI NAGDEN (moo-ee nahg-den)

This North African casserole is a filling dish and is especially satisfying when served piping hot from the oven.

1-pound beef round steak, ½ inch thick
2 tablespoons vegetable oil
1 cup water
1 bay leaf
1 teaspoon salt
⅛ to ¼ teaspoon crushed red pepper
1 can (16 ounces) red kidney beans, drained
1 cup uncooked regular rice
2 medium green peppers, cut into 1-inch pieces
1 medium onion, chopped
1½ teaspoons salt
½ to 1 teaspoon curry powder
¼ teaspoon pepper

Cut beef into 1-inch pieces. Heat oil in 10-inch skillet until hot. Cook and stir beef in oil over medium heat until brown on all sides, about 15 minutes. Add water, bay leaf, 1 teaspoon salt and the red pepper. Heat to boiling; reduce heat. Cover and simmer 45 minutes.

Drain beef, reserving broth. Add enough water to reserved broth to measure 2 cups. Mix beef, broth and remaining ingredients. Pour into ungreased 2-quart casserole. Cover and cook in 350° oven until liquid is absorbed, 45 to 50 minutes. Serve with sliced tomatoes if desired.

6 servings

PER SERVING: Calories 330; Protein 22 g; Carbohydrate 45 g; Fat 10 g; Cholesterol 35 mg; Sodium 1100 mg

BRAISED BEEF ESTERHAZY

ROSTELYOS ESTERHAZY (rosh-teh-yosh ester-haze-zee)

This hearty braised beef dish, with its rich sour cream gravy and its elegant garnish of brightly colored vegetables, is worthy of its aristocratic name.

1½ pounds beef boneless round steak, ½ inch thick
3 tablespoons all-purpose flour
2 tablespoons vegetable oil
1 can (10½ ounces) condensed beef broth
½ cup water
3 carrots, cut into strips, 3 × ½ inch
3 medium parsnips, cut into strips, 3 × ½ inch
2 medium onions, sliced
1 teaspoon salt
¼ teaspoon pepper
¼ teaspoon dried thyme leaves
3 sweet gherkin pickles, cut lengthwise into ¼-inch strips
1 cup dairy sour cream

Sprinkle one side of beef with half the flour; pound in. Turn beef; pound in remaining flour. Cut into 6 serving pieces. Heat oil in 12-inch skillet until hot. Cook 3 or 4 pieces of beef at a time in oil over medium heat until brown on both sides, about 15 minutes; drain.

Add beef broth and water. Heat to boiling; reduce heat. Cover and simmer 15 minutes. Add carrots, parsnips and onions. Sprinkle with salt, pepper and thyme. Cover and simmer until beef and vegetables are tender, 40 to 60 minutes. Add gherkins during last 5 minutes.

Remove beef and vegetables to heated platter. Skim fat from broth if necessary; stir in sour cream. Heat just until hot. Serve gravy with beef and vegetables.

6 servings

PER SERVING: Calories 350; Protein 25 g; Carbohydrate 25 g; Fat 19 g; Cholesterol 75 mg; Sodium 770 mg

STEAK AND KIDNEY PIE

This authentic and popular pie is a relative to another old English favorite, the pasty. Here, tender morsels of kidney bake in a rich and savory sauce beneath a golden, flaky crust. Steak and Kidney Pie is a perennial pub favorite.

1 pound beef boneless round steak
1 beef kidney (about ¾ pound)
⅓ cup all-purpose flour
¼ cup vegetable oil
1 cup water
2 medium onions, chopped
4 ounces mushrooms, sliced
1½ teaspoons salt
1 teaspoon Worcestershire sauce
½ teaspoon dried thyme leaves
¼ teaspoon pepper
Pastry Topping (page 137)
¼ cup cold water
2 tablespoons all-purpose flour

Cut beef into ¾-inch cubes. Remove membrane from kidney; cut kidney into halves. Remove white veins and fat with kitchen scissors. Cut kidney into ¾-inch cubes. Coat beef and kidney with ⅓ cup flour. Heat oil in 10-inch skillet over medium heat until hot. Cook meat in hot oil until brown on all sides. Add 1 cup water, the onions, mushrooms, salt, Worcestershire sauce, thyme and pepper. Heat to boiling; reduce heat. Cover and simmer 1 hour. Prepare Pastry Topping.

Mix ¼ cup water and 2 tablespoons flour; stir into meat mixture. Heat to boiling, stirring constantly. Boil and stir 1 minute. Pour mixture into ungreased 1½-quart casserole. Place baked crust on meat mixture in casserole.

6 servings

PER SERVING: Calories 470; Protein 26 g; Carbohydrate 28 g; Fat 29 g; Cholesterol 180 mg; Sodium 800 mg

PASTRY TOPPING

⅓ cup plus 1 tablespoon shortening
1 cup all-purpose flour
½ teaspoon salt
2 to 3 tablespoons cold water

Cut shortening into flour and salt until particles are size of small peas. Sprinkle in water, 1 tablespoon at a time, tossing with fork until all flour is moistened and pastry almost cleans sides of bowl (1 to 2 teaspoons water can be added if necessary).

Gather pastry into a ball; shape into flattened round on lightly floured cloth-covered board (see Note). Roll out to fit top of casserole. Cut 1-inch slits in pastry. Bake on ungreased cookie sheet in 400° oven until crust is golden brown, 25 to 30 minutes.

NOTE: For individual casseroles, divide pastry into 6 equal parts; pat each to fit top of 8-ounce casserole. Cut slits in pastry. Bake on ungreased cookie sheet at 400° oven 25 to 30 minutes. Divide cooked meat mixture among six 8-ounce casseroles; place baked crusts on meat mixture in casseroles.

KOREAN BARBECUED BEEF
BUL-KO-KEE (buhl-<u>koh</u>-kee)

Korean dishes make great use of that Oriental favorite, sesame oil. A dark sesame oil is one made from seeds that have been toasted, and it has a richer, more pronounced flavor than the paler oil.

1-pound beef boneless top loin or sirloin steak
¼ cup soy sauce
3 tablespoons sugar
2 tablespoons sesame or vegetable oil
¼ teaspoon pepper
3 green onions, finely chopped
2 cloves garlic, chopped

Trim fat from beef; cut beef diagonally across grain into ⅛-inch slices. (For ease in cutting, partially freeze beef about 1½ hours.) Mix remaining ingredients; stir in beef until well coated. Cover and refrigerate 30 minutes.

Drain beef; stir-fry in 10-inch skillet or wok over medium heat until light brown, 2 to 3 minutes. Serve beef with hot cooked rice if desired.

4 servings

PER SERVING: Calories 310; Protein 23 g; Carbohydrate 12 g; Fat 19 g; Cholesterol 65 mg; Sodium 1080 mg

SUKIYAKI

(soo-kee-yah-kee)

This traditional dish is served hot and bubbly from the skillet, with separate bowls for hot cooked rice. The bamboo shoots are a somewhat unfamiliar—though delectable—note among the crunchy vegetables here.

1 teaspoon instant beef bouillon
½ cup hot water
⅓ cup soy sauce
2 tablespoons sugar
1-pound beef tenderloin or boneless sirloin,
　1 inch thick
2 tablespoons vegetable oil
3 stalks celery, cut diagonally into ¼-inch slices
2 carrots, cut diagonally into ⅛-inch slices
1 bunch green onions, cut diagonally into 2-inch
　pieces
8 ounces mushrooms, thinly sliced (about 4 cups)
1 can (about 8½ ounces) bamboo shoots, drained
4 ounces spinach, stems removed (4 cups)
2 cups hot cooked rice

Dissolve bouillon in hot water; stir in soy sauce and sugar. Reserve. Cut beef into ⅛-inch slices. (For ease in cutting, partially freeze beef about 1 hour.) Heat oil in 12-inch skillet until hot. Place half each of the celery, carrots, green onions, mushrooms and bamboo shoots in separate areas in skillet. Pour half the reserved soy sauce mixture into skillet.

Simmer uncovered until vegetables are crisp-tender, turning vegetables gently, 8 to 10 minutes. Push vegetables to side of skillet; add half each of the beef and spinach. Cook beef to desired doneness, about 3 minutes. Repeat with remaining vegetables and beef.

4 servings

PER SERVING: Calories 470; Protein 29 g; Carbohydrate 49 g; Fat 20 g; Cholesterol 65 mg; Sodium 2180 mg

---

BEEF IN PEPPER SAUCE

ZILZIL ALECHA (tzeel-tzeel ah-lay-khah)

A mark of Ethiopian cooking is peppery, piquant flavor. Jalapeño peppers, garlic and gingerroot help fire this braised beef specialty, which is complemented by the fragrance of cardamom, turmeric and dry white wine. In Ethiopia, thin round breads called *buddeena* are commonly served with this dish; *buddeena* makes an easy wrap for bite-size morsels. Pocket Bread (page 293) is also a tasty accompaniment.

2 pounds beef boneless sirloin or top loin
　steak, ¾ inch thick
2 medium red peppers, coarsely chopped
2 jalapeño peppers, seeded and chopped
3 cloves garlic, cut into fourths
⅓ cup dry white wine
1 tablespoon chopped gingerroot
1½ teaspoons salt
1 teaspoon ground turmeric
½ teaspoon ground cardamom
1 tablespoon margarine or butter
1 tablespoon vegetable oil
2 medium onions, chopped
1 medium red pepper, cut into ½-inch strips
4 cups hot cooked rice

Beef in Pepper Sauce, shown with Ethiopian flatbread (*buddeena*)

Trim fat from beef; cut beef across grain into strips, 1½ × ½ inch. (For ease in cutting, partially freeze beef about 1½ hours.)

Place chopped peppers, jalapeño peppers, garlic, wine, gingerroot, salt, turmeric and cardamom in blender container. Cover and blend on medium-high speed, stopping blender occasionally to scrape sides, until mixed, about 45 seconds.

Heat margarine and oil in 12-inch skillet until hot. Cook and stir beef over medium-high heat until all liquid from beef is evaporated and beef is brown, about 15 minutes; remove beef with slotted spoon. Cook and stir onions and pepper strips in remaining oil mixture over medium heat until tender. Add blended pepper mixture and the beef. Heat to boiling; reduce heat. Simmer uncovered, stirring occasionally, until beef is hot and sauce is slightly thickened, about 10 minutes. Serve with rice.

8 servings

PER SERVING: Calories 340; Protein 22 g; Carbohydrate 34 g; Fat 14 g; Cholesterol 55 mg; Sodium 860 mg

AFRICAN BEEF AND VEGETABLE SOUP

NKRAKRA (N'krah-krah)

The stock for this Ghanan soup can be made with anything from lamb shanks to fish or other seafood. Our recipe calls for little more than beef, tomatoes, baby limas and Hubbard squash, and a dash of ground ginger and red pepper for seasoning.

1½ pounds beef boneless chuck, tip or round, cut into ¾-inch cubes
2 cups water
2 teaspoons salt
¼ teaspoon ground ginger
⅛ to ¼ teaspoon ground red pepper
1½ pounds Hubbard squash, pared and cut into 1-inch cubes*
2 medium tomatoes, chopped
1 package (10 ounces) frozen baby lima beans

Heat beef, water, salt, ginger and red pepper to boiling in Dutch oven; reduce heat. Cover and simmer 1½ hours. Add squash; cover and cook until beef and squash are tender, 30 to 45 minutes longer.

Remove squash; mash or purée in blender. Return squash to Dutch oven. Add tomatoes and beans. Heat to boiling; reduce heat. Cover and simmer until beans are tender, about 15 minutes. Top each serving with hot cooked rice if desired.

6 servings

*1 package (12 ounces) frozen cooked squash, thawed, can be substituted for the fresh squash; add with tomatoes.

PER SERVING: Calories 205; Protein 18 g; Carbohydrate 18 g; Fat 9 g; Cholesterol 45 mg; Sodium 420 mg

RUSSIAN BEET SOUP

BORSCHT (borsh't)

This thick, creamy soup has many variations to its theme, but most remain true to two ingredients: beets and sour cream. The beet lends its brilliant color, sour cream its silky texture, to this traditional soup. Red wine vinegar adds tongue-tingling tartness as well.

6 cups water
4 ounces dried navy beans (about ½ cup)
1 pound beef boneless chuck, tip or round, cut into ½-inch cubes
1 smoked pork hock
1 can (10½ ounces) condensed beef broth
2½ teaspoons salt
¼ teaspoon pepper
6 medium beets, cooked
2 medium onions, sliced
2 cloves garlic, chopped
2 medium potatoes, cut into ½-inch cubes
3 cups shredded cabbage
2 teaspoons dill seed or 1 sprig dill weed
1 tablespoon pickling spice
¼ cup red wine vinegar
1 cup dairy sour cream

Heat water and beans to boiling in Dutch oven; boil 2 minutes. Remove from heat; cover and let stand 1 hour. Add beef, pork, beef broth, salt and pepper to beans. Heat to boiling; reduce heat. Cover and simmer until beef is tender, 1 to 1½ hours. Shred beets or cut into ¼-inch strips.

Remove pork from Dutch oven; cool slightly. Remove pork from bone and trim fat; cut into bite-size pieces. Add pork, beets, onions, garlic, potatoes and cabbage to beef mixture. Tie dill seed and pickling spice in cheesecloth bag or place in tea ball; add to beef mixture. Cover and simmer 2 hours. Stir in vinegar; simmer 10 minutes. Remove spice bag. Serve with sour cream; sprinkle with snipped dill weed, if desired.

6 servings

PER SERVING: Calories 480; Protein 28 g; Carbohydrate 31 g; Fat 30 g; Cholesterol 95 mg; Sodium 1330 mg

BRAZILIAN BLACK BEAN STEW

FEIJOADA (fay-zhwah-duh)

Beef tongue, chorizo, bacon and black beans stewed all together in a hot chili sauce make up this national dish from Brazil. Orange sections are a sweet accompaniment to this unique stew.

1 smoked beef tongue (3 to 4 pounds)
8 cups cold water
2 packages (12 ounces each) dried black beans (4 cups)
½ pound dried beef
4 smoked chorizos or highly seasoned smoked Italian sausages (reserve 1 chorizo for Sauce)
½ pound sliced bacon, cut into 1-inch pieces
Sauce (right)
1 large orange, thinly sliced
6 to 7 cups hot cooked rice

Place beef tongue in Dutch oven; add enough water to cover beef. Heat to boiling; reduce heat. Cover and simmer until tender, about 3 hours.

Heat water and beans to boiling in Dutch oven or large kettle; boil gently 2 minutes. Remove from heat; cover and let stand 1 hour. Heat to boiling; reduce heat. Cover and simmer 1 hour. Remove and mash 2 cups beans and liquid; reserve mashed beans for Sauce.

Plunge beef tongue into cold water. Cut lengthwise slashes in skin; peel off skin. Remove any fat and cartilage. Cut beef tongue into ¼-inch slices; stir into unmashed beans. Cut dried beef into bite-size pieces; prick chorizos thoroughly with fork. Stir dried beef, chorizos and bacon into beans and tongue.

Add just enough water to cover. Heat to boiling; reduce heat. Cover and simmer 1 hour.

Prepare Sauce. Stir half the Sauce into meat-bean mixture. Cover and cook until beans are mushy, about 1 hour. (Add ½ to 1 cup water if necessary.) Heat remaining Sauce over low heat. Arrange beef tongue slices in center of platter; arrange remaining chorizos around tongue slices. Pour Sauce over meats. Cut orange slices into halves; arrange around meats. Pour remaining beans into tureen; serve with rice.

12 to 14 servings

PER SERVING: Calories 615; Protein 40 g; Carbohydrate 71 g; Fat 24 g; Cholesterol 95 mg; Sodium 1460 mg

SAUCE

1 chorizo, cooked with the beans (left)
4 jalapeño peppers, finely chopped
2 large tomatoes, chopped
1 large onion, chopped
2 cloves garlic, finely chopped
¼ teaspoon salt
⅛ teaspoon ground red pepper

Cut reserved chorizo into 1-inch pieces. Cook and stir chorizo and remaining ingredients in 10-inch skillet over medium heat 3 minutes. Stir 2 cups reserved beans into chorizo mixture; heat until hot.

HEARTY PULSE AND BEEF SOUP

MAUSHAWA (mah-<u>shah</u>-wah)

Pulses, or legumes, are invaluable sources of protein, especially when they are served together with whole grains. They are a staple in many Middle Eastern and Asian diets, where meat is not available in plenty. In Afghanistan, this filling pulse soup is sometimes made with spiced beef or lamb meatballs. The recipe below uses chunks of spiced beef, with beans and rice. Yogurt both thickens and garnishes the soup in the Afghan tradition.

6 cups water
½ cup dried red kidney beans
½ cup dried green split peas
⅓ cup uncooked regular rice
1 medium onion, chopped
2 tablespoons vegetable oil
½ pound beef boneless round steak, cut into
    ½-inch pieces
1 can (16 ounces) whole tomatoes (with liquid)
1 teaspoon salt
½ teaspoon ground red pepper
2 cartons (8 ounces each) plain yogurt
1 tablespoon snipped dill weed

Heat water and beans to boiling in Dutch oven; boil 2 minutes. Remove from heat; cover and let stand 1 hour.

Heat beans and water to boiling; reduce heat. Cover and simmer 1 hour. (Do not boil or beans will burst.) Add peas. Heat to boiling; reduce heat. Cover and simmer 30 minutes.

Stir in rice. Heat to boiling; reduce heat. Cover and simmer until beans and rice are tender, about 20 minutes.

Cook and stir onion in oil in 10-inch skillet over medium heat until tender; remove with slotted spoon. Add beef to skillet; cook and stir until brown on all sides, about 10 minutes. Stir in tomatoes, salt, red pepper and onions; break up tomatoes with fork. Heat to boiling; reduce heat. Cover and simmer, stirring occasionally, until beef is tender, about 45 minutes.

Stir beef mixture, yogurt and dill weed into bean mixture. Cook uncovered over low heat until hot (add more water, if necessary, until of soup consistency). Garnish with dollops of yogurt topped with sprigs of dill weed, and serve with Indian Flat Bread (page 287) if desired.

6 servings (about 1⅓ cups each)

PER SERVING: Calories 275; Protein 19 g; Carbohydrate 37 g; Fat 9 g; Cholesterol 20 mg; Sodium 550 mg

---

Pulses

Legumes are pulses, rich in protein and usually purchased as dried beans. An exception to the drying rule is the mung bean, a small green bean that harbors the potential to become a bean sprout, the sort made famous by the health-food movement of the 1970s. Pulses include garbanzo beans (chick-peas), kidney beans and split peas of all colors. Middle Eastern and Indian cooking in particular have relied on pulses as a nutritional mainstay.

PUNGENT JAVANESE BEEF

SEMUR DAGING (seh-moor dah-gheeng)

Semur means "braise" or "stew," specifically with sugar, soy sauce, clove, nutmeg and pepper. In *Semur Daging*, almost every taste sensation—sweet and sour, salty and bitter—is excited. Plain boiled rice is the perfect accompaniment here.

1 large onion, finely chopped
2 cloves garlic, finely chopped
2 teaspoons finely chopped gingerroot
2 tablespoons vegetable oil
1½ pounds beef boneless chuck, tip or round,
    cut into 1½-inch cubes
1¼ cups water
1 tablespoon tamarind powder or pulp or
    2 tablespoons lemon juice
2 tablespoons dark soy sauce
2 teaspoons packed brown sugar
¼ teaspoon ground cardamom
¼ teaspoon ground cinnamon
¼ teaspoon pepper
⅛ teaspoon ground nutmeg
⅛ teaspoon ground cloves
2 cups hot cooked rice

Cook and stir onion, garlic and gingerroot in oil in 10-inch skillet over medium heat until onion is tender; remove with slotted spoon. Add beef to skillet. Cook, stirring frequently, until all liquid is evaporated and beef is brown, about 25 minutes.

Stir in onion mixture and remaining ingredients except rice. Heat to boiling; reduce heat. Cover and simmer, stirring occasionally, until beef is tender and sauce is thickened, about 1½ hours. Skim off fat. Serve with rice.

4 servings

PER SERVING: Calories 775; Protein 44 g; Carbohydrate 36 g; Fat 51 g; Cholesterol 145 mg; Sodium 1020 mg

RED COOKED BEEF

HUNG SHAO NIU JO (hwung shah-oo nee-oh rwo)

Succulent strips of beef are stir-fried in an aromatic, slightly sweetened sauce of soy, gingerroot, white wine and garlic, then simmered. It is the generous amount of soy sauce that gives this Chinese dish its red color.

2 pounds beef boneless chuck, tip or round
3 tablespoons peanut or vegetable oil
1½ cups water
¼ cup soy sauce
2 tablespoons dry white wine or sherry
1 thin slice fresh or canned gingerroot or
    1 teaspoon ground ginger
1 green onion, cut lengthwise into halves
1 clove garlic, cut into halves
1 tablespoon sugar
⅛ teaspoon pepper
Fresh cilantro (optional)
2 teaspoons toasted sesame seed

Trim fat from beef; cut beef into 1½-inch cubes. Heat 2 tablespoons of the oil in wok or 12-inch skillet until hot. Stir-fry half the beef cubes until brown on all sides, about 2 minutes. Remove beef to 3-quart saucepan. Repeat with remaining oil and beef.

Mix water, soy sauce, wine, gingerroot, green onion, garlic, sugar and pepper; add to beef. Heat to boiling; reduce heat. Cover and simmer, stirring occasionally, until beef is tender, about 1 hour. Garnish with small sprigs of cilantro; sprinkle with sesame seed. Serve with hot cooked Chinese noodles if desired.

8 servings

PER SERVING: Calories 330; Protein 31 g; Carbohydrate 3 g; Fat 22 g; Cholesterol 90 mg; Sodium 590 mg

HUNGARIAN BEEF GOULASH
BOGRACS GULYAS (boh-grotch goo-l'yosh)

Loosely translated, *Bogracs Gulyas* means "a cauldron of meat." This dish is the quintessential Hungarian stew, filled with potatoes, beef and tomatoes, and seasoned with caraway and paprika.

2 tablespoons vegetable oil or bacon fat
1½ pounds beef boneless chuck, tip or round,
   cut into ¾-inch cubes
2 cups water
1 can (8 ounces) tomatoes (with liquid)
3 medium onions, chopped
1 clove garlic, chopped
2 teaspoons paprika
2 teaspoons salt
1 teaspoon instant beef bouillon
½ teaspoon caraway seed
¼ teaspoon pepper
2 medium potatoes, cut into 1½-inch pieces
2 medium green peppers, cut into 1-inch pieces
French bread or rolls

Heat oil in Dutch oven or 12-inch skillet until hot. Cook and stir beef in hot oil until brown, about 15 minutes; drain. Add water, tomatoes, onions, garlic, paprika, salt, bouillon, caraway seed and pepper. Break up tomatoes with fork. Heat to boiling; reduce heat. Cover and simmer 1 hour.

Add potatoes; cover and simmer until beef and potatoes are tender, about 30 minutes. Add green peppers; cover and simmer until tender, 8 to 10 minutes. Serve in soup bowls with French bread for dipping into hot broth.

6 servings

PER SERVING: Calories 565; Protein 31 g; Carbohydrate 31 g; Fat 35 g; Cholesterol 95 mg; Sodium 1290 mg

BEEF STEW PROVENÇALE
DAUBE DE BOEUF À LA PROVENÇALE
(dohb duh buhf ah lah proh-vahng-sal)

Daube is a French word for a meat stew cooked in a tightly covered dish. Salt pork adds lusty country flavor to the stock.

¼ pound salt pork
1½ pounds beef boneless chuck, tip or round
1 cup dry red wine
½ cup water
2 cloves garlic, chopped
½ teaspoon salt
½ teaspoon dried thyme leaves
¼ teaspoon dried rosemary leaves, crushed
¼ teaspoon pepper
1 bay leaf
6 medium carrots, cut into 1-inch pieces
2 medium onions, cut into fourths
½ cup pitted ripe olives
Snipped parsley
French bread

Remove rind from salt pork; cut pork into ¼-inch slices. Cut beef into 1-inch cubes. (For ease in cutting, partially freeze beef about 1 hour.) Fry salt pork in Dutch oven over medium heat until crisp; remove with slotted spoon. Drain on paper towels. Cook and stir beef in hot fat until brown, about 15 minutes. Drain fat. Add wine, water, garlic, salt, thyme, rosemary, pepper and bay leaf. Heat to boiling; reduce heat. Cover and simmer 1 hour.

Stir in salt pork, carrots, onions and olives. Cover and simmer until beef and vegetables are tender, about 40 minutes. Remove bay leaf. Sprinkle with parsley. Serve in bowls with French bread for dipping.

6 servings

PER SERVING: Calories 600; Protein 32 g; Carbohydrate 26 g; Fat 41 g; Cholesterol 105 mg; Sodium 700 mg

BEEF AND ONION STEW

STIFADO (stee-fah-doh)

This aromatic stew showcases sweet and tender pearl onions. It is a Greek specialty with a tomato base, touched with cinnamon, and is served with a bold feta cheese topping.

1 medium onion, chopped
2 cloves garlic, finely chopped
3 tablespoons olive or vegetable oil
2 pounds beef boneless chuck, tip or round, cut into 1-inch cubes
½ cup dry red wine
2 tablespoons red wine vinegar
½ teaspoon salt
¼ teaspoon coarsely ground pepper
1 bay leaf
1 stick cinnamon
1 can (8 ounces) tomato sauce
1½ pounds pearl onions, peeled
Crumbled feta cheese

Cook and stir chopped onion and garlic in oil in Dutch oven over medium heat until onion is tender; remove with slotted spoon. Cook beef in remaining oil, stirring frequently, until all liquid is evaporated and beef is brown on all sides, about 25 minutes; drain fat.

Return onion and garlic to Dutch oven. Stir in remaining ingredients except onions and cheese. Heat to boiling; reduce heat. Cover and simmer 1 hour and 15 minutes.

Add white onions. Cover and simmer until beef and white onions are tender, about 30 minutes. Remove bay leaf and cinnamon. Garnish with cheese. Serve with Spinach with Lemon Dressing (page 254) if desired.

6 servings

PER SERVING: Calories 475; Protein 43 g; Carbohydrate 16 g; Fat 26 g; Cholesterol 130 mg; Sodium 620 mg

THREE-MEAT STEW

KARJALAN PAISTI (kahr-yah-lan pie-stee)

From Finland comes a stew that reflects the Russian influence on its eastern border. Here the flavors of beef, lamb and pork are enhanced with simple seasonings and boiled potatoes. In Finland this dish would cook overnight. Our recipe produces the same succulent stew in a couple of hours.

1 pound beef boneless chuck or round
1 pound lamb boneless shoulder
1 pound pork boneless shoulder
2 tablespoons all-purpose flour
¾ teaspoon salt
½ teaspoon pepper
½ teaspoon ground allspice
2 large onions, sliced
1 bay leaf
1½ cups hot water
8 medium boiled potatoes, cut in halves

Trim fat from meats; cut meats into 1-inch cubes. Toss meats, flour, salt, pepper and allspice. Alternate layers of meat and onions in Dutch oven. Add bay leaf. Pour hot water over meat and onion mixture. Cover and cook in 350° oven 2½ hours.

Uncover and cook, stirring occasionally, until meat is tender and broth is slightly thickened, about 30 minutes. Remove bay leaf. Serve with potatoes.

8 servings

PER SERVING: Calories 640; Protein 42 g; Carbohydrate 29 g; Fat 41 g; Cholesterol 145 mg; Sodium 300 mg

Beef and Onion Stew and Spinach with Lemon Dressing (page 254)

FLEMISH BEEF AND BEER STEW

CARBONNADES À LA FLAMMANDE
(kahr-bohn-<u>nahd</u> ah la flah-<u>mahnd</u>)

Bacon and a dark-hued beer are the mark of a *carbonnade*. Use a lighter beer for a less assertive beer flavor. This is delicious over hot, buttery noodles.

1½-pound beef boneless chuck or round steak, 1 inch thick
¼ pound bacon
4 medium onions, sliced
1 clove garlic, chopped
3 tablespoons all-purpose flour
1 cup water
1 can (12 or 16 ounces) light or dark beer
1 bay leaf
1 tablespoon packed brown sugar
2 teaspoons salt
½ teaspoon dried thyme leaves
¼ teaspoon pepper
1 tablespoon vinegar
Snipped parsley
3 cups hot cooked noodles

Cut beef into ½-inch slices; cut slices into 2-inch strips. (For ease in cutting, partially freeze beef about 1½ hours.) Cut bacon into ¼-inch pieces; fry in Dutch oven until crisp. Remove bacon with slotted spoon; drain. Pour off fat and reserve. Cook and stir onions and garlic in 2 tablespoons of the reserved bacon fat until onion is tender, about 10 minutes. Remove onions. Cook and stir beef in remaining bacon fat until brown, about 15 minutes.

Stir in flour to coat beef; gradually stir in water. Add onions, beer, bay leaf, brown sugar, salt, thyme and pepper. Add just enough water to cover beef if necessary. Heat to boiling; reduce heat. Cover and simmer until beef is tender, 1 to 1½ hours. Remove bay leaf. Stir in vinegar; sprinkle with bacon and parsley. Serve with noodles.

6 servings

PER SERVING: Calories 555; Protein 34 g; Carbohydrate 34 g; Fat 33 g; Cholesterol 125 mg; Sodium 1000 mg

---

DEVILED SHORT RIBS

These simple, mouth-watering ribs are deviled with dry mustard, Indian curry, spicy red pepper and a generous splash of Worcestershire sauce. They are much admired in Great Britain, especially when accompanied by hot, buttery vegetables.

2 tablespoons vegetable oil
4 pounds beef short ribs, cut into pieces
2 medium onions, sliced
1 tablespoon dry mustard
1 tablespoon Worcestershire sauce
1 teaspoon salt
1 teaspoon curry powder
¼ teaspoon ground red pepper
¾ cup water

Heat oil in Dutch oven until hot. Cook beef over medium heat until brown on all sides; drain. Add onions. Mix remaining ingredients except water; stir in water. Pour over beef. Cover and cook in 350° oven until tender, about 2 hours.

6 servings

PER SERVING: Calories 740; Protein 32 g; Carbohydrate 4 g; Fat 66 g; Cholesterol 140 mg; Sodium 450 mg

KOREAN BRAISED SHORT RIBS

In Japan, Koreans are sometimes referred to as "the garlic eaters." Indeed, garlic plays a big role in flavoring these ribs, as do Chinese gingerroot, sesame seed and soy sauce. Hot cooked cellophane noodles, dipped into the cooking sauce, would make a delicious second lead.

4 pounds beef short ribs, cut into pieces
2 cloves garlic, chopped
½ cup soy sauce
¼ cup chopped onion
2 tablespoons sugar
2 tablespoons ground sesame seed (see Note)
2 teaspoons chopped gingerroot or ½ teaspoon ground ginger
½ teaspoon pepper

Trim fat from beef ribs; place beef in shallow glass or plastic dish. Mix remaining ingredients; pour over beef. Cover and refrigerate, turning occasionally, 24 hours.

Drain beef, reserving marinade. Cook beef in 4-quart Dutch oven over medium heat until brown; drain. Pour marinade over beef. Cover and cook in 350° oven until tender, about 2 hours.

6 servings

PER SERVING: Calories 695; Protein 32 g; Carbohydrate 2 g; Fat 62 g; Cholesterol 135 mg; Sodium 420 mg

NOTE: Ground sesame seed is available in Oriental food specialty stores and some supermarkets. Whole sesame seed can be ground in the blender; 1 tablespoon whole sesame seed yields 2 tablespoons ground.

SHORT RIBS WITH HORSERADISH SAUCE
TAFELSPITZ (tah-fehl-shpeetz)

Austria has a rich and varied cultural heritage, which is reflected in its music and fine cuisine. This recipe for short ribs will inspire the Mozart in all of us.

2 tablespoons vegetable oil
4 pounds beef short ribs, cut into pieces
4 cups water
1 large onion, sliced
1 large carrot, cut into 1-inch pieces
1 stalk celery, cut into 1-inch pieces
1 medium turnip, cut into 1-inch pieces
1½ teaspoons salt
10 to 12 whole black peppercorns
1 bay leaf
Snipped parsley
Horseradish Sauce (below)

Heat oil in Dutch oven until hot. Cook beef ribs over medium heat until brown on all sides; drain fat. Add remaining ingredients except parsley and Horseradish Sauce. Heat to boiling; reduce heat. Cover and simmer until beef is tender, about 2 hours.

Sprinkle with parsley. Serve with Horseradish Sauce.

6 servings

PER SERVING: Calories 780; Protein 32 g; Carbohydrate 14 g; Fat 66 g; Cholesterol 135 mg; Sodium 630 mg

HORSERADISH SAUCE

1 cup applesauce
1 to 2 tablespoons prepared horseradish

Mix applesauce and horseradish.

SPANISH BRAISED OXTAILS

RABO DE TORO A LA ANDALUZA
(<u>rah</u>-boh deh <u>tor</u>-roh ah lah ahn-dah-<u>loo</u>-zah)

Andalucia is that part of Spain where the most fervent homage is paid to bullfighting.

3 pounds oxtails, cut into 2-inch pieces
1 tablespoon olive or vegetable oil
1 teaspoon salt
½ teaspoon dried thyme leaves
¼ teaspoon pepper
1 medium onion, cut into fourths
1 bay leaf
4 cups water
1 medium onion, chopped
2 cloves garlic, finely chopped
2 tablespoons olive or vegetable oil
2 tablespoons all-purpose flour
1 cup dry red wine
Snipped parsley

Cook oxtails in 1 tablespoon oil in Dutch oven over medium heat until brown on all sides, about 15 minutes. Sprinkle with salt, thyme and pepper; add onion fourths, bay leaf and water. Heat to boiling; reduce heat. Cover and simmer 3 hours.

Remove oxtails with slotted spoon; remove bay leaf. Pour liquid into bowl; skim off fat. Reserve 1 cup of the liquid. Cook and stir chopped onion and garlic in 2 tablespoons oil in Dutch oven over medium heat until onion is tender. Stir in flour. Gradually stir in wine and reserved cooking liquid. Heat to boiling, stirring constantly; boil and stir 1 minute. Reduce heat; add oxtails. Cover and simmer until oxtails are tender, 1 to 1½ hours. Sprinkle with parsley.

4 servings

PER SERVING: Calories 445; Protein 24 g; Carbohydrate 9 g; Fat 35 g; Cholesterol 80 mg; Sodium 600 mg

Spanish Braised Oxtails

PORTUGUESE LIVER WITH BACON

ISCAS (eesh-<u>kahsh</u>)

In Portugal, this classic dish is usually made with pork liver. The recipe that follows recommends the more delicately flavored and accessible calf's liver. Accompany the dish with either boiled or panfried potatoes.

½ cup dry red wine
1 tablespoon red wine vinegar
¼ teaspoon salt
Dash of pepper
3 cloves garlic, finely chopped
2 bay leaves, crumbled
1 pound calf liver, sliced ¼ to ½ inch thick
1 tablespoon olive or vegetable oil
4 slices bacon, cut into 1-inch pieces
Snipped parsley

Mix wine, vinegar, salt, pepper, garlic and bay leaves; pour over liver in shallow glass or plastic dish. Cover and refrigerate 1 hour. Drain liver; strain. Reserve wine mixture. Pat liver dry.

Heat oil in 12-inch skillet until hot. Fry bacon in oil over medium heat until crisp; remove with slotted spoon and drain. Cook liver in oil and bacon fat until brown, about 4 minutes on each side. Arrange liver on platter; keep warm. Drain fat from skillet. Add reserved wine mixture to skillet. Heat to boiling, stirring constantly to loosen browned bits; reduce heat. Simmer uncovered until liquid is reduced to about ¼ cup. Pour sauce over liver; sprinkle with bacon and parsley.

4 servings

PER SERVING: Calories 190; Protein 21 g; Carbohydrate 4 g; Fat 10 g; Cholesterol 315 mg; Sodium 290 mg

RAVIOLI

As any Italian knows, the best ravioli is made at home. The filling in this recipe is flavored with beef, cheese and spinach.

Tomato Sauce* (right)
Ravioli Dough (right)
¾ pound ground beef
1 small onion, finely chopped
1 package (10 ounces) frozen chopped spinach, thawed and well drained
1 egg
½ cup grated Parmesan cheese
1 teaspoon salt
¼ teaspoon pepper
6 quarts water
2 tablespoons salt

Prepare Tomato Sauce. Prepare Ravioli Dough. While dough is resting, cook and stir beef and onion over medium heat until beef is light brown and finely crumbled; drain. Squeeze any remaining moisture from spinach. Stir spinach, egg, cheese, 1 teaspoon salt and pepper into beef and onion.

Divide dough into 6 equal parts. (Cover dough with plastic wrap to prevent drying.) Roll one part of the dough as thin as possible on lightly floured surface into about 13-inch square. Trim edges to make 12-inch square; fold in half. (Cover with plastic wrap.) Repeat with a second part of dough, but do not fold.

Mound about 1 teaspoon beef filling about 1½ inches apart in checkerboard pattern on unfolded sheet of dough; make 16 mounds. Dip pastry brush into water; brush in straight lines between filling mounds and around edge of dough. Unfold folded sheet of dough over filled half. Starting at center, press with fingertips and side of hand between mounds of filling and around edges to seal. Cut pasta between mounds into squares with pastry wheel or knife. Separate squares; place on waxed paper. Repeat twice with remaining dough to make 48 squares.

Heat water and 2 tablespoons salt to boiling in large kettle. Add ravioli; stir to prevent sticking. Cook uncovered until tender, about 12 minutes; remove to colander with slotted spoon. Serve with Tomato Sauce.

8 servings (48 ravioli)

*1 cup margarine or butter, melted, and ½ cup grated Parmesan cheese can be substituted for the Tomato Sauce; toss with ravioli.

PER SERVING: Calories 385; Protein 22 g; Carbohydrate 50 g; Fat 13 g; Cholesterol 215 mg; Sodium 2140 mg

TOMATO SAUCE

2 cans (16 ounces each) tomatoes (with liquid)
1 can (15 ounces) tomato sauce
1 large onion, chopped
2 cloves garlic, chopped
2 teaspoons sugar
1 teaspoon dried basil leaves
½ teaspoon salt
¼ teaspoon pepper

Break up tomatoes with fork. Heat tomatoes and remaining ingredients to boiling; reduce heat. Simmer uncovered until thickened, about 30 minutes.

RAVIOLI DOUGH

3 cups all-purpose flour
3 egg yolks
3 eggs
1 tablespoon salt
¼ to ½ cup water

Make a well in center of flour. Add egg yolks, eggs and salt; mix thoroughly with fork. Mix in water, 1 tablespoon at a time, until dough forms a ball. Turn dough onto well-floured cloth-covered board; knead until smooth and elastic, about 5 minutes. Cover; let rest 10 minutes.

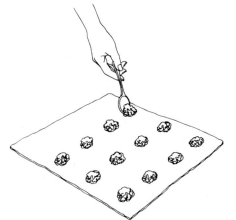

Mound filling by teaspoonfuls on pasta, about 1½ inches apart.

Press down between mounds with side of hand to form ravioli squares; moistened areas of pasta will seal fillings into squares.

Separate squares with pastry wheel, ravioli cutter or sharp knife.

SWEDISH MEATBALLS
KOTTBULLAR (chutt-boo-lahr)

These tempting bits of beef and pork are irresistible when blanketed in a velvety sauce. Serve them with parsleyed potatoes.

1 pound ground beef
½ pound ground pork
¾ cup dry bread crumbs
¼ cup milk
1 egg
1 small onion, finely chopped
1½ teaspoons salt
¼ teaspoon ground nutmeg
¼ teaspoon pepper
3 tablespoons all-purpose flour
¾ cup water
1 cup half-and-half
1 teaspoon instant beef bouillon
½ teaspoon salt
Snipped parsley

Mix beef, pork, bread crumbs, milk, egg, onion, 1½ teaspoons salt, the nutmeg and pepper. Shape mixture into 1-inch balls. (For easy shaping, dip hands into cold water from time to time.) Place meatballs on ungreased jelly roll pan, 15½ × 10½ × 1 inch, or in 2 oblong pans, 13 × 9 × 2 inches. Cook uncovered in 350° oven until light brown, about 20 minutes.

Remove meatballs to serving dish; keep warm. Place 3 tablespoons pan drippings in saucepan; stir in flour. Cook over low heat, stirring constantly, until mixture is smooth and bubbly. Remove from heat. Stir in water, half-and-half, bouillon and ½ teaspoon salt. Heat to boiling, stirring constantly. Boil and stir 1 minute. Pour gravy over meatballs; sprinkle with parsley.

6 to 8 servings (about 48 meatballs)

PER SERVING: Calories 375; Protein 25 g; Carbohydrate 16 g; Fat 24 g; Cholesterol 120 mg; Sodium 1090 mg

Baked Stuffed Papayas and Haitian Bread (page 296)

BAKED STUFFED PAPAYAS

The Hawaiian papaya found in most American markets is sometimes sweeter than its south-of-the-border cousin. Here, the exotic papaya is filled—just like any small winter squash—with a highly seasoned ground beef and jalapeño pepper mixture.

1 pound ground beef
1 medium onion, chopped
1 clove garlic, finely chopped
1 can (16 ounces) whole tomatoes, drained
1 jalapeño pepper, finely chopped
½ teaspoon salt
¼ teaspoon pepper
4 papayas (about 12 ounces each)
2 tablespoons grated Parmesan cheese

Cook and stir beef, onion and garlic in 10-inch skillet over medium heat until beef is light brown; drain. Stir in tomatoes, jalapeño pepper, salt and pepper; break up tomatoes with fork. Heat to boiling; reduce heat. Simmer uncovered until most of the liquid is evaporated, about 10 minutes.

Cut papayas lengthwise into halves; remove seeds. Place about ⅓ cup beef mixture in each papaya half; sprinkle with cheese. Arrange in shallow roasting pan. Pour very hot water into pan to within 1 inch of tops of papaya halves. Cook uncovered in 350° oven until papayas are very tender and hot, about 30 minutes.

4 servings

PER SERVING: Calories 375; Protein 25 g; Carbohydrate 37 g; Fat 18 g; Cholesterol 65 mg; Sodium 560 mg

---

Papaya

Known also as the *tree melon* and, archaically, as the *pawpaw*, the papaya is a tropical fruit. Papaya fruits have been recorded as large as a massive ten pounds, but it is more usual for them to weigh in at a modest twelve to sixteen ounces. The skin of this creamy orange-colored fruit is a vibrant light green that ripens to yellow. When ready to eat raw, the fruit yields to gentle pressure. Cut a papaya in half lengthwise and scoop out the small, shiny (and inedible) black seeds. For cooking, a firm—not rock hard—fruit is preferable. Like another tropical fruit to which it is often compared, the mango, the papaya makes for luscious chutneys and pickles.

BAKED BEEF CURRY WITH CUSTARD TOPPING

BOBOTIE (boh-<u>boh</u>-tee)

Though *Bobotie* is popular fare in South Africa, its origin lies in India. Dutch traders brought exotic Indian spices to their Cape Town way station, en route from Bombay to Amsterdam.

1½ pounds ground beef or lamb
1 cup soft bread crumbs (about 1½ slices bread)
1 cup milk
1 egg
1 medium onion, chopped
¼ cup slivered almonds, chopped
¼ cup raisins
1 tablespoon lemon juice
2 to 3 teaspoons curry powder
1½ teaspoons salt
¼ teaspoon pepper
2 eggs, beaten
1 cup milk
Paprika

Mix beef, bread crumbs, 1 cup milk, 1 egg, the onion, almonds, raisins, lemon juice, curry powder, salt and pepper. Spread mixture in ungreased 2-quart casserole. Cook uncovered in 325° oven 45 minutes; drain excess fat. Mix beaten eggs and 1 cup milk; pour over beef mixture. Sprinkle with paprika. Place casserole in oblong pan, 13 × 9 × 2 inches on oven rack. Pour very hot water (1 inch) into pan.

Cook uncovered until beef is done and custard is set, about 30 minutes. Garnish with lemon slices and pimiento if desired. Cut into wedges to serve.

8 servings

PER SERVING: Calories 280; Protein 21 g; Carbohydrate 12 g; Fat 17 g; Cholesterol 135 mg; Sodium 520 mg

STUFFED CABBAGE ROLLS

KALDOLMAR (kohl-doll-mahr)

Cabbage rolls prevail in Northern Europe, where they have as many names as they have variations. In Scandinavia, one such variation presents these rice- and beef-filled rolls with a delicate sauce.

1 large head cabbage (about 2 pounds)
1½ pounds ground beef
⅓ cup uncooked regular rice
½ cup milk
1 medium onion, chopped
1 egg
2 teaspoons salt
¼ teaspoon pepper
¼ teaspoon ground allspice
½ cup water
½ cup half-and-half
1 tablespoon all-purpose flour
½ teaspoon instant beef bouillon

Remove core from cabbage. Cover cabbage with cold water; let stand about 10 minutes. Remove 12 cabbage leaves. Cover leaves with boiling water. Cover and let stand until leaves are limp, about 10 minutes; drain.

Mix beef, rice, milk, onion, egg, salt, pepper and allspice. Place about ⅓ cup beef mixture at stem end of each leaf. Roll leaf around beef mixture, tucking in sides. Place cabbage rolls, seam sides down, in ungreased oblong baking dish, 13½ × 9 × 2 inches. Pour water over rolls.

Cover and cook in 350° oven until beef is done, about 1 hour. Remove cabbage rolls with slotted spoon; keep warm. Drain liquid from baking dish, reserving ½ cup liquid; skim fat.

Gradually stir half-and-half into flour in saucepan until smooth. Stir in reserved liquid and the bouillon. Heat to boiling, stirring constantly. Boil and stir 1 minute. Serve sauce with cabbage rolls.

6 servings (2 rolls each)

PER SERVING: Calories 370; Protein 27 g; Carbohydrate 25 g; Fat 20 g; Cholesterol 110 mg; Sodium 940 mg

SCANDINAVIAN HAMBURGERS

BIFF À LA LINDSTROM (beef ah lah leend-struhm)

These filling burgers are a warm and welcome meal on a blustery evening. Pickled beets give them a Swedish sweet-sour crunch.

1 pound ground beef
1 egg
½ cup cold mashed potatoes
½ teaspoon salt
¼ teaspoon pepper
¼ cup finely chopped pickled beets
2 tablespoons finely chopped onion
2 tablespoons capers

Mix beef, egg, potatoes, salt and pepper. Stir in remaining ingredients. Shape mixture into 4 patties, each about 1 inch thick.

Set oven control to broil or 550°. Broil patties with tops about 4 inches from heat until desired doneness, 6 to 8 minutes on each side for medium. Top each patty with fried egg if desired.

4 servings

PER SERVING: Calories 285; Protein 23 g; Carbohydrate 9 g; Fat 18 g; Cholesterol 120 mg; Sodium 440 mg

BAKED MACARONI WITH BEEF AND CHEESE

PASTICCIO (pah-<u>sti</u>-zoh)

This Greek dish bakes in a cinnamon-spiced tomato sauce, all topped with a golden layer of sheep's milk Kasseri cheese.

7 ounces uncooked ziti or elbow macaroni
  (about 2 cups)
¾ pound ground beef
1 small onion, chopped
1 can (15 ounces) tomato sauce
1 teaspoon salt
1½ cups grated Kasseri, Parmesan or Romano
  cheese (6 ounces)
⅛ teaspoon ground cinnamon
1¼ cups milk
3 tablespoons margarine or butter
2 eggs, beaten
⅛ teaspoon ground nutmeg

Cook macaroni as directed on package; drain. Cook and stir beef and onion in 10-inch skillet until beef is light brown; drain. Stir in tomato sauce and salt. Spread half the macaroni in greased square baking dish, 8 × 8 × 2 inches; cover with beef mixture. Mix ½ cup of the cheese and the cinnamon; sprinkle over beef mixture. Cover with remaining macaroni.

Cook and stir milk and margarine in 2-quart saucepan until margarine is melted. Remove from heat. Stir at least half the milk mixture gradually into beaten eggs. Blend into milk mixture in saucepan; pour over macaroni. Sprinkle with remaining 1 cup cheese. Cook uncovered in 325° oven until brown and center is set, about 50 minutes. Sprinkle with nutmeg. Garnish with parsley if desired.

6 servings

PER SERVING: Calories 450; Protein 28 g; Carbohydrate 35 g; Fat 23 g; Cholesterol 125 mg; Sodium 1420 mg

BEEF WITH OLIVES AND ALMONDS

PICADILLO (pee-kah-<u>dee</u>-yoh)

Mexican *Picadillo* is a colorful mélange of ground beef, green pepper, tomato and pimiento-stuffed olive. It is seasoned with garlic and perfumed with cinnamon and cloves. Raisins and almonds are added treats to this minced meat hash, which often fills tortillas, pies and whole peppers.

1 pound ground beef
1 medium onion, chopped
1 clove garlic, chopped
2 medium tomatoes, chopped
1 medium green pepper, chopped
¼ cup raisins
1½ teaspoons salt
⅛ teaspoon ground cinnamon
⅛ teaspoon ground cloves
¼ cup slivered almonds
¼ cup sliced pimiento-stuffed olives
Hot cooked rice

Cook and stir beef, onion and garlic in 10-inch skillet until beef is light brown; drain. Add tomatoes, green pepper, raisins, salt, cinnamon and cloves. Cover and simmer 10 minutes.

Cook and stir almonds over medium heat until golden, 2 to 3 minutes. Stir almonds and olives into beef mixture. Serve with rice.

4 servings

PER SERVING: Calories 465; Protein 28 g; Carbohydrate 45 g; Fat 19 g; Cholesterol 70 mg; Sodium 1090 mg

ALSATIAN PORK WITH SAUERKRAUT

CHOUCROUTE GARNIE À L'ALSACIENNE
(shoo-kroot gar-nee ah lahl-zahs-s'yehn)

A wonderful aspect of Alsace-Lorraine is its intriguing blend of French and German cuisine. Tender pork chops and frankfurters stew in bacon drippings and a pungent sauce made with sauerkraut, apples and brown sugar.

4 slices bacon, cut into 1-inch pieces
1 medium onion, chopped
1 can (16 ounces) sauerkraut, drained
1 to 2 tablespoons packed brown sugar
2 medium potatoes, cut into fourths
2 tart apples, sliced
12 juniper berries (optional)
6 black peppercorns
2 whole cloves
1 sprig parsley
1 bay leaf
4 smoked pork chops, ½ inch thick
4 frankfurters, slashed diagonally
2 cups chicken broth

Cook and stir bacon and onion in Dutch oven or 12-inch skillet until bacon is crisp; drain. Stir in sauerkraut and brown sugar. Add potatoes and apples.

Tie juniper berries, peppercorns, cloves, parsley and bay leaf in cheesecloth bag or place in tea ball; add to sauerkraut. Add pork chops and frankfurters. Pour chicken broth over meat. Heat to boiling; reduce heat. Cover and simmer until meat is done and potatoes are tender, about 30 minutes. Remove spice bag. Remove sauerkraut, potatoes and apples to large platter with slotted spoon. Arrange meat around edge.

4 servings

PER SERVING: Calories 455; Protein 25 g; Carbohydrate 33 g; Fat 28 g; Cholesterol 70 mg; Sodium 2380 mg

PORK CHOPS WITH KNOCKWURST

SCHWEINSKOTELETTEN MIT KNACKWURST UND KARTOFFELN
(shvein-skoht-lehtt'n mit k'nack-voorst oont kahr-toff'ln)

The knockwurst is a mainstay of German cooking. This recipe takes fried pork chops and adds a bouquet of vegetables and spicy knockwurst.

4 pork loin or rib chops, about ½ inch thick
1 tablespoon vegetable oil
1 medium onion, chopped
1 medium carrot, chopped
1 stalk celery, sliced
2 sweet pickles, finely chopped
6 ounces knockwurst, cut into ¼-inch slices
2 teaspoons caraway seed
½ teaspoon salt
½ teaspoon pepper
¾ cup water
3 medium potatoes, cut into ⅛-inch slices

Trim excess fat from pork. Heat oil in 10-inch skillet until hot. Cook pork over medium heat until brown on both sides, about 15 minutes; remove pork.

Cook and stir onion, carrot, celery, pickles and knockwurst in skillet until onion is tender, about 5 minutes. Arrange pork on vegetable mixture; sprinkle with caraway seed, salt and pepper. Pour water over pork. Arrange potato slices on top. Heat to boiling; reduce heat. Cover and simmer until pork and potatoes are tender, about 45 minutes. Garnish with snipped parsley or chives if desired.

4 servings

PER SERVING: Calories 525; Protein 27 g; Carbohydrate 23 g; Fat 37 g; Cholesterol 95 mg; Sodium 820 mg

Knockwurst

Knockwurst is a fat and juicy German link sausage, commonly about 1½ to 2 inches around and about 6 inches long. Knockwurst is mildly spiced and traditionally accompanied by sauerkraut. Because knockwurst is already cooked, it needs only to be warmed through before eating.

DANISH PORK TENDERLOINS

FYLDT SVINEMØRBRAD (fewlt <u>svee</u>-neh-mewl-brahl)

In the recipe that follows, we use sweet dried prunes and apples to stuff and flavor tender pork loin. The Danes are great fans of the concentrated sweetness of rich dried fruits.

12 dried prunes
2 pork tenderloins (¾ to 1 pound each)
Salt and pepper
1 tart apple, chopped
¾ cup water
¼ cup cold water
2 tablespoons all-purpose flour
¼ teaspoon salt
⅛ teaspoon pepper

Cook prunes in boiling water 5 minutes; drain. Remove pits. Cut tenderloins lengthwise almost in half. Sprinkle cut sides with salt and pepper. Place half each of the prunes and apple down center of one side of each tenderloin; cover with the other side. Fasten with metal skewers; lace with string. Place on rack in shallow roasting pan. Insert meat thermometer horizontally so tip is in center of thickest part of pork and does not rest in stuffing. Roast in 325° oven until thermometer registers 170°, 1¼ to 1½ hours.

Remove pork to warm platter; keep warm. Add ¾ cup water to roasting pan; stir to loosen browned bits. Pour into 1-quart saucepan; heat to boiling. Shake ¼ cup water and the flour in tightly covered container; stir gradually into drippings. Heat to boiling, stirring constantly. Add ¼ teaspoon salt and ⅛ teaspoon pepper. Boil and stir 1 minute. Cut pork into slices; serve with gravy.

6 to 8 servings

PER SERVING: Calories 240; Protein 33 g; Carbohydrate 16 g; Fat 6 g; Cholesterol 105 mg; Sodium 340 mg

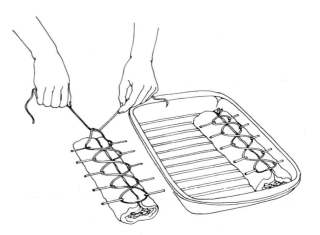

Fasten stuffed tenderloin with metal skewers; lace with string.

YUCATAN ROAST PORK

COCHINITA PIBIL (coh-chee-<u>nee</u>-tah pee-beel)

Originally this dish was prepared by the Mayans in ovens dug into the earth and lined with stones. The meat was wrapped in either seaweed or banana leaves and left to roast slowly in its own juices. Eat this succulent meat wrapped up in flour tortillas with Sweet Pickled Onions.

2 tablespoons annatto seed
18 whole black peppercorns
4 large cloves garlic, cut into fourths
½ cup orange juice
2 teaspoons ground cumin
1 teaspoon salt
¾ teaspoon dried oregano leaves
4-pound pork shoulder roast
Sweet Pickled Onions (right)
Sixteen 8-inch flour tortillas, warmed

Cover annatto seed with boiling water. Cover and let stand at least 12 hours; drain.

Place annatto seed, peppercorns, garlic, orange juice, cumin, salt and oregano in blender container. Cover and blend with on/off motions, scraping sides occasionally, until annatto seeds are chopped, about 1 minute. Make several deep cuts in pork roast. Place pork in shallow glass or plastic dish. Pour marinade over pork; rub into cuts. Cover and refrigerate at least 12 hours. Prepare Sweet Pickled Onions. Place pork and marinade in Dutch oven. Cover and cook in 325° oven, turning pork and spooning marinade over pork occasionally, until very tender, about 3 hours. Remove pork; let stand 30 minutes.

Remove bones and fat from pork; pull pork into shreds. Skim fat from marinade. Return pork to marinade. Heat to boiling; reduce heat. Cover and simmer until pork is hot, about 10 minutes. Spoon about ⅓ cup of the pork mixture onto each warm tortilla; top with Sweet Pickled Onions. Fold in sides of tortillas. Serve with Baked Plantains (page 254) if desired.

8 servings

PER SERVING: Calories 1030; Protein 62 g; Carbohydrate 54 g; Fat 64 g; Cholesterol 190 mg; Sodium 690 mg

SWEET PICKLED ONIONS

2 large onions, sliced
¼ cup vinegar
1 tablespoon sugar

Cover onions with water in skillet. Heat to boiling; reduce heat. Cover and simmer 5 minutes; drain. Mix onions, vinegar and sugar. Cover and refrigerate at least 6 hours.

Yucatan Roast Pork (showing Sweet Pickled Onions)

CITRUS-MARINATED PORK ROAST

Tender pork roast marinates in a tangy sauce of orange and lime juice, then is roasted to crisp perfection on a bed of fresh vegetables. The roasted vegetables are puréed to make a mouthwatering citrus sauce.

1 cup orange juice
¼ cup lime juice
3-pound pork boneless loin roast
3 cloves garlic, finely chopped
1 teaspoon dried oregano leaves
½ teaspoon coarsely ground pepper
1 large onion, chopped
2 stalks celery, sliced
1 large carrot, sliced
1 teaspoon salt
½ cup orange juice

Mix 1 cup orange juice and the lime juice; pour over pork roast in glass or plastic bowl. Cover and refrigerate, turning pork occasionally, at least 4 hours.

Remove pork from juice; reserve juice. Pat pork dry. Mix garlic, oregano and pepper; rub evenly over pork. Place onion, celery and carrot in shallow roasting pan; sprinkle with salt. Pour reserved juice over vegetables. Place pork on top of vegetables. Insert meat thermometer so tip is in center of thickest part of pork and does not rest in fat. Roast uncovered in 325° oven, spooning juices over pork occasionally, until thermometer registers 170°, about 2½ hours.

Remove pork; cover with aluminum foil and let stand 15 to 20 minutes before carving. Place vegetable mixture and ½ cup orange juice in blender container. Cover and blend on medium-high speed, stopping blender occasionally to scrape sides, until well blended, about 1 minute. Heat to boiling. Serve with pork.

8 to 10 servings

PER SERVING: Calories 585; Protein 42 g; Carbohydrate 9 g; Fat 43 g; Cholesterol 140 mg; Sodium 360 mg

ROAST FRESH HAM WITH ONION STUFFING

In Wales, the intrepid coal miners welcome a savory roast ham after long hours in the mines. Sweet onion stuffing tempts even the most finicky appetites.

4-pound pork boneless leg (fresh ham)
Salt
3 cups water
6 medium onions, chopped
2 cups soft bread cubes
1 egg, beaten
2 tablespoons margarine or butter
1 tablespoon dried sage leaves, crushed
1 teaspoon salt
¼ teaspoon pepper

Spread pork flat; sprinkle lightly with salt. Heat water to boiling; add onions. Cook 5 minutes; drain. Mix onions and remaining ingredients. Spread half of onion mixture on pork; roll up. Fasten with metal skewers.

Place pork, fat side down, on rack in shallow roasting pan. Spoon any remaining stuffing over top of pork. Insert meat thermometer so tip is in center of thickest part of pork and does not rest in stuffing. Roast uncovered in 325° oven until thermometer registers 170°, 3 to 3½ hours.

8 to 10 servings

PER SERVING: Calories 735; Protein 59 g; Carbohydrate 12 g; Fat 51 g; Cholesterol 240 mg; Sodium 620 mg

PORK WITH RICE AND OLIVES

ARROZ CON CARNE DE CERDO
(ar-rohs kohn kar-neh deh sehr-doh)

Though *Arroz con Carne de Cerdo* is a traditional casserole from the Dominican Republic, it hints of Africa. In Africa, highly seasoned combinations of rice and meat are common, a penchant thought to have been introduced to both Africa and the West Indies by Spanish adventurers.

1½ pounds pork boneless shoulder
¼ cup vinegar
1 medium onion, chopped
2 cloves garlic, chopped
⅛ to ¼ teaspoon crushed red pepper
3 slices bacon
2 cups boiling water
1 cup uncooked regular rice
¼ cup sliced pimiento-stuffed olives
2 tablespoons snipped parsley
1½ teaspoons salt

Trim fat from pork; cut pork into ¾-inch cubes. Mix pork, vinegar, onion, garlic, and red pepper in glass or plastic bowl. Cover and refrigerate, stirring occasionally, at least 6 hours.

Fry bacon until crisp; drain. Remove pork from marinade, reserving marinade. Cook and stir pork in bacon fat until all liquid has evaporated and pork is brown on all sides; drain. Mix pork, reserved marinade, the bacon and remaining ingredients in ungreased 2-quart casserole. Cover and cook in 350° oven until liquid is absorbed, 25 to 30 minutes.

4 servings

PER SERVING: Calories 605; Protein 51 g; Carbohydrate 41 g; Fat 27 g; Cholesterol 155 mg; Sodium 1220 mg

SPARERIBS AND CABBAGE

ZEBERKA WIEPRZOWENA Z KAPUSTA
(z'behr-kah vee-ehp-sor-vee-nah z kah-poo-stah)

The piquant flavor of caraway seed and the pungent aroma of vinegar characterize many East European dishes, especially those from Poland, where pork and cabbage dishes abound. Serve our spareribs and cabbage with mashed or boiled potatoes, if you like.

1 tablespoon vegetable oil
4½ pounds fresh pork spareribs, cut into 6 pieces
1 large onion, sliced
1 large carrot, sliced
2 teaspoons instant beef bouillon
½ teaspoon salt
½ teaspoon caraway seed
¼ teaspoon coarsely ground pepper
1 bay leaf
2 cups water
½ cup vinegar
1 small head green cabbage, cut into 6 wedges
Freshly ground pepper

Heat oil in Dutch oven until hot. Cook pork spareribs, a few pieces at a time, over medium heat until brown on all sides, about 15 minutes; drain fat. Add onion, carrot, bouillon, salt, caraway seed, ¼ teaspoon pepper and the bay leaf. Pour water and vinegar over pork mixture. Heat to boiling; reduce heat. Cover and simmer 1½ hours.

Add cabbage; sprinkle with pepper. Cover and simmer until cabbage is tender, about 45 minutes. Remove bay leaf. Arrange spareribs and vegetables on serving platter. Garnish with snipped parsley if desired.

6 servings

PER SERVING: Calories 540; Protein 30 g; Carbohydrate 12 g; Fat 43 g; Cholesterol 120 mg; Sodium 710 mg

MOU SHU PORK WITH MANDARIN PANCAKES

Mou Shu Pork is like a tiny smorgasbord inside a thin pancake. We fill our pancakes with pork strips cooked in flavorful sesame oil, along with garlic and soy sauce. Then we add a tasty sampling of Chinese vegetables: bamboo shoots, green onions and dried mushrooms.

Mandarin Pancakes (right)
1 pound pork boneless loin*
2 teaspoons soy sauce
1 teaspoon cornstarch
6 large dried mushrooms
1 tablespoon sesame or vegetable oil
2 eggs, slightly beaten
¼ teaspoon salt
2 tablespoons sesame or vegetable oil
1 can (8 ounces) bamboo shoots, drained and cut into ¼-inch strips
¼ cup water
3 tablespoons soy sauce
1 clove garlic, finely chopped
1 teaspoon sugar
1 tablespoon cold water
1 teaspoon cornstarch
2 green onions (with tops), cut diagonally into ¼-inch pieces

Prepare Mandarin Pancakes. Cut pork into slices, 2 × ⅛ inch. (For ease in cutting, partially freeze pork about 1 hour.) Stack slices; cut lengthwise into strips. Mix 2 teaspoons soy sauce and 1 teaspoon cornstarch in glass bowl; stir in pork. Cover and refrigerate 30 minutes. Soak mushrooms in warm water until soft, about 30 minutes.

Preceding pages: Spareribs and Cabbage (page 163), Apples and Potatoes (page 263) and Dark Pumpernickel Bread (page 291)

Drain mushrooms. Remove and discard stems; cut caps into thin slices. Heat 1 tablespoon oil in 10-inch skillet or wok until hot. Mix eggs and salt. Cook eggs until firm, turning once. Remove eggs; cut into thin strips.

Heat 2 tablespoons oil in skillet until hot. Cook and stir pork in oil until no longer pink. Add mushrooms, bamboo shoots, ¼ cup water, 3 tablespoons soy sauce, the garlic and sugar. Heat to boiling. Mix 1 tablespoon water and 1 teaspoon cornstarch; stir into pork mixture. Cook and stir until thickened, about 1 minute. Add egg strips and green onions; cook and stir 30 seconds.

Pour pork filling into serving bowl; arrange hot pancakes on platter. To serve, unfold each pancake and spoon about ¼ cup filling down center. Roll up; fold one end over to contain filling.

6 servings (3 pancakes each)

*1½ pounds pork chops can be substituted for the boneless pork.

PER SERVING: Calories 445; Protein 28 g; Carbohydrate 37 g; Fat 22 g; Cholesterol 140 mg; Sodium 710 mg

MANDARIN PANCAKES

2 cups all-purpose flour
¾ cup boiling water
¼ teaspoon salt
Sesame or vegetable oil

Mix flour, water and salt until dough holds together (add 2 tablespoons water if necessary); shape into a ball. Knead on lightly floured board until smooth, about 8 minutes. Shape dough into 9-inch roll; cut into 1-inch slices. Cut each slice into halves. (Cover pieces of dough with plastic wrap to prevent drying.)

Shape each piece of dough into a ball; flatten slightly. Roll each ball into 3-inch circle on lightly floured surface. Brush top of one circle with oil; top with another circle. Roll each double circle into 6- or 7-inch circle on lightly floured surface. Stack circles between pieces of waxed paper to prevent drying. Repeat with remaining pieces of dough.

Heat skillet over medium heat until warm. Cook one circle at a time in ungreased skillet, turning frequently, until pancake is blistered by air pockets and becomes slightly translucent, about 2 minutes. (Do not brown or overcook, or pancake will become brittle.) Carefully separate into 2 pancakes. Fold each pancake into fourths. (Keep covered.) Repeat with remaining pancakes.

Reheat pancakes by placing on heatproof plate or rack in steamer. Cover and steam over boiling water 10 minutes. (A steamer can be improvised by using a large skillet or wok. A plate can be supported above water on trivet or canning jar rings.)

DO-AHEAD TIP: Prepare Mandarin Pancakes, stack and cover until completely cool. Wrap in aluminum foil, label and freeze no longer than 2 weeks. Heat frozen wrapped pancakes in 325° oven 30 minutes.

Brush one circle with sesame oil; cover with another circle.

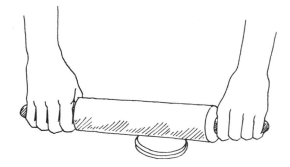

Roll two circles together into a 6-inch circle.

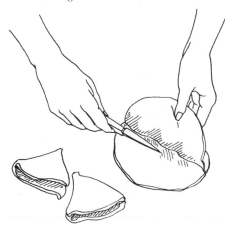

Separate cooked pancake with tip of knife into two pancakes.

PORK AND CHICKEN, FILIPINO STYLE

ADOBO (aw-<u>doh</u>-boh)

This tart pork and chicken stew is influenced by the tastes of Southeast Asia as well as by the Spanish who colonized the Philippines. From Asia comes the love of soy sauce; from Spain, the love of vinegar. Both regions adore the fragrance of garlic.

1½ pounds pork boneless shoulder
1½ pounds chicken legs or thighs
¾ cup water
⅓ cup white wine vinegar
3 cloves garlic, chopped
2 tablespoons soy sauce
1 teaspoon salt
¼ teaspoon pepper
2 tablespoons vegetable oil
4 cups hot cooked rice

Trim fat from pork; cut pork into 1-inch cubes. Heat pork, chicken, water, vinegar, garlic, soy sauce, salt and pepper to boiling in Dutch oven; reduce heat. Cover and simmer until pork and chicken are done, 45 to 55 minutes.

Remove pork and chicken from Dutch oven. Skim fat from broth if necessary. Cook broth uncovered until reduced to about 1 cup. Heat oil in 10-inch skillet until hot. Cook chicken in oil over medium heat until brown on all sides. Add pork; cook and stir until brown. Serve pork, chicken and broth over rice. Garnish with snipped parsley and tomato wedges if desired.

8 servings

PER SERVING: Calories 455; Protein 37 g; Carbohydrate 30 g; Fat 21 g; Cholesterol 115 mg; Sodium 1010 mg

FRENCH BEAN CASSEROLE WITH PORK

CASSOULET (kah-soo-<u>lay</u>)

The name *cassoulet* comes from *cassole d'Issel*, an earthenware pot in which early versions of *cassoulet* were made. Variations exist made with such country fare as partridge and goose. Our version uses meaty pork shoulder.

4 cups water
1 pound dried Great Northern or navy beans
   (about 2½ cups)
1½ pounds pork boneless shoulder
1 pound link sausage, cut into 1-inch pieces
6 slices bacon, cut into 2-inch pieces
4 medium carrots, sliced
2 medium onions, sliced
2 cloves garlic, chopped
2 bay leaves
1 can (6 ounces) tomato paste
2 teaspoons salt
½ teaspoon dried thyme leaves
½ teaspoon dry mustard
¼ teaspoon pepper
Snipped parsley

Heat water and beans to boiling in Dutch oven; boil 2 minutes. Remove from heat; cover and let stand 1 hour. Add enough water to cover beans if necessary. Heat to boiling; reduce heat. Cover and simmer until almost tender, about 1½ hours (do not boil or beans will burst). Drain, reserving liquid.

Trim fat from pork; cut pork into ¾-inch cubes. Cook and stir pork, sausage and bacon over medium heat until brown; drain. Place beans, meat mixture, carrots, onions, garlic and bay leaves in ungreased 4-quart bean pot, casserole or Dutch oven.

Add enough water to reserved bean liquid to measure 2 cups. Mix reserved liquid, the tomato paste, salt, thyme, mustard and pepper; pour over beans. Add water to almost cover mixture. Cover and cook in 325° oven, stirring occasionally, 1 hour. Uncover and cook until beans are of desired consistency, about 30 minutes. Remove bay leaves. Garnish with parsley.

8 servings

PER SERVING: Calories 695; Protein 46 g; Carbohydrate 45 g; Fat 42 g; Cholesterol 120 mg; Sodium 1560 mg

PORK WITH CORIANDER

AFELIA (ah-<u>fee</u>-l'yah)

Cypriot cuisine is marked by a preference for coriander seeds.

2 pounds pork boneless shoulder
1 tablespoon vegetable oil
1 cup dry white wine
1 tablespoon ground coriander
1 teaspoon salt
¼ teaspoon pepper
1 pound new potatoes, cut into halves
8 ounces mushrooms, cut into halves

Trim fat from pork; cut pork into 1-inch cubes. Heat oil in Dutch oven until hot. Cook pork over medium heat, stirring occasionally, until all liquid is evaporated and pork is brown, about 25 minutes; drain fat.

Stir in wine, coriander, salt and pepper. Heat to boiling; reduce heat. Cover and simmer 45 minutes. Stir in potatoes and mushrooms. Heat to boiling; reduce heat. Cover and simmer until pork and potatoes are tender, 15 to 20 minutes. Serve with Cracked Wheat Pilaf (page 269) and tossed green salad if desired.

5 servings

PER SERVING: Calories 700; Protein 46 g; Carbohydrate 21 g; Fat 49 g; Cholesterol 150 mg; Sodium 520 mg

SERBIAN SKILLET PORK

MUCKALICA (muh-<u>koll</u>-ee-kah)

This honest Yugoslavian stew is seasoned with little more than paprika and red pepper. A feta cheese topping lends it an air of simple elegance.

1½ pounds pork boneless shoulder
2 tablespoons vegetable oil
¼ cup water
3 medium onions, sliced
1 medium tomato, chopped
1½ teaspoons salt
½ teaspoon paprika
¼ teaspoon pepper
⅛ to ¼ teaspoon crushed red pepper
1 medium green pepper, cut into strips
2 ounces feta cheese, cut into ¾-inch cubes
2 cups hot cooked rice

Trim fat from pork. Cut pork into ½-inch slices; cut slices into ½-inch strips. (For ease in cutting, partially freeze pork about 1 hour.) Heat oil in 10-inch skillet until hot. Cook and stir pork in oil over medium heat until brown, about 15 minutes; drain. Add water, onions, tomato, salt, paprika, pepper and red pepper. Cover and simmer until pork is tender, about 30 minutes. (Add water if necessary.)

Add green pepper. Cover and simmer until green pepper is crisp-tender, 5 to 10 minutes. Top with cheese. Serve with rice.

4 servings

PER SERVING: Calories 810; Protein 47 g; Carbohydrate 39 g; Fat 53 g; Cholesterol 150 mg; Sodium 1430 mg

PORK STEW WITH BEER

SECO DE CHANCHO (<u>seh</u>-koh deh <u>chahn</u>-choh)

Pungent fresh cilantro, serrano chilies and fragrant spices make this beer-spiked stew from Ecuador intriguing. Accompany this dish with soothing, hot cooked rice.

2 pounds pork boneless shoulder
1 tablespoon olive or vegetable oil
1 medium onion, chopped
2 cloves garlic, finely chopped
1 can (8¼ ounces) whole tomatoes, drained
1 red serrano chili, finely chopped
2 tablespoons snipped fresh cilantro
1 teaspoon salt
1 teaspoon ground cumin
½ teaspoon dried oregano leaves
1 can or bottle (12 ounces) beer
1 large red pepper, cut into 1-inch pieces
2 cups hot cooked rice

Trim fat from pork; cut pork into 1-inch cubes. Heat oil in Dutch oven until hot. Cook pork over medium heat, stirring frequently, until all liquid is evaporated and pork is brown, about 25 minutes; remove with slotted spoon. Drain all but 2 tablespoons of fat from Dutch oven.

Cook and stir onion and garlic in Dutch oven until onion is tender. Add tomatoes, chili, cilantro, salt, cumin and oregano; break up tomatoes with fork. Heat to boiling; reduce heat. Simmer uncovered 10 minutes. Stir in pork and beer. Heat to boiling; reduce heat. Cover and simmer 45 minutes. Stir in red pepper. Heat to boiling; reduce heat. Simmer uncovered until pork is tender and sauce is thickened, about 15 minutes; skim off fat. Serve with rice.

4 servings

PER SERVING: Calories 670; Protein 56 g; Carbohydrate 41 g; Fat 31 g; Cholesterol 170 mg; Sodium 1170 mg

BURMESE CURRIED PORK

WETA HIN (weh-<u>tah</u> hin)

Traditional Burmese curries include onion, garlic, gingerroot, chili peppers and turmeric. In *Weta Hin*, these spices are enhanced by sesame oil, fish sauce and lemon grass.

2 pounds pork boneless shoulder
1 large onion, finely chopped
5 cloves garlic, finely chopped
1 tablespoon finely chopped gingerroot
1 teaspoon ground turmeric
½ teaspoon crushed red pepper
2 tablespoons vegetable oil
1 teaspoon sesame oil
1 can (16 ounces) whole tomatoes, drained
1 stalk fresh lemon grass, finely chopped
1 tablespoon fish sauce
2 cups hot cooked rice

Trim fat from pork; cut pork into 2-inch cubes. Place onion, garlic, gingerroot, turmeric and red pepper in blender container. Cover and blend on medium-high speed, stopping blender frequently to scrape sides, until smooth, about 1 minute.

Heat oils in Dutch oven over medium heat until hot. Gradually and carefully pour vegetable mixture into oil (oil will spatter). Heat to boiling; reduce heat. Cover and simmer, stirring occasionally, 15 minutes. Add pork, tomatoes, lemon grass and fish sauce; break up tomatoes with fork. Heat to boiling; reduce heat. Cover and simmer until pork is tender, about 1½ hours. Serve over rice. Garnish with snipped fresh cilantro if desired.

4 servings

PER SERVING: Calories 975; Protein 59 g; Carbohydrate 39 g; Fat 66 g; Cholesterol 185 mg; Sodium 940 mg

Burmese Curried Pork and Fresh Pineapple Compote (page 320)

PORTUGUESE PORK WITH LEMON

Lemon and garlic are as essential to Iberian cooking as curry is to Indian cooking. This stew contains a good measure of the olives that the Portuguese like so much.

2 pounds pork boneless shoulder
2 cloves garlic, chopped
2 tablespoons lemon juice
1 tablespoon olive or vegetable oil
1 teaspoon salt
¼ teaspoon ground cumin
¼ to ½ teaspoon crushed red pepper
1 tablespoon olive or vegetable oil
¼ cup water
½ cup pitted ripe olives

Trim fat from pork; cut pork into ¾-inch cubes. Toss pork, garlic, lemon juice, 1 tablespoon oil, the salt, cumin and red pepper in glass or plastic bowl. Cover and refrigerate, stirring occasionally, at least 8 hours.

Remove pork from marinade; reserve any remaining marinade. Heat 1 tablespoon oil in skillet until hot. Cook and stir pork in oil over medium heat until liquid has evaporated and pork is brown, about 25 minutes; drain. Add water and reserved marinade. Cover and simmer until pork is tender, about 30 minutes. (Add water if necessary.) Stir in olives. Serve with Green Beans in Tomato Sauce (page 236) and hot cooked rice if desired.

6 servings

PER SERVING: Calories 545; Protein 36 g; Carbohydrate 1 g; Fat 44 g; Cholesterol 125 mg; Sodium 520 mg

JELLIED PORK AND VEAL LOAF

SYLTA (sewl-tah)

Tiny pickled beets make a wonderful garnish for this Swedish smorgasbord specialty.

2 pounds pork boneless shoulder
1 pound veal or beef shanks
4 cups water
1 medium onion, cut into ½-inch slices
6 whole allspice
4 whole cloves
1 bay leaf
1 tablespoon salt
¼ teaspoon pepper
1 envelope unflavored gelatin
¼ cup cold water
1 tablespoon vinegar
1 teaspoon salt

Trim fat from pork. Heat pork, veal, 4 cups water, the onion, allspice, cloves, bay leaf, 1 tablespoon salt and the pepper to boiling in Dutch oven; reduce heat. Cover and simmer until meat is tender, about 1½ hours.

Remove meat from broth; cool meat slightly. Remove meat from bones. Finely chop meat or put through fine blade of food chopper.

Strain broth. Sprinkle gelatin over ¼ cup water in saucepan. Heat over low heat, stirring constantly, until gelatin is dissolved, about 3 minutes.

Mix meat, 2½ cups of the broth, the gelatin, vinegar and 1 teaspoon salt; pour into ungreased loaf pan, 9 × 5 × 3 inches. Cover and refrigerate until firm, at least 6 hours. Unmold onto platter; cut into slices. Garnish with celery leaves and pickled beets if desired.

6 servings

PER SERVING: Calories 650; Protein 57 g; Carbohydrate 2 g; Fat 46 g; Cholesterol 200 mg; Sodium 840 mg

CALZONE

Versatile pizza dough can be rolled and used to make savory turnovers called calzone. Plum tomatoes are a good choice for the filling; they are meaty rather than juicy and add flavor without making the pastry soggy.

Pizza Dough (below)
2 cups shredded mozzarella cheese (8 ounces)
4 ounces salami, cut into thin strips
½ cup ricotta cheese
¼ cup snipped fresh basil
2 Italian plum tomatoes, chopped
Freshly ground pepper
1 egg, slightly beaten

Prepare Pizza Dough. Heat oven to 375°. Punch down dough; divide into 6 equal parts. Roll each part into 7-inch circle on lightly floured surface with floured rolling pin.

Mound some of the mozzarella, salami, ricotta cheese, basil and tomatoes on half of each circle to within 1 inch of edge. Sprinkle each with pepper. Carefully fold dough over filling; pinch edges to seal securely. Place calzones on greased cookie sheets; brush with egg. Bake until golden brown, about 25 minutes.

6 servings

PER SERVING: Calories 415; Protein 23 g; Carbohydrate 42 g; Fat 18 g; Cholesterol 75 mg; Sodium 950 mg

PIZZA DOUGH

1 package active dry yeast
1 cup warm water (105 to 115°)
1 teaspoon sugar
1 teaspoon salt
1 tablespoon vegetable oil
2¼ to 2½ cups all-purpose flour

Dissolve yeast in warm water in large bowl. Stir in sugar, salt, oil and 1 cup of the flour. Beat until smooth. Stir in enough remaining flour to make dough easy to handle.

Turn dough onto lightly floured surface; knead until smooth and elastic, about 5 minutes. Place in greased bowl; turn greased side up. Cover; let rise in warm place until almost double, 30 to 40 minutes.

6 servings

SCOTCH EGGS

These batter-fried egg and sausage fritters can be served for breakfast, the Scottish way, or as appetizing snacks in the British fashion.

8 hard-cooked eggs, peeled
¼ cup all-purpose flour
1 pound bulk pork sausage
¾ cup dry bread crumbs
½ teaspoon ground sage
¼ teaspoon salt
2 eggs, beaten
Vegetable oil

Coat each hard-cooked egg with flour. Divide sausage into 8 equal parts. Pat one part sausage around each egg to cover. Mix bread crumbs, sage and salt. Dip sausage-coated eggs into beaten eggs; roll in bread crumb mixture.

Heat oil (1½ to 2 inches) in 3-quart saucepan to 360°. Fry eggs, 4 at a time, turning occasionally, 5 to 6 minutes; drain. Serve hot or cold.

8 servings

PER SERVING: Calories 315; Protein 14 g; Carbohydrate 11 g; Fat 24 g; Cholesterol 290 mg; Sodium 560 mg

GREEN LASAGNE WITH TWO SAUCES

LASAGNE VERDI AL FORNO
(lah-sah-n'yah vehr-dee ahl for-noh)

Lasagne Verdi is made green with fresh spinach. This is the classic dish that earned for Italy's Bologna the reputation as "the city where one dines well."

Meat Sauce (below)
Green Noodles (right) or 12 spinach lasagne noodles, cooked and drained
Cheese Filling (page 175)
Creamy Sauce (page 175)

Prepare Meat Sauce, Green Noodles, Cheese Filling and Creamy Sauce. Reserve ½ cup of the Cheese Filling. Spread 1 cup of the Meat Sauce in ungreased oblong baking dish, 13½ × 9 × 2 inches. Layer 3 lasagne noodles, ½ of the Creamy Sauce, ½ of the remaining Cheese Filling, 3 lasagne noodles and ½ of the remaining Meat Sauce; repeat. Sprinkle with reserved Cheese Filling. Cook uncovered in 350° oven until hot and bubbly, about 35 minutes. Let stand 10 minutes before cutting.

12 servings

PER SERVING: Calories 280; Protein 12 g; Carbohydrate 26 g; Fat 15 g; Cholesterol 65 mg; Sodium 830 mg

MEAT SAUCE

8 ounces bulk Italian sausage, crumbled
4 ounces smoked sliced chicken or turkey, finely chopped
1 large onion, finely chopped
1 medium stalk celery, finely chopped
1 medium carrot, finely shredded
2 cloves garlic, finely chopped
1¾ cups water
¾ cup dry red wine
⅓ cup tomato paste
½ teaspoon Italian herb seasoning
⅛ teaspoon pepper
Dash of ground nutmeg

Cook and stir sausage until light brown; drain. Stir in remaining ingredients. Heat to boiling; reduce heat. Simmer uncovered, stirring occasionally, 1 hour.

GREEN NOODLES

8 ounces fresh spinach*
2 eggs
1 tablespoon olive or vegetable oil
1 teaspoon salt
2 cups all-purpose flour
4½ quarts water
1 tablespoon salt
1 tablespoon olive or vegetable oil

Remove root ends and imperfect leaves from spinach. Wash several times in water, lifting out each time; drain. Cover and cook with just the water that clings to leaves until tender, 3 to 10 minutes.

Rinse spinach with cold water; drain. Place spinach, eggs, 1 tablespoon oil and 1 teaspoon salt in blender container. Cover and blend until puréed, about 20 seconds.

Make a well in center of flour. Add spinach mixture; stir with fork until mixed. Sprinkle with a few drops water if dry; mix in small amount of flour if sticky. Gather dough into a ball. Knead on lightly floured cloth-covered board until smooth and elastic, about 5 minutes. Let stand 10 minutes.

Divide dough into halves. Roll one half into rectangle, 13 × 12 inches; cut rectangle into 6 strips, 13 × 2 inches each. Repeat with remaining dough. Spread strips on rack; let stand 30 minutes.

Heat water to rapid boiling; stir in 1 tablespoon salt, 1 tablespoon oil and the noodles. Cook uncovered over medium heat until nearly tender, 15 to 20 minutes. Drain; rinse with cold water. Place in single layer between sheets of waxed paper.

*1 package (10 ounces) frozen spinach can be substituted for the fresh spinach. Cook as directed on package.

CHEESE FILLING

2 cups shredded mozzarella cheese
1½ cups grated Parmesan cheese
¼ cup snipped parsley

Toss cheeses and parsley.

CREAMY SAUCE

⅓ cup margarine or butter
⅓ cup all-purpose flour
1 teaspoon salt
Dash of ground nutmeg
3 cups milk

Heat margarine over low heat until melted. Blend in flour, salt and nutmeg. Cook over low heat, stirring constantly, until smooth and bubbly; remove from heat. Stir in milk. Heat to boiling, stirring constantly. Boil and stir 1 minute; cover and keep warm. (If sauce thickens, beat in small amount of milk. Sauce should be the consistency of heavy cream.)

THAI PORK AND PINEAPPLE
MA HO

The engimatic translation of *Ma Ho* is "galloping horses." This dish is an intriguing, not too spicy-hot mixture of fresh fruit and pork.

1 tablespoon vegetable oil
4 cloves garlic, finely chopped
1 pound lean ground pork
1 to 2 jalapeño peppers, finely chopped
2 tablespoons sugar
1 tablespoon fish sauce
¼ cup dry roasted peanuts, chopped
2 tablespoons snipped fresh cilantro
1 small pineapple, pared, cored and cut into
  slices
Snipped fresh cilantro

Heat oil in wok or 10-inch skillet until hot. Stir-fry garlic until light brown. Add pork; stir-fry until brown, 6 to 8 minutes. Spoon off fat. Add peppers, sugar and fish sauce; stir-fry 2 minutes. Add peanuts and 2 tablespoons cilantro; stir-fry 1 minute. Spoon pork mixture onto pineapple slices. Sprinkle with cilantro. Serve with hot cooked rice if desired.

4 servings

PER SERVING: Calories 450; Protein 24 g; Carbohydrate 25 g; Fat 29 g; Cholesterol 70 mg; Sodium 330 mg

CANADIAN PORK PIE

TOURTIÈRE (toor-t'yehr)

Tourtière is a pie that French Canadians traditionally serve following midnight Mass on Christmas Eve.

1 pound ground pork
½ pound ground beef
1 medium onion, chopped
1 clove garlic, chopped
½ cup water
1½ teaspoons salt
½ teaspoon dried thyme leaves
¼ teaspoon ground sage
¼ teaspoon pepper
⅛ teaspoon ground cloves
Egg Pastry (right)

Heat all ingredients except Egg Pastry to boiling, stirring constantly; reduce heat. Cook, stirring constantly, until meat is light brown but still moist, about 5 minutes. Prepare Egg Pastry.

Heat oven to 425°. Gather pastry into a ball; divide into halves and shape into 2 flattened rounds. Place one round on lightly floured cloth-covered board. Roll pastry 2 inches larger than inverted pie plate with floured stockinet-covered rolling pin. Fold pastry into quarters; unfold and ease into plate.

Turn filling into pastry-lined pie plate. Trim overhanging edge of pastry ½ inch from rim of plate. Roll other round of pastry. Fold into quarters; cut slits so steam can escape. Place over filling and unfold. Trim overhanging edge of pastry 1 inch from rim of plate. Fold and roll top edge under lower edge, pressing on rim to seal securely. Press firmly around edge with fork. (Dip fork into flour occasionally to prevent sticking.)

Thai Pork and Pineapple (page 175)

Cover edge with 3-inch strip of aluminum foil; remove foil during last 15 minutes of baking. Bake until crust is brown, 35 to 40 minutes. Let stand 10 minutes before cutting.

8 servings

PER SERVING: Calories 495; Protein 19 g; Carbohydrate 25 g; Fat 36 g; Cholesterol 80 mg; Sodium 710 mg

EGG PASTRY

⅔ cup plus 2 tablespoons shortening
2 cups all-purpose flour
1 teaspoon salt
1 egg, slightly beaten
2 to 3 tablespoons cold water

Cut shortening into flour and salt until particles are size of small peas. Mix egg and 2 tablespoons water; stir into flour mixture until flour is moistened (add remaining tablespoon water if needed).

IRISH STEW

Potatoes are the staple of long standing in Ireland. They make Irish Stew, rich with flavor of lamb, a substantial dish.

2 pounds lamb boneless neck or shoulder
6 medium potatoes (about 2 pounds)
3 medium onions, sliced
2 teaspoons salt
¼ teaspoon pepper
2 cups water
Snipped parsley

Trim fat from lamb; cut lamb into 1-inch cubes. Cut potatoes into ½-inch slices. Layer half each of the lamb, potatoes and onions in Dutch oven; sprinkle with half each of the salt and pepper. Repeat. Add water.

Heat to boiling; reduce heat. Cover and simmer until lamb is tender, 1½ to 2 hours. Skim fat from broth. Sprinkle with parsley. Serve in bowls with pickled red cabbage if desired.

6 servings

PER SERVING: Calories 420; Protein 45 g; Carbohydrate 29 g; Fat 14 g; Cholesterol 140 mg; Sodium 830 mg

---

Tagine

In Morocco, the word *tagine* refers to both a main course and the earthenware casserole in which it is cooked or presented. The tagine is ideal for cooking over low heat; the even heat of a charcoal fire that has burned to glowing coals is perfect for the tagine. As with most ceramic ware, it can safely be used over gas or electric heat only with the aid of a heat diffuser.

LAMB TAGINE WITH DATES
TAGINE DE MOUTON AUX DATTES
(tah-<u>jheen</u> duh moo-<u>tohn</u> oh <u>daht</u>)

The French name barely does justice to the Moroccan derivation of this dish. In Morocco, this fragrantly spiced lamb casserole would be served in an ornate domed serving dish known as a *tagine*. Couscous would be presented as an accompaniment.

3 pounds lamb boneless shoulder
2 tablespoons olive or vegetable oil
1 large onion, chopped
2 cloves garlic, finely chopped
1 teaspoon salt
½ teaspoon coarsely ground pepper
½ teaspoon ground cinnamon
¼ teaspoon saffron
2 cups water
1 tablespoon honey
1 cup whole pitted dates
1 cup whole toasted almonds
Lemon slices

Trim fat from lamb; cut lamb into 1-inch cubes. Heat oil in Dutch oven until hot. Cook and stir lamb in oil until all liquid is evaporated and lamb is brown, about 25 minutes; drain.

Stir in onion, garlic, salt, pepper, cinnamon and saffron; cook and stir over medium heat 5 minutes. Stir in water and honey. Heat to boiling; reduce heat. Cover and simmer, stirring occasionally, until lamb is tender, 1½ to 2 hours.

Stir dates into lamb mixture; simmer uncovered 5 minutes. Spoon onto platter. Garnish with almonds and lemon slices. Serve with couscous if desired.

8 servings

PER SERVING: Calories 675; Protein 42 g; Carbohydrate 24 g; Fat 47 g; Cholesterol 155 mg; Sodium 510 mg

LAMB AND POTATO CURRY

ALOO GOSHT (ah-loo gohsht)

This simple Indian curry combines lamb, potatoes and tomatoes with an aromatic blend of spices. Serve it with hot cooked rice or *Puris* (page 287).

1 large onion, chopped
6 cloves garlic, finely chopped
1 jalapeño pepper, finely chopped
¼ cup vegetable oil
1½ pounds lamb boneless shoulder, cut into
    1-inch cubes
1 can (16 ounces) whole tomatoes (with liquid)
1 tablespoon ground coriander
1 tablespoon ground cumin
2 teaspoons salt
1 teaspoon ground turmeric
1 teaspoon chili powder
3 medium potatoes, cut into fourths
2 cups water
2 tablespoons vinegar
Snipped fresh cilantro

Cook and stir onion, garlic and jalapeño pepper in oil in Dutch oven until onion is tender. Add lamb. Cook and stir over medium-high heat until lamb is light brown, about 15 minutes; drain fat. Stir in tomatoes, coriander, cumin, salt, turmeric and chili powder; break up tomatoes with fork. Heat to boiling; reduce heat. Simmer uncovered, stirring occasionally, until sauce is thick, about 15 minutes.

Add potatoes, water and vinegar. Heat to boiling; reduce heat. Cover and simmer 15 minutes. Uncover and simmer, stirring occasionally, until lamb and potatoes are tender and sauce is thickened, 15 to 20 minutes. Sprinkle with cilantro. Serve with rice and Savory Green Beans with Coconut (page 237) if desired.

6 servings

PER SERVING: Calories 470; Protein 28 g; Carbohydrate 20 g; Fat 32 g; Cholesterol 105 mg; Sodium 920 mg

SKEWERED LAMB AND VEGETABLES

SHISH KABOB (shish kuh-bahb)

In Arabic, *shish* means "skewered," and *kabob* means "meat." These succulent grilled lamb, eggplant and green pepper morsels traditionally are served on a bed of hot cooked rice or rice pilaf, accompanied by Greek olives and Bean and Sesame Seed Spread (page 35).

1 pound lamb boneless shoulder, cut into
    1-inch cubes
¼ cup lemon juice
2 tablespoons olive or vegetable oil
2 teaspoons salt
½ teaspoon dried oregano leaves
¼ teaspoon pepper
1 medium green pepper, cut into 1-inch pieces
1 medium onion, cut into eighths
1 cup cubed eggplant

Place lamb in glass or plastic bowl. Mix lemon juice, oil, salt, oregano and pepper; pour over lamb. Cover and refrigerate, stirring occasionally, at least 6 hours.

Remove lamb; reserve marinade. Thread lamb on four 11-inch metal skewers, leaving a space between each piece of meat. Set oven control to broil or 550°. Broil lamb with tops about 3 inches from heat 5 minutes. Turn; brush with reserved marinade. Broil 5 minutes longer.

Alternate green pepper, onion and eggplant on four 11-inch metal skewers, leaving space between vegetables. Place vegetables on rack in broiler pan with lamb. Turn lamb again; brush lamb and vegetables with reserved marinade. Broil kabobs, turning and brushing twice with marinade, until brown, 4 to 5 minutes. Serve with fresh fruit if desired.

4 servings

PER SERVING: Calories 305; Protein 33 g; Carbohydrate 6 g; Fat 17 g; Cholesterol 105 mg; Sodium 1150 mg

GROUND LAMB KABOBS

KABAB MASHWI (<u>kah</u>-bahb <u>mahsh</u>-wee)

These spiced minced-meat kabobs are grilled on skewers, then tucked into pocket bread for serving.

6 Pocket Breads (page 293)
1½ pounds ground lamb
1 medium onion, chopped
1 cup snipped parsley leaves
1¼ teaspoons salt
½ teaspoon coarsely ground pepper
½ teaspoon ground cumin
½ teaspoon paprika
¼ teaspoon ground nutmeg
Vegetable oil
2 medium tomatoes, chopped
4 green onions (with tops), sliced
Plain yogurt

Prepare Pocket Breads; split and keep warm. Place lamb, chopped onion, parsley, salt, pepper, cumin, paprika and nutmeg in food processor workbowl fitted with steel blade; cover and process with about 20 on/off motions until mixture forms a paste.

Divide lamb mixture into 12 equal parts. Shape each part into a roll, 5 × 1 inch. (For easy shaping, dip hands in cold water from time to time.) Place 2 rolls lengthwise on each of six 14-inch metal skewers. Brush kabobs with oil.

Grill kabobs about 4 inches from medium coals, turning 2 or 3 times, until no longer pink inside, 10 to 12 minutes. Remove kabobs from skewers; serve on Pocket Bread halves topped with tomatoes, green onions and yogurt.

6 servings

PER SERVING: Calories 455; Protein 24 g; Carbohydrate 31 g; Fat 26 g; Cholesterol 75 mg; Sodium 770 mg

Ground Lamb Kabobs, Pocket Bread (page 293) and Cracked Wheat Pilaf (page 269)

KASHMIRI LAMB MEATBALLS

KASHMIRI KOFTA KARI
(kahsh-<u>mee</u>-ree <u>kohf</u>-tah <u>kah</u>-ree)

In traditional Kashmiri cooking, *kofta* are prepared with minced lamb, as beef is not eaten. *Kofta* do not contain onion or garlic, since these are believed to stir unadvisable passions.

2 pounds ground lamb
1 tablespoon plain yogurt
2 teaspoons finely chopped gingerroot
2 teaspoons ground cumin
2 teaspoons ground coriander
1½ teaspoons salt
1 teaspoon garam masala
1 teaspoon chili powder
½ cup vegetable oil
2 cardamom pods
1 stick cinnamon
1 cup water
¼ cup plain yogurt

Mix lamb, 1 tablespoon yogurt, the gingeroot, cumin, coriander, salt, garam masala and chili powder. Shape into ovals, about 2 inches long and 1 inch thick. (For easy shaping, dip hands into cold water from time to time.)

Heat oil in 12-inch skillet until hot. Cook and stir cardamom and cinnamon 10 seconds; reduce heat to medium. Add meatballs. Cook uncovered, turning occasionally, until meatballs are brown, about 15 minutes; drain. Mix water and ¼ cup yogurt; pour over meatballs in skillet. Heat to boiling; reduce heat. Cover and simmer 10 minutes. Uncover and cook over medium heat until most of the liquid is evaporated, about 10 minutes. Remove cardamom and cinnamon. Remove meatballs with slotted spoon. Serve with basmati or white rice if desired.

8 servings (about 48 meatballs)

PER SERVING: Calories 350; Protein 18 g; Carbohydrate 2 g; Fat 30 g; Cholesterol 75 mg; Sodium 460 mg

MOUSSAKA

(moo-sah-<u>kah</u>)

This lamb and eggplant casserole is embraced by much of the Middle East, but the Greeks claim it for their own. It is a wonderfully aromatic stew, topped with a light baked custard that is sometimes made with potato.

1 large eggplant (about 2 pounds)
2 tablespoons margarine or butter
1½ pounds ground lamb or beef
1 medium onion, chopped
1 can (15 ounces) tomato sauce
¾ cup red wine or beef broth
1 tablespoon snipped parsley
2 teaspoons salt
¼ teaspoon pepper
¼ teaspoon ground nutmeg
White Sauce (right)
1 cup grated Parmesan cheese
⅔ cup dry bread crumbs
1 egg, beaten
Tomato Sauce (right)

Cut eggplant crosswise into ½-inch slices. Cook slices in small amount boiling, salted water (½ teaspoon salt to 1 cup water) until tender, 5 to 8 minutes. Drain. Heat margarine in 12-inch skillet until melted. Cook and stir lamb and onion until lamb is light brown; drain. Stir in tomato sauce, wine, parsley, salt, pepper and nutmeg. Cook uncovered over medium heat until half the liquid is absorbed, about 20 minutes. Prepare White Sauce.

Stir ⅔ cup of the cheese, ⅓ cup of the bread crumbs and the egg into meat mixture; remove from heat. Sprinkle remaining bread crumbs evenly in greased oblong baking dish, 13½ × 9 × 2 inches. Arrange half the eggplant slices in baking dish; cover with meat mixture. Sprinkle 2 tablespoons of the remaining cheese over meat

mixture; top with remaining eggplant slices. Pour White Sauce over mixture; sprinkle with remaining cheese. Cook uncovered in 375° oven 45 minutes. Prepare Tomato Sauce. Let moussaka stand 20 minutes before serving. Cut into squares; serve with Tomato Sauce.

8 servings

PER SERVING: Calories 455; Protein 26 g; Carbohydrate 31 g; Fat 28 g; Cholesterol 145 mg; Sodium 2070 mg

WHITE SAUCE

¼ cup margarine or butter
¼ cup all-purpose flour
¾ teaspoon salt
¼ teaspoon ground nutmeg
2 cups milk
2 eggs, slightly beaten

Heat margarine over low heat until melted. Blend in flour, salt and nutmeg. Cook over low heat, stirring constantly, until smooth and bubbly; remove from heat. Stir in milk. Heat to boiling, stirring constantly. Boil and stir 1 minute. Gradually stir at least ¼ of the hot mixture into eggs. Blend back into hot mixture in pan.

TOMATO SAUCE

1 medium onion, finely chopped
1 clove garlic, finely chopped
1 tablespoon olive or vegetable oil
2 cups chopped ripe tomatoes
½ cup water
1½ teaspoons salt
1 teaspoon dried basil leaves
½ teaspoon sugar
¼ teaspoon pepper
1 bay leaf, crushed
1 can (6 ounces) tomato paste

Cook and stir onion and garlic in oil in 3-quart saucepan over medium heat until onion is tender. Add remaining ingredients except tomato paste. Heat to boiling, stirring constantly; reduce heat. Simmer uncovered until thickened, about 30 minutes. Stir in tomato paste. (Add 2 to 3 tablespoons water if necessary for desired consistency.)

STUFFED GRAPE LEAVES
DOLMADES (dohl-<u>mah</u>-dehs)

Dolmades is the Greek name for a dish celebrated throughout the Middle East. These little roll-ups are bold with the flavors of mint, lemon, rice and lamb.

1 jar (9 ounces) grape leaves
4 medium onions, finely chopped
1 teaspoon salt
3 tablespoons olive or vegetable oil
1½ pounds ground lamb or beef
⅔ cup uncooked regular rice
1 teaspoon salt
¼ teaspoon pepper
1 teaspoon snipped mint leaves or ½ teaspoon
   dried mint leaves
1½ cups water
3 eggs
3 tablespoons lemon juice
Lemon slices

Wash and drain grape leaves. Cook and stir onions and 1 teaspoon salt in oil until tender, about 5 minutes. Mix half the cooked onions, the lamb, rice, 1 teaspoon salt, the pepper and mint. Place rounded measuring tablespoon meat mixture on center of double layer of grape leaves. Fold stem ends over filling; fold in sides.

Roll up tightly; place seam side down in 12-inch skillet or two 10-inch skillets. Repeat with remaining meat mixture and grape leaves. Add water and remaining cooked onions. Heat to boiling; reduce heat. Cover and simmer until tender, 50 to 55 minutes. Drain and reserve broth.

Beat eggs until thick and lemon colored, about 3 minutes. Slowly beat in lemon juice. Add enough water to broth from skillet to measure 1 cup if necessary; gradually stir into egg mixture. Pour over grape leaves. Simmer uncovered 10 to 15 minutes. Garnish with lemon slices.

8 servings

PER SERVING: Calories 305; Protein 17 g; Carbohydrate 18 g; Fat 19 g; Cholesterol 135 mg; Sodium 610 mg

DO-AHEAD TIP: Grape leaves can be stuffed, covered and refrigerated no longer than 24 hours before cooking.

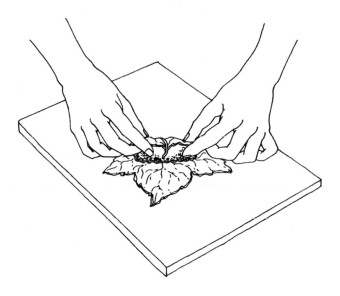

Place meat mixture on center of double layer of grape leaves; fold stem end over mixture.

STUFFED MEAT LOAF

KIBBY BIL SANIEH (<u>kib</u>-beh bil sah-<u>nay</u>-uh)

Kibby or *kibbeh*, as it is known in Arabic, is sometimes prepared as fried meatballs, which are sensational as party food. The recipe below captures all of the traditional flavors loved in *kibby* but is a quicker way to prepare what is ordinarily a time-consuming dish.

1¼ cups bulgur (cracked wheat)
1 pound ground lamb or beef
1 medium onion, finely chopped
1¾ teaspoons salt
⅛ teaspoon pepper
Stuffing (right)
2 tablespoons margarine or butter, melted

Cover bulgur with cold water; let stand 10 minutes. Drain; press bulgur to remove excess water. Mix lamb, onion, salt and pepper; add bulgur. Knead until well mixed. (Dip hands in cold water occasionally while kneading to moisten and soften mixture.) Prepare Stuffing.

Press half the lamb-bulgur mixture evenly in ungreased square pan, 8 × 8 × 2 inches. Cover with stuffing; spread remaining lamb-bulgur mixture evenly over stuffing. Cut diagonal lines across top to make diamond pattern. Pour margarine over meat loaf. Cook uncovered in 350° oven until brown, about 40 minutes. Cut into diamond shapes; serve hot or cold.

6 to 8 servings

PER SERVING: Calories 370; Protein 21 g; Carbohydrate 38 g; Fat 19 g; Cholesterol 60 mg; Sodium 720 mg

STUFFING

¼ pound ground lamb or beef
1 small onion, finely chopped
2 tablespoons pine nuts (pignolia)
⅛ teaspoon ground cinnamon
Dash of ground nutmeg

Cook and stir all ingredients until lamb is light brown, about 5 minutes.

SCOTCH BROTH

This lamb-based, barley-rich broth is a nutritious, meaty-tasting supper—comforting on a cold or stormy night.

1½ pounds lamb boneless shoulder
6 cups water
½ cup barley
1 tablespoon salt
½ teaspoon pepper
3 carrots, sliced
2 stalks celery, sliced
2 medium onions, chopped
1 cup diced rutabaga or turnip
Snipped parsley

Trim fat from lamb; cut lamb into ¾-inch cubes. Heat lamb, water, barley, salt and pepper to boiling in Dutch oven; reduce heat. Cover and simmer 1 hour.

Add vegetables to lamb mixture. Cover and simmer until lamb and vegetables are tender, about 30 minutes. Skim fat if necessary. Sprinkle with parsley.

6 servings

PER SERVING: Calories 310; Protein 35 g; Carbohydrate 22 g; Fat 11 g; Cholesterol 105 mg; Sodium 1180 mg

VEAL WITH TUNA SAUCE
VITELLO TONNATO (vee-<u>tel</u>-loh toh-<u>nah</u>-toh)

In our recipe for this Northern Italian classic, braised veal is flavored with anchovies and then covered in creamy Tuna Sauce. This is an elegant dish, true company fare.

4-pound leg of veal, boned, rolled and tied
1 can (2 ounces) anchovy fillets, drained
3 cloves garlic, sliced
2 cups dry white wine
3 stalks celery (with leaves), cut up
2 medium onions, cut into fourths
2 medium carrots, cut up
4 teaspoons instant chicken bouillon
8 black peppercorns
4 sprigs parsley
2 bay leaves
2 teaspoons salt
½ teaspoon dried thyme leaves
Tuna Sauce (right)
Snipped parsley

Make 10 to 12 deep cuts down length of meat with small knife. Cut 3 anchovy fillets into ¾-inch pieces. Cover and refrigerate remaining anchovies for Tuna Sauce. Stuff a piece of anchovy and a slice of garlic into each cut. Place meat, wine, celery, onions, carrots, bouillon, peppercorns, 4 sprigs parsley, the bay leaves, salt, thyme and enough water to cover in Dutch oven. Heat to boiling; reduce heat. Cover and simmer until meat is tender, 1½ to 2 hours. (Skim foam if necessary.) Remove from heat; cool.

Remove meat from broth; strain and reserve ¼ cup broth for Tuna Sauce. Prepare Tuna Sauce. Pat meat dry; cut into thin slices. Spoon a thin layer of Tuna Sauce into oblong baking dish 13½ × 9 × 2 inches. Arrange meat slices in sauce. Spoon remaining sauce over meat slices. Cover and refrigerate at least 3 hours. Arrange meat slices on platter; spoon Tuna Sauce over meat. Sprinkle with snipped parsley.

10 to 12 servings

PER SERVING: Calories 455; Protein 53 g; Carbohydrate 6 g; Fat 25 g; Cholesterol 230 mg; Sodium 1430 mg

TUNA SAUCE

1 can (3½ ounces) white tuna, drained
1 jar (3¼ ounces) capers, drained
½ cup olive or vegetable oil
¼ cup lemon juice
1 egg yolk
1 clove garlic
Reserved anchovies
Salt and white pepper
¼ cup whipping cream
¼ cup reserved broth

Place tuna, capers, oil, lemon juice, egg yolk, garlic and remaining anchovies in blender container. Cover and blend on low speed just until well blended, about 45 seconds. Season with salt and white pepper. Add whipping cream and reserved broth; blend on low speed just until well blended, about 30 seconds.

VEAL ROLLS, ROMAN STYLE
SALTIMBOCCA ALLA ROMANA
(sahl-teem-<u>bohk</u>-kah ahl-lah roh-<u>mah</u>-nah)

These prosciutto-filled veal steaks are so savory that they practically "jump in the mouth" (*saltimbocca*). They are sautéed with a coating of herbs, then napped with a Marsala wine sauce.

1½-pound veal boneless round steak, ½ inch thick
¼ teaspoon dried sage leaves, crushed
¼ teaspoon pepper
6 thin slices prosciutto or fully cooked smoked or boiled ham
2 tablespoons margarine or butter
1 tablespoon olive or vegetable oil
2 tablespoons all-purpose flour
½ cup Marsala wine or other dry white wine
¾ cup water
¼ teaspoon salt (optional)

Trim excess fat from veal; pound veal until ⅛ inch thick. Sprinkle one side of veal with sage and pepper; cut into 6 pieces, 4 or 5 inches square. Place ham slice on seasoned side of each piece veal. Roll up; secure with picks.

Heat margarine and oil in 10-inch skillet until hot. Cook veal rolls over high heat until brown, 5 to 10 minutes. Remove from heat. Place rolls in single layer in ungreased oblong baking dish, 10 × 6 × 2 inches.

Stir flour into drippings in skillet; stir in wine, water and salt, if desired. (The saltiness of the ham will determine whether salt is desired.) Heat to boiling; pour over rolls. Cover and cook in 325° oven until tender, 35 minutes. Garnish with parsley if desired.

6 servings

PER SERVING: Calories 185; Protein 19 g; Carbohydrate 2 g; Fat 11 g; Cholesterol 80 mg; Sodium 280 mg

KIDNEYS IN SHERRY SAUCE
RIÑONES AL JEREZ (reen-<u>yoh</u>-nehs ahl <u>heh</u>-rehz)

In Spain, kidneys are typically prepared in a sherry sauce. The sherries of Spain are legendary: smooth and rich.

½ cup milk
2 pounds veal kidneys
¼ cup olive or vegetable oil
1 medium onion, chopped
2 cloves garlic, finely chopped
2 tablespoons all-purpose flour
1 cup beef broth
¾ cup dry sherry
½ teaspoon salt
¼ teaspoon pepper
Snipped parsley
3 cups hot cooked rice

Pour milk over kidneys in glass or plastic bowl. Add enough water to cover kidneys. Cover and refrigerate 1 hour. Drain and rinse kidneys; pat dry. Cut kidneys lengthwise into halves. Remove fat and membranes with kitchen scissors. Cut kidneys into 1-inch pieces.

Heat oil in 12-inch skillet until hot. Cook and stir kidneys in oil over medium heat until brown on all sides, about 8 minutes; remove with slotted spoon. Cook and stir onion and garlic in remaining oil until onion is tender. Remove from heat; stir in flour. Gradually stir both into flour mixture. Stir in sherry, salt, pepper and kidneys. Heat to boiling, stirring constantly; reduce heat. Simmer uncovered, stirring occasionally, until kidneys are no longer pink inside and sauce is thickened, about 10 minutes. Sprinkle with parsley. Serve with hot cooked rice.

6 servings

PER SERVING: Calories 360; Protein 23 g; Carbohydrate 37 g; Fat 14 g; Cholesterol 550 mg; Sodium 770 mg

BRAISED VEAL SHANKS, MILAN STYLE

OSSO BUCO (<u>ohs</u>-soh <u>boo</u>-koh)

Milan has two sensational attractions: *Osso Buco* and Leonardo da Vinci's *Last Supper*. It is hard to tell which masterpiece outdoes the other; both are hailed by the Milanese as their own. The veal is served with a sprinkling of pungent Gremolada: lemon peel, garlic and parsley.

4 pounds veal or beef shanks
¼ cup all-purpose flour
3 tablespoons olive or vegetable oil
1 medium onion, chopped
1 medium carrot, chopped
1 stalk celery, chopped
1 clove garlic, chopped
1 bay leaf
1 cup water
½ cup dry white wine
1 teaspoon instant beef bouillon
½ teaspoon dried basil leaves
½ teaspoon salt
¼ teaspoon pepper
Gremolada (optional, right)

Trim excess fat from veal shanks if necessary. Coat veal with flour. Cook veal in oil in Dutch oven over medium heat until brown on all sides, about 20 minutes. Drain fat. Add remaining ingredients except Gremolada. Heat to boiling; reduce heat. Cover and simmer until veal is tender, 1½ to 2 hours.

Arrange veal and vegetables on platter. Skim fat from broth; pour broth over veal. Sprinkle with Gremolada if desired. Serve with Rice, Milan Style (page 273), or hot cooked spaghetti if desired.

6 servings

PER SERVING: Calories 685; Protein 77 g; Carbohydrate 8 g; Fat 39 g; Cholesterol 310 mg; Sodium 650 mg

GREMOLADA

2 tablespoons snipped parsley
1 clove garlic, finely chopped
1 teaspoon grated lemon peel

Mix parsley, garlic and lemon peel.

5

EGGS, CHEESE AND DRIED BEANS

F
ew foods are a better value than eggs, beans or cheese, in terms of both price and nutrition. Nothing beats them for versatility, as the following recipes show.

Eggs are a rich source of protein; when they are topped with cheese (as in Ranch-style Eggs) or combined with meat (as in Eggs with Peppers and Sausage), their nutritional value more than doubles. Hard-cooked, scrambled, poached or fried, the possibilities with a meal planned around eggs are limitless. Scandinavia's Smoked Fish Omelet is a must for Sunday-morning brunches, and Malaysian Omelet and Italian Zucchini Omelet, stuffed with crisp-tender vegetables, are delicious any time of day.

We have included banner recipes from around the world for those times when cheese is the order of the day. Cheese is everybody's favorite, and we take great pleasure in presenting not only international classics but uncommon, perhaps unfamiliar, cheeses as well. Try Cheese-stuffed Chilies for an unusual, tongue-tingling dish. Swiss Cheese Fondue is smooth and warming on chilly evenings, while Spinach Cheese Pie is light and ideal for summer entertaining. And, when the craving is for a hearty bean stew or bowl of hot, nourishing soup, Middle Eastern Lentil and Vegetable Stew, Dutch Split Pea Soup or creamy Cheddar Cheese Soup will fill the bill with style.

Clockwise from top: Spanish Crullers (page 345), Portuguese Herbed Potatoes (page 262) and Baked Eggs with Ham, Sausage and Peas (page 190)

BAKED EGGS WITH HAM, SAUSAGE AND PEAS

HUEVOS À LA FLAMENCA
(weh-vohs ah lah flah-mehn-kah)

Spain's Andalucía is known for its gypsy past and boldly flavored dishes. Here, vegetables and spiced meats are lightly cooked to form a base for baked eggs.

1 medium onion, finely chopped
1 clove garlic, finely chopped
1 tablespoon olive oil
1 can (16 ounces) tomatoes (with liquid)
½ teaspoon sugar
¼ teaspoon paprika
4 ounces fully cooked smoked ham, diced
1 smoked chorizo sausage (about 2 ounces), cut into ¼-inch slices
4 eggs
¼ cup cooked green peas
2 tablespoons chopped pimiento
1 tablespoon snipped parsley

Cook and stir onion and garlic in oil in 2-quart saucepan until onion is tender. Add tomatoes, sugar and paprika; break up tomatoes with fork. Heat to boiling; reduce heat. Simmer uncovered, stirring occasionally, 15 minutes.

Cook and stir ham and chorizo sausage in 8-inch skillet until sausage is done, about 5 minutes; drain. Divide tomato mixture evenly among 4 ungreased 10-ounce custard cups. Break 1 egg over mixture in each cup. Arrange ham mixture, peas and pimiento around each egg. Sprinkle with parsley. Cook uncovered in 400° oven until eggs are set, 12 to 15 minutes. Serve in custard cups.

4 servings

PER SERVING: Calories 285; Protein 17 g; Carbohydrate 11 g; Fat 19 g; Cholesterol 240 mg; Sodium 700 mg

SCRAMBLED EGGS WITH PEPPERS AND TOMATOES

PIPÉRADE BASQUAISE (peep-eh-rahd bahs-kehz)

The Basques live on either side of the border dividing Spain and France. Their version of *pipérade*—a mixture of bell pepper, tomato and egg—features a separately cooked scrambled egg mixture served on top of the vegetables.

2 medium green peppers, sliced
1 medium onion, sliced
1 clove garlic, chopped
½ teaspoon salt
½ teaspoon dried thyme leaves
3 tablespoons olive oil or margarine
2 medium tomatoes, coarsely chopped
8 eggs
½ cup milk
½ cup ¼-inch strips fully cooked smoked ham
1½ teaspoons salt
¼ teaspoon pepper

Cook and stir green peppers, onion, garlic, ½ teaspoon salt and the thyme in 1 tablespoon of the oil in 10-inch skillet over medium heat until green peppers are crisp-tender, about 8 minutes. Add tomatoes; heat until hot, about 2 minutes. Drain excess liquid from vegetables; place vegetables on platter. Keep warm.

Heat remaining oil in same skillet over medium heat until hot. Mix remaining ingredients; pour into skillet. Cook uncovered over low heat, stirring frequently, until eggs are thickened throughout but still moist, 3 to 5 minutes. Mound scrambled eggs in center of vegetables. Sprinkle with snipped parsley if desired.

4 to 6 servings

PER SERVING: Calories 330; Protein 18 g; Carbohydrate 11 g; Fat 24 g; Cholesterol 440 mg; Sodium 1380 mg

ITALIAN ZUCCHINI OMELET

FRITTATA DI ZUCCHINE
(freet-tah-tah dee dzook-kee-nee)

The top of this *frittata* is run under the broiler, eliminating the sometimes breathtaking step when an omelet must be carefully folded or turned. The Italians often use a variety of vegetables in the place of zucchini.

6 eggs
¼ cup water
3 tablespoons snipped parsley
3 tablespoons soft bread crumbs
1 teaspoon salt
1 clove garlic, finely chopped
2 tablespoons olive or vegetable oil
1 medium zucchini, cut in ¼-inch slices (about 1 cup)
All-purpose flour
2 tablespoons grated Parmesan cheese

Beat eggs, water, parsley, bread crumbs, salt and garlic. Heat oil in 8-inch broiler-proof skillet over medium heat until hot. Coat zucchini with flour; cook until golden, about 2 minutes on each side. Pour egg mixture over zucchini.

Cook until eggs are thickened throughout but still moist, 3 to 5 minutes. Gently lift edge with fork so that uncooked portion can flow to bottom. Sprinkle with cheese. Set oven control to broil or 550°. Broil omelet with top 5 inches from heat until golden brown, 3 to 4 minutes. Loosen edge with spatula; slip omelet, cheese side up, onto serving plate.

3 servings

PER SERVING: Calories 290; Protein 15 g; Carbohydrate 13 g; Fat 20 g; Cholesterol 430 mg; Sodium 950 mg

EGGS WITH PEPPERS AND SAUSAGE

These fried eggs are served over a savory sausage and vegetable preparation similar to Hungarian *lecsó*. Good-quality paprika, indispensable to the Hungarian kitchen, adds a rich, complex flavor.

1 large onion, sliced
1 pound Italian sweet peppers or banana peppers, seeded and cut into strips
¼ cup vegetable oil
2 large tomatoes, seeded and cut into wedges
1 tablespoon paprika
1 teaspoon sugar
½ pound fully cooked smoked sausage links, cut into thin slices
6 fried eggs

Cook onion and peppers in oil in 12-inch skillet, stirring occasionally, until tender, about 15 minutes. Stir in tomatoes, paprika and sugar. Cover and cook over low heat 15 minutes. Stir in sausage; cook uncovered until sausage is hot, about 5 minutes. Top with fried egg.

6 servings

PER SERVING: Calories 285; Protein 9 g; Carbohydrate 13 g; Fat 22 g; Cholesterol 190 mg; Sodium 370 mg

AUSTRIAN EGG CAKE
EIERKUCHEN (eye-er-koo-kh′n)

Here is a breakfast dish that couldn't be more easygoing. Soft bread crumbs add body.

6 eggs, beaten
1½ cups milk
1 teaspoon salt
Dash of pepper
2½ cups soft bread crumbs (see Note)
2 green onions (with tops), chopped

Mix eggs, milk, salt and pepper; stir in bread crumbs and green onions. Pour into greased square baking dish, 8 × 8 × 2 inches. Cook uncovered in 325° oven until set and top is light brown, about 40 minutes.

4 servings

PER SERVING: Calories 395; Protein 20 g; Carbohydrate 52 g; Fat 12 g; Cholesterol 330 mg; Sodium 1130 mg

NOTE: For soft bread crumbs, tear 3½ slices bread into pieces. Place in blender container, one slice at a time. Cover and blend until crumbled, about 3 seconds.

CHEESE SOUFFLÉ
SOUFFLÉ AU FROMAGE (soo-flay oh froh-mahj)

Many soufflés are easy to prepare and require little as an accompaniment. Serve this soufflé with a lightly dressed lettuce salad and some good, crusty bread.

¼ cup margarine or butter
¼ cup all-purpose flour
½ teaspoon salt
Dash of ground red pepper
1 cup milk
1 cup shredded Swiss or Gruyère cheese (4 ounces)
4 eggs, separated
¼ teaspoon cream of tartar

Heat margarine in 2-quart saucepan over low heat until melted. Blend in flour, salt and red pepper. Cook over low heat, stirring constantly until mixture is smooth and bubbly; remove from heat. Stir in milk. Heat to boiling, stirring constantly. Boil and stir 1 minute. Stir in cheese until melted; remove from heat.

Heat oven to 325°. Beat egg whites and cream of tartar in large mixer bowl until stiff but not dry. Beat egg yolks in small mixer bowl until very thick and lemon-colored, about 5 minutes; stir into cheese mixture. Stir about ¼ of the egg whites into cheese mixture. Fold cheese mixture into remaining egg whites.

Carefully pour into greased 1½-quart soufflé dish or casserole. Cook uncovered in oven until knife inserted halfway between center and edge comes out clean, 50 to 60 minutes. Serve immediately.

4 servings

PER SERVING: Calories 335; Protein 17 g; Carbohydrate 11 g; Fat 25 g; Cholesterol 240 mg; Sodium 580 mg

MALAYSIAN OMELET

TELURDADAR BIASA (teh-loor-dah-dahr bee-yah-sah)

In Malaysia this omelet is hardly a formal dish and is sometimes offered as a snack. Peanut oil will not brown excessively as butter and margarine often do with long cooking. Serve this thin omelet in wedges, as Malaysians do.

2 cups mixed thinly sliced eggplant, green
   pepper and onion
1 tablespoon peanut oil
1 medium onion, finely chopped
1 green chili, seeded and finely chopped (about
   1 tablespoon)
1 red chili, seeded and finely chopped (about
   1 tablespoon)
1 clove garlic, finely chopped
2 tablespoons peanut oil
4 eggs, beaten
¼ teaspoon salt
¼ teaspoon pepper

Cook 2 cups vegetables in 1 tablespoon oil until tender; reserve.

Cook chopped onion, chilies and garlic in 2 tablespoons oil in 10-inch skillet until tender. Mix eggs, salt and pepper; pour into skillet. Cover and cook over low heat until eggs are set and light brown on bottom, about 8 minutes. Cut eggs into wedges; spoon reserved vegetable mixture over omelet.

4 servings

PER SERVING: Calories 195; Protein 7 g; Carbohydrate 8 g; Fat 15 g; Cholesterol 215 mg; Sodium 200 mg

SMOKED FISH OMELET

This omelet is a nice way to stretch the wonderful flavor of your favorite smoked fish. The Scandinavians have long favored smoked fishes of many kinds, and fresh dill weed complements that heritage.

6 eggs
½ cup milk
1 teaspoon all-purpose flour
⅛ teaspoon pepper
2 tablespoons margarine or butter
2 tablespoons snipped dill weed
¾ pound smoked fish, cut into 6 pieces
¼ cup sliced radishes

Beat eggs, milk, flour and pepper. Heat margarine in 10-inch skillet over medium heat until hot. Pour egg mixture into skillet; sprinkle with 1 tablespoon of the dill weed.

Cook until eggs are thickened throughout but still moist, 3 to 5 minutes, gently lifting edge with fork so that uncooked portion can flow to bottom. Arrange fish on eggs; place radishes in center of eggs. Sprinkle omelet with remaining dill weed. Cut into wedges to serve.

6 servings

PER SERVING: Calories 185; Protein 21 g; Carbohydrate 3 g; Fat 10 g; Cholesterol 260 mg; Sodium 550 mg

Following pages: Smoked Fish Omelet, *right*, and Spinach-Cheese Pie (page 199)

SCRAMBLED EGGS WITH SMOKED SALMON

ÄGGRÖRA MED RÖKT LAX
(eh-guh-ruh myeht ruhkt lahx)

Salmon has a rich, assertive flavor that stands out. Serve these eggs as part of a very special Swedish breakfast.

1 tablespoon margarine or butter
4-ounce chunk smoked salmon, flaked
4 eggs
¼ cup water
¼ teaspoon pepper
1 tablespoon snipped dill weed
4 slices toast
Lemon slices
Dill weed

Heat margarine in 10-inch skillet over medium heat until hot and bubbly; cook and stir salmon 1 minute. Beat eggs, water and pepper; pour into skillet. Cook uncovered over low heat, stirring occasionally, until eggs are thickened throughout but still moist, 3 to 5 minutes; sprinkle with snipped dill weed. Serve eggs on toast; garnish with lemon slices and dill weed.

4 servings

PER SERVING: Calories 200; Protein 14 g; Carbohydrate 14 g; Fat 10 g; Cholesterol 220 mg; Sodium 450 mg

SPANISH POTATO OMELET

TORTILLA ESPAÑOLA (tohr-tee-yah ehs-pahn-yoh-lah)

In Spain the *Tortilla Española* may be had at any hour of the day, thanks to the ubiquitous *tapas* bars. In Spain, *tortilla* does not refer to the Mexican flatbread or flour or corn, but to a savory round based on potatoes or eggs.

¾ cup olive oil
4 medium potatoes, pared and cut into ⅛-inch slices (about 1½ pounds)
1 medium onion, cut into ⅛-inch slices
4 eggs
½ teaspoon salt
¼ teaspoon pepper

Heat oil in 10-inch nonstick skillet until hot; layer potato and onion slices alternately in skillet. Cook over medium-low heat, turning frequently, until potatoes are tender but not brown, about 12 minutes. Remove potatoes and onion with slotted spoon; drain, reserving 3 tablespoons oil in skillet.

Beat eggs, ¼ teaspoon of the salt and the pepper in large bowl; gently stir in potatoes and onion. Sprinkle remaining salt over potatoes. Heat oil in skillet until hot; pour egg and potato mixture into skillet. Cook uncovered over medium-low heat until potatoes begin to brown on bottom and edge of omelet is firm (center will be wet), about 7 minutes. (Shake pan occasionally to prevent omelet from sticking.) Place large plate over skillet; invert omelet on plate. Slide omelet back into skillet. Continue to cook over medium-low heat until eggs are set and potatoes are golden brown, about 2 minutes longer. Turn onto serving plate; cut into wedges to serve.

4 servings

PER SERVING: Calories 555; Protein 8 g; Carbohydrate 27 g; Fat 46 g; Cholesterol 210 mg; Sodium 340 mg

STIR-FRIED EGGS WITH MUSHROOMS

The earthy flavor of dried mushrooms is nice here with the Chinese accents of green onion, fresh ginger, rice wine and soy sauce. In the Orient, eggs are viewed not so much as a breakfast but as a vegetarian food.

3 dried black Chinese mushrooms
2 tablespoons peanut oil
½ cup sliced green onions (with tops)
1 teaspoon finely chopped gingerroot
½ cup sliced oyster mushrooms
6 eggs, beaten
2 tablespoons rice wine (sake)
1 tablespoon soy sauce
Sesame oil

Cover black mushrooms with warm water; let stand 20 minutes. Drain and rinse. Remove and discard stems from mushrooms. Cut mushrooms into thin strips; reserve.

Heat peanut oil in 10-inch skillet or wok until hot. Cook onions and gingerroot until tender; stir in reserved black mushrooms and oyster mushrooms. Mix eggs, wine and soy sauce; pour into skillet. As mixture begins to set at bottom and sides, gently lift cooked portions with spatula so that thin, uncooked portion can flow to bottom. Avoid constant stirring. Cook until eggs are thickened throughout but still moist, 3 to 5 minutes. Sprinkle with sesame oil; serve immediately.

4 servings

PER SERVING: Calories 210; Protein 10 g; Carbohydrate 6 g; Fat 16 g; Cholesterol 320 mg; Sodium 360 mg

SWISS CHEESE FONDUE

FONDUE NEUFCHÂTELOISE
(fawn-<u>doo</u> nuhf-shah-teh-<u>l'wahz</u>)

Fondue—the word comes from French for "melted"—is quintessentially Swiss. Made with dry white wine, this version is called *Neufchâteloise* for the Neufchâtel canton (region) of Switzerland, known for its white wines.

2 cups shredded natural (not process) Swiss cheese (8 ounces)
2 cups shredded Gruyère cheese* (8 ounces)
1 tablespoon cornstarch
1 clove garlic, cut into halves
1 cup dry white wine
1 tablespoon lemon juice
3 tablespoons kirsch or dry sherry
½ teaspoon salt
⅛ teaspoon white pepper
French bread, cut into 1-inch cubes

Toss cheeses with cornstarch until coated. Rub garlic on bottom and side of heavy saucepan or skillet; add wine. Heat over low heat just until bubbles rise to surface (wine should not boil). Stir in lemon juice.

Gradually add cheeses, about ½ cup at a time, stirring constantly with wooden spoon over low heat until cheeses are melted. Stir in kirsch, salt and white pepper. Remove to earthenware fondue dish; keep warm over low heat. Spear bread cubes with fondue forks; dip and swirl in fondue with stirring motion. If fondue becomes too thick, stir in ¼ to ½ cup heated wine.

4 to 6 servings

*An additional 2 cups shredded Swiss cheese can be substituted for the Gruyère cheese.

PER SERVING: Calories 570; Protein 36 g; Carbohydrate 34 g; Fat 32 g; Cholesterol 100 mg; Sodium 830 mg

ALPINE CHEESE SUPPER
RACLETTE (rah-<u>klett</u>)

This winter dish is simple: cheese, pickles, potatoes and onions. The traditional Swiss way with raclette is to place the wheel of cheese on the hearth, close enough to the fire so that the cheese begins to melt. Raclette is scraped (*racler* means "to scrape," in French) from the wheel as it melts and served with the vegetables.

2 pounds new potatoes (12 to 14)
1 pound imported Swiss raclette cheese*
Freshly ground pepper
1 jar (8 ounces) midget dill pickles or gherkins
1 jar (8 ounces) pickled cocktail onions

Heat 1 inch salted water (1 teaspoon salt to 1 cup water) to boiling. Add potatoes. Heat to boiling; reduce heat. Cover and cook until tender, 20 to 25 minutes; drain. Keep warm.

Cut cheese into 4 pieces; divide among 4 individual ovenproof casseroles. Heat in 400° oven until cheese is melted, about 10 minutes.

Place each hot casserole on a dinner plate. Sprinkle potatoes with pepper, then swirl in melted cheese. Eat the potatoes alternately with pickles and onions.

4 servings

*Other cheeses that melt smoothly and easily, such as Gruyère, Muenster, Fontina, Swiss or Monterey Jack, can be substituted for the raclette cheese.

PER SERVING: Calories 670; Protein 37 g; Carbohydrate 61 g; Fat 31 g; Cholesterol 105 mg; Sodium 920 mg

PASTA WITH THREE CHEESES
PASTA AL TRE FORMAGGI
(<u>pahs</u>-tah ahl treh for-<u>mahj</u>-jee)

Thomas Jefferson, an exceedingly well-traveled statesman for his day, brought the early American forerunner of macaroni and cheese to the United States. This Italian dish may well have inspired him. Use Fontina for more pronounced flavor.

2 tablespoons margarine or butter
2 tablespoons all-purpose flour
½ teaspoon salt
⅛ teaspoon pepper
2 cups milk
1 cup shredded Fontina or mozzarella cheese (4 ounces)
1 cup shredded Gruyère or Swiss cheese (4 ounces)
½ cup grated Parmesan cheese
10 ounces (6 cups) uncooked egg noodles
3 tablespoons dry bread crumbs
1 tablespoon margarine or butter

Heat 2 tablespoons margarine in 2-quart saucepan over low heat until melted. Blend in flour, salt and pepper. Cook over low heat, stirring constantly, until smooth and bubbly; remove from heat. Gradually stir in milk. Heat to boiling, stirring constantly. Boil and stir 1 minute. Stir in cheeses; keep warm over low heat.

Cook noodles as directed on package; drain. Alternate layers of noodles and cheese mixture in ungreased 2-quart casserole. Stir bread crumbs and 1 tablespoon margarine over medium heat until crumbs are toasted; sprinkle over noodles. Cook uncovered in 350° oven until bubbly, about 20 minutes.

8 servings

PER SERVING: Calories 330; Protein 16 g; Carbohydrate 30 g; Fat 16 g; Cholesterol 65 mg; Sodium 600 mg

NOODLE AND CHEESE CASSEROLE

LAZANKI S TVOROGOM I SMETANOI (RUSSIAN);
LOKSHYNA, ZAPECHENA Z SYROM (UKRANIAN)
(la-sahn-ki s tvo-roh-gom ee-smje-tah-noy)

The distinctive diamond shape of the pasta speaks of Russian heritage. This warming casse-role is rich with eggs and cheese.

12 ounces fresh lasagne noodles
1 pound farmer cheese
1 cup dairy sour cream
4 egg yolks
½ teaspoon salt
¼ teaspoon pepper
2 tablespoons margarine or butter
¼ cup dry bread crumbs
1 tablespoon margarine or butter

Cut lasagne noodles into diamond shapes, about 1 inch wide. Cook noodles in 3 quarts boiling water until tender, about 3 minutes, drain. Mix cheese, sour cream, egg yolks, salt and pepper in large bowl; gently stir in cooked noodles.

Heat oven to 375°. Grease 2-quart shallow casserole with 2 tablespoons margarine; sprinkle with bread crumbs. Pour noodle mixture into casserole; dot with 1 tablespoon margarine. Bake uncovered until hot, 25 to 30 minutes.

6 servings

PER SERVING: Calories 475; Protein 20 g; Carbohydrate 51 g; Fat 21 g; Cholesterol 180 mg; Sodium 600 mg

SPINACH-CHEESE PIE

SPANOKOPITA (spah-noh-koh-pit-ah)

Phyllo is an elegant Greek contribution to the food world. This pie may be cut into bite-size pieces for serving as an appetizer.

10 ounces fresh spinach (about 6 cups)
6 ounces feta cheese, crumbled (about 1 cup)
1 cup small-curd cottage cheese
1 small onion, chopped
2 tablespoons snipped parsley
2 teaspoons dried dill weed
½ teaspoon salt
3 eggs, beaten
1 tablespoon margarine or butter, softened
½ package (16-ounce size) frozen phyllo leaves, thawed
½ cup margarine or butter, melted

Wash spinach; drain and chop. Cover and cook with just the water that clings to the leaves until tender, about 3 minutes; drain. Mix spinach, feta cheese, cottage cheese, onion, parsley, dill weed and salt; stir into eggs.

Brush bottom and sides of oblong baking dish, 12 × 7½ × 2 inches, with softened margarine. Unfold phyllo leaves. Remove 10 leaves; cut crosswise into halves. (Cover completely with a sheet of waxed paper, then a damp towel to prevent drying. Wrap and refreeze remaining phyllo leaves.) Gently separate 1 half leaf; place in baking dish, folding edges over to fit bottom of dish. Brush lightly with melted margarine. Repeat 9 times.

Heat oven to 350°. Spread spinach-egg mixture evenly over phyllo leaves. Layer 10 more phyllo leaves over filling, spreading each leaf with margarine and tucking in sides around edges to cover filling. Cut through top layer of phyllo leaves with sharp knife into 6 squares. Cook uncovered until golden, about 35 minutes. Let stand 10 minutes. Cut through scored lines to serve.

6 servings

PER SERVING: Calories 405; Protein 14 g; Carbohydrate 29 g; Fat 26 g; Cholesterol 130 mg; Sodium 920 mg

EGGPLANT WITH TWO CHEESES

MELANZANE CON DUE FORMAGGI
(meh-lahn-tsah-reh kon doo-ay for-mahj-jee)

Luscious eggplant, tomato sauce and oregano are a time-honored combination that is well loved in Italy.

¼ cup olive or vegetable oil
⅓ cup all-purpose flour
¼ teaspoon garlic salt
1 medium eggplant (about 1½ pounds), cut into
 ½-inch slices
1 can (15 ounces) tomato sauce
⅓ cup grated Parmesan cheese
½ teaspoon dried oregano leaves
2 cups shredded mozzarella cheese (8 ounces)

Heat oil in 12-inch skillet until hot. Mix flour and garlic salt; coat eggplant with flour mixture. Cook over medium heat, turning once, until golden brown. (Add more oil if necessary.)

Pour half the tomato sauce into ungreased oblong baking dish, 13½ × 9 × 2 inches. Add eggplant; sprinkle with Parmesan cheese. Pour remaining tomato sauce over eggplant; sprinkle with oregano and mozzarella cheese. Cook uncovered in 325° oven until hot and bubbly, about 25 minutes.

4 servings

PER SERVING: Calories 430; Protein 22 g; Carbohydrate 27 g; Fat 26 g; Cholesterol 35 mg; Sodium 1130 mg

CHEESE-STUFFED EGGPLANT

Half of a smallish, stuffed eggplant is perfect for one serving. The Jordanian addition of peanuts to the cheese filling adds crunch and enhances the protein value of the dish.

2 small eggplants (about 1 pound each)
1 medium onion, chopped
2 cloves garlic, finely chopped
¼ cup olive or vegetable oil
8 ounces mushrooms, thinly sliced
2 medium tomatoes, cut into wedges
1 cup salted peanuts
1½ cups soft bread crumbs
2 tablespoons snipped parsley
½ teaspoon salt
½ teaspoon ground marjoram
½ teaspoon ground oregano
⅔ cup grated Parmesan cheese

Cut eggplants lengthwise into halves. Cut out and cube enough eggplant from shells to measure about 4 cups, leaving a ½-inch wall on side and bottom of each shell; reserve shells. (To remove eggplant from shell easily, cut around side with a grapefruit knife.) Cook and stir eggplant cubes, onion and garlic in oil in 10-inch skillet over medium heat 5 minutes. Add remaining ingredients except reserved shells and cheese. Cover and cook over low heat 10 minutes.

Place eggplant shells in ungreased shallow pan; spoon peanut mixture into shells. Sprinkle cheese over filled shells. Cook uncovered in 350° oven until eggplant is tender, 30 to 40 minutes.

4 servings

PER SERVING: Calories 660; Protein 23 g; Carbohydrate 57 g; Fat 38 g; Cholesterol 10 mg; Sodium 960 mg

ENCHILADAS WITH GREEN SAUCE

ENCHILADAS VERDES (ehn-chee-<u>lah</u>-dahs <u>vehr</u>-dehs)

These Mexican *enchiladas* are gently seasoned with mild green chilies. The classic recipe for green sauce is based on *tomatillos*, vegetables that look like bright, acid-green tomatoes in miniature. Spinach, more widely available in the United States, is used here.

Cheese Filling (below)
Green Sauce (right)
8 six-inch corn tortillas

Prepare Cheese Filling and Green Sauce. Heat tortillas, one at a time, in ungreased hot skillet until softened, about 30 seconds. (Cover hot tortillas to prevent drying.) Dip each tortilla into Green Sauce to coat both sides. Spoon about ¼ cup Cheese Filling onto each tortilla; roll tortilla around filling to form enchilada.

Arrange enchiladas, seam sides down, in ungreased oblong baking dish, 12 × 7½ × 2 inches. Pour remaining sauce over enchiladas. Cook uncovered in 350° oven until bubbly, about 20 minutes. Garnish with shredded Cheddar or Monterey Jack cheese and lime wedges if desired.

4 servings

PER SERVING: Calories 690; Protein 30 g; Carbohydrate 34 g; Fat 48 g; Cholesterol 130 mg; Sodium 1740 mg

CHEESE FILLING

2 cups shredded Monterey Jack cheese
  (8 ounces)
1 cup shredded Cheddar cheese (4 ounces)
1 medium onion, chopped
½ cup dairy sour cream
2 tablespoons snipped parsley
1 teaspoon salt
¼ teaspoon pepper

Mix all ingredients.

GREEN SAUCE

10 ounces fresh spinach* (about 6 cups)
2 tablespoons margarine or butter
2 tablespoons all-purpose flour
¼ teaspoon salt
½ cup milk
1½ cups chicken broth
1 to 2 tablespoons chopped canned green chilies
1 small onion, chopped
1 clove garlic, finely chopped
¾ teaspoon ground cumin
⅔ cup dairy sour cream

Wash spinach; cover and cook with just the water that clings to leaves until tender, 3 to 5 minutes. Drain and pat dry; chop coarsely.

Heat margarine over low heat until melted. Blend in flour and salt. Cook over low heat, stirring constantly, until smooth and bubbly; remove from heat. Stir in milk and ½ cup of the chicken broth; heat to boiling, stirring constantly. Boil and stir 1 minute. Stir in remaining chicken broth. Cook and stir over low heat until hot; remove from heat. Stir in spinach and remaining ingredients.

*1 packaged (10 ounces) frozen chopped spinach, cooked and well drained, can be substituted for the fresh spinach.

Cheese-stuffed Chilies

Ingredients for Cheese-stuffed Chilies

CHEESE-STUFFED CHILIES

CHILES RELLENOS (<u>chee</u>-lehs ray-<u>yeh</u>-nohs)

Poblano chilies are the perfect size for stuffing, and, though they are somewhat less sturdy when they have been blistered and peeled, they will not fall to pieces. These Mexican chilies are filled with a mixture of two cheeses, then coated with crumbs and fried.

8 poblano chilies, 3½ to 4½ inches long
8 tablespoons shredded Monterey Jack cheese
    (about 2 ounces)
8 tablespoons shredded Cheddar cheese (about
    2 ounces)
½ cup dry bread crumbs
4 eggs, separated
¼ teaspoon salt
¼ teaspoon cream of tartar
Vegetable oil
Mexican Sauce (page 207)
1 cup dairy sour cream
Snipped fresh cilantro

Set oven control to broil or 550°. Place chilies on rack in broiler pan. Broil with tops 4 to 5 inches from heat, turning frequently, until skins blister all around, up to 15 minutes. Place in plastic bags and close tightly; let stand 20 minutes. Carefully peel chilies, starting at stem end. Cut lengthwise slit down side of each chili. Carefully remove seeds and membranes; rinse. Fill each chili with 1 tablespoon Monterey Jack cheese and 1 tablespoon Cheddar cheese; coat with bread crumbs. Cover and refrigerate 20 minutes.

Beat egg whites, salt and cream of tartar in large bowl until stiff. Beat egg yolks until thick and lemon-colored, about 5 minutes; fold into egg whites. Heat 1 to 1½ inches oil to 375° in Dutch oven. Coat each chili again with bread crumbs; dip into egg mixture. Fry 1 or 2 chilies at a time, turning once, until puffy and golden brown, about 4 minutes. Drain chilies; keep warm in oven.

Prepare Mexican Sauce; pour over chilies. Garnish with sour cream and cilantro.

8 servings

PER SERVING: Calories 270; Protein 9 g; Carbohydrate 13 g; Fat 20 g; Cholesterol 140 mg; Sodium 570 mg

SPICED COTTAGE CHEESE WITH GREENS

GOMEN KITFO (goh-mehn kut-foh)

Seasoned cheese and collard greens make up this Ethiopian dish. The crunch of the greens is nice with the smooth, ginger-scented cheese.

1 carton (12 ounces) cottage cheese
2 tablespoons Ghee (page 237), margarine or
  butter
1 clove garlic, cut into halves
½ teaspoon ground cardamom
¼ teaspoon ground ginger
⅛ teaspoon ground cinnamon
⅛ teaspoon ground cloves
2 tablespoons finely chopped onion
1 green chili, seeded and finely chopped
1 to 2 teaspoons grated gingerroot
2 pounds fresh collard greens or spinach,
  coarsely chopped
2 tablespoons Ghee (page 237), margarine or
  butter

Mix cottage cheese, 2 tablespoons Ghee, the garlic, cardamom, ginger, cinnamon and cloves in medium bowl. Let stand 15 minutes; remove garlic. Cook onion, chili, gingerroot and collard greens in 2 tablespoons Ghee in Dutch oven until tender; drain. Serve collard greens over cottage cheese.

6 servings

PER SERVING: Calories 165; Protein 10 g; Carbohydrate 9 g; Fat 10 g; Cholesterol 10 mg; Sodium 420 mg

CHEDDAR CHEESE SOUP

Cheddar cheese originally came from the English town of the same name, where it was made as early as the sixteenth century. The soup is popular in Canada, New Zealand, Australia and across Great Britain. After adding the shredded cheese, be careful not to let the mixture boil, or it might separate.

1 small onion, chopped
1 medium stalk celery, thinly sliced
2 tablespoons margarine or butter
2 tablespoons all-purpose flour
¼ teaspoon pepper
¼ teaspoon dry mustard
1 can (10¾ ounces) condensed chicken broth
1 cup milk
2 cups shredded Cheddar cheese (8 ounces)
Paprika

Cover and simmer onion and celery in margarine in 2-quart saucepan until onion is tender, about 5 minutes. Stir in flour, pepper and mustard. Cook over low heat, stirring constantly until smooth and bubbly; remove from heat. Add chicken broth and milk. Heat to boiling over medium heat, stirring constantly. Boil and stir 1 minute. Stir in cheese; heat over low heat, stirring occasionally, just until cheese is melted. Sprinkle soup with paprika.

4 servings

PER SERVING: Calories 360; Protein 20 g; Carbohydrate 9 g; Fat 27 g; Cholesterol 65 mg; Sodium 920 mg

Creamy Stilton Soup and Crumpets (page 298)

CREAMY STILTON SOUP

Here is another cheese soup, rich and satisfying. Stilton cheese is the great English blue-veined cheese that ages to ivory–pale gold perfection.

½ cup finely chopped onion
½ cup finely chopped carrot
1 bay leaf
¼ cup margarine or butter
¼ cup all-purpose flour
¼ teaspoon white pepper
2 cups chicken broth
1½ cups half-and-half
1½ cups crumbled Stilton cheese (6 ounces)
Snipped parsley

Cook onion, carrot and bay leaf in margarine in 3-quart saucepan until onion and carrot are tender, about 5 minutes. Stir in flour and white pepper. Cook over low heat, stirring constantly until smooth and bubbly; remove from heat. Stir in broth and half-and-half. Heat to boiling over medium heat, stirring constantly; boil and stir 1 minute. Stir in cheese; heat over low heat, stirring constantly, just until cheese is melted. Remove bay leaf; sprinkle soup with parsley.

6 servings

PER SERVING: Calories 315; Protein 11 g; Carbohydrate 11 g; Fat 25 g; Cholesterol 50 mg; Sodium 850 mg

EGGS FLORENTINE

OEUFS À LA FLORENTINE (eu ah lah flaw-rawn-<u>teen</u>)

When a dish is styled *à la Florentine*, you may be sure that it is made with spinach. This French preparation, with a traditional Mornay Sauce (a white sauce flavored with cheese), is lovely for late breakfast or simple lunch.

1 package (10 ounces) frozen chopped spinach
Mornay Sauce (below)
4 Poached Eggs (right)
2 tablespoons grated Parmesan cheese
1 tablespoons dry bread crumbs

Cook spinach as directed on package; drain. Place spinach in ungreased shallow 1-quart baking dish; keep warm. Prepare Mornay Sauce and Poached Eggs. Place eggs on spinach. Cover with Mornay Sauce; sprinkle with cheese and bread crumbs. Set oven control to broil or 550°. Broil with top about 5 inches from heat until light brown, about 1 minute.

4 servings

PER SERVING: Calories 215; Protein 12 g; Carbohydrate 8 g; Fat 15 g; Cholesterol 240 mg; Sodium 220 mg

MORNAY SAUCE

2 teaspoons margarine or butter
2 teaspoons all-purpose flour
½ teaspoon instant chicken bouillon
Dash of ground nutmeg
Dash of ground red pepper
¾ cup half-and-half
¼ cup shredded Swiss cheese

Heat margarine in 1-quart saucepan until melted. Blend in flour, bouillon, nutmeg and red pepper. Cook over low heat, stirring constantly, until mixture is smooth and bubbly. Stir in half-and-half. Heat to boiling, stirring constantly. Boil and stir 1 minute. Add cheese; stir until cheese is melted.

POACHED EGGS

Heat water (1½ to 2 inches) to boiling; reduce to simmer. Break each egg into saucer; holding saucer close to water's surface, slip 1 egg at a time into water. Cook until desired doneness, 3 to 5 minutes. Remove eggs from water with slotted spoon.

GOUDA CHEESE AND EGG CASSEROLE

Gouda is a Dutch cheese usually found sealed in a brightly colored, waxy coating. This casserole is like a savory bread pudding, baked until the top is golden brown.

4 eggs, slightly beaten
1¼ cups half-and-half
1¼ cups soft bread crumbs
1 cup shredded Gouda cheese (4 ounces)
¾ teaspoon salt
¼ teaspoon pepper
Paprika

Mix all ingredients except paprika; pour into greased 1-quart casserole. Sprinkle with paprika. Cook uncovered in 325° oven until center is set, 45 to 50 minutes.

4 servings

PER SERVING: Calories 390; Protein 19 g; Carbohydrate 27 g; Fat 23 g; Cholesterol 270 mg; Sodium 1000 mg

RANCH-STYLE EGGS

HUEVOS RANCHEROS (<u>weh</u>-vohs rahn-<u>cheh</u>-rohs)

Strictly speaking, *huevos rancheros* means any Mexican egg dish made with tortillas. This, the most popular version, serves up fried eggs on corn tortillas with a topping of tomato–green chili sauce.

Mexican Sauce (right)
Vegetable oil
8 4-inch corn tortillas
Vegetable oil
8 eggs
Salt and pepper
1 cup shredded Monterey Jack cheese (4 ounces)

Prepare Mexican Sauce. Heat oil (⅛ inch) in 6- or 8-inch skillet until hot. Cook tortillas until crisp and light brown, about 1 minute on each side. Drain; keep warm.

Heat oil (⅛ inch) in 12-inch skillet until hot. Break each egg into measuring cup or saucer; carefully slip 4 eggs, 1 at a time, into skillet. Immediately reduce heat. Cook slowly, spooning oil over eggs until whites are set and a film forms over the yolks. (Or, turn eggs over gently when whites are set and cook to desired doneness.) Sprinkle with salt and pepper. Repeat with remaining eggs.

Spoon 1 tablespoon sauce over each tortilla; place 1 egg on each. Spoon sauce over white of eggs; sprinkle yolks with cheese.

4 servings

PER SERVING: Calories 520; Protein 23 g; Carbohydrate 24 g; Fat 37 g; Cholesterol 450 mg; Sodium 500 mg

MEXICAN SAUCE

1 medium onion, chopped
½ medium green pepper, chopped
1 clove garlic, finely chopped
1 tablespoon vegetable oil
2 cups chopped ripe tomatoes*
¼ to ½ cup chopped green chilies
5 drops red pepper sauce
½ teaspoon sugar
⅛ teaspoon salt

Cook and stir onion, green pepper and garlic in oil in 2-quart saucepan until green pepper is tender, about 5 minutes. Stir in remaining ingredients. Heat to boiling; reduce heat. Simmer uncovered until slightly thickened, about 15 minutes.

*1 can (16 ounces) tomatoes (with liquid) can be substituted for the ripe tomatoes. Break up tomatoes with fork.

CHEESE AND RICE CASSEROLE

RISO E FORMAGGIO (<u>ree</u>-soh eh fohr-<u>mahj</u>-joh)

This easy casserole features two Italian cheeses: mozzarella and Parmesan.

2 cups water
1 cup uncooked regular rice
1 teaspoon salt
½ teaspoon dry mustard
½ teaspoon red pepper sauce
¼ teaspoon pepper
1 medium onion, chopped
1 medium green pepper, chopped
2 cups shredded mozzarella or Cheddar cheese (8 ounces)
4 eggs, slightly beaten
2½ cups milk
½ cup grated Parmesan cheese

Heat water, rice, salt, mustard, red pepper sauce and pepper to boiling, stirring once or twice; reduce heat. Cover and simmer 14 minutes. (Do not lift cover or stir.) Remove from heat. Fluff rice lightly with fork; cover and let steam 5 to 10 minutes.

Lay half each of the rice, onion, green pepper and mozzarella cheese in greased oblong baking dish, 11 × 7 × 1½ inches; repeat. Mix eggs and milk; pour over rice mixture. Sprinkle with Parmesan cheese. (Casserole can be covered and refrigerated up to 24 hours at this point.) Cook uncovered in 325° oven until set, 45 to 50 minutes. Let stand 10 minutes. Cut into squares.

8 servings

PER SERVING: Calories 275; Protein 17 g; Carbohydrate 27 g; Fat 11 g; Cholesterol 130 mg; Sodium 580 mg

BEAN SOUP WITH PASTA

PASTA E FAGIOLI (<u>pahs</u>-tah eh fah-<u>joh-lee</u>)

This famous hearty soup from Italy has many variations.

5 cups water
8 ounces dried great northern or navy beans (about 1¼ cups)
1 large onion, chopped
1 large tomato, chopped, or 1 can (8 ounces) tomato sauce
2 medium stalks celery, sliced
2 cloves garlic, chopped
¼ pound salt pork, chopped (see Note)
2 teaspoons instant beef bouillon
½ teaspoon salt
¼ teaspoon pepper
½ cup uncooked macaroni (shells, bows, or elbow macaroni)
⅓ cup grated Parmesan cheese

Heat water and beans to boiling in Dutch oven; boil 2 minutes. Remove from heat; cover and let stand 1 hour.

Add onion, tomato, celery, garlic, salt pork, bouillon, salt and pepper to beans. Heat to boiling; reduce heat. Cover and simmer until beans are tender, about 2 hours (do not boil or beans will burst). Skim fat if necessary.

Stir macaroni into soup. Cover and simmer until macaroni is tender, 10 to 15 minutes. Sprinkle with cheese.

5 servings (about 1⅓ cups each)

NOTE: ¼ to ½ pound fully cooked smoked ham, chopped (1 to 2 cups), can be added with the salt pork.

PER SERVING: Calories 250; Protein 10 g; Carbohydrate 21 g; Fat 14 g; Cholesterol 20 mg; Sodium 1140 mg

CUBAN BLACK BEAN SOUP

SOPA DE FRIJOL NEGRO (<u>soh</u>-pah deh free-<u>hohl</u> <u>nay</u>-groh)

A dash of rum and dusky-tasting cumin give this version of black bean soup a hint of sophistication. Garnish each serving of this dramatically dark soup with the bright yellow and white of hard-cooked egg and chopped onions or, if preferred, finely chopped green onions.

1 cup chopped onion
3 cloves garlic, finely chopped
2 tablespoons vegetable oil
1 pound dried black beans (about 2⅔ cups)
3 cups beef broth
3 cups water
1 cup finely chopped fully cooked smoked ham
1 cup chopped green pepper
1 large tomato, chopped
¼ cup dark rum
1½ teaspoons ground cumin
1½ teaspoons dried oregano leaves
4 hard-cooked eggs, chopped
1 small onion, chopped

Cook 1 cup onion and the garlic in oil in Dutch oven until tender. Add remaining ingredients except chopped eggs and onions; heat to boiling. Boil 2 minutes; reduce heat. Cover and simmer until beans are tender, about 2 hours. Serve with chopped eggs and onions.

8 servings

PER SERVING: Calories 345; Protein 21 g; Carbohydrate 43 g; Fat 10 g; Cholesterol 120 mg; Sodium 450 mg

DUTCH SPLIT PEA SOUP

ERWTENSOEP (<u>ehrt</u>-tuhn-soop)

The Dutch like this soup very thick. Serve it with a fresh loaf of pumpernickel and some smoked Dutch cheese. Cooking the split peas with ham hocks gives them loads of added flavor.

9 cups water
1 pound dried green split peas (about 2¼ cups)
2 pounds smoked pork hocks
6 leeks, sliced
4 stalks celery (with leaves), sliced
2 cloves garlic, chopped
1½ teaspoon crushed dried savory leaves
1½ teaspoon salt
½ teaspoon pepper
½ pound cooked smoked sausage*

Heat water and peas to boiling in Dutch oven; boil 2 minutes. Remove from heat; cover and let stand 1 hour. Add remaining ingredients except sausage to peas. Heat to boiling; reduce heat. Cover and simmer until pork is tender, about 2 hours. Skim fat if necessary.

Remove pork hocks; cool slightly. Trim fat and bone from pork. Cut pork into ½-inch pieces. Stir pork and sausage into soup. Heat to boiling; reduce heat. Cover and simmer until sausage is hot, 15 minutes. Remove sausage and slice. Serve sausage with pumpernickel bread and prepared mustard if desired or return to soup.

8 servings (about 1½ cups each).

*Dutch-type smoked sausage, Polish kielbasa, knackwurst or frankfurters.

PER SERVING: Calories 540; Protein 32 g; Carbohydrate 42 g; Fat 27 g; Cholesterol 70 mg; Sodium 1480 mg

SPICY SPLIT PEAS WITH VEGETABLES

SAMBAR (sahm-bahr)

Indian *dal* is a spiced lentil, split pea, farina or dried bean mixture that is cooked almost to a smooth texture. *Sambar* takes *dal* several steps further, adding a variety of fresh vegetables. This version of *sambar* is flavored with just a sampling of the spices loved by the Indians: coriander, fenugreek, cinnamon and tamarind.

4 cups water
1 cup dried yellow split peas
2 tablespoons shredded or flaked coconut
1 teaspoon coriander seed
½ teaspoon fenugreek seed
1 stick cinnamon, ½ inch long
1 tablespoon Ghee (page 237) or vegetable oil
¼ teaspoon salt
⅛ to ¼ teaspoon cayenne pepper
3 medium carrots, diced
2 medium zucchini, diced
1 medium onion, finely chopped
1 small eggplant, diced
2 tablespoons Ghee (page 237) or vegetable oil
2 tablespoons water
1 tablespoon tamarind pulp
2 cups hot cooked rice
Snipped fresh cilantro

Heat 4 cups water and the peas to boiling in 2-quart saucepan; reduce heat. Cover and simmer 45 minutes. Cook and stir coconut, coriander, fenugreek and cinnamon in 1 tablespoon Ghee in 8-inch skillet until coconut is light brown. Remove from heat; stir in salt and cayenne pepper. Crush coconut mixture with mortar and pestle until finely ground; reserve.

Cook carrots, zucchini, onion and eggplant in 2 tablespoons Ghee in 12-inch skillet, stirring occasionally, until tender. Stir 2 tablespoons water into tamarind pulp until softened. Stir tamarind mixture, coconut mixture and peas into skillet. Cook and stir over low heat, adding water until of consistency of soup, if necessary, until hot and well blended. Serve over rice; garnish with cilantro.

6 servings

PER SERVING: Calories 315; Protein 11 g; Carbohydrate 52 g; Fat 7 g; Cholesterol 0 mg; Sodium 450 mg

---

Fenugreek

The tiny, brown seeds of the fenugreek plant are most commonly added to dishes, whether knowingly or not, in "curry powder" combinations. Commercial curry powder blends nearly always contain fenugreek, and it is a frequent component of the freshly toasted curry spices ground in Indian homes. These squarish seeds, both whole and ground, flavor foods all the way from Russia to South Africa. Fenugreek has a special affinity for fish, and it is sometimes known as "the fish herb." It has a warm, maple-like flavor.

MARINATED BLACK-EYED PEAS

SALADA DE FEIJÃO FRADE
(sah-lah-dah deh fay-jhaoh frah-deh)

This salad is a variation on the rustic Portuguese bean dishes popular around Lisbon. Marjoram is the expected herb, and we have added the fresh, citric punch of cilantro, too.

3 cups water
½ pound dried black-eyed peas (about 1½ cups)
1 cup finely chopped onion
¼ cup chopped green pepper
¼ cup olive oil
2 cloves garlic, finely chopped
2 tablespoons snipped fresh cilantro
2 tablespoons red wine vinegar
½ teaspoon salt
½ teaspoon marjoram leaves
¼ teaspoon pepper
3 hard-cooked eggs, sliced

Heat water and peas to boiling in 3-quart saucepan. Boil 2 minutes; reduce heat. Cover and simmer until tender, 50 to 60 minutes; drain. Mix peas and remaining ingredients except 1 hard-cooked egg in large bowl. Cover and refrigerate 3 hours.

Arrange remaining egg on top of mixture; sprinkle with additional snipped cilantro if desired.

5 servings

PER SERVING: Calories 320; Protein 14 g; Carbohydrate 32 g; Fat 15 g; Cholesterol 130 mg; Sodium 260 mg

LENTIL AND VEGETABLE STEW

MJEDDRAH (m'jed-duh-ruh)

Lentils come in a rainbow of colors: red, yellow, orange, green and brown. Choose any of them for this vegetable stew. Lentil soups are entrenched in the history of the Middle East; it is speculated that Esau's biblical pottage (thick vegetable soup) was made with lentils.

3 cups water
8 ounces dried lentils (about 1¼ cups)
2 medium potatoes, cut into 1-inch cubes
1 medium onion, chopped
1 stalk celery, chopped
2 cloves garlic, finely chopped
1 tablespoon finely snipped parsley
1 tablespoon instant beef bouillon
1 teaspoon salt
1 teaspoon ground cumin
2 medium zucchini, cut into ½-inch slices
Lemon wedges

Heat water and lentils to boiling in Dutch oven; reduce heat. Cover and cook until lentils are almost tender, about 30 minutes. Stir in potatoes, onion, celery, garlic, parsley, bouillon, salt and cumin. Cover and cook until potatoes are tender, about 20 minutes.

Stir in zucchini; cover and cook until zucchini is tender, 10 to 15 minutes. Serve with lemon wedges.

4 or 5 servings

PER SERVING: Calories 300; Protein 18 g; Carbohydrate 55 g; Fat 1 g; Cholesterol 0 mg; Sodium 1510 mg

SAVORY LENTILS

DAL (dul)

Dal is the perfect accompaniment to spicy-hot foods. It is popular in India and in Southeast Asia. Sometimes, as in Sri Lanka, it is served over rice to make a side dish of heartier proportions.

3 cups water
1 cup dried lentils or split peas
1 teaspoon salt
1 teaspoon ground turmeric
1 medium onion, finely chopped
2 cloves garlic, finely chopped
1 teaspoon ground cumin
¼ teaspoon ground cardamom
2 tablespoons Ghee (page 237) or vegetable oil
Lime wedges

Heat water and lentils to boiling in 2-quart saucepan. Stir in salt and turmeric. Cover and simmer until lentils are tender, about 45 minutes. Cook and stir onion, garlic, cumin and cardamom in Ghee until onion is tender; stir into lentils. Cook uncovered over low heat, stirring frequently, until thickened, 20 to 30 minutes. Serve with lime wedges.

5 servings

PER SERVING: Calories 195; Protein 10 g; Carbohydrate 25 g; Fat 6 g; Cholesterol 0 mg; Sodium 430 mg

Lentils

Dried lentils give the impression of needing the same long cooking process that most dried beans require, but that is not so. After less than an hour of cooking, they are quite tender. Lentils in cans, of course, have already been cooked and need only to be heated through. Lentils come in a rainbow of colors: yellow, orange, red, brown and green; they may be used interchangeably.

INDIAN SPICED LENTILS

DHULI MAAH KI DAAL (<u>doo</u>-lee <u>ma</u>'ah kee dahl)

This recipe for tender, separate (rather than soupy) lentils is a side dish with character. Feature it as part of an all-Indian-food menu, if you like. Just before serving, top it with crisp-fried onions.

1 medium onion, chopped
1 clove garlic, finely chopped
2 tablespoons Ghee (page 237), margarine or butter
6 ounces dried red lentils (about 1 cup)
2 tablespoons ground coriander
2 teaspoons grated gingerroot
½ teaspoon salt
¼ teaspoon ground turmeric
⅛ to ¼ teaspoon ground red pepper
2½ cups water
2 tablespoons vegetable oil
2 cups finely sliced onions

Cook chopped onion and garlic in Ghee in 2-quart saucepan until tender. Stir in remaining ingredients except water, oil and sliced onions; cook and stir over medium heat 2 minutes. Add water. Heat to boiling; reduce heat. Cover and simmer until lentils are tender and most of liquid is absorbed, about 30 minutes.

Cook onion slices in oil until crisp and dark brown. Top each serving of lentils with fried onions. Serve with Naan (page 287) if desired.

4 servings

PER SERVING: Calories 330; Protein 13 g; Carbohydrate 40 g; Fat 13 g; Cholesterol 0 mg; Sodium 340 mg

Clockwise from top: Spicy Split Peas with Vegetables (page 210), Fava Bean Rounds (page 216) and Indian Spiced Lentils

SWEDISH BROWN BEANS
BRUNA BÖNOR (brew-nah buh-nohr)

Scandinavian groceries and some of the larger supermarkets carry these beans, which look much like Mexican pink beans.

2½ cups water
½ pound dried Swedish brown beans (1 cup)
⅓ cup packed brown sugar
2 tablespoons vinegar
¾ teaspoon salt

Heat water and beans to boiling in Dutch oven; boil 2 minutes. Remove from heat; cover and let stand 1 hour.

Add enough water to cover beans if necessary. Heat to boiling; reduce heat. Cover and simmer 1 hour. Stir in remaining ingredients. Cover and simmer until beans are tender, 50 to 60 minutes. (Add a small amount water if mixture becomes dry.)

4 servings

PER SERVING: Calories 230; Protein 11 g; Carbohydrate 46 g; Fat 0 g; Cholesterol 0 mg; Sodium 410 mg

Turmeric

Turmeric is related to ginger. It is a rhizome, difficult to grind, that is most frequently purchased already in its powder form. Even small quantities of turmeric give food a bright yellow-orange color; when the color—but not the expense—of saffron is wanted, turmeric is the substitute. Turmeric gives curry mixtures their color. It has an agreeable musty flavor of its own. The use of this spice is widespread, but it is especially popular in India, Africa, Morocco and the Middle East.

AFRICAN VEGETABLE STEW
VEGETABLE BIRYANI (beer-yah-nee)

A dollop of yogurt is a nice counterpoint to the richly seasoned broth.

1 cup chopped onion
½ cup snipped parsley
2 cloves garlic, finely chopped
1 teaspoon ground cinnamon
½ teaspoon ground turmeric
½ teaspoon pepper
¼ teaspoon ground ginger
2 tablespoons margarine or butter
5 cups water
1 cup sliced carrots
½ cup dried lentils
1 cup uncooked regular rice
1 can (16 ounces) whole tomatoes (with liquid)
¾ teaspoon salt
1 package (10 ounces) frozen green peas
1 package (9 ounces) frozen sliced green beans
3 sprigs fresh mint, snipped
¾ to 1 cup plain yogurt

Cook and stir onion, parsley, garlic, cinnamon, turmeric, pepper and ginger in margarine in Dutch oven until onion is tender. Stir in water, carrots and lentils. Heat to boiling; reduce heat. Cover and cook 25 minutes.

Add rice, tomatoes and salt. Heat to boiling; reduce heat. Cover and cook 20 minutes. Stir in peas, green beans and mint. Heat to boiling; reduce heat. Cover and cook until peas and beans are tender, about 5 minutes. Serve with yogurt.

6 to 8 servings

PER SERVING: Calories 320; Protein 12 g; Carbohydrate 57 g; Fat 5 g; Cholesterol 5 mg; Sodium 510 mg

African Vegetable Stew, *top,* and Marinated Black-eyed Peas (page 211)

FAVA BEAN ROUNDS

FALAFEL (fah-<u>lah</u>-fel)

Egypt claims *Falafel* as its own, though it is popular throughout the Middle East. They are commonly eaten tucked into pocket bread.

2 cups water
1 cup dried white fava or garbanzo beans*
1 egg
1 small red onion, finely chopped
3 tablespoons snipped parsley
2 tablespoons all-purpose flour
2 teaspoons finely chopped garlic
1 teaspoon salt
1 teaspoon ground coriander
¾ teaspoon ground cumin
¼ teaspoon baking powder
Dash of ground red pepper
Vegetable oil

Heat water and beans to boiling in 2-quart saucepan; boil 2 minutes. Remove from heat; cover and let stand 1 hour. Add enough water to cover beans if necessary. Heat to boiling; reduce heat. Cover and simmer until tender, 1 to 1½ hours. Drain, reserving liquid.

Mash beans with fork; add 2 to 3 tablespoons reserved liquid if necessary. (Do not purée beans in blender or food processor.) Stir in remaining ingredients except oil. (Mixture should be thick.) Cover and let stand 1 hour.

Pinch off 1-inch pieces; shape into rounds and flatten. Let stand 30 minutes. Heat oil (2 inches) in 3-quart saucepan to 375°. Fry 4 or 5 rounds at a time in hot oil, turning once, until golden brown, 2 to 3 minutes; drain on paper towels.

4 to 6 servings

*2 cans (15 ounces each) garbanzo beans, drained (reserve liquid), can be substituted. Mash beans with fork and continue as directed.

PER SERVING: Calories 340; Protein 11 g; Carbohydrate 34 g; Fat 18 g; Cholesterol 55 mg; Sodium 580 mg

MOROCCAN GARBANZO BEANS WITH RAISINS

Turmeric gives the squash sensational yellow color. This is a dramatic dish of many textures: grains of rice and smooth squash, tender beans and chewy raisins.

1 large onion, sliced
1 medium onion, chopped
1 clove garlic, finely chopped
2 tablespoons peanut oil
1 cup diced acorn or butternut squash
1 cup chicken broth
½ cup raisins
1 teaspoon ground turmeric
1 teaspoon ground cinnamon
½ teaspoon ground ginger
1 can (15 ounces) garbanzo beans, drained
2 cups hot cooked rice

Cook onions and garlic in oil in 3-quart saucepan, stirring frequently, until tender, about 7 minutes. Add remaining ingredients except garbanzo beans and rice. Heat to boiling; reduce heat. Cover and cook until squash is tender, about 8 minutes. Stir in garbanzo beans. Serve over rice.

4 servings

PER SERVING: Calories 440; Protein 12 g; Carbohydrate 75 g; Fat 10 g; Cholesterol 0 mg; Sodium 770 mg

BAKED KIDNEY BEANS AND RICE
RIZ ET POIS ROUGES (<u>rees</u> eh pwah <u>roojh</u>)

The French influence in Haiti is not to be denied. Literally translated, *Riz et Pois Rouges* means "rice and red peas." There is nothing French, though, about the use of cumin and crushed red pepper here.

1 medium onion, chopped
2 to 4 cloves garlic, finely chopped
1 medium green pepper, chopped
2 tablespoons vegetable oil
1 cup uncooked regular rice
2 cans (15 ounces each) kidney beans, drained
4 ounces fully cooked smoked ham, diced
½ teaspoon ground cumin
¼ teaspoon salt
¼ teaspoon dried oregano leaves
⅛ to ¼ teaspoon crushed red pepper
2½ cups boiling water

Cook and stir onion, garlic and green pepper in oil until tender. Mix onion mixture and remaining ingredients in ungreased 2-quart casserole. Cover and cook in 350° oven until liquid is absorbed and rice is tender, about 55 minutes. Stir before serving.

5 to 6 servings

PER SERVING: Calories 420; Protein 19 g; Carbohydrate 63 g; Fat 10 g; Cholesterol 15 mg; Sodium 610 mg

BROILED BEAN CURD
TOFU DENGAKU (<u>toh</u>-fu dehn-<u>gah</u>-ku)

Dengaku (the Japanese name for a sort of fair) refers to any number of different foods, all of which are threaded on skewers before cooking. It harkens back both to street foods and to the stilts on which fair performers entertained the crowds. Here, tofu is marinated in a savory mixture sparked with fresh ginger.

¼ cup sake
2 tablespoons soy sauce
2 tablespoons sesame paste
1 tablespoon mirin (sweet Japanese cooking wine)
1 teaspoon grated gingerroot
1 pound firm bean curd (tofu)
Tempura Sauce (page 71), Hot Mustard Sauce (page 16) or Teriyaki sauce

Mix sake, soy sauce, sesame paste, mirin and gingerroot in ungreased oblong baking dish, 10 × 6 × ½ inches. Cut bean curd into 1-inch cubes; arrange in sake mixture. Cover; refrigerate, turning bean curd once, 1 hour. Soak six 8-inch bamboo or wooden skewers in water.

Thread 4 bean curd cubes on each skewer. Set oven control to broil or 550°. Broil bean curd with tops abut 4 inches from heat until light brown, 2 to 3 minutes; turn. Brush with marinade; broil 2 to 3 minutes. Serve with Tempura Sauce.

6 servings

PER SERVING: Calories 190; Protein 15 g; Carbohydrate 10 g; Fat 10 g; Cholesterol 0 mg; Sodium 1290 mg

6

SALADS, VEGETABLES, PASTA AND GRAINS

I n Europe, salads rarely open the meal. They are more frequently enjoyed after the main course. In addition to classic, green Athenian Salad and other traditional leafy fare, our salad selection includes the smooth and creamy salads popular in the Middle East and the Mediterranean like Cucumber Salad with mint, and Eggplant Salad, along with popular grain-based salads like Cracked Wheat and Parsley Salad from Turkey. South-of-the-border dishes like Cactus Salad, Avocado and Tomato Salad and Mexico's traditional Christmas Eve Salad attest to that region's bright and festive fare. From Asia, where lettuce is commonly steamed over broth or lightly "cooked" under a blanket of hot vegetables, we offer Indonesian Salad with spicy-sweet Coconut-Peanut Dressing.

Our collection of vegetables is a veritable greengrocer's assortment. Choose French Vegetable Ragout for a warming dish, Honeyed Carrots for sweet simplicity or Red Cabbage with Apples to make the most of pork roasts or chops. A few dishes, Bok Choy with Bean Curd and Tofu with Green Onion Sauce, for example, are substantial while others—hot and spicy Korean Vegetable Pickle, aromatic African Squash and Yams and savory Baked Plantains—make uncommon accompaniments.

Here too is a passel of easy grain and pasta side dishes. Curried Indian Fried Rice, with raisins and almonds, Polenta with Cheese, and Cracked Wheat Pilaf are but a few of the recipes featured. Fettuccine with Wild Mushrooms and Cellophane Noodles with Vegetables are brilliant stars, guaranteed to win raves.

Clockwise from top left: Prosciutto-stuffed Artichokes (page 235), Roasted Pepper Salad (page 220) and Green Rice (page 274)

ROASTED PEPPER SALAD
PIMENTOS ASSADOS (pee-mehn-tohs ah-sah-dohs)

Even in the smallest, most remote Italian trattoria, there is little question that roasted peppers will be on the menu. They are adored, not just in Italy, but all around the Mediterranean and up into Portugal (where they are known as *pimentos assados*). Blistering peppers is a small chore in return for the mouthwatering result.

6 large green, red or yellow peppers (or combination)
¼ cup olive or vegetable oil
1 tablespoon white wine vinegar
½ teaspoon salt
⅛ teaspoon coarsely ground pepper

Set oven control to broil or 550°. Arrange peppers on rack in broiler pan. Broil with tops about 5 inches from heat, turning frequently, until blistered on all sides, about 20 minutes. Place peppers in plastic bag; seal bag. Let stand until peppers can be peeled easily, about 20 minutes.

Remove skin, stems and seeds from peppers. Cut peppers into ½-inch wide strips, and place in glass or plastic bowl. Shake remaining ingredients in tightly covered jar; pour over peppers. Cover and refrigerate at least 4 hours. Remove from refrigerator 30 minutes before serving.

6 servings

PER SERVING: Calories 115; Protein 1 g; Carbohydrate 7 g; Fat 9 g; Cholesterol 0 mg; Sodium 180 mg

CRACKED WHEAT AND PARSLEY SALAD
TABOOLEY, TABULEH (tah-boo-lee)

Drain the softened bulgur thoroughly, so that the grains will absorb all the good flavor of the lemony dressing. Even such a small quantity of fresh mint as 2 tablespoons makes an exciting change from Western-style seasoning. This bulgur salad from the Middle East would benefit from a scattering of marinated olives.

¾ cup bulgur (cracked wheat)
1½ cups snipped parsley
3 medium tomatoes, chopped
⅓ cup chopped green onions (with tops)
2 tablespoons snipped fresh mint leaves, or 2 teaspoons crushed dried mint leaves
¼ cup olive or vegetable oil
¼ cup lemon juice
1 teaspoon salt
¼ teaspoon pepper

Cover bulgur with cold water; let stand 30 minutes. Drain; press out as much water as possible. Place bulgur, parsley, tomatoes, green onions and mint in glass or plastic bowl. Mix remaining ingredients; pour over bulgur mixture. Toss. Cover and refrigerate at least 1 hour. Garnish with ripe olives if desired.

6 servings

PER SERVING: Calories 210; Protein 4 g; Carbohydrate 26 g; Fat 10 g; Cholesterol 0 mg; Sodium 380 mg

NOTE: For a softer texture, cover bulgur with boiling water; let stand 1 hour.

Fresh Herb and Tomato Salad, *top* (page 226), and Cracked Wheat and Parsley Salad

ATHENIAN SALAD

SALATA ATHENAS (sah-<u>lah</u>-tah ah-<u>thee</u>-nahs)

Whether it is served as a first course or after the soup and before the main dish (Greek fashion), Athenian Salad is refreshing with the lively flavors of anchovy and feta cheese.

1 medium head lettuce
1 bunch romaine
10 radishes, sliced
1 medium cucumber, sliced
6 green onions (with tops), cut into ½-inch
  pieces
½ cup olive or vegetable oil
⅓ cup wine vinegar
1 teaspoon salt
1 teaspoon dried oregano leaves
24 Greek or ripe green olives
¼ cup crumbled feta cheese (about 1 ounce)
1 can (2 ounces) rolled anchovies with capers,
  drained

Tear lettuce and romaine into bite-size pieces. Place lettuce, romaine, radishes, cucumber and green onions in large plastic bag. Close bag tightly and refrigerate. Shake oil, vinegar, salt and oregano in tightly covered jar; refrigerate.

Just before serving, shake dressing. Add dressing and olives to vegetables in bag. Close bag tightly and shake until ingredients are well coated. Pour salad into large bowl; top with cheese and anchovies.

8 servings

PER SERVING: Calories 190; Protein 4 g; Carbohydrate 5 g; Fat 17 g; Cholesterol 10 mg; Sodium 810 mg

ITALIAN GREEN BEAN SALAD

Fresh, bright green beans—not limp and overcooked—are summer's delight. When green beans aren't available, try yellow or wax beans in their stead.

1 pound green beans
Vinaigrette Dressing (below)
Lettuce (optional)
2 medium tomatoes, cut into wedges
1 small onion, sliced
¼ cup grated Parmesan cheese
Ripe olives (optional)

Remove ends from beans. If beans are large, cut French style into lengthwise strips. Heat beans and 1 inch salted water (½ teaspoon salt to 1 cup water) to boiling. Cook uncovered 5 minutes. Cover and cook until tender, 10 to 15 minutes, French style 5 to 10 minutes; drain.

Prepare Vinaigrette Dressing. Pour over warm beans and toss. Cover and refrigerate at least 2 hours. Remove beans to lettuce-lined plate with slotted spoon. Add tomatoes and onion. Sprinkle with cheese; garnish with olives.

4 to 6 servings

PER SERVING: Calories 245; Protein 4 g; Carbohydrate 12 g; Fat 20 g; Cholesterol 5 mg; Sodium 650 mg

VINAIGRETTE DRESSING

⅓ cup olive or vegetable oil
2 tablespoons wine vinegar
1 clove garlic, chopped
1 teaspoon salt
½ teaspoon prepared dark mustard
Dash of pepper

Mix all ingredients.

FRESH MUSHROOM SALAD

SIENISALAATTI (see-ehn-ee-sah-lah-tee)

In Finland they dress just about everything with cream. Here, domestic mushrooms get their turn and are sparked with snipped fresh chives.

1 pound mushrooms, sliced
2 tablespoons snipped chives
¼ cup whipping cream or half-and-half
2 teaspoons sugar
½ teaspoon salt
Dash of pepper

Heat 1 inch salted water (½ teaspoon salt to 1 cup water) to boiling. Add mushrooms. Heat to boiling; reduce heat. Cover and simmer 1 minute. Drain and chill.

Add chives. Mix remaining ingredients. Pour over mushrooms and chives; toss. Serve in lettuce cups if desired.

4 servings

PER SERVING: Calories 85; Protein 2 g; Carbohydrate 8 g; Fat 5 g; Cholesterol 15 mg; Sodium 280 mg

Eggplant

Apparently when Europeans saw their first eggplant, they were at a loss for a name until someone pointed out that it is egg-shaped. This may seem silly; after all, the difference in size between a hen's egg and the large, meaty purple eggplant so popular here in the United States can't be overlooked. It must be remembered, though, that there are many varieties of eggplant of different sizes, from two-pounders down to the little Japanese eggplants. Store eggplant in a cool, dry place.

EGGPLANT SALAD

CAPONATA (kah-poh-nah-tah)

Eggplant, onion and tomato are given a luscious bath of flavorful olive oil with herbs in this salad. *Caponata* is popular in Italy as part of an antipasto.

1 medium eggplant (about 1½ pounds)
1 small onion, chopped
2 tablespoons white wine vinegar
1 clove garlic, chopped
½ teaspoon dried oregano leaves
½ teaspoon salt
¼ teaspoon pepper
1 medium tomato, chopped
¼ cup snipped parsley
¼ cup olive or vegetable oil

Cut eggplant into ¾-inch cubes (about 5 cups). Heat small amount salted water (½ teaspoon salt to 1 cup water) to boiling. Add eggplant. Heat to boiling; reduce heat. Cover and cook until tender, about 10 minutes; drain.

Place eggplant and onion in glass or plastic bowl. Mix vinegar, garlic, oregano, salt and pepper; pour over eggplant and onion. Toss. Stir in tomato and parsley. Cover and refrigerate at least 6 hours. Just before serving, stir in oil.

4 to 6 servings

PER SERVING: Calories 185; Protein 2 g; Carbohydrate 13 g; Fat 14 g; Cholesterol 0 mg; Sodium 750 mg

CACTUS SALAD

ENSALADA DE NOPALITOS
(ehn-sah-<u>lah</u>-dah deh noh-pah-<u>lee</u>-tohs)

No salad is more characteristic of Mexico than Cactus Salad. *Nopal* or prickly pear cactus paddles are fleshy little wedges that are delicious tossed with a vinaigrette. The dressing below features aromatic cilantro.

2 jars (11 ounces each) sliced or diced cactus
   in water, drained
2 medium tomatoes, coarsely chopped
1 small onion, chopped
2 tablespoons snipped fresh cilantro
3 tablespoons vegetable oil
4 teaspoons white wine vinegar
¼ teaspoon salt
¼ teaspoon dried oregano leaves
Dash of pepper

Place cactus, tomatoes, onion and cilantro in glass or plastic bowl. Shake remaining ingredients in tightly covered jar. Pour over vegetables; toss. Cover and refrigerate at least 4 hours. Serve on lettuce leaves if desired.

6 servings

PER SERVING: Calories 90; Protein 2 g; Carbohydrate 5 g; Fat 7 g; Cholesterol 0 mg; Sodium 380 mg

CUCUMBERS AND TOMATOES IN YOGURT

RAITA (<u>right</u>-tuh)

Raitas are cooling yogurt dishes, invented by Indian cooks who wanted relief from incendiary foods. Many *raitas* are smooth, the ingredients turned into a purée. This *Raita* has juicy pieces of summer's finest vegetables.

Cactus Salad, *top*, and Orange and Jícama Salad (page 231)

2 medium cucumbers
2 green onions (with tops), chopped
1 teaspoon salt
2 medium tomatoes, chopped
½ clove garlic, finely chopped
2 tablespoons snipped cilantro or parsley
½ teaspoon ground cumin
⅛ teaspoon pepper
1 cup plain yogurt

Cut cucumbers lengthwise into halves. Scoop out seeds; chop cucumbers. Mix cucumbers, green onions and salt; let stand 10 minutes. Add tomatoes. Mix remaining ingredients except yogurt; toss with cucumber mixture. Cover and refrigerate at least 1 hour. Drain thoroughly. Just before serving, fold in yogurt.

6 servings

PER SERVING: Calories 55; Protein 3 g; Carbohydrate 8 g; Fat 1 g; Cholesterol 5 mg; Sodium 390 mg

Nopales

These cacti are not so viciously spined as many others. The paddles (leaves) are the edible portion, a great favorite in Mexican cooking. Called *nopalitos*, they are boiled and eaten crisp-tender, dressed in salads, or served tender and hot, as a cooked vegetable. Their little spines must be removed before cooking. Look in specialty stores featuring Mexican groceries for cans of cooked *nopalitos*.

CUCUMBER SALAD WITH MINT

CACIK (chudge-chik)

The Turks have devised a delicious way to survive the searing heat waves of summer: minty salads. A splash of lemon juice makes this salad all the more refreshing.

1 cup plain yogurt
2 tablespoons finely snipped fresh mint leaves
    or ½ teaspoon dried mint leaves
1 tablespoon lemon juice
1 clove garlic, finely chopped
Dash of white pepper
1 medium cucumber, thinly sliced

Mix all ingredients except cucumber; cover and refrigerate. Just before serving, stir in cucumber. Place in serving dish; garnish with additional mint if desired.

4 servings

PER SERVING: Calories 50; Protein 3 g; Carbohydrate 7 g; Fat 1 g; Cholesterol 5 mg; Sodium 45 mg

ASIAN CUCUMBER SALAD

Lime juice, cilantro and red-hot jalapeño pepper give this salad a fiery, Thai brand.

2 tablespoons lime juice
1 tablespoon water
1 teaspoon sugar
¼ teaspoon salt
1 large cucumber, cut lengthwise into halves,
    seeded and thinly sliced

1 small onion, thinly sliced
1 red jalapeño pepper, seeded and chopped
Snipped fresh cilantro

Mix lime juice, water, sugar and salt in glass or plastic bowl. Add cucumber, onion and pepper; toss. Cover and refrigerate, stirring occasionally, at least 1 hour. Sprinkle with cilantro.

4 to 6 servings

PER SERVING: Calories 30; Protein 1 g; Carbohydrate 6 g; Fat 0 g; Cholesterol 0 mg; Sodium 140 mg

FRESH HERB AND TOMATO SALAD

SABZI KHORDAN (sahb-zee yor-den)

Choose the reddest, ripest tomatoes you can find for this variation of an Iranian dish, a celebration of summer's most tempting herbs.

3 large tomatoes, sliced
⅓ cup flat-leaf parsley or curly parsley leaves
¼ cup fresh cilantro leaves
¼ cup fresh mint leaves
2 tablespoons fresh tarragon leaves
2 green onions (with tops), thinly sliced
¼ cup crumbled feta cheese
1 cup plain yogurt

Arrange tomatoes on serving platter. Mix remaining ingredients except cheese and yogurt; sprinkle over tomatoes. Sprinkle cheese over herbs. Serve with yogurt.

6 servings

PER SERVING: Calories 65; Protein 4 g; Carbohydrate 8 g; Fat 2 g; Cholesterol 10 mg; Sodium 95 mg

AVOCADO AND TOMATO SALAD

ENSALADA DE GUACAMOLE
(ehn-sah-lah-dah deh wah-kah-moh-lay)

Central America dotes on creamy, ripe avocados. In the United States, *guacamole* is frequently an avocado purée. This salad keeps the vegetables chunky and adds a little taste of bacon.

6 slices bacon
3 tablespoons vegetable oil
1 tablespoon vinegar
½ teaspoon salt
⅛ teaspoon pepper
3 drops red pepper sauce
2 medium avocados, peeled and cubed
2 medium tomatoes, cut into ½-inch pieces
1 small onion, chopped
4 to 6 cups bite-size salad greens

Fry bacon until crisp; drain and crumble. Mix oil, vinegar, salt, pepper and red pepper sauce; pour over avocados. Toss. Stir in bacon, tomatoes and onion. Cover and refrigerate about 2 hours. Just before serving, place on salad greens with slotted spoon.

4 to 6 servings

PER SERVING: Calories 335; Protein 6 g; Carbohydrate 12 g; Fat 19 g; Cholesterol 10 mg; Sodium 440 mg

---

FRENCH POTATO SALAD

The French like to flavor their potatoes with wine, *naturellement*. The dressing includes tarragon and dark mustard, both traditional elements of an herbal vinaigrette.

6 medium potatoes (about 2 pounds)
1 clove garlic, cut into halves
¼ teaspoon instant beef or chicken bouillon
⅓ cup hot water
⅓ cup dry white wine
Tarragon Dressing (below)
3 tablespoons snipped parsley

Heat 1 inch salted water (½ teaspoon salt to 1 cup water) to boiling. Add potatoes. Heat to boiling; reduce heat. Cover and cook until tender, 30 to 35 minutes. Drain and cool.

Rub 2-quart bowl with garlic; discard garlic. Cut potatoes into ¼-inch slices; place in bowl. Dissolve bouillon in hot water; add wine. Pour over potatoes. Cover and refrigerate, stirring once or twice; drain.

Prepare Tarragon Dressing; gently toss with potatoes. Sprinkle with parsley. Garnish with tomato wedges and sliced cooked luncheon meat if desired.

4 to 6 servings

PER SERVING: Calories 285; Protein 4 g; Carbohydrate 45 g; Fat 10 g; Cholesterol 0 mg; Sodium 1110 mg

TARRAGON DRESSING

3 tablespoons olive or vegetable oil
2 tablespoons tarragon vinegar
2 teaspoons snipped chives
1 teaspoon salt
1 teaspoon dark prepared mustard
½ teaspoon dried tarragon leaves
⅛ teaspoon pepper

Shake all ingredients in tightly covered jar.

Ingredients for Peruvian Potato Salad

Peruvian Potato Salad

PERUVIAN POTATO SALAD
PAPAS À LA HUANCAINA (<u>pah</u>-pahs ah lah whan-<u>kie</u>-nah)

In Peru, the potato (or potatoes, as they have many different varieties) is lavished with attention. Here, chunks of potato are dressed with a creamy sauce of cheese and fiery serrano chilies.

1 small onion, thinly sliced and separated into
   rings
3 tablespoons lemon juice
½ teaspoon salt
⅛ teaspoon ground red pepper
1½ pounds new potatoes
2 packages (3 ounces each) cream cheese, softened and cut into ½-inch cubes
½ cup half-and-half
2 small serrano chilies, seeded and finely
   chopped
¼ teaspoon salt
¼ teaspoon ground turmeric
Bibb lettuce leaves
12 Greek olives
3 hard-cooked eggs, peeled and cut into fourths

Mix onion, lemon juice, ½ teaspoon salt and the red pepper; cover and reserve.

Heat 1 inch salted water (1 teaspoon salt to 1 cup water) to boiling. Add potatoes. Heat to boiling; reduce heat. Cover and cook until tender, 20 to 25 minutes; drain and cool. Pare potatoes; cut into fourths.

Heat cream cheese, half-and-half, chilies, ¼ teaspoon salt and the turmeric over low heat, stirring frequently, until mixture is smooth, 10 to 12 minutes.

Arrange potatoes on lettuce leaves. Spoon cheese mixture over potatoes. Drain onion; arrange on cheese and potatoes. Garnish with olives and eggs.

6 servings

PER SERVING: Calories 290; Protein 9 g; Carbohydrate 28 g; Fat 16 g; Cholesterol 150 mg; Sodium 840 mg

ONION AND TOMATO SALAD

SALATA BONJON-E-RHUMI-E-PIAZ
(sah-lah-tah bohn-john eh rooh-mee eh pee-yahz)

This Afghan salad is fresh-tasting, sprinkled with cilantro and bits of serrano chili spark.

2 large tomatoes, thinly sliced
1 medium onion, thinly sliced
1 serrano chili, seeded and finely chopped
1 clove garlic, finely chopped
2 tablespoons lemon juice
½ teaspoon salt
2 tablespoons snipped fresh cilantro

Alternate slices of tomatoes and onions on serving plate. Mix remaining ingredients except cilantro; spoon over vegetables. Sprinkle with cilantro. Cover and refrigerate at least 1 hour.

6 servings

PER SERVING: Calories 30; Protein 1 g; Carbohydrate 6 g; Fat 0 g; Cholesterol 0 mg; Sodium 190 mg

RADISH AND WATERCRESS SALAD

RADIS RÂPÉ (rah-dee rah-pay)

The French name for this salad indicates that the radishes are shredded; here, they are simply sliced to the same crunchy effect.

8 ounces watercress
3 tablespoons olive or vegetable oil
1 tablespoon white wine vinegar
¼ teaspoon salt
Freshly ground pepper
12 radishes, sliced

Remove tough stems from watercress; break sprigs into bite-size pieces. Arrange watercress on plates. Mix oil, vinegar, salt and pepper. Pour over radishes; toss. Spoon radish mixture over watercress.

6 servings

PER SERVING: Calories 70; Protein 1 g; Carbohydrate 1 g; Fat 7 g; Cholesterol 0 mg; Sodium 105 mg

TOMATO AND GREEN PEPPER SALAD

In Morocco, a salad with crunch is more likely to be made up of chunky vegetables than lettuces. This salad is almost Continental in flavor; only the jalapeño pepper and cumin give it away.

3 large tomatoes, coarsely chopped
3 medium green peppers, coarsely chopped
1 medium cucumber, seeded and coarsely chopped
1 clove garlic, finely chopped
1 jalapeño pepper, finely chopped
¼ cup snipped parsley
3 tablespoons olive or vegetable oil
1 tablespoon lemon juice
½ teaspoon salt
½ teaspoon ground cumin
⅛ teaspoon pepper

Mix all ingredients in glass or plastic bowl. Cover and refrigerate at least 4 hours.

8 to 10 servings

PER SERVING: Calories 75; Protein 1 g; Carbohydrate 7 g; Fat 5 g; Cholesterol 0 mg; Sodium 140 mg

CHRISTMAS EVE SALAD

ENSALADA DE NOCHE BUENA
(ehn-sah-lah-dah deh noh-chay bway-nah)

Christmas is a high celebration in Mexico. This festive, brilliantly colored salad is an example of that exuberance. The vegetables take on a rosy hue, thanks to the beet juice.

2 medium oranges, pared and sectioned
2 medium bananas, sliced
1 can (8¼ ounces) sliced beets, drained (reserve liquid)
1 can (8 ounces) pineapple chunks in juice, drained (reserve juice)
½ jícama, pared and sliced, or 1 can (8 ounces) water chestnuts, drained and sliced
2 tablespoons lemon juice
2 tablespoons sugar
½ teaspoon salt
3 cups shredded lettuce
1 lime, cut into wedges
¼ cup chopped peanuts
⅓ cup pomegranate seeds or sliced radishes
1 tablespoon anise seed
1 tablespoon sugar

Place oranges, bananas, beets, pineapple and jícama in bowl. Mix reserved beet liquid, pineapple juice, the lemon juice, 2 tablespoons sugar and the salt; pour over fruit. Let stand 10 minutes; drain.

Arrange fruit on shredded lettuce. Garnish with lime, peanuts and pomegranate seeds. Mix anise seed and 1 tablespoon sugar; sprinkle over salad.

8 to 10 servings

PER SERVING: Calories 150; Protein 3 g; Carbohydrate 28 g; Fat 3 g; Cholesterol 0 mg; Sodium 200 mg

ORANGE AND JÍCAMA SALAD

PICO DE GALLO NARANJAS (pee-koh deh guy-yoh nah-rahn-hahs)

The Southwest loves its oranges and jícama, and this salad from Mexico adds sweet red onion to that crisp-juicy combination.

3 tablespoons vegetable oil
2 tablespoons vinegar
½ teaspoon salt
3 medium oranges, pared and sectioned
1 small red onion, thinly sliced and separated into rings
1 medium green, red or yellow pepper, cut into 1-inch pieces
8 ounces jícama, pared and cut into 1½ × ½-inch strips
Chili powder or paprika

Mix oil, vinegar and salt in large bowl. Add remaining ingredients except chili powder; toss. Sprinkle lightly with chili powder. Serve on lettuce leaves if desired.

6 to 8 servings

PER SERVING: Calories 120; Protein 1 g; Carbohydrate 13 g; Fat 7 g; Cholesterol 0 mg; Sodium 180 mg

INDONESIAN SALAD

GADO-GADO (<u>gah</u>-doh <u>gah</u>-doh)

Indonesia was historically a stopping point for explorers and trade ships, and her cuisine reflects the influence of other cultures.

Coconut-Peanut Dressing (below)
1 cup bean sprouts
1 cup shredded cabbage
4 ounces bean curd (tofu), drained and cut into 1-inch pieces
2 tablespoons peanut or vegetable oil
1 cup sliced cooked potatoes
1 cup cooked cut green beans
1 cup cooked sliced carrots
1 medium cucumber, sliced
2 hard-cooked eggs, peeled and sliced

Prepare Coconut-Peanut Dressing. Pour enough boiling water over bean sprouts and cabbage to cover; let stand 2 minutes. Drain.

Cook bean curd in oil in 10-inch skillet over medium heat, turning pieces gently, until light brown. Remove with slotted spoon; drain. Cook potatoes in same skillet until light brown; drain.

Arrange bean sprouts, cabbage, bean curd, potatoes and remaining ingredients on platter. Pour dressing over salad.

6 to 8 servings

PER SERVING: Calories 380; Protein 14 g; Carbohydrate 25 g; Fat 25 g; Cholesterol 70 mg; Sodium 380 mg

COCONUT-PEANUT DRESSING

½ cup flaked coconut
1 cup hot water
1 small onion, chopped
1 clove garlic, finely chopped

Indonesian Salad with Coconut-Peanut Dressing

1½ teaspoons peanut oil or Ghee (page 237)
⅔ cup peanut butter
½ cup water
1 tablespoon sugar
½ teaspoon salt
¼ to ½ teaspoon chili powder
⅛ teaspoon ground ginger

Place coconut in blender container; add 1 cup water. Cover and blend on high speed about 30 seconds.

Cook and stir onion and garlic in oil in 2-quart saucepan about 5 minutes. Stir in coconut and remaining ingredients. Heat to boiling, stirring constantly; reduce heat. Simmer uncovered, stirring occasionally, until slightly thickened, about 3 minutes. Serve warm.

Coconut Milk

The liquid inside a coconut is not coconut milk. Coconut milk is made from the fresh coconut meat, shredded and blended with hot water, then strained. A less concentrated milk can be made by repeating the process with the used coconut meat. It is possible to make coconut milk with dried, unsweetened coconut, too. The dried flakes are heated in a mixture of whole milk and water, cooled and blended, then strained as above. Coconut milk is rich. Store freshly made coconut milk in the refrigerator, tightly covered; a rich coconut cream will rise to the top in a few hours. The cream may be skimmed for an exceptionally rich treat, or it may be mixed back into the milk before using.

Thai cooking is known for its lavish use of coconut and coconut milk, but both are prized ingredients wherever the coconut palm is a native.

ORANGE SALAD WITH ONION AND OLIVES

Orange salads are beloved of many cultures, and this one, with its wafer-thin onion rings and juicy olives, is no exception. This dramatic-looking dish could be found anywhere in North Africa and the Middle East.

2 large oranges, pared and thinly sliced
2 cups shredded lettuce
1 large onion, thinly sliced
8 Greek olives, sliced
2 tablespoons olive or vegetable oil
2 tablespoons lemon juice
⅛ teaspoon salt
Dash of ground red pepper

Arrange orange slices on lettuce; top with onion and olives. Shake remaining ingredients in tightly covered container; drizzle over salad.

4 servings

PER SERVING: Calories 140; Protein 2 g; Carbohydrate 15 g; Fat 8 g; Cholesterol 0 mg; Sodium 260 mg

FRUIT AND CABBAGE SALAD

KÅL-OCH APPELSALLAD (kohl-oh eppel-sah-lahd)

Shreds of cabbage nestle lightly dressed fresh fruit in this Scandinavian salad.

2 oranges, pared and sectioned
2 apples, chopped
2 cups shredded green cabbage (about ¼ medium head)
1 cup seedless green grapes
½ cup whipping cream
1 tablespoon sugar
1 tablespoon lemon juice
¼ teaspoon salt
¼ cup mayonnaise or salad dressing

Place oranges, apples, cabbage and grapes in bowl. Beat whipping cream in chilled bowl until stiff. Fold whipped cream, sugar, lemon juice and salt into mayonnaise. Stir into fruit mixture.

6 servings

PER SERVING: Calories 285; Protein 1 g; Carbohydrate 21 g; Fat 22 g; Cholesterol 30 mg; Sodium 210 mg

PINEAPPLE SALAD

This fresh pineapple salad is drenched with the sweet-salty flavor that Thailand is famed for.

⅓ cup olive or vegetable oil
2 tablespoons lemon juice
1 tablespoon soy sauce
1 to 2 teaspoons packed brown sugar
1 small pineapple
1 tart red apple, diced
3 green onions (with tops), sliced
1 small bunch romaine, shredded

Shake oil, lemon juice, soy sauce and brown sugar in tightly covered jar. Cut top off pineapple; cut pineapple into fourths. Cut fruit from rind; remove core and any "eyes." Slice each fourth lengthwise; cut crosswise into chunks.

Toss pineapple chunks, apple and green onions with dressing. Place romaine in shallow bowl; mound fruit mixture in center.

6 servings

PER SERVING: Calories 180; Protein 1 g; Carbohydrate 17 g; Fat 12 g; Cholesterol 0 mg; Sodium 180 mg

PROSCIUTTO-STUFFED ARTICHOKES

CARCIOFI RIPIENI CON PROSCIUTTO
(kahr-<u>choh</u>-fee ree-p'<u>yeh</u>-nee kohn proh-<u>shoo</u>-toh)

These dramatic vegetables, once relieved of their prickly "chokes," are terrific natural containers for savory stuffings. Nibble the meaty bases of the leaves first and then go on to enjoy the prosciutto-flavored stuffing.

4 medium artichokes
1 quart water
1 tablespoon lemon juice
¼ pound prosciutto or fully cooked smoked ham, finely chopped
¼ cup dry bread crumbs
1 small onion, finely chopped
1 clove garlic, finely chopped
2 tablespoons snipped parsley
¼ teaspoon pepper
2 cups dry white wine
2 tablespoons olive or vegetable oil

Trim stems even with base of artichokes. Cutting straight across, slice 1 inch off tops; discard tops. Snip off points of remaining leaves with scissors. Rinse artichokes under cold water. Mix 1 quart water and the lemon juice; submerge artichokes in mixture to prevent discoloration, then drain.

Mix prosciutto, bread crumbs, onion, garlic, parsley and pepper. Spread artichoke leaves open; dig out the fuzzy purple choke of each artichoke with the point of a knife or a pointed spoon. Discard chokes. Spoon prosciutto mixture into center of each artichoke. Place artichokes upright in Dutch oven. Pour wine over artichokes; drizzle with oil. Heat to boiling; reduce heat. Cover and simmer until bottoms of artichokes are tender when pierced with a knife,

about 1 hour. Spoon liquid over each artichoke before serving.

4 servings

PER SERVING: Calories 240; Protein 11 g; Carbohydrate 22 g; Fat 12 g; Cholesterol 20 mg; Sodium 440 mg

SAUTÉED ARTICHOKE HEARTS

ALCACHOFAS SALTEADAS CON JAMÓN
(ahl-kah-<u>choh</u>-fahs sahl-tay-<u>yah</u>-dahs kohn hah-<u>mohn</u>)

These Spanish artichoke hearts sautéed in olive oil take on an almost buttery flavor. Made with either Italian prosciutto or Spanish Serrano ham, Sautéed Artichoke Hearts is an elegant side dish.

1 can (14 ounces) artichoke hearts, drained
2 tablespoons olive or vegetable oil
¼ cup chopped prosciutto or Serrano ham
⅛ teaspoon coarsely ground pepper
Snipped parsley

Cut artichoke hearts into halves. Heat oil in 10-inch skillet until hot. Cook and stir artichoke hearts and prosciutto in oil over medium heat until hot and hearts are light golden brown, 6 to 8 minutes. Stir in pepper. Sprinkle with parsley.

3 or 4 servings

PER SERVING: Calories 175; Protein 5 g; Carbohydrate 10 g; Fat 13 g; Cholesterol 10 mg; Sodium 380 mg

ASPARAGUS WITH GRUYÈRE

ASPERGES À LA GRUYÈRE (ahs-<u>pehr′jh</u> ah lah gree-<u>yair</u>)

The woody end of asparagus stems poses but a small problem. Rather than cut them off, guessing at what point on the stalk the asparagus becomes tender, simply bend the stalk near the base until it snaps.

1½ pounds asparagus*
½ teaspoon salt
¼ cup margarine or butter
½ cup grated Gruyère or Parmesan cheese

Break off tough ends of asparagus as far down as stalks snap easily. Wash asparagus. Arrange in single layer in ungreased oblong baking dish, 11 × 7 × 1½ inches. Sprinkle with salt. Cover with aluminum foil and cook in 350° oven until tender, about 25 minutes.

Heat margarine over low heat until light brown. Drizzle over asparagus; sprinkle with cheese. Place in oven just until cheese softens, 5 to 8 minutes.

6 servings

*2 packages (10 ounces each) frozen asparagus spears can be substituted for the fresh asparagus. Rinse asparagus under running cold water to separate; drain. Cover and cook in oven about 35 minutes.

PER SERVING: Calories 130; Protein 5 g; Carbohydrate 5 g; Fat 10 g; Cholesterol 10 mg; Sodium 290 mg

GREEN BEANS IN TOMATO SAUCE

Basil brings out the summery best in tomatoes, and a little bit of sugar helps, too. This green bean preparation is popular in Portugal and northern Spain.

1 medium onion, chopped
1 clove garlic, chopped
2 tablespoons olive or vegetable oil
1½ pounds green beans, cut into 3-inch pieces (about 5 cups)
3 medium tomatoes, chopped
¼ cup snipped parsley
1 teaspoon sugar
1 teaspoon salt
½ teaspoon dried basil leaves
⅛ teaspoon pepper

Cook and stir onion and garlic in oil in 3-quart saucepan until onion is tender. Add remaining ingredients. Cover and simmer over low heat until beans are tender, 15 to 20 minutes. Sprinkle with grated Parmesan cheese, if desired.

6 servings

PER SERVING: Calories 100; Protein 2 g; Carbohydrate 12 g; Fat 5 g; Cholesterol 0 mg; Sodium 380 mg

SAVORY GREEN BEANS WITH COCONUT

SAME KI BHAJI (sah-mee kay bah-jee)

Don't expect these beans to be barely cooked and crisp. They are gently stewed in clarified butter with coconut and aromatic Indian spices. This would be delicious with curries or a simple pork roast.

¼ cup Ghee (right)
½ cup flaked coconut
½ cup water
1½ pounds green beans
1 medium onion, sliced
1 teaspoon ground coriander
½ teaspoon ground turmeric
½ teaspoon ground ginger
1½ teaspoons salt

Prepare Ghee. Place coconut and water in blender container. Cover and blend on high speed until coconut is finely chopped, about 10 seconds. Cut beans lengthwise into halves; cut halves lengthwise into halves.

Cook and stir onion, coriander, turmeric and ginger in Ghee in 10-inch skillet over medium heat until onion is coated. Stir coconut mixture, beans and salt into onion mixture. Cover and cook over medium heat, stirring occasionally, until beans are tender, 20 to 30 minutes.

4 or 5 servings

PER SERVING: Calories 225; Protein 3 g; Carbohydrate 17 g; Fat 16 g; Cholesterol 35 mg; Sodium 850 mg

GHEE

1 pound unsalted butter

Cut butter into pieces. Heat over low heat until melted. Increase heat to medium; heat to boiling. Immediately remove from heat and stir gently.

Return to heat; slowly heat to simmering. Simmer uncovered until butter separates into transparent substance on top and milk solids on bottom, 30 to 40 minutes. Remove from heat; let stand 5 minutes. Strain through cheesecloth into container. Cover and refrigerate no longer than 2 months.

Ghee

Ghee is an everyday ingredient in Eastern cooking, Indian above the rest. The Western world has its version—clarified butter— but true *ghee* is cooked more slowly and has a stronger flavor. To make *ghee*, butter is heated until the milk solids separate out. The solids are skimmed off and saved and are sometimes used for flavoring vegetables. What is left after the solids are removed is a clear, yellow liquid: *ghee. Ghee* doesn't burn at high temperatures, and it does not go rancid nearly as quickly as whole butter.

BEETS IN ORANGE SAUCE

Russia and neighboring Finland are where beets often put in an appearance with oranges. Vinegar and brown sugar make a sweet and sour sauce that is hard to resist.

5 medium beets (about 1¼ pounds)
6 cups water
1 teaspoon salt
1 tablespoon packed brown sugar
2 teaspoons cornstarch
½ teaspoon salt
Dash of pepper
¾ cup orange juice
2 teaspoons vinegar

Cut off all but 2 inches of beet tops. Leave beets whole with root ends attached. Heat water and 1 teaspoon salt to boiling in 3-quart saucepan. Add beets. Heat to boiling; reduce heat. Cover and cook until tender, 35 to 45 minutes; drain. Run cold water over beets; slip off skins and remove root ends. Cut beets into ¼-inch slices.

Mix brown sugar, cornstarch, ½ teaspoon salt and the pepper in 2-quart saucepan. Stir orange juice gradually into cornstarch mixture; stir in vinegar. Cook, stirring constantly, until mixture thickens and boils. Boil and stir 1 minute. Stir in beets; heat until hot.

4 servings

PER SERVING: Calories 60; Protein 1 g; Carbohydrate 14 g; Fat 0 g; Cholesterol 0 mg; Sodium 830 mg

BOK CHOY WITH BEAN CURD

This is a pale dish that shows the bright color of green onions to advantage. Bean curd, or tofu, is protein-rich and sometimes thought of as a meat substitute. Oyster sauce gives it salty savor.

1 pound bean curd (tofu)
4 medium stalks bok choy
4 green onions (with tops)
¼ cup vegetable oil
1 can (4 ounces) button mushrooms, drained (reserve liquid)
3 tablespoons oyster sauce
½ teaspoon instant chicken bouillon
1 tablespoon cold water
1 tablespoon cornstarch

Cut bean curd into ¾-inch cubes; drain thoroughly. Cut bok choy (with leaves) into ¼-inch slices. Cut green onions into 2-inch pieces.

Heat 2 tablespoons of the oil in wok or 10-inch skillet over medium-high heat until hot. Cook bean curd, stirring carefully, 3 to 5 minutes. Remove bean curd. Add remaining oil and the bok choy to wok; stir-fry over medium-high heat 2 minutes. Add mushrooms.

Add enough water to reserved liquid to measure ½ cup. Stir liquid, the oyster sauce and bouillon into vegetables; heat to boiling.

Mix water and cornstarch; stir into vegetable mixture. Cook and stir until thickened, about 1 minute. Stir in bean curd and green onions; heat until hot.

6 to 8 servings

PER SERVING: Calories 175; Protein 8 g; Carbohydrate 6 g; Fat 13 g; Cholesterol 0 mg; Sodium 550 mg

BRUSSELS SPROUTS WITH SOUR CREAM

These cabbages in miniature, grown like buds along the length of a thick stalk, are much loved in Eastern Europe. They were reputedly developed in Belgium more than four hundred years ago. The assertive flavor of Brussels sprouts is deliciously complemented by onion and smoky bacon in this Hungarian recipe.

1½ pounds Brussels sprouts*
3 slices bacon, cut into 1-inch pieces
1 small onion, chopped
1 cup dairy sour cream
⅛ teaspoon coarsely ground pepper

Heat 1 inch salted water (½ teaspoon salt to 1 cup water) to boiling. Add Brussels sprouts. Heat to boiling; reduce heat. Cover and cook until tender, 8 to 10 minutes; drain.

Fry bacon in 10-inch skillet over medium heat until crisp. Remove bacon with slotted spoon; reserve. Cook and stir onion in hot bacon fat until tender. Stir in Brussels sprouts, sour cream and pepper; heat until hot. Sprinkle with bacon.

6 to 8 servings

*2 packages (8 ounces each) frozen Brussels sprouts can be substituted for fresh Brussels sprouts; cook as directed on package.

PER SERVING: Calories 155; Protein 6 g; Carbohydrate 12 g; Fat 9 g; Cholesterol 30 mg; Sodium 90 mg

RED CABBAGE WITH APPLES

The Danes and the Germans cook frequently with red cabbage. Cooked, the flavor of cabbage mellows. Here it is tender and mild, tossed with tart apples. The sweet-sour sauce is just the sort the Pennsylvania Dutch brought with them from Germany to the United States hundreds of years ago.

2 tart red apples, sliced
3 tablespoons margarine or butter
1 medium head red cabbage, coarsely shredded (about 8 cups)
¼ cup water
¼ cup red wine vinegar
2 tablespoons sugar
1 teaspoon salt
¼ teaspoon pepper

Cook and stir apples in margarine in Dutch oven over medium heat 5 minutes. Stir in remaining ingredients. Heat to boiling; reduce heat. Cover and simmer until cabbage is tender, 35 to 40 minutes.

6 servings

PER SERVING: Calories 135; Protein 1 g; Carbohydrate 19 g; Fat 6 g; Cholesterol 0 mg; Sodium 450 mg

Ingredients for Korean Vegetable Pickle

Korean Vegetable Pickle

KOREAN VEGETABLE PICKLE

KIMCHEE (kihm-chee)

Korean cooks are about as fond of pickled condiments as are Indian cooks. This mixture of carrot, celery cabbage and cauliflower is spicy-hot, a bright accompaniment to Oriental meats.

1 cup ¼-inch slices carrot
1 cup 1-inch pieces celery cabbage
1 cup cauliflowerets
2 teaspoons salt
3 green onions (with tops), finely chopped
1 thin slice gingerroot, finely chopped
2 teaspoons salt
½ teaspoon garlic salt
¼ teaspoon crushed red pepper

Sprinkle carrot, celery cabbage and cauliflowerets with 2 teaspoons salt; toss. Let stand 20 min-utes; rinse with cold water and drain. Toss drained vegetables with remaining ingredients. Cover tightly and refrigerate at least 48 hours but no longer than 4 days.

3 or 4 servings

PER SERVING: Calories 35; Protein 1 g; Carbohy-drate 8 g; Fat 0 g; Cholesterol 0 mg; Sodium 1780 mg

Celery Cabbage

This vegetable is related to the cabbage family though it does not look much like a cabbage. It is commonly used in Chinese, Japanese and Korean cooking. The heads are usually a bit thicker than those of bok choy and feature the same broad, thick stems that spread into darker, slightly ruffled leaves.

SPICY CABBAGE

This Sephardic dish is spiced with elements that tell of its Indian and Middle Eastern origins: jalapeño peppers, cumin, coriander and turmeric. Spicy Cabbage might traditionally be served with *Kofta* (page 181) and rice.

2 tablespoons vegetable oil
1 medium onion, chopped
2 cloves garlic, finely chopped
2 jalapeño peppers, seeded and chopped
1 medium green or red pepper, chopped
½ teaspoon ground cumin
½ teaspoon ground coriander
½ teaspoon ground turmeric
½ teaspoon salt
2 medium tomatoes, coarsely chopped
1 small head green cabbage (about 1½ pounds), thinly sliced
1 tablespoon vinegar

Heat oil in 12-inch skillet until hot. Cook and stir onion, garlic, jalapeño peppers, green pepper, cumin, coriander, turmeric and salt over medium heat until onion is tender, about 5 minutes. Stir in tomatoes and cabbage. Heat to boiling; reduce heat. Cover and simmer until cabbage is tender, about 12 minutes. Stir in vinegar.

8 servings

PER SERVING: Calories 80; Protein 2 g; Carbohydrate 9 g; Fat 4 g; Cholesterol 0 mg; Sodium 160 mg

VIENNESE CABBAGE

The city of Wien (Vienna) is known for its sparkle and elegance. The Viennese take what is wholly Austrian, treat it with their own particular flair, and mark it as their own. Here, cabbage with cream and a touch of vinegar, is given royal Viennese treatment: it is stewed in champagne.

2 tablespoons margarine or butter
1 large onion, chopped
1 medium head green cabbage, coarsely shredded
1 cup champagne
1 tablespoon white wine vinegar
1 teaspoon sugar
½ teaspoon salt
Dash of pepper
¼ cup whipping cream

Heat margarine in 12-inch skillet until hot. Cook and stir onion in margarine over medium heat until tender. Add cabbage; cook and stir until slightly limp, about 5 minutes. Stir in remaining ingredients except whipping cream.

Heat to boiling; reduce heat. Cover and simmer 5 minutes. Uncover and cook over medium heat, stirring occasionally, until cabbage is crisp-tender and liquid is evaporated, about 15 minutes. Stir in whipping cream. Sprinkle with caraway seed if desired.

8 servings

PER SERVING: Calories 100; Protein 1 g; Carbohydrate 8 g; Fat 5 g; Cholesterol 10 mg; Sodium 190 mg

HONEYED CARROTS

These glazed carrots take on not only a sweet nature, but the distinctive flavor of the honey used as well. Simple clover honey is delicious, but consider trying a strong honey such as buckwheat. This popular Middle Eastern dish is thought to have its roots in ancient Egypt.

12 medium carrots (about 1½ pounds), sliced
⅓ cup honey
2 tablespoons vegetable oil
1 teaspoon lemon juice
½ teaspoon salt

Heat 1 inch salted water (½ teaspoon salt to 1 cup water) to boiling. Add carrots. Heat to boiling; reduce heat. Cover and cook until tender, 12 to 15 minutes; drain.

Cook and stir remaining ingredients in 10-inch skillet until bubbly; add carrots. Cook uncovered over low heat, stirring occasionally, until carrots are glazed, 2 to 3 minutes.

6 servings

PER SERVING: Calories 165; Protein 1 g; Carbohydrate 29 g; Fat 5 g; Cholesterol 0 mg; Sodium 270 mg

---

Black Mustard Seed

Black mustard seed is usually more of a dark brown color than a true black. It has a stronger mustard flavor than the yellow mustard seed more familiar to American cooks. The light-colored seed is used to make yellow mustard; the dark seed, to make grainy mustards. Dried, ground mustard uses both as a blend. Like the yellow seed, black mustard seed is used as a pickling spice. It flavors many Indian dishes, where, like most spices, it is cooked in fat first to bring up the flavor.

CAULIFLOWER WITH SPICES

BAGHARI PHOOL GOBI (bah-hah-ree fool goh-bee)

This Indian dish is gilded with the characteristic bright yellow of turmeric. If black mustard seed is unavailable, yellow mustard seed may be substituted.

¼ cup vegetable oil
2 teaspoons black mustard seed
1 teaspoon fennel seed
2 cloves garlic, finely chopped
¼ teaspoon ground turmeric
⅛ teaspoon ground red pepper
1 small head cauliflower (about 2½ pounds), separated into flowerets
¼ cup water
½ teaspoon salt

Heat oil in 12-inch skillet until hot. Cook and stir mustard and fennel seeds over medium heat until mustard seed pops, about 2 minutes. Add garlic, turmeric and red pepper. Cook and stir until garlic is light brown.

Stir in remaining ingredients. Heat to boiling; reduce heat. Simmer uncovered, stirring occasionally, until cauliflower is crisp-tender and liquid is evaporated, 18 to 20 minutes.

6 servings

PER SERVING: Calories 95; Protein 1 g; Carbohydrate 2 g; Fat 9 g; Cholesterol 0 mg; Sodium 190 mg

Following pages (clockwise from top): Spicy Cabbage (page 242), Cauliflower with Spices, Mushrooms with Tomatoes and Peas (page 250) and Fried Bread Puffs (page 287)

CELERY, MILAN STYLE

In the larger European cities, capitals of elegance and style, it was common to braise vegetables simply in broth. This recipe turns celery from an incidental vegetable into a star.

6 large stalks celery
¾ cup water
½ teaspoon instant chicken bouillon
2 tablespoons margarine or butter
¼ cup grated Parmesan cheese
Snipped parsley

Cut celery into 2-inch pieces (about 4 cups). Heat celery, water and bouillon to boiling; reduce heat. Cover and cook until celery is crisp-tender, about 15 minutes; drain. Dot with margarine; cover and let stand until margarine is melted. Sprinkle with grated cheese and parsley.

4 to 6 servings

PER SERVING: Calories 90; Protein 3 g; Carbohydrate 4 g; Fat 7 g; Cholesterol 5 mg; Sodium 400 mg

DANISH PICKLED CUCUMBERS

SYLTEDE AGURKER (sewlt-eh-deh ah-goor-kehr)

Here is a very quick pickle. It can be made in the morning and enjoyed at lunch! The Danish love their pickles, which are a lovely feature of the famous Danish open-face sandwiches.

2 medium cucumbers, thinly sliced
⅓ cup cider vinegar
⅓ cup water
2 tablespoons sugar
½ teaspoon salt
⅛ teaspoon pepper
Snipped dill weed or parsley

Place cucumbers in glass or plastic bowl. Mix vinegar, water, sugar, salt and pepper; pour over cucumbers. Cover and refrigerate, stirring occasionally, at least 3 hours. Drain; sprinkle with dill weed.

6 servings

PER SERVING: Calories 10; Protein 0 g; Carbohydrate 4 g; Fat 0 g; Cholesterol 0 mg; Sodium 25 mg

MEXICAN CORN PUDDING

Made with evaporated milk and eggs, this pudding is rich. It doesn't feature any of the strong spices associated with Mexican food, so as a side dish it would be appropriate with just about any non-creamy main dish, whether Mexican or not.

1 can (12 ounces) evaporated milk
¼ cup all-purpose flour
2 cans (about 16 ounces each) cream-style corn
4 eggs, slightly beaten
½ cup sugar
¼ cup raisins
1 teaspoon baking soda
1 teaspoon salt
1 teaspoon vanilla

Shake ½ cup of the milk and the flour in tightly covered container. Mix milk mixture, remaining milk and the remaining ingredients. Pour into greased square pan, 9 × 9 × 2 inches. Cook uncovered in 350° oven until knife inserted halfway between center and edge comes out clean, about 1 hour.

8 servings

PER SERVING: Calories 275; Protein 10 g; Carbohydrate 45 g; Fat 6 g; Cholesterol 115 mg; Sodium 820 mg

CORN WITH OKRA AND TOMATOES

This is a Caribbean dish that spotlights the okra that came to this part of the world from Africa at the outset of the international slave trade. Okra has always been popular in the American South, and especially in Creole recipes.

6 ears corn*
2 cups cut-up okra† (about 1 pound)
⅓ cup margarine or butter
2 tablespoons margarine or butter
3 medium tomatoes, chopped
1 tablespoon sugar
1½ teaspoons salt
¼ teaspoon pepper

Cut corn from cobs (about 4 cups). Cook and stir okra in ⅓ cup margarine in 12-inch skillet over medium heat until tender, about 7 minutes. Add corn and 2 tablespoons margarine. Cook uncovered until tender, 10 to 12 minutes.

Stir in remaining ingredients. Cook uncovered until tomatoes are hot, about 3 minutes.

8 servings

*2 cans (16 ounces each) whole-kernel corn, drained, can be substituted for the fresh corn.

†1 package (10 ounces) frozen okra can be substituted for the fresh okra. Rinse under running cold water to separate; cut crosswise into slices. Cook as directed above.

PER SERVING: Calories 200; Protein 3 g; Carbohydrate 22 g; Fat 11 g; Cholesterol 0 mg; Sodium 540 mg

EGGPLANT WITH YOGURT SAUCE

BONJAN BORANI (bon-jon bohr-<u>ah</u>-nee)

Yogurt is indispensable to the cooking of Afghanistan. This sauce combines garlic and fresh mint, two vivacious seasonings that seem to go in opposite directions but are in fact delicious together. Eggplant dishes of all sorts are naturals with lamb.

1 medium onion, sliced
¼ cup olive or vegetable oil
1 medium eggplant (about 1½ pounds), cut into
    ½-inch slices
1 cup plain yogurt
3 tablespoons snipped fresh mint leaves or 1½
    teaspoons crushed dried mint leaves
2 cloves garlic, finely chopped
½ teaspoon salt
Dash of pepper
Paprika

Cook and stir onion in oil in 12-inch skillet until tender; remove onion. Cook half the eggplant over medium-high heat, turning once, until tender and golden brown, about 10 minutes. Repeat with remaining eggplant. (Add more oil if necessary.)

Arrange onion and eggplant slices on ovenproof platter or in ungreased oblong baking dish, 11 × 7 × 1½ inches. Mix remaining ingredients except paprika; pour over eggplant. Sprinkle with paprika. Heat in 350° oven until hot and bubbly, 10 to 15 minutes.

6 servings

PER SERVING: Calories 145; Protein 3 g; Carbohydrate 11 g; Fat 10 g; Cholesterol 5 mg; Sodium 210 mg

CUCUMBER AND TOMATO SKILLET

The Germans cook cucumbers—we usually eat them raw—to give them an extra measure of succulence. Fresh dill weed is the time-honored herb to season tomatoes and cucumbers.

2 medium cucumbers, cut into 1-inch pieces
1 medium onion, sliced and separated into rings
2 tablespoons margarine or butter
4 medium tomatoes, cut into wedges
½ teaspoon salt
Dash of pepper
1 tablespoon snipped fresh dill weed or 1 teaspoon dried dill weed

Cook and stir cucumbers and onion in margarine in 12-inch skillet until cucumbers are crisp-tender, about 5 minutes. Stir in tomatoes; sprinkle with salt and pepper. Cook, stirring occasionally, just until tomatoes are heated through. Sprinkle with dill weed.

6 to 8 servings

PER SERVING: Calories 70; Protein 1 g; Carbohydrate 8 g; Fat 4 g; Cholesterol 0 mg; Sodium 230 mg

GREENS WITH BACON

COUVE A MINEIRA (kuh-ve a mi-neh-ra)

The Brazilian way with tough, raw greens is to cook them in bacon fat until they are tender and have taken on a delicious hint of pork. This method is used in the American South as well.

2 pounds collard greens or kale
6 slices bacon, cut into 1-inch pieces
1 clove garlic, finely chopped
½ teaspoon salt
Freshly ground pepper

Remove stems from collard greens; cut leaves into ½-inch wide strips. Pour boiling water over collard greens. Let stand 5 minutes. Drain thoroughly.

Fry bacon in 10-inch skillet until crisp; remove with slotted spoon and reserve. Stir garlic and collard greens into bacon fat; cook and stir 2 minutes. Cover and cook over low heat until collard greens are tender, about 15 minutes longer. Stir in salt and pepper. Garnish with reserved bacon.

6 servings

PER SERVING: Calories 85; Protein 4 g; Carbohydrate 11 g; Fat 3 g; Cholesterol 5 mg; Sodium 310 mg

MUSHROOMS WITH SOUR CREAM

The Polish have a deep love of mushrooms. This luxurious mushroom dish is fresh with dill weed and extremely quick to prepare.

8 ounces mushrooms, sliced
2 tablespoons margarine or butter
1 teaspoon all-purpose flour
½ cup dairy sour cream
¼ teaspoon salt
Dash of pepper
Snipped dill weed or parsley

Cook and stir mushrooms in margarine 3 minutes. Stir in flour; cook and stir 1 minute. Stir in sour cream, salt and pepper. Heat, stirring occasionally, just until hot. Sprinkle with dill weed.

4 servings

PER SERVING: Calories 125; Protein 2 g; Carbohydrate 4 g; Fat 11 g; Cholesterol 20 mg; Sodium 210 mg

---

GRILLED MUSHROOMS
MANITARIA STI SKHARA (ma-nee-<u>ta</u>-rea stee <u>skah</u>-ra)

Grilled Mushrooms is a Cyprian celebration of large, meaty mushrooms. They are simply dressed with olive oil and lemon juice.

1 pound very large mushrooms (about 2½ inches)
Olive or vegetable oil
Salt to taste
2 tablespoons olive or vegetable oil
2 tablespoons lemon juice
Snipped parsley

Brush mushrooms with oil; sprinkle with salt. Cook mushrooms on grill 5 to 6 inches from medium coals, turning once or twice, until hot and golden brown, 10 to 15 minutes. Place mushrooms in serving bowl. Shake 2 tablespoons oil and lemon juice in tightly covered jar; pour over mushrooms. Sprinkle with parsley.

4 servings

PER SERVING: Calories 155; Protein 2 g; Carbohydrate 5 g; Fat 14 g; Cholesterol 0 mg; Sodium 270 mg

---

GOLDEN PANFRIED MUSHROOMS

This Polish recipe fries mushrooms that have been dipped into crumbs. The result: mushrooms that are crunchy and golden outside, juicy inside.

1 pound small mushrooms
1 egg, beaten
½ cup dry bread crumbs
1 medium onion, chopped
⅓ cup margarine or butter

Dip mushrooms into egg; coat with bread crumbs. Cook mushrooms and onion in margarine in 12-inch skillet, turning occasionally, until mushrooms are tender and golden brown, 7 to 8 minutes.

4 servings

PER SERVING: Calories 235; Protein 5 g; Carbohydrate 16 g; Fat 17 g; Cholesterol 55 mg; Sodium 290 mg

MUSHROOMS WITH TOMATOES AND PEAS

This is an opulent Indian side dish that would be just as delicious with Western food. Ginger adds a wonderful fragrance.

1 medium onion, sliced
½ to 1 teaspoon ground turmeric
¼ teaspoon ground ginger
1 tablespoon Ghee (page 237) or vegetable oil
1 package (10 ounces) frozen green peas, thawed and drained
8 ounces whole mushrooms
2 teaspoons lemon juice
1¼ teaspoons salt
2 medium tomatoes, cut into wedges

Cook and stir onion, turmeric and ginger in Ghee in 10-inch skillet over medium heat until onion is tender, about 3 minutes. Stir in peas, mushrooms, lemon juice and salt. Cook uncovered, stirring occasionally, until peas are tender, about 8 minutes. Stir in tomatoes; heat just until hot.

6 servings

PER SERVING: Calories 85; Protein 3 g; Carbohydrate 11 g; Fat 3 g; Cholesterol 0 mg; Sodium 490 mg

SPICY OKRA AND TURNIP GREENS

The fiery red jalapeño peppers make no secret of the origin of this African dish. The okra, once cut, will thicken the sauce as it cooks.

1 pound turnip or collard greens
12 okra
1 medium onion, chopped
1 jar (1 ounce) pine nuts (about ¼ cup)
2 tablespoons vegetable oil
3 red jalapeño peppers, seeded and finely chopped
¼ cup water
¼ teaspoon salt

Remove stems from turnip greens; cut leaves into ¼-inch slices. Remove ends from okra; cut okra crosswise into halves.

Cook and stir onion and pine nuts in oil in Dutch oven over medium heat until onion is tender, about 5 minutes. Stir in turnip greens, okra and remaining ingredients. Heat to boiling; reduce heat. Cover and simmer until turnip greens are tender, 18 to 20 minutes.

6 servings

PER SERVING: Calories 115; Protein 2 g; Carbohydrate 9 g; Fat 8 g; Cholesterol 0 mg; Sodium 110 mg

ROASTED ONIONS

With long cooking, onions become quite sweet. These large onions are served with an Italian-inspired rosemary butter.

4 large yellow onions (each about 3½ inches in diameter), unpeeled
Vegetable oil
¼ cup margarine or butter
1 teaspoon dried rosemary, crushed, or 1 tablespoon snipped fresh rosemary

Trim both ends from onion; prick each onion several times with fork. Brush with oil. Place onions in greased baking dish, 10 × 6 × 1½ inches. Cook uncovered in 350° oven until tender, about 1¼ hours.

Carefully remove skin from onions; place onions upright in serving dish. Cut each onion about halfway through into fourths; separate slightly. Heat margarine and rosemary until margarine is hot. Pour over onions.

4 servings

PER SERVING: Calories 220; Protein 2 g; Carbohydrate 13 g; Fat 18 g; Cholesterol 0 mg; Sodium 140 mg

---

Hearts of Palm

Known variously as *palm heart* and *swamp cabbage*, heart of palm is the core of a palm tree. The flesh is a creamy color and has fibers that run the length of the stalk. The most tender hearts of palm come from young palm trees. They can be cut into strips and eaten raw, as cabbage is, but more frequently they are cooked and canned commercially. Canned hearts of palm are a distinctive addition to salads.

HEARTS OF PALM IN TOMATO SAUCE

PALMITO GUISADO (pahl-<u>mee</u>-toh ghee-<u>sah</u>-doh)

The cabbage palmetto tree, when young, yields at the center of its stem a fibrous meat that is nearly white and absolutely delicious. Canned hearts of palm have been boiled. In the Dominican Republic, this exotic vegetable is stewed in a tomato sauce with ham and jalapeño peppers.

1 medium onion, chopped
2 cloves garlic, finely chopped
1 jalapeño pepper, seeded and chopped
4 ounces fully cooked smoked ham, coarsely chopped (about ⅔ cup)
2 tablespoons vegetable oil
1 can (16 ounces) whole tomatoes (with liquid)
2 tablespoons snipped parsley
1 teaspoon vinegar
⅛ teaspoon pepper
2 cans (14 ounces each) hearts of palm, rinsed, drained and sliced ½ inch thick
¼ cup grated Parmesan cheese

Cook and stir onion, garlic, jalapeño peppers and ham in oil in 10-inch skillet over medium heat until onion is tender. Add tomatoes, parsley, vinegar and pepper; break up tomatoes with fork. Heat to boiling; reduce heat. Simmer uncovered, stirring occasionally, until mixture is thickened, about 15 minutes. Stir in hearts of palm. Cover and simmer, stirring occasionally, until hearts of palm are hot, about 5 minutes. Sprinkle with cheese.

6 servings

PER SERVING: Calories 205; Protein 10 g; Carbohydrate 16 g; Fat 11 g; Cholesterol 15 mg; Sodium 640 mg

FRENCH GARDEN PEAS

In France, the arrival of the first tiny sweet peas (*petits pois*) is cause for celebration. The French stew them with butter and a sprinkling of sugar and stir in gala ribbons of tender, pale lettuce.

1½ cups shelled fresh green peas* (1½ pounds in pods)
1 cup shredded lettuce
3 green onions, sliced
2 tablespoons water
2 tablespoons margarine or butter
½ teaspoon salt
¼ teaspoon sugar
Dash of pepper

Heat all ingredients to boiling; reduce heat. Cover and simmer until peas are tender. About 8 minutes.

4 servings

*1 package (10 ounces) frozen green peas can be substituted for the fresh peas.

PER SERVING: Calories 105; Protein 3 g; Carbohydrate 8 g; Fat 6 g; Cholesterol 0 mg; Sodium 380 mg

CURRIED PEAS AND RICE

This is a popular West Indian combination, straightforward with the heady aroma of curry powder.

1 package (10 ounces) frozen green peas
1 tablespoon vegetable oil
1 tablespoon margarine or butter
1 small onion, chopped
1 teaspoon curry powder
¼ teaspoon salt
¾ cup cold cooked rice

Rinse peas under running cold water to separate; drain. Heat oil and margarine in 10-inch skillet until hot. Cook and stir onion, curry powder and salt in oil mixture over medium heat until onion is tender. Add peas and rice. Cook, stirring frequently, until mixture is hot and peas are tender, about 8 minutes.

6 servings

PER SERVING: Calories 105; Protein 3 g; Carbohydrate 14 g; Fat 4 g; Cholesterol 0 mg; Sodium 250 mg

Clockwise from left: French Garden Peas, French Potato Salad (page 227) and Radish and Watercress Salad (page 230)

BAKED PLANTAINS

Latin kitchens frequently cook the plantain as a starchy vegetable. It has much the same flavor, though not the sweetness, of a banana. Here the plantain is baked almost like a potato.

4 ripe plantains
Vegetable oil
Margarine or butter, melted
Salt

Cut tip off each end of plantains. Cut lengthwise slit through peel on one side of each plantain. Rub peel of plantains with oil.

Arrange plantains, cut sides up, in ungreased oblong baking dish, 13 × 9 × 2 inches. Cook uncovered in 350° oven until tender when pierced with fork, about 35 minutes. Make 1 or 2 lengthwise cuts through peel; remove peel. Serve plantains with margarine and salt.

8 servings

PER SERVING: Calories 205; Protein 1 g; Carbohydrate 37 g; Fat 6 g; Cholesterol 0 mg; Sodium 310 mg

SPINACH WITH LEMON DRESSING

HORTA (hohrr-tah)

The ages-old Greek treatment of greens is to toss them with lemon juice and fruity olive oil. The Greeks choose from poppy leaves, mustard greens, dandelion greens, rock samphire, charlock, and other greens more familiar to Western cooks. Take care to wash fresh spinach very thoroughly to remove all of the grit.

1½ pounds fresh spinach
2 tablespoons olive or vegetable oil
1 tablespoon lemon juice
¼ teaspoon salt
Freshly ground pepper

Wash spinach and remove stems; drain. Place spinach leaves and just the water that clings to them in Dutch oven. Cover and cook until tender, 7 to 8 minutes; drain thoroughly. Shake oil, lemon juice and salt in tightly covered jar; toss with spinach. Sprinkle with pepper.

6 servings

PER SERVING: Calories 70; Protein 2 g; Carbohydrate 4 g; Fat 5 g; Cholesterol 0 mg; Sodium 160 mg

AFRICAN GREEN PEPPER AND SPINACH

Chunks of fresh tomato melt into a sauce that is given an African twist with peanut butter. The flavor of peanuts is nice with celery and bananas, and equally good with crisp-tender green pepper.

1 medium onion, chopped
1 medium green pepper, chopped
1 tablespoon vegetable oil
1 medium tomato, chopped
1 pound fresh spinach*
¾ teaspoon salt
⅛ teaspoon pepper
¼ cup peanut butter

Cook and stir onion and green pepper in oil in 3-quart saucepan until onion is tender. Add tomato and spinach. Cover and simmer until spinach is tender, about 5 minutes. Stir in salt, pepper and peanut butter; heat just until hot.

4 servings

PER SERVING: Calories 190; Protein 7 g; Carbohydrate 13 g; Fat 12 g; Cholesterol 0 mg; Sodium 550 mg

AFRICAN SQUASH AND YAMS

FUTARI (foo-tah-ree)

Winter squash and creamy yams get special treatment with the sweet trio of coconut milk, cinnamon and cloves.

1 small onion, chopped
2 tablespoons vegetable oil
1 pound Hubbard squash, pared and cut into 1-inch pieces
2 medium yams or sweet potatoes (about ¾ pound), pared and cut into 1-inch pieces
1 cup Coconut Milk (page 72)
½ teaspoon salt
½ teaspoon ground cinnamon
¼ teaspoon ground cloves

Cook and stir onion in oil in 10-inch skillet over medium heat until tender. Stir in remaining ingredients. Heat to boiling; reduce heat. Cover and simmer 10 minutes. Simmer uncovered, stirring occasionally, until vegetables are tender, about 5 minutes longer.

6 to 8 servings

PER SERVING: Calories 200; Protein 2 g; Carbohydrate 17 g; Fat 14 g; Cholesterol 0 mg; Sodium 190 mg

FINNISH RUTABAGA CASSEROLE

LANTTULAATIKKO (lahn-too-lah-tee-koh)

In the tradition of hearty, warming fare from bone-chilling Lapland, this casserole makes a sturdy root vegetable shine. Nutmeg emphasizes the slight sweetness of this creamy dish.

2 medium rutabagas (about 2 pounds)
2 eggs, beaten
¼ cup dry bread crumbs
¼ cup half-and-half
2 teaspoons sugar or corn syrup
1 teaspoon salt
¼ teaspoon ground nutmeg
2 tablespoons margarine or butter

Slice and pare rutabagas; cut into ½-inch cubes. Heat 1 inch salted water (½ teaspoon salt to 1 cup water) to boiling. Add rutabagas. Heat to boiling; reduce heat. Cover and cook until tender, about 20 minutes.

Drain rutabagas, reserving ¼ cup cooking liquid. Mash rutabagas with reserved liquid or purée through food mill (see Note). Stir remaining ingredients except margarine into rutabagas. Pour into greased 1½-quart casserole; dot with margarine. Cook in 350° oven until top is light brown, 45 to 50 minutes.

6 to 8 servings

PER SERVING: Calories 135; Protein 4 g; Carbohydrate 14 g; Fat 7 g; Cholesterol 75 mg; Sodium 480 mg

NOTE: Rutabagas can be puréed in blender. Place half the cubes at a time in blender container; add 2 tablespoons reserved liquid. Cover and blend until of uniform consistency. Repeat.

TOMATOES, PEPPERS AND ONIONS

PEPERONATA (peh-pehr-oh-<u>nah</u>-tah)

This is a Roman favorite, hot or cold. Toss marinated olives into this dish if you like.

2 medium onions, sliced
2 tablespoons olive or vegetable oil
3 medium green peppers, cut into strips
1 teaspoon dried basil leaves
1 teaspoon red wine vinegar
½ teaspoon salt
¼ teaspoon pepper
2 medium tomatoes, coarsely chopped (about 2 cups)

Cook and stir onions in oil in 10-inch skillet until tender; add remaining ingredients except tomatoes. Cover and cook over low heat 10 minutes. Add tomatoes. Cover and simmer until green pepper is tender, about 5 minutes. Garnish with ripe olives if desired.

4 servings

PER SERVING: Calories 120; Protein 2 g; Carbohydrate 12 g; Fat 7 g; Cholesterol 0 mg; Sodium 280 mg

VEGETABLE CASSEROLE

GRÖNSAKSGRATIN (gruhn-sahks-grah-<u>teng</u>)

Because the vegetables can be prepared in advance, this Scandinavian casserole is a great dish for parties; all that remains is to pour over the hot sauce, sprinkle with cheese and broil.

3 medium carrots, sliced (about 1½ cups)
8 ounces green beans, cut into 1-inch pieces
½ small head cauliflower, separated into flowerets (about 2 cups)
1 small onion, sliced
2 tablespoons margarine or butter
2 tablespoons all-purpose flour
½ teaspoon salt
⅛ teaspoon pepper
½ cup whipping cream
¼ cup grated Parmesan cheese

Heat 1 inch salted water (½ teaspoon salt to 1 cup water) to boiling. Add carrots, beans, cauliflower and onion. Heat to boiling; reduce heat. Cover and simmer until tender, 12 to 15 minutes. Drain vegetables, reserving 1 cup liquid. Place vegetables in ungreased oblong baking dish, 11 × 7 × 1½ inches, or square baking dish, 8 × 8 × 2 inches.

Heat margarine over low heat until melted. Blend in flour, salt and pepper. Cook over low heat, stirring constantly, until mixture is smooth and bubbly; remove from heat.

Stir in reserved liquid and the whipping cream. Heat to boiling, stirring constantly. Boil and stir 1 minute; remove from heat. Pour sauce over vegetables; sprinkle with cheese.

Set oven control to broil or 550°. Broil until top is light brown and bubbly, 3 to 5 minutes.

6 servings

PER SERVING: Calories 150; Protein 3 g; Carbohydrate 10 g; Fat 11 g; Cholesterol 25 mg; Sodium 320 mg

Tofu with Green Onion Sauce

TOFU WITH GREEN ONION SAUCE

TOFU CINA (doh-foo see-nah)

This Chinese preparation celebrates, rather than smothers, the subtle flavor of bean curd. Cilantro adds a note of citrus.

1 pound bean curd (tofu)
1 tablespoon vegetable oil
6 green onions (with tops), sliced
3 tablespoons soy sauce
Snipped fresh cilantro

Drain bean curd; pat dry. Cut bean curd into 1-inch cubes; arrange on serving plate.

Heat oil in 8-inch skillet until hot. Cook and stir green onions over medium heat until crisp-tender, 2 to 3 minutes; remove from heat. Stir in soy sauce. Pour mixture over bean curd. Sprinkle with cilantro.

6 to 8 servings

PER SERVING: Calories 95; Protein 7 g; Carbohydrate 3 g; Fat 6 g; Cholesterol 0 mg; Sodium 520 mg

FRENCH VEGETABLE RAGOUT

RATATOUILLE (rah-tah-twee)

In the south of France, this summery casserole of vegetables features the greenest, deepest-tasting olive oil to be found. This is a gorgeous dish, bright with color.

1 small eggplant (about 1 pound)
1 medium onion, sliced
1 clove garlic, chopped
2 tablespoons olive or vegetable oil
4 medium tomatoes, cut into fourths
1 medium zucchini, sliced
1 medium green pepper, cut into strips
¼ cup snipped parsley
1 teaspoon salt
½ teaspoon dried basil leaves
¼ teaspoon pepper

Cut eggplant into ½-inch cubes (about 5 cups). Cook and stir onion and garlic in oil in 12-inch skillet until onion is tender. Add eggplant and remaining ingredients. Heat to boiling; reduce heat. Cover and simmer, stirring occasionally, until vegetables are crisp-tender, about 10 minutes.

8 servings

PER SERVING: Calories 80; Protein 1 g; Carbohydrate 10 g; Fat 4 g; Cholesterol 0 mg; Sodium 280 mg

RUMANIAN MIXED VEGETABLES

GHIVECI (gee-vetch-ee)

This, the national dish of Rumania, is traditionally cooked in a *guvens*, a special casserole.

2 medium potatoes, (about ⅔ pound), cut into ½-inch cubes
2 medium carrots, sliced
8 ounces green beans, cut into 1-inch pieces
2 medium onions, chopped
2 cloves garlic, chopped
2 tablespoons olive or vegetable oil
4 medium tomatoes, chopped
2 cups cauliflowerets
1 stalk celery, sliced
2 teaspoons salt
¼ teaspoon dried thyme leaves
¼ teaspoon ground marjoram
¼ teaspoon pepper
1 medium zucchini, sliced
1 medium green pepper, chopped

Heat 1 inch water to boiling in 3-quart saucepan. Add potatoes, carrots and beans. Heat to boiling; reduce heat. Cover and simmer 10 minutes; drain. Cook and stir onions and garlic in oil in 10-inch skillet over medium heat until almost tender. Add tomatoes, cauliflowerets, celery, salt, thyme, marjoram and pepper. Cover and cook 5 minutes.

Place potato mixture in greased 3-quart casserole. Spread half the tomato mixture over top. Layer zucchini and green pepper over tomato mixture. Top with remaining tomato mixture. Cover and cook in 350° oven until vegetables are tender, 50 to 60 minutes.

8 servings

PER SERVING: Calories 120; Protein 3 g; Carbohydrate 18 g; Fat 4 g; Cholesterol 0 mg; Sodium 570 mg

DILLED ZUCCHINI

In Hungary, vegetables are often dressed with sour cream, cream or yogurt. This is a fresh-tasting dish, relatively low in calories.

6 small zucchini (about 1½ pounds), cut into
   ½-inch slices
1 clove garlic, finely chopped
2 tablespoons olive or vegetable oil
1 small onion, sliced and separated into rings
½ teaspoon salt
Dash of pepper
½ cup plain yogurt
3 tablespoons snipped fresh dill weed or 1 teaspoon dried dill weed

Cook and stir zucchini and garlic in oil in 10-inch skillet over medium heat until zucchini is light brown, 5 to 8 minutes. Stir in onion; heat just until hot. Sprinkle with salt and pepper; remove from heat. Mix yogurt and dill weed; stir into zucchini mixture.

6 servings

PER SERVING: Calories 80; Protein 2 g; Carbohydrate 7 g; Fat 5 g; Cholesterol 0 mg; Sodium 200 mg

6 medium baking potatoes (about 2 pounds)
¼ cup margarine or butter, melted
Salt
Pepper
¼ cup grated Parmesan cheese
2 tablespoons dry bread crumbs
Paprika

Cut potatoes crosswise into ⅛-inch slices, cutting only ¾ through. Place cut side up in greased oblong baking dish, 11 × 7 × 1½ inches. Brush with margarine; sprinkle with salt and pepper.

Bake in 375° oven, brushing with margarine once or twice, 45 minutes (see Note). Mix cheese and bread crumbs; sprinkle on potatoes. Sprinkle with paprika. Bake until tender, 20 to 30 minutes.

6 servings

PER SERVING: Calories 230; Protein 4 g; Carbohydrate 33 g; Fat 9 g; Cholesterol 5 mg; Sodium 530 mg

NOTE: Potatoes can be baked with a roast at 325° for 1 hour. Brush with meat drippings; sprinkle with cheese mixture. Bake until tender, about 30 minutes.

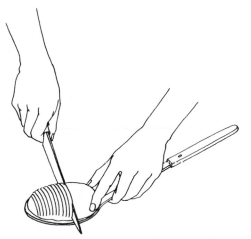

Place each potato in the bowl of a large spoon before slicing. The rim of the spoon prevents the knife from cutting too deeply into the potato.

HASSELBACK POTATOES

Cut partially through, these Swedish potatoes roast to an extra-crispy texture. It is easy to keep from slicing the potatoes all the way through: Place each potato in the bowl of a large spoon. Holding the knife blade perpendicular to the kitchen surface, slice into the potato. The rim of the spoon will stop the knife before it cuts through entirely.

CRUSTY POTATO CAKE

POMMES DE TERRE ANNA (pohm duh <u>tehr</u> ah-<u>nah</u>)

This famous nineteenth-century dish was named in honor of a fashionable French lady. Layers of thinly sliced potato bake into a golden, crisp cake that is elegantly served in wedges.

6 medium baking potatoes (about 2 pounds), thinly sliced
1 teaspoon salt
Pepper
⅓ cup margarine or butter, melted

Arrange layer of potato slices in bottom of generously greased 9-inch pie plate. Sprinkle with small amount of salt and dash of pepper. Repeat until all potatoes have been layered, sprinkling each layer with small amount of salt and dash of pepper. Pour margarine over potatoes. Cook uncovered in 400° oven until potatoes are tender, about 50 minutes.

Loosen edge and bottom of potato cake with wide spatula. Place inverted platter over pie plate; invert potatoes onto platter. Cut into wedges to serve.

6 servings

PER SERVING: Calories 225; Protein 3 g; Carbohydrate 31 g; Fat 10 g; Cholesterol 0 mg; Sodium 480 mg

SCOTTISH SKILLET POTATOES

STOVIES (<u>stoh</u>-vees)

The Scottish name for this dish describes its casual nature. Stovies frequently are whipped up to accompany a supper of cold meats.

2 tablespoons bacon fat, margarine or butter
6 medium potatoes (about 2 pounds), thinly sliced (about 4 cups)
2 medium onions, sliced
1½ teaspoons salt
¼ teaspoon pepper
¼ cup snipped parsley
¾ cup water

Heat bacon fat in 10-inch skillet until hot. Layer half each of the potato and onion slices in skillet. Sprinkle with half each of the salt, pepper and parsley. Repeat. Add water. Cover and simmer over low heat until potatoes are tender and liquid is absorbed, about 30 minutes. (Add water if necessary.)

6 servings

PER SERVING: Calories 155; Protein 2 g; Carbohydrate 28 g; Fat 4 g; Cholesterol 0 mg; Sodium 590 mg

HUNGARIAN POTATO AND EGG CASSEROLE

RAKOTT KRUMPLI (<u>rah</u>-koht <u>kroom</u>-plee)

This chunky potato salad is rich and filling. Serve it in the place of plain old American-style scalloped potatoes.

6 medium potatoes (about 2 pounds)
1 medium onion, chopped
2 tablespoons vegetable oil
1 cup dairy sour cream
1½ teaspoons salt
¼ teaspoon pepper
2 hard-cooked eggs, peeled and sliced
2 tablespoons dry bread crumbs
Paprika

Heat 1 inch salted water (½ teaspoon salt to 1 cup water) to boiling. Add potatoes. Heat to boiling; reduce heat. Cover and cook until tender, 30 to 35 minutes. Drain; cool slightly.

Cook onion in oil until tender. Mix onion, oil, sour cream, salt and pepper. Peel potatoes; cut into ¼-inch slices. Gently mix potatoes and sour cream mixture.

Arrange half the potatoes in greased oblong baking dish, 10 × 6 × 1½ inches, or 1½-quart casserole. Arrange eggs on top; add remaining potatoes. Sprinkle with bread crumbs and paprika. Cook uncovered in 325° oven until light brown, 30 to 40 minutes. Garnish with snipped parsley if desired.

6 servings

PER SERVING: Calories 285; Protein 6 g; Carbohydrate 34 g; Fat 14 g; Cholesterol 100 mg; Sodium 910 mg

SUGAR-BROWNED POTATOES

Denmark's sweet tooth favors these little golden brown potatoes.

2 pounds new potatoes
¼ cup margarine or butter
¼ cup sugar
½ teaspoon salt
3 tablespoons water

Heat 1 inch salted water (1 teaspoon salt to 1 cup water) to boiling. Add potatoes. Heat to boiling; reduce heat. Cover and cook until tender, 20 to 25 minutes; drain.

Cook and stir margarine, sugar and salt in 10-inch skillet over medium heat until mixture starts to turn golden brown. Remove from heat; cool slightly. Stir in water until blended. Add

potatoes. Cook over low heat, turning potatoes to coat with sugar mixture.

4 to 6 servings

PER SERVING: Calories 355; Protein 4 g; Carbohydrate 58 g; Fat 12 g; Cholesterol 0 mg; Sodium 910 mg

POTATOES WITH ROSEMARY
PASTEL DE PATATA CON ROMERO
(pah-stehl deh pah-tah-tah kohn roh-meh-roh)

Potatoes and tender onion slices are layered in this creamy Spanish casserole.

¼ cup margarine or butter
2 large onions, thinly sliced
2 teaspoons snipped fresh rosemary leaves
½ teaspoon salt
¼ teaspoon coarsely ground pepper
4 medium baking potatoes (about 1⅓ pounds) thinly sliced
1 cup half-and-half

Heat margarine in 10-inch skillet until melted. Stir in onions, rosemary, salt and pepper. Cook over low heat, stirring frequently, until onion is very soft and begins to brown, about 20 minutes.

Arrange half of the potato slices in bottom of greased pie plate, 10 × 1½ inches. Top with half the onion mixture. Repeat layers. Pour half-and-half over top.

Cover with aluminum foil, and cook in 350° oven 1 hour. Uncover and cook until top is golden brown, about 20 minutes longer. Cut into wedges to serve.

6 to 8 servings

PER SERVING: Calories 210; Protein 3 g; Carbohydrate 23 g; Fat 12 g; Cholesterol 15 mg; Sodium 290 mg

PORTUGUESE HERBED POTATOES

BATATAS CON LOURO (bah-tah-tahs kohn loh-roh)

Sometimes it seems that the bay leaf is relegated to nothing more than flavoring tomato sauces. Its pungent flavor makes this bubbly potato casserole unusual.

1½ pounds new potatoes
6 bay leaves
2 tablespoons olive or vegetable oil
2 tablespoons margarine or butter
½ teaspoons salt
Dash of pepper

Pare a narrow strip around center of each potato. Heat 1 inch salted water (1 teaspoon salt to 1 cup water) to boiling. Add potatoes and bay leaves. Heat to boiling; reduce heat. Cover and cook until potatoes are tender, 20 to 25 minutes; drain.

Heat oil and margarine in 10-inch skillet until margarine is melted and bubbly. Add potatoes and bay leaves; stir to coat with oil mixture. Sprinkle with salt and pepper. Cook uncovered over medium heat, turning potatoes frequently, until golden brown, 10 to 12 minutes. Remove bay leaves.

4 servings

PER SERVING: Calories 265; Protein 3 g; Carbohydrate 34 g; Fat 13 g; Cholesterol 0 mg; Sodium 710 mg

SWISS FRIED POTATOES

RÖSTI (ruh-stee)

Potatoes are cooked, shredded and flavored with Gruyère cheese, and then pressed to form a flat, crisp cake that is famous the world over.

4 medium potatoes (about 1½ pounds)
¼ cup margarine or butter
1 small onion, chopped
½ cup diced Gruyère or Swiss cheese
½ teaspoon salt
¼ teaspoon pepper
2 tablespoons water

Heat 1 inch salted water (½ teaspoon salt to 1 cup water) to boiling. Add potatoes. Heat to boiling; reduce heat. Cover and cook until tender, 30 to 35 minutes. Peel and shred potatoes or cut into ¼-inch strips.

Heat margarine in 10-inch skillet until melted. Add potatoes, onion and cheese. Sprinkle with salt and pepper. Cook uncovered over medium heat, turning frequently, until potatoes start to brown, about 10 minutes. (Add 1 to 2 tablespoons margarine to prevent sticking if necessary.)

Press potatoes with spatula to form flat cake; sprinkle with water. Cover and cook over low heat, without stirring, until bottom is golden brown and crusty, about 10 minutes. Place inverted platter over skillet; invert potatoes onto platter.

4 to 6 servings

PER SERVING: Calories 265; Protein 6 g; Carbohydrate 27 g; Fat 15 g; Cholesterol 10 mg; Sodium 710 mg

APPLES AND POTATOES

HIMMEL UND ERDE (<u>him</u>-m'l oont <u>ehr</u>-deh)

The German name for this dish is "heaven and earth," referring to the tree-borne apple and the earthy potato. Traditionally this bacon-scented combination is served with blood sausage.

4 medium potatoes (about 1½ pounds), cut
   into 1-inch cubes (about 4 cups)
2 tart apples, sliced
1 tablespoon sugar
4 slices bacon, cut into 1-inch pieces
1 medium onion, sliced
1 tablespoon margarine or butter, softened
Dash of ground nutmeg

Heat 1 inch salted water (1 teaspoon salt to 1 cup water) to boiling. Add potatoes, apples and sugar. Heat to boiling; reduce heat. Cover and cook until potatoes are tender, 10 to 15 minutes; drain.

Fry bacon until crisp; drain. Cook and stir onion in bacon fat until tender. Place potatoes and apples in serving bowl. Dot with margarine; sprinkle with nutmeg. Top with onion and bacon.

4 to 6 servings

PER SERVING: Calories 240; Protein 5 g; Carbohydrate 42 g; Fat 6 g; Cholesterol 5 mg; Sodium 460 mg

MASHED POTATOES WITH CABBAGE

COLCANNON (kohl-<u>can</u>-non)

For this Irish dish, tender, cooked cabbage is stirred into creamy mashed potatoes—simple and delicious.

6 medium potatoes (about 2 pounds)
½ small head green cabbage, shredded (about
   3 cups)
6 scallions (with tops), chopped
¼ cup water
⅛ teaspoon salt
⅓ to ½ cup milk
¼ cup margarine or butter, softened
1 teaspoon salt
Dash of pepper
Margarine or butter

Heat 1 inch salted water (½ teaspoon salt to 1 cup water) to boiling. Add potatoes. Heat to boiling; reduce heat. Cover and cook until tender, 30 to 35 minutes; drain. Heat cabbage, scallions, water and ⅛ teaspoon salt to boiling; reduce heat. Cover and simmer until crisp-tender, 5 to 10 minutes; drain.

Mash potatoes until no lumps remain. Beat in milk in small amounts. Add ¼ cup margarine, 1 teaspoon salt and the pepper; beat until potatoes are light and fluffy. Stir in cabbage and scallions; dot with margarine.

6 servings

PER SERVING: Calories 220; Protein 3 g; Carbohydrate 29 g; Fat 10 g; Cholesterol 0 mg; Sodium 800 mg

OVEN-FRIED POTATOES WITH BACON

TATWS RHOST (<u>tah</u>-tuss rroast)

This Welsh dish is something of a historic artifact. The recipe is virtually unchanged from the way these potatoes were cooked many hundreds of years ago. Today, unless we are camping out or "roughing it," we needn't cook them in a covered kettle over an open fire.

6 medium potatoes (about 2 pounds), thinly
  sliced
6 green onions (with tops), chopped
⅓ cup water
6 slices bacon
Coarsely ground pepper

Arrange potato slices in greased oblong baking dish, 13 × 9 × 2 inches; sprinkle with green onions. Pour water over potatoes and onions. Arrange bacon slices on top; sprinkle with pepper. Cover and cook in 400° oven 35 minutes. Uncover and cook until potatoes are tender and bacon is slightly crisp, about 15 minutes longer.

6 servings

PER SERVING: Calories 145; Protein 4 g; Carbohydrate 25 g; Fat 3 g; Cholesterol 5 mg; Sodium 110 mg

GERMAN POTATO PANCAKES

KARTOFFELPUFFER (kahr-<u>tof</u>-f'l-poof-f'r)

Applesauce is the classic accompaniment to potato pancakes. To serve these pancakes as a dessert, hold the onions.

4 medium potatoes (about 1½ pounds)
4 eggs, beaten
1 small onion, finely chopped (optional)
¼ cup all-purpose flour
1 teaspoon salt
¼ cup bacon fat, margarine or butter

Shred enough potatoes to measure 4 cups; drain. Mix potatoes, eggs, onion, flour and salt. Heat 2 tablespoons of the bacon fat in 12-inch skillet over medium heat until hot. Pour in about ¼ cup potato mixture for each pancake and spread with spatula to about 4 inches in diameter.

Cook pancakes until golden brown, about 2 minutes on each side. Keep warm. Repeat with remaining batter. (Add remaining bacon fat as needed to prevent sticking.)

16 pancakes

PER PANCAKE: Calories 75; Protein 2 g; Carbohydrate 8 g; Fat 4 g; Cholesterol 55 mg; Sodium 180 mg

German Potato Pancakes and Red Cabbage with Apples (page 239)

ARMENIAN NOODLES AND RICE
PILAV (pee-lahv)

The texture of egg noodles is nice with long grain rice. Fresh parsley can play a more flavorful role than that of garnish; sprinkle with as much as you like.

1 cup uncooked fine egg noodles
¼ cup margarine or butter
2½ cups water
1 cup uncooked long grain rice
1¼ teaspoons salt
Dash of pepper
Snipped parsley

Break noodles into 1-inch pieces if necessary. Cook and stir noodles in margarine in 2-quart saucepan 5 minutes. Stir in remaining ingredients except parsley. Heat to boiling, stirring once or twice; reduce heat. Cover and simmer 14 minutes. (Do not lift cover or stir.) Remove from heat. Fluff mixture lightly with fork; cover and let steam 5 to 10 minutes. Sprinkle with parsley.

8 servings

PER SERVING: Calories 155; Protein 2 g; Carbohydrate 23 g; Fat 6 g; Cholesterol 5 mg; Sodium 400 mg

PASTA WITH PESTO SAUCE
PASTA CON PESTO (pah-stah kohn peh-stoh)

Genoa is said to be the birthplace of pesto, a fragrant sauce of olive oil, fresh basil, pine nuts, garlic and freshly grated Parmesan cheese. A similar sauce is native to provincial France, too; along the Riviera, it is known as *pistou*.

⅔ cup packed coarsely chopped basil leaves
⅓ cup grated Parmesan cheese
⅓ cup olive or vegetable oil
2 tablespoons pine nuts or walnuts
½ teaspoon salt
⅛ teaspoon pepper
1 clove garlic
10 ounces uncooked spaghetti or noodles
2 tablespoons margarine or butter

Place all ingredients except spaghetti and margarine in blender container. Cover and blend on high speed until mixture is of uniform consistency. Cook spaghetti as directed on package; drain. Toss spaghetti with basil mixture and the margarine. Serve with additional Parmesan cheese if desired.

6 servings

PER SERVING: Calories 365; Protein 9 g; Carbohydrate 40 g; Fat 19 g; Cholesterol 5 mg; Sodium 500 mg

---

Pine Nuts

Pine nuts are sweet, and because they are oil-rich, it is advisable to keep them frozen until they are needed (a measure of prevention to keep them from going rancid too quickly). Known also as *pignolis*, these little oval nuts have a delicious, distinctive flavor. If they are not available, substitute unsalted sunflower nuts, almonds or walnuts. Pine nuts are favored in the Mediterranean and the Middle East.

Cold Noodles with Dipping Sauce, *top*, and Cellophane Noodles with Vegetables (page 268)

COLD NOODLES WITH DIPPING SAUCE

SOBA (<u>so</u>-bah)

A refreshing Japanese dish, these cold noodles are at once hearty and light-tasting. Use a cautious hand with wasabi until you are familiar with its power. It is delicious but can have a truly sinus-clearing effect.

1 package (8½ ounces) soba (buckwheat
   noodles)
1 cup water
¼ cup soy sauce
3 tablespoons sugar
¼ teaspoon hon-dashi (dashi granules)
1 green onion (with top), thinly sliced
1 teaspoon grated gingerroot
1 tablespoon wasabi powder
1 tablespoon water

Cook noodles as directed on package; drain. Cover and refrigerate until chilled. Heat water, soy sauce, sugar and hon-dashi to boiling; remove from heat. Cool; stir in onion and gingerroot. Mix wasabi powder and water to a paste.

Divide noodles among 8 small bowls. Pour soy mixture into 8 small dipping bowls. Serve with wasabi paste. Stir small amounts of wasabi paste into soy mixture to taste.

8 servings

PER SERVING: Calories 115; Protein 4 g; Carbohydrate 27 g; Fat 0 g; Cholesterol 0 mg; Sodium 620 mg

FETTUCCINE WITH WILD MUSHROOMS

PASTA AL FUNGHI (pah-stah ahl foon-ghee)

Dried porcini have an intensely earthy flavor that, combined with cream, is indisputably luscious. The Italians and the French consider dried wild mushrooms to be worth their weight in gold. Because the flavor is so strong, a little dried mushroom added to a soup, stew or sauce can go a long way.

1 cup hot water
1 package (about 1 ounce) dried porcini or cèpe mushrooms
1 small onion, chopped
2 cloves garlic, finely chopped
2 tablespoons olive or vegetable oil
1 cup whipping cream
½ teaspoon salt
8 ounces uncooked fettuccine
Coarsely ground pepper

Pour water over mushrooms. Let stand 30 minutes; drain. Cut mushrooms into ¼-inch strips.

Cook and stir mushrooms, onion and garlic in oil in 10-inch skillet over medium heat until onion is tender. Add whipping cream and salt. Heat to boiling; reduce heat. Simmer uncovered, stirring occasionally, until slightly thickened, 3 to 5 minutes.

Cook fettuccine as directed on package; drain. Pour sauce over hot fettuccine, tossing until fettuccine is well coated. Serve with pepper.

6 servings

PER SERVING: Calories 300; Protein 6 g; Carbohydrate 28 g; Fat 18 g; Cholesterol 75 mg; Sodium 360 mg

CELLOPHANE NOODLES WITH VEGETABLES

Yellow bean paste is available in Chinese groceries and specialty shops.

1 package (3¾ ounces) cellophane noodles
3 tablespoons water
1 tablespoon yellow bean paste
1 teaspoon cornstarch
1 teaspoon sugar
1 teaspoon soy sauce
2 tablespoons vegetable oil
1 medium carrot, cut into 2 × ¼-inch strips
1 clove garlic, finely chopped
1 teaspoon finely chopped gingerroot
1 medium zucchini, cut into 2 × ¼-inch strips
1 green onion (with top), sliced

Cover noodles with hot water. Let stand 10 minutes; drain. Cut into 2-inch lengths. Mix 3 tablespoons water, the bean paste, cornstarch, sugar and soy sauce; reserve.

Heat oil in wok or 10-inch skillet until hot. Add carrot, garlic and gingerroot. Stir-fry 1 minute. Add zucchini; stir-fry 2 minutes. Add noodles and bean paste mixture; stir-fry 45 seconds. Sprinkle with green onion.

4 to 6 servings

PER SERVING: Calories 145; Protein 1 g; Carbohydrate 20 g; Fat 7 g; Cholesterol 0 mg; Sodium 360 mg

CRACKED WHEAT PILAF

BULGUR PILAV (buhl-gahr pee-lahv)

This grain dish is typical of uncomplicated Turkish food. Flavor the bulgur with beef or chicken bouillon to complement the main dish.

1 cup bulgur (cracked wheat)
1 medium onion, chopped
2 tablespoons margarine or butter
2¼ cups water
2 teaspoons instant beef or chicken bouillon
½ teaspoon salt

Cook and stir bulgur and onion in margarine until onion is tender. Stir in remaining ingredients. Heat to boiling; reduce heat. Cover and simmer until bulgur is tender but firm, 20 to 25 minutes.

6 servings

PER SERVING: Calories 175; Protein 5 g; Carbohydrate 30 g; Fat 4 g; Cholesterol 0 mg; Sodium 650 mg

BARLEY WITH MUSHROOMS

This grain dish has most of the elements of a Scotch broth, but it is much heartier.

8 ounces mushrooms, sliced
2 medium onions, chopped
2 tablespoons margarine or butter
3¼ cups boiling water
1 cup barley
2 teaspoons instant chicken bouillon
½ teaspoon salt
Dash of pepper

Cook and stir mushrooms and onions in margarine 5 minutes; place in ungreased 1½-quart casserole. Stir in remaining ingredients. Cover and cook in 375° oven, stirring once, until barley is tender, about 1¼ hours.

6 servings

PER SERVING: Calories 175; Protein 4 g; Carbohydrate 31 g; Fat 4 g; Cholesterol 0 mg; Sodium 650 mg

POLENTA WITH CHEESE

The Rumanians have their own version of this Italian classic; *mamaliga*. Fried, polenta can be enjoyed as either a sweet or savory treat.

1 cup yellow cornmeal
¾ cup water
3¼ cups boiling water
2 teaspoons salt
1 tablespoon margarine or butter
1 cup grated Parmesan cheese
⅓ cup shredded Swiss or Kashkaval cheese (about 1½ ounces)

Mix cornmeal and ¾ cup water in 2-quart saucepan. Stir in 3¼ cups water and the salt. Cook, stirring constantly, until mixture thickens and boils; reduce heat. Cover and simmer, stirring occasionally, 10 minutes. Remove from heat; stir until smooth.

Spread ⅓ of the mixture in greased 1½-quart casserole. Dot with ⅓ of the margarine; sprinkle with ⅓ of the Parmesan cheese. Repeat twice. Sprinkle with Swiss cheese. Cook uncovered in 350° oven until hot and bubbly, 15 to 20 minutes.

6 servings

PER SERVING: Calories 185; Protein 9 g; Carbohydrate 19 g; Fat 8 g; Cholesterol 15 mg; Sodium 1000 mg

BRAISED BUCKWHEAT KERNELS

KASHA (<u>kah</u>-shah)

In Russia and Eastern Europe, this grain (sometimes called groats) is a mainstay. It is quickly prepared and very hearty.

1 cup medium buckwheat kernels (kasha)
1 egg
2½ cups boiling water
2 tablespoons margarine or butter
2½ teaspoons instant beef bouillon
¼ teaspoon salt
¼ teaspoon pepper

Mix buckwheat kernels and egg; cook in ungreased skillet over medium-high heat, stirring constantly, until kernels separate and brown. Stir in water, margarine, bouillon, salt and pepper; reduce heat. Cover and simmer until liquid is absorbed and buckwheat kernels are tender, about 5 minutes.

6 servings

PER SERVING: Calories 115; Protein 3 g; Carbohydrate 14 g; Fat 5 g; Cholesterol 35 mg; Sodium 680 mg

---

Kasha

This is the Russian preparation of buckwheat kernels (groats). Kasha is a nutritious food that benefits from the addition of flavorful ingredients. Served as a porridge or sort of pilaf, groats takes on an enhanced flavor when cooked in stock or broth. Served as a sturdy, sweetened dessert, groats assume a note of luxury with the addition of heavy cream. Sometimes groats themselves are labeled "kasha." Like cooked rice, they can be the base of delicious stuffings for poultry and fish.

ROMAN FARINA DUMPLINGS

GNOCCHI ALLA ROMANA
(<u>n'yoh</u>-kee ah-lah roh-<u>mah</u>-nah)

In Italy, *gnocchi* are sometimes made from cooked, mashed potatoes, too. These dumplings have a delightful, chewy texture and cook up golden brown.

3 cups milk
1 cup farina or semolina
2 eggs, well beaten
1 tablespoon margarine or butter
1 teaspoon salt
Dash of pepper
¼ cup margarine or butter
1 cup grated Parmesan cheese

Heat milk to scalding in 2-quart saucepan; reduce heat. Sprinkle farina slowly into hot milk, stirring constantly. Cook, stirring constantly, until thick, about 5 minutes (spoon will stand upright in mixture); remove from heat.

Stir in eggs, 1 tablespoon margarine, the salt and pepper; beat until smooth. Spread in greased oblong pan, 13 × 9 × 2 inches; cool. Cover and refrigerate until firm, 2 to 3 hours.

Cut farina mixture into 1½-inch squares or circles. (Dip knife in cold water to prevent sticking.) Place cakes, overlapping, in ungreased baking dish. Dot with ¼ cup margarine; sprinkle with cheese. Bake uncovered in 350° oven until crisp and golden, about 30 minutes.

6 servings

PER SERVING: Calories 340; Protein 15 g; Carbohydrate 29 g; Fat 18 g; Cholesterol 90 mg; Sodium 800 mg

NOTE: For a browner top, set oven control to broil or 550°. Broil dumplings with tops 2 or 3 inches from heat until golden brown, about 3 minutes.

GREEK TOMATO PILAF

Beef-flavored rice is cooked with fresh toma-toes for a savory pilaf.

2 medium tomatoes, coarsely chopped
2 tablespoons chopped onion
2 tablespoons margarine or butter
2 cups water
1 cup uncooked regular rice
1 teaspoon instant beef bouillon
¾ teaspoon salt
⅛ teaspoon pepper

Cook and stir tomatoes and onions in mar-garine in 2-quart saucepan over medium heat 2 minutes. Stir in remaining ingredients. Heat to boiling, stirring once or twice, reduce heat. Cover and simmer 14 minutes. (Do not lift cover or stir.) Remove from heat. Fluff rice lightly with fork; cover and let steam 5 to 10 minutes. Serve with grated Parmesan cheese if desired.

8 servings

PER SERVING: Calories 125; Protein 2 g; Carbohy-drate 22 g; Fat 3 g; Cholesterol 0 mg; Sodium 400 mg

Chayote

Mild-flavored chayote, a squash the size of a large pear, weighs on the average about 10 to 12 ounces. In typical squash fashion, it grows on vines. Chayote is usually creamy jade in color; there are chayotes that are quite white, and some are nearly as dark as avocados. It is popular in every corner of the world, from Australia and New Zealand to Africa. In the United States alone it has three names in addition to *chayote: mirliton* (frequently heard in the South), *christophine* (of Caribbean derivation) and *vegetable pear* (widely used).

RICE WITH CHAYOTE

FRITANGA (free-tahn-gah)

In Antigua, where this dish is often enjoyed, chayote might be more commonly known as *christophine*. With the addition of tomato, this is a classic in Guatemala, too.

2 tablespoons vegetable oil
1 medium chayote (about 8 ounces), pared and
  cut into ½-inch pieces
1 medium onion, chopped
2 cloves garlic, chopped
1 tablespoon vegetable oil
4 cups cooked rice
1 medium tomato, coarsely chopped
¼ teaspoon salt
Dash of pepper
Snipped chives

Heat 2 tablespoons oil in 12-inch skillet until hot. Cook and stir chayote over medium heat until crisp-tender, about 5 minutes; remove with slotted spoon.

Cook and stir onion and garlic in 1 tablespoon oil until onion is tender, about 5 minutes. Stir in rice; cook and stir until hot, about 8 minutes. Stir in chayote, tomato, salt and pepper. Cook and stir until tomato is hot, 3 to 5 minutes. Sprinkle with chives.

6 to 8 servings

PER SERVING: Calories 265; Protein 4 g; Carbohy-drate 44 g; Fat 8 g; Cholesterol 0 mg; Sodium 610 mg

INDONESIAN YELLOW RICE

NASI KUNING (nah-<u>see</u> koh-<u>neeg</u>)

Coconut milk, lemon grass and turmeric are the key elements that flavor this fluffy rice.

2 cups Coconut Milk (page 72)
1 cup uncooked regular rice
1 piece lemon grass, about 2 inches long
½ teaspoon salt
¼ teaspoon ground turmeric

Heat all ingredients to boiling in 2-quart saucepan, stirring once or twice; reduce heat. Cover and simmer 14 minutes. (Do not lift cover or stir.) Remove from heat. Fluff rice lightly with fork; cover and let steam 5 to 10 minutes. Remove lemon grass.

6 servings

PER SERVING: Calories 285; Protein 4 g; Carbohydrate 29 g; Fat 17 g; Cholesterol 0 mg; Sodium 190 mg

GARLIC FRIED RICE

SINANGAG (see-<u>nah</u>-nahg)

With so few ingredients making up this rice dish from the Philippines, the flavor of garlic comes through loud and clear. First, chopped garlic seasons the oil; then, when the rice is done, it is served with a sprinkling of the golden, crunchy garlic bits.

2 tablespoons vegetable oil
2 cloves garlic, chopped
3 cups cold cooked rice

Heat oil in 10-inch skillet until hot. Cook and stir garlic in oil over medium heat until golden brown; remove with slotted spoon and reserve.

Golden Rice Cake, *top* (page 275), and Indonesian Yellow Rice

Add rice to remaining oil in skillet. Cook and stir until rice is hot, about 5 minutes. Sprinkle with garlic.

6 servings

PER SERVING: Calories 175; Protein 3 g; Carbohydrate 29 g; Fat 5 g; Cholesterol 0 mg; Sodium 390 mg

RICE, MILAN STYLE

RISOTTO ALLA MILANESE
(ree-<u>soh</u>-toh ah-lah mee-lah-<u>nay</u>-seh)

In Italy they make their risotto with a short, fat grain of rice called *arborio*, which absorbs broth in such a way as to make the resulting risotto especially creamy. Our version uses the rice most commonly available to us, and it is delicious. Beef marrow and saffron give this dish its big-city distinction.

1 cup uncooked regular rice
1 small onion, chopped
1 tablespoon chopped beef marrow (optional)
3 tablespoons margarine or butter
2 cups water
2 teaspoons instant chicken bouillon
¼ teaspoon salt
Dash of ground saffron
¼ cup grated Parmesan cheese

Cook and stir rice, onion and beef marrow in margarine in 2-quart saucepan until rice is golden, 4 to 5 minutes. Stir in remaining ingredients except cheese. Heat to boiling, stirring once or twice; reduce heat. Cover and simmer 14 minutes. (Do not lift cover or stir.) Remove from heat. Gently stir in cheese with fork; cover and let steam 5 to 10 minutes. Serve rice with additional Parmesan cheese if desired.

6 servings

PER SERVING: Calories 190; Protein 4 g; Carbohydrate 28 g; Fat 7 g; Cholesterol 5 mg; Sodium 640 mg

LEMON AND CELERY PILAF

This Portuguese pilaf adds the zip of mustard and red pepper sauce to lemon's fresh effect. The result is a fluffy dish that is great with broiled or baked fish.

1 small onion, chopped
1 small clove garlic, finely chopped
¼ cup margarine or butter
2 cups water
1 cup uncooked regular rice
2 stalks celery, sliced
2 teaspoons instant chicken bouillon
2 teaspoons finely shredded lemon peel
½ teaspoon salt
¼ teaspoon dry mustard
⅛ teaspoon red pepper sauce
2 tablespoons snipped parsley

Cook and stir onion and garlic in margarine in 3-quart saucepan until onion is tender. Stir in remaining ingredients except parsley. Heat to boiling, stirring once or twice; reduce heat. Cover and simmer 14 minutes. (Do not lift cover or stir.) Remove from heat. Stir in parsley lightly with fork; cover and let steam 5 to 10 minutes.

7 servings

PER SERVING: Calories 175; Protein 3 g; Carbohydrate 25 g; Fat 7 g; Cholesterol 0 mg; Sodium 610 mg

GREEN RICE

ARROZ VERDE (ah-rros vehr-deh)

The lusty poblano chili is much used in Mexican cooking. This is a very pretty dish, flecked with fresh parsley and cilantro.

2 cups water
½ cup snipped parsley
½ cup snipped fresh cilantro
1 teaspoon salt
Dash of pepper
2 poblano chilies, seeded and coarsely chopped
2 cloves garlic, cut into fourths
1 small onion, cut into fourths
1 cup uncooked regular rice
2 tablespoons vegetable oil

Place water, parsley, cilantro, salt, pepper, chilies, garlic and onion in blender container. Cover and blend on medium-high speed until smooth, about 30 seconds. Strain; reserve liquid.

Cook and stir rice in oil in 2-quart saucepan over medium heat until rice is well coated, about 1 minute. Pour reserved liquid over rice.

Heat rice mixture to boiling, stirring once or twice; reduce heat. Cover and simmer 14 minutes. (Do not lift cover or stir.) Remove from heat. Fluff rice lightly with fork; cover and let steam 5 to 10 minutes. Garnish with sliced pimiento if desired.

6 servings

PER SERVING: Calories 175; Protein 3 g; Carbohydrate 30 g; Fat 5 g; Cholesterol 0 mg; Sodium 360 mg

INDIAN FRIED RICE
PULAO (pooh-lah'oh)

This rice dish is made festive with raisins, almonds and curry powder, and brilliant with turmeric. Indian Fried Rice is especially good with poultry dishes.

1 cup uncooked regular rice
1 medium onion, chopped
½ cup Ghee (page 237), margarine or butter
½ cup raisins (optional)
2 teaspoons instant chicken bouillon
1 teaspoon curry powder
½ teaspoon salt
2¼ cups boiling water
¼ cup toasted slivered almonds

Cook and stir rice and onion in Ghee until rice is yellow and onion is tender. Stir in raisins, bouillon, curry powder and salt. Pour into ungreased 1½-quart casserole. Stir in water. Cover and cook in 350° oven until liquid is absorbed, 25 to 30 minutes. Stir in almonds.

6 servings

PER SERVING: Calories 300; Protein 4 g; Carbohydrate 30 g; Fat 18 g; Cholesterol 0 mg; Sodium 780 mg

GOLDEN RICE CAKE
KATEH (kah-teh)

The basmati rice praised by the Indians is loved in Iran, too. With its mild fragrance, it gives this crusty fried rice patty exotic distinction.

1½ cups uncooked basmati or regular rice (see Note)
2¾ cups water
1 teaspoon salt
3 tablespoons Ghee (page 237), margarine or butter

Heat rice, water and salt to boiling in 3-quart saucepan, stirring once or twice; reduce heat. Cover and simmer 14 minutes. (Do not lift cover or stir.) Remove from heat. Fluff rice lightly with fork; cover and let steam 5 to 10 minutes. Stir in Ghee.

Smooth top of rice; gently press in saucepan. Cover and cook over low heat until rice is light golden brown on bottom, about 30 minutes. Set saucepan in bowl of iced water 10 minutes. Loosen edge with spatula. Unmold on serving plate; cut into wedges. Serve warm or cold.

6 servings

PER SERVING: Calories 230; Protein 4 g; Carbohydrate 40 g; Fat 6 g; Cholesterol 0 mg; Sodium 430 mg

NOTE: Rinse rice thoroughly if using bulk basmati.

7

BREADS

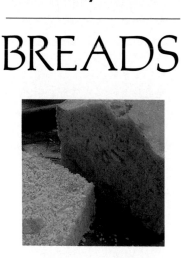

An interesting feature of the collection of breads that follows is that it captures the essence of how different societies fashion, flavor and serve this staple. In China, where rice predominates, there are few yeast breads. Rice cakes, often steamed, are usually the rule. However, in the northernmost regions of that vast country, where a semitropical climate yields to a more arid one, grains are a more common resource, and certain wheat-based breads, like Chinese Green Onion Circles, are popular fare.

As we move south and west along the Asian continent, the category of bread embraces unique forms and flavors. In Sri Lanka, for example, coconut adds its faintly sweet and nutty flavor to Sri Lankan Flat Bread. In India and the Middle East, the breads are customarily small and round, whether they are baked and split like Pocket Bread, deep-fried like *Puris* (Fried Bread Puffs) or rolled paper-thin like Indian Flat Bread.

In Europe, where commercial bakeries abound in cities and towns, breads honor the grains and hearty fare of the countryside. Russian Rye Bread and Dark Pumpernickel Bread are delicious and true to the spirit of the traditional recipes. Gruyère Cheese Ring and Brioche give a nod to some of the fancier, more refined baked goods famed in central Europe.

Clockwise from top left: Turkish Bread Rings (page 302), Yugoslavian Coffee Cake (page 302) and Coconut Corn Bread (page 278)

COCONUT CORN BREAD

Cornmeal gives this tropically flavored loaf from the Dominican Republic crunch. Spices, fresh coconut, coconut milk and rum flavor this sweet bread, studded with candied fruit.

½ cup diced mixed candied fruit
2 tablespoons dark rum
⅓ cup sugar
⅓ cup margarine or butter, softened
2 eggs
1 cup coconut cream
1 cup yellow cornmeal
1 cup all-purpose flour
1½ teaspoons baking powder
½ teaspoon salt
½ teaspoon ground cinnamon
¼ teaspoon ground cloves
1 cup shredded fresh coconut

Heat oven to 375°. Mix candied fruit and rum in small bowl; reserve. Beat sugar and margarine in large bowl; add eggs, one at a time, beating until well blended. Stir in remaining ingredients except candied fruit mixture and coconut; beat until smooth, about 30 strokes by hand. Fold in candied fruit mixture and coconut. Pour into greased loaf pan, 8½ × 4½ × 2½ inches. Bake until top is golden brown and wooden pick inserted in center comes out clean, 40 to 45 minutes. Cool 20 minutes; remove from pan. Cool completely before slicing.

1 loaf (24 slices)

PER SLICE: Calories 135; Protein 2 g; Carbohydrate 16 g; Fat 7 g; Cholesterol 20 mg; Sodium 115 mg

BANANA BREAD
PÃO DE BANANO (pow day bah-nah-noh)

Banana quick breads are widely popular. Americans tend to load theirs with walnuts. This Guatemalan version is distinctive with lime, allspice and cinnamon. Many quick breads are versatile enough to go from the breakfast table to the dinner table; this one is sweet enough to serve as a teacake.

2½ cups all-purpose flour
½ cup granulated sugar
½ cup brown sugar
3½ teaspoons baking powder
1 teaspoon salt
½ teaspoon ground cinnamon
½ teaspoon ground allspice
1¼ cups mashed bananas (2 large bananas)
¼ cup milk
3 tablespoons vegetable oil
1 egg
1½ teaspoons grated lime peel
1 tablespoon lime juice

Heat oven to 350°. Grease bottom only of loaf pan, 9 × 5 × 3 inches, or 2 loaf pans, 8½ × 4½ × 2½ inches. Mix all ingredients; beat 30 seconds. Pour into pan. Bake until wooden pick inserted in center comes out clean, 9-inch loaf 70 to 80 minutes, 8½-inch loaves 55 to 60 minutes. Cool slightly. Loosen sides of loaf from pan; remove from pan. Cool completely before slicing. To store, wrap and refrigerate no longer than 1 week.

1 loaf (26 slices)

PER SLICE: Calories 100; Protein 1 g; Carbohydrate 20 g; Fat 2 g; Cholesterol 10 mg; Sodium 140 mg

MEXICAN DATE BREAD

PAN DE DATIL MOLEGE (pahn deh dah-<u>teel</u> moh-leh-<u>heh</u>)

This sweet, egg-rich loaf is thick with dates and pecans, and fragrant with a good Mexican shake of cinnamon. The egg yolks and whites are beaten separately for more tender results. Serve this dense date bread with cream cheese for a sweet snack or with ice cream for a full-blown dessert.

6 eggs, separated
½ cup sugar
½ cup margarine or butter, melted and cooled
1 cup all-purpose flour
1 tablespoon ground cinnamon
1 teaspoon ground nutmeg
2 cups cut-up dates
1 cup chopped pecans
Powdered sugar

Heat oven to 350°. Grease and flour loaf pan, 9 × 5 × 3 inches. Beat egg whites in large bowl on high speed until soft peaks form.

Gradually beat sugar into egg yolks in medium bowl; beat on high speed until thick and lemon colored, about 3 minutes. Beat in margarine on medium speed until well blended. Fold egg yolk mixture into egg whites. Gently stir in flour, cinnamon and nutmeg just until moistened; stir in dates and pecans. Pour into pan. Bake until wooden pick inserted in center comes out clean, 55 to 60 minutes. Cool 5 minutes; remove from pan. Cool completely; sprinkle top with powdered sugar.

1 loaf (26 slices)

PER SLICE: Calories 155; Protein 2 g; Carbohydrate 19 g; Fat 8 g; Cholesterol 50 mg; Sodium 55 mg

PARAGUAYAN CORN BREAD

SOPA PARAGUAYA (<u>soh</u>-pah pah-rah-<u>gwy</u>-yah)

This cheese-laden loaf is boldly spiced, and in Paraguay it often accompanies a hearty beef soup. Every slice is peppered with moist corn kernels.

1½ cups boiling water
1 cup cornmeal
2 tablespoons margarine or butter, softened
3 eggs, separated
½ cup milk
½ cup (4 ounces) cottage cheese
1 teaspoon salt
1 teaspoon baking powder
¼ teaspoon ground cumin
⅛ teaspoon ground allspice
⅛ teaspoon ground red pepper
1 can (8 ounces) whole-kernel corn, drained
1 cup shredded Monterey Jack cheese (4 ounces)
1 small onion, chopped

Heat oven to 375°. Stir boiling water into cornmeal in 3-quart bowl; continue stirring until smooth. Blend in margarine and egg yolks. Stir in remaining ingredients except egg whites. Beat egg whites just until soft peaks form; fold into batter. Pour into greased 2-quart casserole. Bake until knife inserted near the center comes out clean, 45 to 50 minutes.

9 to 12 servings

PER SERVING: Calories 185; Protein 9 g; Carbohydrate 17 g; Fat 9 g; Cholesterol 85 mg; Sodium 520 mg

┌─ *Gruyère* ─┐

Although Gruyère cheese is often likened to Swiss cheeses, Emmenthaler usually, it has a stronger and more mellow flavor. It is a firm, French cheese, with small holes and a hard rind. Gruyère is indispensable in making the classic French Gougère (this page). Gruyère is delicious nibbled on its own or with fresh fruit and is perfect for picnics. The slightly nutty flavor of Gruyère is very nice in quiches and sandwiches; the popular French street snacks *croque monsieur* and *croque madame* are topped with Gruyère.

GRUYÈRE RING
GOUGÈRE (goo-<u>jehr</u>)

This light puff of bread is said to have been first baked in the Burgundy region of France, but it is now popular across the country. It can stand on its own as a light luncheon dish, served with nothing more than a salad. The dough, made using the same technique as that for cream puff dough, may be dropped from a spoon or piped into mounds, to be baked as little hors d'oeuvres and served hot.

1 cup milk
½ cup margarine or butter
1 cup all-purpose flour
4 eggs, slightly beaten
1 cup shredded Gruyère cheese (about 3 ounces)

Heat oven to 400°. Heat milk and margarine to rolling boil in 2-quart saucepan. Stir in flour. Stir vigorously over low heat until mixture forms a ball, about 1 minute; remove from heat. Beat in 4 eggs all at once; continue beating until smooth.

Fold in ⅔ cup of the cheese. Drop dough by tablespoonfuls onto greased cookie sheet to form 8-inch ring; smooth with spatula. Sprinkle with remaining cheese. Bake until puffed and golden, 50 to 60 minutes.

8 to 10 servings

PER SERVING: Calories 260; Protein 10 g; Carbohydrate 14 g; Fat 18 g; Cholesterol 120 mg; Sodium 220 mg

IRISH SODA BREAD

The history of this bread goes back hundreds of years, to a time before brick ovens were a common kitchen convenience. Then, this bread was baked in an early sort of Dutch oven—an iron kettle that could be covered. It is delicious warm, spread with butter and jam, or cooled, when it can be more easily sliced.

3 tablespoons margarine or butter, softened
2½ cups all-purpose flour
2 tablespoons sugar
1 teaspoon baking soda
1 teaspoon baking powder
½ teaspoon salt
⅓ cup raisins (optional)
¾ cup buttermilk

Cut margarine into flour, sugar, baking soda, baking powder and salt until mixture resembles fine crumbs. Stir in raisins and enough buttermilk to make a soft dough.

Turn onto lightly floured surface; knead until smooth, 1 to 2 minutes. Shape into round loaf, about 6½ inches in diameter. Place on greased cookie sheet. Cut an X about ¼ through center of loaf with floured knife. Bake in 375° oven until golden brown, 35 to 45 minutes. Brush with margarine if desired.

1 loaf (16 slices)

PER SLICE: Calories 95; Protein 2 g; Carbohydrate 17 g; Fat 2 g; Cholesterol 5 mg; Sodium 170 mg

CURRANT CREAM SCONES

Scones are short biscuits especially favored by the British, who love them at teatime. Only faintly sweet, they are wonderful with butter and jam. The legendary British "cream tea" offers thick, clotted Devonshire cream to spread on the scones.

⅓ cup margarine, butter or shortening
1¾ cups all-purpose flour
3 tablespoons sugar
2½ teaspoons baking powder
½ teaspoon salt
1 egg, beaten
½ cup currants or raisins
4 to 6 tablespoons half-and-half
1 egg, beaten

Heat oven to 400°. Cut margarine into flour, sugar, baking powder and salt until mixture resembles fine crumbs. Stir in 1 egg, the currants and just enough half-and-half so dough leaves side of bowl. Turn dough onto lightly floured surface. Knead lightly 10 times. Roll ½ inch thick.

Cut dough into 2¼-inch circles with floured cutter. Place on ungreased cookie sheet. Brush with 1 egg. Bake until golden, 10 to 12 minutes. Immediately remove from cookie sheet.

10 to 12 scones

PER SCONE: Calories 195; Protein 4 g; Carbohydrate 27 g; Fat 8 g; Cholesterol 45 mg; Sodium 290 mg

SCOTTISH OATCAKES

Oatcakes are a wonderful breakfast invention, perfect plain or with honey, butter or jam. They are useful as an hors d' oeuvre or savory snack, too, topped with smoked fish or meat, or cheese.

½ cup shortening
1 cup regular oats or quick-cooking oats
1 cup all-purpose flour
½ teaspoon baking soda
¼ teaspoon salt
2 to 3 tablespoons cold water

Cut shortening into oats, flour, baking soda and salt until mixture resembles fine crumbs. Add water, 1 tablespoon at a time, until mixture forms a stiff dough.

Roll until ⅛ inch thick on lightly floured surface. Cut into 2½-inch rounds or squares. Place on ungreased cookie sheet. Bake in 375° oven until oatcakes start to brown, 12 to 15 minutes. Cool on wire rack.

18 oatcakes

PER OATCAKE: Calories 90; Protein 1 g; Carbohydrate 8 g; Fat 6 g; Cholesterol 0 mg; Sodium 50 mg

OATCAKE COOKIES: Prepare as directed above except add ⅓ cup sugar with the flour.

GERMAN APPLE PANCAKES
APFELPFANNKUCHEN (ahp-f'l-p'fann-koo-kh'n)

Apfelpfannkuchen is literally a "pan cake," an eggy mixture poured into pans and baked. Like soufflés, these pancakes should be served as soon as they are pulled hot from the oven, as they will not stay impressively puffed long. They are an easy brunch dish, requiring no last-minute attention.

4 eggs
¾ cup all-purpose flour
¾ cup milk
½ teaspoon salt
¼ cup margarine or butter
2 medium apples, thinly sliced
¼ cup sugar
¼ teaspoon ground cinnamon

Heat oven to 400°. Place 2 round layer pans, 9 × 1½ inches, in oven. Beat eggs, flour, milk and salt in small mixer bowl on medium speed 1 minute. Remove pans from oven. Place 2 tablespoons margarine in each pan; rotate pans until margarine is melted and coats sides of pans.

Arrange half the apple slices in each pan; divide batter evenly between pans. Mix sugar and cinnamon; sprinkle 2 tablespoons sugar mixture over batter in each pan. Bake uncovered until puffed and golden brown, 20 to 25 minutes.

2 large pancakes (4 servings)

PER SERVING: Calories 380; Protein 10 g; Carbohydrate 44 g; Fat 18 g; Cholesterol 220 mg; Sodium 490 mg

LITTLE GERMAN NOODLE DUMPLINGS
SPÄTZLE (shpeh-ts'leh)

These free-form dumplings make an unusual side dish, sprinkled with grated cheese or toasted bread crumbs. They can be made in hot broth instead of water, and some recipes instruct forcing the *Spätzle* dough directly into a boiling soup to cook, just minutes before the soup is brought to the table.

2 eggs, beaten
¼ cup milk or water
1 cup all-purpose flour
½ teaspoon salt
Dash of pepper
2 quarts water*
1 teaspoon salt
2 tablespoons margarine or butter, melted

Mix eggs, milk, flour, ½ teaspoon salt and the pepper. (Batter will be thick.) Heat water and 1 teaspoon salt to boiling in Dutch oven. Press batter through colander (preferably one with large holes), a few tablespoons at a time, into boiling water. Stir once or twice while boiling to prevent sticking.

Cook until dumplings rise to surface and are tender, about 5 minutes; drain. Pour margarine over dumplings. Serve with Sauerbraten (page 126), meatballs, chicken or sauerkraut.

4 to 6 servings

*Beef or chicken broth may be used in place of the water.

PER SERVING: Calories 210; Protein 7 g; Carbohydrate 25 g; Fat 9 g; Cholesterol 110 mg; Sodium 640 mg

COCONUT PANCAKES
KANOM KLUK (ko-nohm kluk)

The Thais are known for their inventiveness with coconut—the meat, the milk and coconut cream. These sweet pancakes, light with rice flour, are offered fresh and warm in Thai markets. They are delicate, thinner than American pancakes and more like crèpes.

1 cup rice flour
¼ cup sugar
½ teaspoon salt
1 can (14 ounces) unsweetened coconut milk
4 eggs
¾ cup shredded coconut
Vegetable oil
Red and green food colors
1 cup sweetened condensed milk
¾ cup shredded coconut

Beat flour, sugar, salt, coconut milk and eggs in medium bowl until smooth. Stir in ¾ cup coconut. Divide batter equally among 3 bowls. Tint one part of batter pale pink with red food color, and one part pale green with green food color; leave third part untinted. Lightly oil 8-inch nonstick skillet; heat until hot. For each pancake, pour scant ¼ cup batter into skillet; immediately rotate skillet until batter covers bottom.

Cook until top is almost dry and bottom is light brown. Run wide spatula around edge to loosen; turn and cook other side until light brown. Roll up pancake, and place on heatproof platter; keep warm. Drizzle with sweetened condensed milk, and sprinkle with coconut.

About 18 pancakes

PER PANCAKE: Calories 200; Protein 4 g; Carbohydrate 24 g; Fat 10 g; Cholesterol 50 mg; Sodium 120 mg

Following pages: German Apple Pancake, *left* (page 282) and Coconut Pancakes

FRIED POTATO BREAD

LEFSE (leff-seh)

The unusual dough for this Norwegian bread is rolled out into large, thin circles and fried on a hot griddle. The resulting bread, which is soft, is extremely versatile. It is eaten warm or cold, plain or spread with butter or sprinkled with brown sugar. To serve *Lefse,* fold each circle into quarters or roll up.

5 cups hot mashed potatoes (no milk, margarine or salt added)
¼ cup shortening
2 tablespoons milk
1½ teaspoons salt
2 cups all-purpose flour

Beat mashed potatoes, shortening, milk and salt until no lumps remain. Cover and refrigerate until completely chilled, at least 4 hours.

Turn potato mixture onto floured surface; knead in flour. (Dough will be soft.) Divide into 20 equal parts; shape each part into a ball. (For best results, work with 4 or 5 balls at a time; cover and refrigerate remaining balls until needed.)

Shape each ball into a flattened round on heavily floured board. Roll each round as thin as possible into 10- to 12-inch circle with floured stockinet-covered rolling pin or lefse rolling pin. Lift dough occasionally with spatula to make sure it is not sticking, adding flour as needed.

Heat ungreased griddle or lefse baker to 400°. Cook until blisters form and brown spots appear on bottom, about 1 minute on each side. (Do not overcook. Lefse should be soft, not crisp.) Stack cooked lefse between two towels to prevent drying. Wrap in plastic wrap and refrigerate no longer than 3 days or freeze no longer than 1 month.

20 lefse

PER LEFSE: Calories 110; Protein 2 g; Carbohydrate 19 g; Fat 3 g; Cholesterol 0 mg; Sodium 170 mg

---

SRI LANKAN FLATBREAD

ROTIS (roh-tis)

Coconut flavors this flatbread, cooked golden brown on a griddle.

¾ cup fine coconut*
2¼ cups self-rising flour
1 to 1¼ cups cold water
Ghee (page 237) or vegetable oil

Mix coconut and flour in medium bowl. Gradually add water, stirring until dough is soft and smooth and cleans side of bowl. Turn dough onto floured surface. Cover; let rest 30 minutes.

Heat griddle to 375°. Divide dough into 12 equal parts; flatten each part with floured hands into thin rounds, about 5 inches in diameter, on floured surface. Brush griddle with Ghee. Cook breads on both sides until golden brown, about 2 minutes on each side. Serve hot.

12 breads

*If fine coconut is unavailable, place shredded coconut in blender container; cover, and blend until finely ground.

PER BREAD: Calories 120; Protein 2 g; Carbohydrate 21 g; Fat 3 g; Cholesterol 0 mg; Sodium 15 mg

INDIAN FLAT BREAD
NAAN (non)

Humble *Naan* is an everyday bread, common in India, Pakistan and central Asia.

2 cups all-purpose flour
¼ cup plain yogurt
1 egg, slightly beaten
1½ teaspoons baking powder
1 teaspoon sugar
¼ teaspoon salt
⅛ teaspoon baking soda
½ cup milk
Ghee (page 237) or vegetable oil
Poppy seed

Mix all ingredients except milk, Ghee and poppy seed. Stir in enough milk to make a soft dough. Turn dough onto lightly floured surface; knead until smooth, about 5 minutes. Place in greased bowl; turn greased side up. Cover; let rest in warm place 3 hours.

Divide dough into 6 or 8 equal parts. Flatten each part on lightly floured surface, rolling it into a 6 × 4-inch leaf shape (round at one end, tapered at the other) about ¼ inch thick. Brush with Ghee; sprinkle with poppy seed.

Place 2 cookie sheets in oven; heat oven to 450°. Remove cookie sheets from oven; place breads on hot cookie sheets. Bake until firm, 6 to 8 minutes.

6 or 8 breads

PER BREAD: Calories 200; Protein 6 g; Carbohydrate 35 g; Fat 4 g; Cholesterol 40 mg; Sodium 230 mg

FRIED BREAD PUFFS
PURIS (poo-rrees)

Puris is perhaps the most spectacular of all Indian breads. Some restaurants serve enormous *Puris,* eight or more inches across, but the *Puris* below are more manageable. Because they deflate as they cool, it is advisable to bring them promptly to the table where their spectacle can be enjoyed.

1 cup whole wheat flour
1 cup all-purpose flour
½ teaspoon salt
3 tablespoons Ghee (page 237) or vegetable oil
½ to ¾ cup water
Vegetable oil

Mix flour, salt and Ghee until mixture resembles fine crumbs. Stir in just enough water to make a very stiff dough. Turn dough onto lightly floured surface; knead until smooth and elastic, 5 to 8 minutes. Cover; let rest 20 minutes.

Shape dough by rounded teaspoonfuls into 1-inch balls. Roll into 3- to 4-inch circles ⅛ inch thick on lightly floured surface. (Cover to prevent drying.)

Heat oil (1½ to 2 inches) to 370°. Fry 1 to 3 puris at a time, turning once, until golden brown and evenly puffed, 1½ to 2 minutes; drain. (Keep puris submerged in hot oil with spoon if necessary, to insure even puffing.)

About 24 puffs

PER PUFF: Calories 70; Protein 1 g; Carbohydrate 8 g; Fat 4 g; Cholesterol 0 mg; Sodium 45 mg

Chinese Green Onion Circles

CHINESE GREEN ONION CIRCLES

T'SUNG YU PING (tzoong yuh bing)

These coiled little pastries taste faintly of sesame oil, but green onions are the dominant flavor. *T'sung Yu Ping* comes from northern China, where it is one of the few breads that is not steamed.

3 cups all-purpose flour
1½ teaspoons baking powder
1 teaspoon salt
1 tablespoon sesame oil
1 cup plus 1 to 2 tablespoons cold water
Sesame oil

¾ cup chopped green onions
Vegetable oil

Mix flour, baking powder and salt in medium bowl; stir in 1 tablespoon sesame oil and enough water to make a smooth, soft dough. Turn dough onto floured surface; knead 3 minutes. Divide dough into 6 equal parts; keep covered. Roll each part into circle, about 7 inches in diameter. Brush each circle with sesame oil, and sprinkle with about 2 tablespoons of the green onions. Roll each circle up tightly, pinching side and ends to seal. Shape into rope, about 12 inches long. Roll to form a coil, tucking end under coil; flatten into circle, about 7 inches in diameter.

Heat 2 tablespoons vegetable oil in 8-inch skillet until hot. Cook 1 circle over medium heat until golden brown, about 8 minutes on each side. Repeat with additional oil and remaining circles. Cut into wedges; serve hot.

6 circles (24 wedges)

PER WEDGE: Calories 90; Protein 2 g; Carbohydrate 12 g; Fat 4 g; Cholesterol 0 mg; Sodium 115 mg

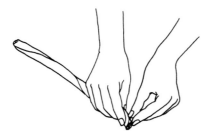

Roll each circle up tightly, pinching side and ends to seal.

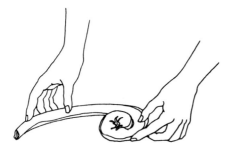

Shape rope to form a coil; tuck end under coil.

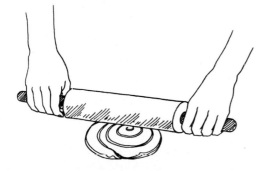

Flatten coil into a circle about 7 inches in diameter.

AFRICAN CORIANDER BREAD

PAIN NORD AFRICAIN AU CORIANDRE
(<u>pan</u> nohr ahf-ree-<u>cangh</u> oh kohr-ree-<u>ahn</u>-druh)

Here is a marriage of Moroccan–North African flavorings with a European yeast-raised bread. This bread is thought to be a product of French colonials in northern Africa.

2 packages active dry yeast
1½ cups lukewarm milk (scalded, then cooled)
½ cup honey
½ cup margarine or butter, melted and cooled
1 tablespoon ground coriander
1 tablespoon grated orange peel
1 teaspoon salt
½ teaspoon ground ginger
¼ teaspoon ground cinnamon
1 egg
1½ cups whole wheat flour
4 to 4½ cups all-purpose flour

Dissolve yeast in warm milk in large bowl. Stir in remaining ingredients except all-purpose flour. Stir in enough all-purpose flour to make dough easy to handle. Turn dough onto lightly floured surface; knead until smooth and elastic, 5 to 10 minutes. Place in greased bowl; turn greased side up. Cover; let rise until double, about 1 hour. (Dough is ready if indentation remains when touched.)

Punch down dough; divide into halves. Shape each half into a loaf, 8 inches long. Place loaves in 2 greased loaf pans, 9 × 5 × 3 inches. Cover; let rise until double, 40 to 45 minutes.

Heat oven to 375°. Cut lengthwise slash in top of each loaf. Bake until loaves are golden brown and sound hollow when tapped, 35 to 40 minutes; remove from pans. Cool on wire racks.

2 loaves (16 slices each)

PER SLICE: Calories 125; Protein 3 g; Carbohydrate 21 g; Fat 3 g; Cholesterol 5 mg; Sodium 105 mg

FINNISH RYE BREAD

SUOMALAISRUISLEIPÄ (<u>soo</u>-oh-mah-lais-<u>roo</u>-is-<u>lay</u>-pah)

To serve, cut this round loaf into wedges. It is at its best warm, spread with butter or soft, mild cheese.

1 package active dry yeast
1¼ cups warm water* (105 to 115°)
1 tablespoon packed brown sugar
1 tablespoon vegetable oil
1½ teaspoons salt
1¼ cups medium rye flour
1½ to 2 cups all-purpose flour
Margarine or butter, softened

Dissolve yeast in warm water in large bowl. Stir in brown sugar, oil, salt and 1 cup of the rye flour. Beat until smooth. Stir in enough all-purpose flour to make the dough easy to handle.

Turn dough onto surface that has been sprinkled with the remaining rye flour. Cover; let rest 10 to 15 minutes. Knead until smooth and elastic, about 5 minutes. Place in greased bowl; turn greased side up. Cover; let rise in warm place until double, about 1 hour. (Dough is ready if indentation remains when touched.)

Punch down dough; shape into a round, slightly flat loaf. Place in greased round pan, 9 × 1½ inches. Cover; let rise until double, about 1 hour.

Heat oven to 375°. Bake until loaf sounds hollow when tapped, 40 to 50 minutes. Immediately remove from pan. Brush top of loaf with margarine; cool on wire rack.

1 loaf (12 slices)

*Potato water (water in which potatoes have been cooked) can be substituted for the water. This is traditional for Finnish Rye Bread.

PER SLICE: Calories 120; Protein 3 g; Carbohydrate 22 g; Fat 2 g; Cholesterol 0 mg; Sodium 280 mg

RUSSIAN RYE BREAD

This round bread has a deep, mysterious flavor. Dark molasses, fennel seed and coffee add to the no-nonsense quality of rye flour. Serve this rye bread with full-flavored soups.

2 packages active dry yeast
2 cups warm water (105 to 115°)
¼ cup margarine or butter, softened
¼ cup dark molasses
1 tablespoon freeze-dried instant coffee
2 tablespoons honey
1 teaspoon salt
1 teaspoon fennel seed, crushed
4 cups medium rye flour
1½ to 1¾ cups whole wheat flour
1 egg, slightly beaten

Dissolve yeast in warm water in large bowl. Stir in margarine, molasses, coffee, honey, salt, fennel seed and rye flour. Beat until smooth. Stir in enough whole wheat flour to make dough easy to handle (dough will be stiff but slightly sticky). Turn dough onto generously floured surface; knead until smooth, about 5 minutes. Place in greased bowl; turn greased side up. Cover; let rise in warm place until double, about 1 hour. (Dough is ready if indentation remains when touched.)

Punch down dough; divide into halves. Shape each half into a round loaf about 5 inches in diameter. Place loaves on greased cookie sheet. Cover; let rise until double, about 1 hour. Heat oven to 350°. Brush each loaf with egg. Sprinkle with fennel seed if desired. Bake until loaves are dark brown and sound hollow when tapped, about 1 hour; cool on wire racks.

2 loaves (12 slices each)

PER SLICE: Calories 130; Protein 3 g; Carbohydrate 23 g; Fat 3 g; Cholesterol 10 mg; Sodium 120 mg

SWEDISH RYE BREAD

LIMPA (lim-pah)

This bread is often associated with holidays. The flavorings (molasses, orange peel and anise seed) are delicate but definite.

2 packages active dry yeast
1½ cups warm water (105 to 115°)
⅓ cup packed brown sugar
⅓ cup molasses
1 tablespoon salt
1 tablespoon anise seed or fennel seed, crushed
1 tablespoon finely shredded orange peel
2 tablespoons vegetable oil
2½ cups medium rye flour
2¼ to 2¾ cups all-purpose or unbleached flour

Dissolve yeast in warm water in large bowl. Stir in brown sugar, molasses, salt, anise seed, orange peel, oil and rye flour. Beat until smooth. Stir in enough all-purpose flour to make a soft dough.

Turn dough onto lightly floured surface. Cover; let rest 10 to 15 minutes. Knead until smooth and elastic, about 5 minutes. Place in greased bowl; turn greased side up. Cover; let rise in warm place until double, about 1 hour. (Dough is ready if indentation remains when touched.)

Punch down dough; divide into halves. Shape each half into a round, slightly flat loaf. Place loaves in opposite corners of greased cookie sheet. Cover; let rise until double, about 1 hour.

Heat oven to 375°. Bake until loaves sound hollow when tapped, 40 to 50 minutes. Brush with margarine or butter if desired. Cool on wire racks.

2 loaves (12 slices each)

PER SLICE: Calories 120; Protein 2 g; Carbohydrate 24 g; Fat 2 g; Cholesterol 0 mg; Sodium 270 mg

DARK PUMPERNICKEL BREAD

German pumpernickel uses a blend of rye and wheat flours. Unsweetened cocoa powder adds dimension to the flavor of this round loaf.

3 packages active dry yeast
1¾ cups warm water (105 to 115°)
½ cup dark molasses
2 tablespoons vegetable oil
1 tablespoon caraway seed
1 tablespoon salt
2½ cups dark rye flour
1 cup shreds of wheat bran cereal
¼ cup cocoa
2 to 2½ cups all-purpose flour
Cornmeal
Margarine or butter, softened

Dissolve yeast in warm water in large bowl. Stir in molasses, oil, caraway seed, salt, rye flour, cereal and cocoa. Beat until smooth. Stir in enough all-purpose flour to make dough easy to handle.

Turn dough onto lightly floured surface. Cover; let rest 10 to 15 minutes. Knead until smooth, about 5 minutes. Place in greased bowl; turn greased side up. Cover; let rise in warm place until double, about 1 hour. (Dough is ready if indentation remains when touched.)

Grease cookie sheet; sprinkle with cornmeal. Punch down dough; divide into halves. Shape each half into a round, slightly flat loaf. Place loaves in opposite corners of cookie sheet. Brush tops lightly with margarine; let rise until double, 40 to 50 minutes. Heat oven to 375°. Bake until loaves sound hollow when tapped, 30 to 35 minutes. Cool on wire racks.

2 loaves (12 slices each)

PER SLICE: Calories 140; Protein 3 g; Carbohydrate 25 g; Fat 3 g; Cholesterol 0 mg; Sodium 290 mg

Australian Damper Bread

AUSTRALIAN DAMPER BREAD

This bread dates back to the early days of the Australian colonies. Damper bread, scarcely more complicated than biscuit, reflects that early simplicity. The bread may have been named for one William Dampier, an early explorer of the land.

1 package active dry yeast
¼ cup warm water (105 to 115°)
2 tablespoons sugar
3 cups all-purpose flour
1 tablespoon baking powder
¾ teaspoon salt
¼ cup shortening
1 cup buttermilk

Dissolve yeast in warm water; stir in sugar. Mix flour, baking powder and salt in large bowl; cut in shortening until mixture resembles fine crumbs. Stir in yeast mixture and buttermilk until soft dough forms. Turn dough onto lightly floured surface; gently knead until smooth, about 1 minute. Cover; let rest 10 minutes. Shape dough into a round loaf, about 7 inches in diameter. Place on greased cookie sheet. Cover; let rise in warm place 30 minutes.

Heat oven to 375°. Cut an X about ½ inch deep in top of bread. Bake until golden brown, about 35 minutes. Serve warm. Tear bread into pieces to serve.

1 loaf (12 slices)

PER SLICE: Calories 170; Protein 4 g; Carbohydrate 27 g; Fat 5 g; Cholesterol 0 mg; Sodium 250 mg

FRENCH BREAD

Brushing the loaf with cold water before baking encourages a crackly crust.

1 package active dry yeast
1¼ cups warm water (105 to 115°)
1 tablespoon sugar
1½ teaspoons salt
2¾ to 3 cups all-purpose flour
1 tablespoon cornmeal
1 egg white
2 tablespoons cold water

Dissolve yeast in warm water in large bowl. Stir in sugar, salt and 2 cups of the flour. Beat until smooth. Stir in enough remaining flour to make dough easy to handle.

Turn dough onto lightly floured surface; knead until smooth and elastic, about 5 minutes. Place in greased bowl; turn greased side up. Cover with damp cloth; let rise in warm place until double, 1½ to 2 hours. (Dough is ready if indentation remains when touched.)

Punch down dough; cover and let rest 15 minutes. Grease cookie sheet; sprinkle with cornmeal. Roll dough into rectangle, 15 × 10 inches. Roll up tightly, beginning at 15-inch side; seal edge. Roll gently back and forth to taper ends. Place on cookie sheet. Make ¼-inch slashes in loaf at 2-inch intervals or make 1 lengthwise slash. Brush top of loaf with cold water. Let rise uncovered until double, 1½ hours.

Heat oven to 375°. Brush loaf with cold water. Bake 20 minutes. Mix egg white and 2 tablespoons water; brush over loaf. Bake until loaf is deep golden brown and sounds hollow when tapped, about 25 minutes.

1 loaf (12 slices)

PER SLICE: Calories 110; Protein 3 g; Carbohydrate 24 g; Fat 0 g; Cholesterol 0 mg; Sodium 270 mg

POCKET BREAD

There are many Middle Eastern names for this bread: pita, Arab bread, Israeli flatbread and Armenian bread. It's a bread very handy for stuffing, and like the tortillas of Mexico, it can be cut into wedges for scooping, too.

1 package active dry yeast
1⅓ cups warm water (105 to 115°)
1 tablespoon vegetable oil
1 teaspoon sugar
1 teaspoon salt
3 to 3½ cups all-purpose or unbleached flour

Dissolve yeast in warm water in large bowl. Stir in oil, sugar, salt and 2 cups of the flour. Beat until smooth. Stir in enough remaining flour to make dough easy to handle.

Turn dough onto lightly floured surface; knead until smooth and elastic, about 10 minutes. Place in greased bowl; turn greased side up. Cover; let rise in warm place until double, about 1 hour. (Dough is ready if indentation remains when touched.)

Punch down dough; divide into 6 equal parts. Shape into balls. Cover; let rise 30 minutes. Roll each ball into a 6- to 7-inch circle ⅛ inch thick on floured surface. Place 2 circles in opposite corners of each of 3 cookie sheets. Cover; let rise 30 minutes.

Heat oven to 450°. Bake until loaves are puffed and golden brown, about 10 minutes.

6 pocket breads

PER BREAD: Calories 250; Protein 7 g; Carbohydrate 49 g; Fat 3 g; Cholesterol 0 mg; Sodium 360 mg

ITALIAN FOCACCIA

Focaccia is as flavorful as a simple country bread can get. Olive oil and fresh rosemary give this yeast-raised flatbread its glorious Italian flavor.

1 package active dry yeast
1 cup warm water (105 to 115°)
2 to 3 tablespoons snipped fresh rosemary
3 tablespoons olive oil
2 teaspoons salt
2½ to 3 cups all-purpose flour
Olive oil
Coarsely ground pepper (optional)

Dissolve yeast in warm water in large bowl. Stir in rosemary, 3 tablespoons oil, the salt and enough flour to make dough easy to handle. Turn dough onto lightly floured surface; knead until smooth and elastic, 5 to 10 minutes. Place in greased bowl; turn greased side up. Cover; let rise in warm place until double, about 1 hour. (Dough is ready if indentation remains when touched.)

Heat oven to 400°. Punch down dough. Press in oiled 12-inch pizza pan. Make depressions, with fingers about 2 inches apart, on top of dough. Brush with oil; sprinkle with pepper. Let rise uncovered 30 minutes. Bake until golden brown, 20 to 25 minutes. Brush with additional oil. Serve warm.

1 focaccia (12 pieces)

PER PIECE: Calories 145; Protein 3 g; Carbohydrate 20 g; Fat 6 g; Cholesterol 0 mg; Sodium 360 mg

---

Rosemary

Rosemary is an herb used both fresh and dried. Unlike many herbs, even in its dried form rosemary has powerful flavor; crush the dried leaves in your fingers before adding it to foods to release even more. It is hugely popular around the Mediterranean and is as delectable with olives and olive oil as it is with poultry, fish and countless vegetables. The long, narrow, dusky green leaves are pretty. Sprigs of fresh rosemary make a fragrant, handsome garnish.

BRIOCHE

(bree-ohsh)

Brioche dough is full of eggs and butter and is very soft, but an electric mixer makes handling it a breeze. The French bake their brioche both as large loaves and as individual brioches, for sophisticated breakfast rolls. Brioche has a tender crust and feathery interior.

1 package active dry yeast
¼ cup warm water (105 to 115°)
2 tablespoons sugar
1 teaspoon salt
4 eggs
1 egg white
1 cup butter, softened
3½ cups all-purpose flour
1 egg yolk
1 tablespoon water

Dissolve yeast in warm water in large mixer bowl. Add sugar, salt, 4 eggs, egg white, butter and 2 cups of the flour. Beat on low speed, scraping bowl constantly, 30 seconds. Beat on medium speed, scraping bowl occasionally, 10 minutes. Stir in remaining flour until smooth. Scrape batter from side of bowl. Cover with plastic wrap; let rise in warm place until double, about 1 hour.

Stir down batter by beating about 25 strokes. Cover bowl tightly with plastic wrap; refrigerate at least 8 hours.

Stir down batter. (Batter will be soft and slightly sticky.) Divide batter into halves. Cover and refrigerate one half until ready to use. Shape ¼ of the batter into a ball on lightly floured surface. Shape remaining ¾ batter into a 3½-inch flattened round. Repeat with refrigerated batter.

Grease two 5-cup brioche pans or two 1½-quart ovenproof bowls. Place large rounds in pans, patting to fit. Make indentation about 2 inches in diameter in center of each; place smaller balls in indentations. Cover and let rise until double, about 1½ hours.

Heat oven to 375°. Beat egg yolk and 1 tablespoon water slightly; brush over tops. (Do not let egg-yolk mixture accumulate around edges of pans.) Bake until golden brown, 25 to 30 minutes. Immediately remove from pans.

2 brioche loaves (12 slices each)

PER SLICE: Calories 155; Protein 3 g; Carbohydrate 15 g; Fat 9 g; Cholesterol 65 mg; Sodium 150 mg

INDIVIDUAL BRIOCHES: Grease 24 individual brioche pans or muffin cups, 2½ × 1¼ inches. Divide chilled batter into halves; refrigerate one half. Shape remaining half into roll about 7½ inches long. Cut into 15 slices about ½ inch thick.

Working quickly with floured hands (batter will be soft and slightly sticky), shape 12 of the slices into balls; place in pans. Flatten and make a deep indentation in center of each. Cut each of the remaining 3 slices into 4 equal parts. Shape each part into a small ball; place a ball in each indentation. Repeat with refrigerated batter. Cover and let rise until double, about 40 minutes.

Heat oven to 375°. Beat egg yolk and 1 tablespoon water slightly; brush over tops. (Do not let egg-yolk mixture accumulate around edges of pans.) Bake until golden brown, 15 to 20 minutes. Immediately remove from pans.

24 brioches

JEWISH EGG BRAID

CHALLAH (kha-lah)

This exquisite bread is traditionally made for the Sabbath and holidays. If there is any left over, it makes delicious toast and French toast.

1 package active dry yeast
¾ cup warm water (105 to 115°)
2 tablespoons sugar
1 teaspoon salt
1 egg
1 tablespoon vegetable oil
2½ to 2¾ cups all-purpose flour
Vegetable oil
1 egg yolk
2 tablespoons cold water
Poppy seed

Dissolve yeast in warm water in large bowl. Stir in sugar, salt, 1 egg, 1 tablespoon oil and 1¼ cups of the flour. Beat until smooth. Stir in enough remaining flour to make dough easy to handle.

Turn dough onto lightly floured surface; knead until smooth and elastic, about 5 minutes. Place in greased bowl; turn greased side up. Cover; let rise in warm place until double, 1½ to 2 hours. (Dough is ready if indentation remains when touched.)

Punch down dough; divide into 3 equal parts. Roll each part into a rope, 14 inches long. Place ropes close together on lightly greased cookie sheet. Braid ropes gently and loosely; do not stretch. Pinch ends to fasten; tuck under braid securely. Brush with oil. Let rise until double, 40 to 50 minutes.

Heat oven to 375°. Mix egg yolk and 2 tablespoons water; brush braid with egg-yolk mixture. Sprinkle with poppy seed. Bake until golden brown, 25 to 30 minutes.

1 loaf (16 slices)

PER SLICE: Calories 105; Protein 3 g; Carbohydrate 17 g; Fat 3 g; Cholesterol 25 mg; Sodium 140 mg

HAITIAN BREAD

PAIN HAÏTIEN (panh eye-ee-see-yan)

In French-speaking Haiti, this bread is to be found baked both with and without the benefit of yeast. The version below uses yeast for a lighter, more tender result. Nutmeg is a warming accent in this pull-apart bread.

2 packages active dry yeast
1½ cups warm water (105 to 115°)
¼ cup honey
2 tablespoons peanut or vegetable oil
1 teaspoon salt
¾ teaspoon ground nutmeg
4 to 4½ cups all-purpose flour
¼ teaspoon freeze-dried instant coffee
2 tablespoons milk

Dissolve yeast in warm water in large bowl. Stir in honey, oil, salt, nutmeg and 2 cups of the flour. Beat until very smooth, about 1 minute. Gradually add enough of the remaining flour to make a stiff dough. Turn dough onto lightly floured surface; knead until smooth, about 5 minutes. Place in greased bowl; turn greased side up. Cover; let rise in warm place until double, about 50 minutes. (Dough is ready if indentation remains when touched.)

Punch down dough. Press in greased jelly roll pan, 15½ × 10½ × 1 inch. Cut dough into about 2½-inch squares with sharp knife, cutting two-thirds of the way through dough. Cover; let rise until double, about 30 minutes.

Heat oven to 350°. Dissolve instant coffee in milk; brush over dough. Bake until bread is golden brown, about 35 minutes. Break bread into squares to serve.

24 squares

PER SQUARE: Calories 95; Protein 2 g; Carbohydrate 19 g; Fat 1 g; Cholesterol 0 mg; Sodium 90 mg

BROWN SUGAR ROLLS

CHORREADAS (choh-rray-ah-dahs)

The Mexican name for these rolls means "dirty faces," referring to the dark smudge of Brown Sugar Glaze.

½ cup packed dark brown sugar
⅓ cup lard
2 teaspoons salt
1¾ cups hot water
1 package active dry yeast
Dash of granulated or dark brown sugar
¼ cup warm water (105 to 115°)
2 cups whole wheat flour
3¾ to 4 cups all-purpose flour
1 egg, slightly beaten
Brown Sugar Glaze (right)

Place brown sugar, lard and salt in large bowl. Stir in 1¾ cups hot water until brown sugar is dissolved. Dissolve yeast and granulated sugar in ¼ cup warm water; stir into brown sugar

mixture. Beat in whole wheat flour and enough all-purpose flour to make dough stiff enough to knead. Turn dough onto lightly floured surface; knead until smooth and elastic, about 10 minutes. Place in greased bowl; turn greased side up. Cover; let rise in warm place until double, about 2 hours. (Dough is ready if indentation remains when touched.)

Line 2 cookie sheets with aluminum foil; grease. Punch down dough. Turn onto lightly floured surface; knead until smooth. Shape into roll, 10 inches long; cut into 10 slices. Shape each slice into smooth ball. Place on foil-covered cookie sheets; flatten into circles, 3½ to 4 inches in diameter. Cover; let rise until double, about 30 minutes.

Heat oven to 375°. Brush rolls with egg. Spread Brown Sugar Glaze on centers of rolls. Make diagonal or crisscross cuts in tops of rolls with tip of sharp knife. Bake until rolls are brown and sound hollow when tapped, 20 to 25 minutes. Immediately remove rolls; cool on wire racks.

10 rolls

PER ROLL: Calories 410; Protein 9 g; Carbohydrate 75 g; Fat 8 g; Cholesterol 20 mg; Sodium 440 mg

BROWN SUGAR GLAZE

½ cup packed dark brown sugar
2 to 3 teaspoons water

Mix brown sugar and water until of spreading consistency.

CRUMPETS

Crumpets are British griddle cakes. The batter is poured into metal rings, and when the cakes have "set" the rings are removed so that the crumpets can be turned over. Crumpets have large holes—just right for catching lots of marmalade or butter—and, like many fried foods, are most delicious when they are hot.

1 package active dry yeast
¼ cup warm water (105 to 115°)
½ cup lukewarm milk (scalded, then cooled)
1 tablespoon margarine or butter
1 teaspoon sugar
¾ teaspoon salt
1 egg
1 cup all-purpose flour

Dissolve yeast in warm water in medium bowl. Stir in remaining ingredients; beat until smooth. Cover; let rise in warm place until double, 40 to 60 minutes.

Grease griddle or heavy skillet and insides of four to six 3-inch flan rings or crumpet rings.* Place rings on griddle over medium heat until hot. Pour about 2 tablespoons batter into each ring. Cook until tops form bubbles and bottoms are golden brown, 1 to 2 minutes. Remove rings; turn crumpets to brown other side, 1 to 2 minutes. Repeat with remaining batter, greasing insides of rings each time. Serve with margarine or butter and jam or marmalade if desired.

12 crumpets

*6½-ounce tuna, minced clam or shrimp cans, tops and bottoms removed, can be substituted for the flan rings.

PER CRUMPET: Calories 70; Protein 2 g; Carbohydrate 9 g; Fat 3 g; Cholesterol 20 mg; Sodium 170 mg

SPANISH HARD ROLLS

BOLILLOS (boh-<u>lee</u>-yohs)

The shape of *Bolillos*—oblong and pointed at both ends—marks them as an unmistakable specialty of Spanish bakeries. They are ideal dinner rolls, with a straightforward flavor and crunchy crust.

1 package active dry yeast
2 cups warm water (105 to 115°)
1 tablespoon honey
1 teaspoon salt
5½ to 6 cups all-purpose flour
1 tablespoon cornstarch
2½ teaspoons water

Dissolve yeast in 2 cups warm water in large bowl. Stir in honey, salt and 3 cups of the flour. Beat until smooth. Stir in enough remaining flour to make dough easy to handle. Turn dough onto floured surface; knead until smooth and elastic, about 5 minutes. Place in greased bowl; turn greased side up. Cover; let rise in warm place until double, about 1 hour. (Dough is ready if indentation remains when touched.)

Punch down dough. Cover; let rest 15 minutes. Divide dough into 16 equal parts. Shape each part into oblong, about 5 inches long; pinch ends to form points. Place on greased cookie sheets. Make slash about 3 inches long and ½ inch deep the length of each roll. Cover; let rise until double, 45 to 60 minutes.

Heat oven to 375°. Mix cornstarch and 2½ teaspoons water; brush on rolls. Bake until rolls are golden brown, 35 to 40 minutes. Serve warm.

16 rolls

PER ROLL: Calories 155; Protein 4 g; Carbohydrate 35 g; Fat 0 g; Cholesterol 0 mg; Sodium 135 mg

SWEDISH LUCIA BUNS

Cardamom and orange peel flavor these distinctive S-shaped buns. There are popular variations, some flavored with saffron, and as many shapes as there are Swedish cooks. Tradition dictates that the youngest woman or girl of the household offer these buns to guests, in honor of the Queen of Light Festival at the outset of the Christmas season.

2 packages active dry yeast
½ cup warm water (105 to 115°)
⅔ cup lukewarm milk (scalded, then cooled)
½ cup sugar
½ cup margarine or butter, softened
2 eggs
1 teaspoon ground cardamom
1 teaspoon salt
1 teaspoon grated orange peel
5 to 5½ cups all-purpose flour
½ cup raisins
Margarine or butter, softened
1 egg, slightly beaten
1 tablespoon water
2 tablespoons sugar

Dissolve yeast in warm water in large bowl. Stir in milk, ½ cup sugar, ½ cup margarine, 2 eggs, the cardamom, salt, orange peel and 3 cups of the flour. Beat until smooth. Stir in enough remaining flour to make dough easy to handle.

Turn dough onto lightly floured surface; knead until smooth and elastic, about 5 minutes. Place in greased bowl; turn greased side up. Cover; let rise in warm place until double, 1½ to 2 hours. (Dough is ready if indentation remains when touched.)

Punch down dough; divide into 4 equal parts. Cut each part into 6 equal pieces. Shape each piece into a smooth rope, 10 to 12 inches long. Shape each rope into an S; curve both ends into a coil. Place a raisin in center of each coil. Place on greased cookie sheets. Brush tops lightly with margarine; let rise until double, 35 to 45 minutes.

Heat oven to 350°. Mix 1 egg and 1 tablespoon water; brush buns lightly with egg mixture. Sprinkle with 2 tablespoons sugar. Bake until golden brown, 15 to 20 minutes.

24 buns

PER BUN: Calories 180; Protein 4 g; Carbohydrate 28 g; Fat 6 g; Cholesterol 30 mg; Sodium 160 mg

Following pages (from left): Scandinavian Christmas Fruit Bread (page 311), Danish Kringle (page 306) and Swedish Lucia Buns

TURKISH BREAD RINGS

SIMIT (s'<u>miht</u>)

These sesame rings can be bought on the street, where they are displayed on sticks.

2 packages active dry yeast
1½ cups warm water (105 to 115°)
1½ cups lukewarm milk (scalded, then cooled)
2 tablespoons sugar
1 tablespoon salt
2 tablespoons vegetable oil
6½ to 7 cups all-purpose flour
1 egg
2 teaspoons water
¾ cup sesame seed

Dissolve yeast in warm water in large bowl. Stir in milk, sugar, salt, oil and 3 cups of the flour. Beat until smooth. Stir in enough remaining flour to make dough easy to handle. Turn dough onto generously floured surface; knead until smooth and elastic, about 5 minutes. Place in greased bowl; turn greased side up. Cover; let rise in warm place until double, about 45 minutes. (Dough is ready if indentation remains when touched.)

Punch down dough; divide into 8 equal parts. Roll and shape each part into a rope about 24 inches long; moisten ends with water. Bring ends of rope together, and pinch to form a ring about 6 inches in diameter. Beat egg and 2 teaspoons water with fork. Spread sesame seed on dinner plate. Brush each ring with egg mixture; dip into sesame seed. Place rings, sesame seed side up, on large greased cookie sheets. Cover loosely; let rise until double, about 30 minutes.

Heat oven to 400°. Bake until rings are golden brown, 18 to 20 minutes.

8 bread rings

PER RING: Calories 520; Protein 16 g; Carbohydrate 85 g; Fat 13 g; Cholesterol 30 mg; Sodium 840 mg

YUGOSLAVIAN COFFEE CAKE

POTICA (<u>poh</u>-tee-kah)

Walnut-filled dough is wound into a snail shape. Slices of this sweet coffee cake are spectacularly traced with the filling.

1 package active dry yeast
¼ cup warm water (105 to 115°)
¾ cup lukewarm milk (scalded, then cooled)
½ cup margarine or butter, softened
3 eggs
¼ cup sugar
½ teaspoon salt
4½ to 5 cups all-purpose flour
Walnut Filling (page 303)
Glaze (page 307)

Dissolve yeast in warm water in large bowl. Stir in milk, margarine, eggs, sugar, salt and 3 cups of the flour. Beat until smooth. Stir in enough remaining flour to make dough easy to handle.

Turn dough onto lightly floured surface; knead until smooth and elastic, about 5 minutes. Place in greased bowl; turn greased side up. Cover; let rise in warm place until double, 1 to 1½ hours. (Dough is ready if indentation remains when touched.)

Punch down dough; divide into halves. Roll each half into rectangle, 15 × 12 inches, on lightly floured surface. Spread half the Walnut

Filling over each rectangle. Roll up tightly, beginning at 15-inch side. Pinch edge of dough into each roll to seal well. Stretch rolls to make even. With sealed edges down, coil into snail shapes on lightly greased cookie sheets. Cover; let rise until double, about 1 hour. Heat oven to 350°. Bake until golden brown, 35 to 45 minutes. Brush with margarine if desired; spread with Glaze.

2 coffee cakes (18 servings each)

PER SERVING: Calories 190; Protein 4 g; Carbohydrate 21 g; Fat 10 g; Cholesterol 25 mg; Sodium 90 mg

WALNUT FILLING

2½ cups finely chopped walnuts
1 cup packed brown sugar
⅓ cup margarine or butter, softened
1 egg
2 teaspoons ground cinnamon

Mix all ingredients.

PORTUGUESE SWEET BREAD

PÃO DÔCE (pow <u>doh</u>-say)

Up and down the northeastern seaboard of the United States are fans of this melt-in-your-mouth bread. Some say it came to our shores with the influx of Portuguese sailors at the outset of the American whaling boom. *Pão Dôce* is still popular in Portugal today.

2 packages active dry yeast
¼ cup warm water (105 to 115°)
1 cup lukewarm milk (scalded, then cooled)
¾ cup sugar
1 teaspoon salt
3 eggs
½ cup margarine or butter, softened
5½ to 6 cups all-purpose flour
1 egg
1 teaspoon sugar

Dissolve yeast in warm water in large bowl. Stir in milk, ¾ cup sugar, the salt, 3 eggs, the margarine and 3 cups of the flour. Beat until smooth. Stir in enough remaining flour to make dough easy to handle.

Turn dough onto lightly floured surface; knead until smooth and elastic, about 5 minutes. Place in greased bowl; turn greased side up. Cover; let rise in warm place until double, 1½ to 2 hours. (Dough is ready if indentation remains when touched.)

Punch down dough; divide into halves. Shape each half into a round, slightly flat loaf. Place each loaf in greased round layer pan, 9 × 1½ inches. Cover; let rise until double, about 1 hour. Heat oven to 350°. Beat 1 egg slightly; brush over loaves. Sprinkle with 1 teaspoon sugar. Bake until loaves are golden brown, 35 to 45 minutes.

2 loaves (12 slices each)

PER SLICE: Calories 175; Protein 4 g; Carbohydrate 29 g; Fat 5 g; Cholesterol 35 mg; Sodium 150 mg

SNAIL LOAVES (CARACOIS): After dividing dough into halves, roll each half into a rope about 25 × 1½ inches. Coil each to form a snail shape in greased round layer pan, 9 × 1½ inches. Continue as directed.

ITALIAN SWEET BREAD WITH RAISINS

SCHIACCIATA CON ZIBIBBO
(sk'yah-<u>chah</u>-tah kohn zee-<u>bee</u>-boh)

Muscat raisins are often fatter than common raisins. A sprinkling of sugar baked into the crust makes this sweet bread irresistible to children.

1 package active dry yeast
1 cup warm water (105 to 115°)
1 cup muscat raisins
½ cup sugar
3 tablespoons olive oil
1 tablespoon grated orange peel
1 egg, beaten
3½ to 4 cups all-purpose flour
Milk
Sugar

Dissolve yeast in warm water in large bowl. Stir in raisins, sugar, oil, orange peel, egg and enough flour to make a soft dough. Turn dough onto generously floured surface; knead until smooth and elastic, 10 to 15 minutes. Place in greased bowl; turn greased side up. Cover; let rise in warm place until double, about 1 hour.

Punch down dough. Shape into round, slightly flat loaf about 9 inches in diameter. Place on greased cookie sheet. Cover; let rise 45 minutes.

Heat oven to 350°. Brush loaf with milk; sprinkle with sugar. Bake until bread is golden brown, 30 to 35 minutes. Remove from cookie sheet; cool on wire rack.

1 loaf (12 wedges)

PER WEDGE: Calories 245; Protein 5 g; Carbohydrate 47 g; Fat 4 g; Cholesterol 20 mg; Sodium 10 mg

Preceding pages: Italian Sweet Bread with Raisins, *left,* and Italian Coffee Cake (page 310)

DANISH KRINGLE

The Danes are noted for their love of baked sweets. *Kringle* is a rich pastry that, if not enjoyed year-round by most, is looked forward to at Christmastime by nearly all.

½ cup margarine or butter
2 cups all-purpose flour
1 tablespoon sugar
½ teaspoon salt
1 package active dry yeast
¼ cup warm water (105 to 115°)
1 egg
½ cup lukewarm milk (scalded, then cooled)
Almond or Pecan Filling (page 307)
Glaze (page 307)
¼ cup chopped nuts

Cut margarine into flour, sugar and salt in large bowl until mixture resembles fine crumbs. Dissolve yeast in warm water. Stir yeast mixture, egg and milk into flour mixture; beat until smooth (dough will be very soft). Cover and refrigerate at least 2 hours but no longer than 24 hours.

Prepare Almond Filling. Divide dough into halves; return one half to refrigerator. Roll other half into rectangle, 15 × 6 inches, on floured cloth-covered board with floured stockinet-covered rolling pin. Spread half the filling lengthwise down center of rectangle in 3-inch strip. Fold sides of dough over filling with 1½-inch overlap; pinch edges to seal.

Carefully arrange kringle, seam side down, on greased cookie sheet in oval or horseshoe shape; pinch ends together for the former. Repeat with remaining dough. Cover; let rise in warm place

30 minutes. Heat oven to 375°. Bake until golden brown, 20 to 25 minutes. Spread with Glaze; sprinkle with nuts.

2 coffee cakes (12 servings each)

PER SERVING: Calories 205; Protein 3 g; Carbohydrate 24 g; Fat 11 g; Cholesterol 10 mg; Sodium 140 mg

ALMOND FILLING

1 can (8 ounces) almond paste (1 cup)
½ cup packed brown sugar
½ cup margarine or butter, softened

Mix almond paste, brown sugar and margarine until smooth.

PECAN FILLING

1½ cups chopped pecans
1 cup packed brown sugar
½ cup margarine or butter, softened

Mix pecans, brown sugar and margarine.

GLAZE

1 cup powdered sugar
1 tablespoon water
½ teaspoon vanilla

Mix powdered sugar, water and vanilla until smooth. Stir in additional water if necessary, ½ teaspoon at a time.

POLISH EASTER BREAD

BABKA WIELKANOCNA (bahb-kah veel-kah-notz-nah)

Flavored with lemon and orange peels and cinnamon, Polish Easter Bread is another festive, light-textured sweet bread in the European tradition.

½ cup margarine or butter, softened
½ cup sugar
3 egg yolks
1 package active dry yeast
¼ cup warm water (105 to 115°)
2 teaspoons grated orange peel
1 teaspoon grated lemon peel
1 teaspoon ground cinnamon
½ teaspoon salt
4 cups all-purpose flour
1 cup lukewarm milk (scalded, then cooled)
1 cup golden raisins

Beat margarine and sugar in large bowl until blended. Beat in egg yolks until well blended. Dissolve yeast in warm water. Stir yeast mixture, orange peel, lemon peel, cinnamon and salt into margarine mixture. Stir in flour alternately with the milk, beating well after each addition, until soft dough forms. Stir in raisins, Cover; let rise in warm place until double, about 1½ hours.

Stir down dough; spoon into greased and floured tube pan, 10 × 4 inches, or 12-cup bundt cake pan. Cover; let rise until double, about 1 hour.

Heat oven to 350°. Bake until bread is golden brown, 35 to 40 minutes. Cool 5 minutes. Remove from pan; cool completely. Sprinkle with powdered sugar if desired.

1 loaf (16 slices)

PER SLICE: Calories 235; Protein 4 g; Carbohydrate 39 g; Fat 7 g; Cholesterol 40 mg; Sodium 150 mg

RUSSIAN EASTER BREAD

KULICH (koo-lickh)

Kulich is baked into little towering loaves. It is traditional to make the design "XV" (meaning "Christ is risen") on top of each loaf.

2 packages active dry yeast
½ cup warm water (105 to 115°)
¾ cup lukewarm milk (scalded, then cooled)
⅓ cup sugar
1 teaspoon salt
2 eggs
½ cup shortening
½ cup raisins
½ cup cut-up mixed candied fruit
¼ cup chopped blanched almonds
1 teaspoon grated lemon peel
4½ to 5 cups all-purpose flour
Lemon Icing (right)

Dissolve yeast in warm water in large bowl. Stir in milk, sugar, salt, eggs, shortening, raisins, candied fruit, almonds, lemon peel and 3 cups of the flour. Beat until smooth. Stir in enough remaining flour to make dough easy to handle.

Turn dough onto lightly floured surface; knead until smooth and elastic, about 5 minutes. Place in greased bowl; turn greased side up. Cover; let rise in warm place until double, 1 to 1½ hours. (Dough is ready if indentation remains when touched.)

Punch down dough; divide into halves. Shape each half into round bun-shaped loaf. Place in two well-greased 3-pound shortening cans.* Let rise until double, 40 to 50 minutes.

Heat oven to 375°. Place cans on low rack so that midpoint of each can is in center of oven. Bake until tops are golden brown, 40 to 45 minutes. (If tops brown too quickly, cover loosely with aluminum foil.) Cool 10 minutes; remove from cans. Spoon Lemon Icing over tops of warm bread, allowing some to drizzle down sides. Trim with tiny decorating candies if desired.

2 loaves (16 slices each)

*Two 46-ounce juice cans can be substituted for the 3-pound shortening cans.

PER SLICE: Calories 145; Protein 3 g; Carbohydrate 24 g; Fat 4 g; Cholesterol 15 mg; Sodium 80 mg

LEMON ICING

1 cup powdered sugar
1 tablespoon warm water
1 teaspoon lemon juice

Mix powdered sugar, water and lemon juice until smooth. (Icing should be glaze consistency. Add 1 to 2 teaspoons water if necessary.)

Russian Easter Bread

ITALIAN COFFEE CAKE

PANETTONE (pah-neh-<u>toh</u>-nee)

This is a festive sweet bread originally from Milan. Recipes for *Panettone* nearly always call for lemon peel, raisins and citron.

2 packages active dry yeast
1 cup warm water (105 to 115°)
½ cup sugar
½ cup margarine or butter, softened
3 eggs
1 teaspoon salt
1 teaspoon grated lemon peel
1 teaspoon vanilla
5 to 5½ cups all-purpose flour
½ cup golden raisins
½ cup chopped citron
2 tablespoons pine nuts or walnuts (optional)
Margarine or butter, softened

Dissolve yeast in warm water in large bowl. Stir in sugar, ½ cup margarine, the eggs, salt, lemon peel, vanilla and 2½ cups of the flour. Beat until smooth. Stir in raisins, citron, pine nuts and enough remaining flour to make dough easy to handle.

Turn dough onto lightly floured surface; knead until smooth and elastic, about 5 minutes. Place in greased bowl; turn greased side up. Cover; let rise in warm place until double, 1½ to 2 hours. (Dough is ready if indentation remains when touched.)

Punch down dough; divide into halves. Shape each half into round loaf, about 7 inches in diameter. Place loaves in 2 ungreased round layer pans, 8 × 1½ inches. Cut a cross ½ inch deep on top of each loaf. Generously grease one side of a strip of heavy brown paper, about 25 × 4 inches. Fit around inside of pan, forming a collar; fasten with paper clip. Repeat with second loaf. Cover, let rise until double, about 1 hour.

Heat oven to 350°. Bake loaves until golden brown, 35 to 45 minutes. Remove paper. Brush tops with margarine. Cool on rack.

2 loaves (12 slices each)

PER SLICE: Calories 190; Protein 4 g; Carbohydrate 30 g; Fat 6 g; Cholesterol 25 mg; Sodium 160 mg

Cardamom

As this spice travels north, from its native home in Sri Lanka and southern portions of India, it is used less frequently for seasoning vegetables and meats, and more often for sweets. Today it is used the world over and, as common as it is, still has managed to retain its exotic aura; the flavor is warm, with light menthol overtones. Tiny cardamom seeds are housed in pea-size pods. The whole pods are convenient for flavoring stews, as they can be fished out before serving. The seeds are ground to a fine powder, which is used extensively in baking.

SCANDINAVIAN CHRISTMAS FRUIT BREAD

JULEKAGE (yoo-leh-<u>kay</u>-yeh)

Featuring the combination of cardamom and dried fruits (one that often speaks of festivity in European cooking), this round sweet bread is covered with a snow-white glaze.

1 package active dry yeast
¼ cup warm water (105 to 115°)
¾ cup lukewarm milk (scalded, then cooled)
¼ cup sugar
½ teaspoon salt
½ teaspoon ground cardamom
1 egg
¼ cup shortening
½ cup raisins
⅓ cup cut-up citron or mixed candied fruit
3¼ to 3½ cups all-purpose flour
Margarine or butter, softened
Glaze (right)

Dissolve yeast in warm water in large mixer bowl. Add milk, sugar, salt, cardamom, egg, shortening, raisins, citron and 2 cups of the flour. Beat on low speed, scraping bowl constantly, 30 seconds. Beat on medium speed, scraping bowl occasionally, 2 minutes. Stir in enough remaining flour to make dough easy to handle.

Turn dough onto lightly floured surface; knead until smooth and elastic, about 5 minutes. Place in greased bowl; turn greased side up. Cover; let rise in warm place until double, 1 to 1½ hours. (Dough is ready if indentation remains when touched.)

Punch down dough; shape into round loaf. Place in greased round layer pan, 9 × 1½ inches. Brush top lightly with margarine; let rise until double, about 45 minutes. Heat oven to 350°. Bake until loaf is golden brown, 35 to 45 minutes. Brush with margarine. Spread with Glaze. Cool on wire rack.

1 loaf (12 slices)

PER SLICE: Calories 275; Protein 5 g; Carbohydrate 50 g; Fat 6 g; Cholesterol 20 mg; Sodium 130 mg

GLAZE

1 cup powdered sugar
1 to 2 tablespoons water

Mix powdered sugar and water until smooth and of desired consistency.

8

DESSERTS

I In the following pages, we begin to explore the sweetest international domain of all: the dessert. Here are the secrets of cakes, tortes, puddings, sorbets and sweet surprises loved around the world, from the shores of the Mediterranean to the Indian Ocean and far beyond.

What follows is a selection of mouth-watering treats to enhance any holiday table or informal gathering. Brandied Honey Cake to celebrate the New Year, rich and creamy Russian Easter Dessert, English Plum Pudding blazing for Christmas, gala Thousand Leaves Torte—these desserts are perfect for crowning seasonal festivities. Tangy, chilled Lemon Ice and Gingered Pear Sorbet are refreshing fare for a scorching summer buffet, whether served on a small city balcony or a rolling green lawn. Smooth Cardamom Fudge and crunchy Greek Crescent Cookies are delicious any time of year. The chocolate lover will delight in the Chocolate-Cinnamon Cake Roll from Mexico and Chocolate Marzipan Slices from Hungary. Those who yearn for the richness of cheesecake will find Italian Ricotta Cheesecake irresistible, while those preferring a lighter finish will relish fragrant Persian Apple Dessert.

Many of these desserts can be whipped up in record time or prepared in advance. From around the world, these delicious sweets are the reason for countless smiles and contented sighs.

Clockwise from top: French Ring Cake (page 342), Molded Strawberry Dessert (page 314), Greek Crescent Cookies (page 349) and Sicilian Cheese and Chocolate Cake (page 341)

MOLDED STRAWBERRY DESSERT

ERDBEEREN ELISABETH (ehrd-beh-rehn eh-lee-zah-beht)

Kirsch flavors this German dessert made of "earth berries." The cream-laden mixture may be chilled in an elaborate mold for a sensational presentation or spooned into little dessert dishes. Garnish with perfect whole berries.

4 cups strawberries
¾ cup sugar
2 tablespoons kirsch
2 envelopes unflavored gelatin
½ cup cold water
½ cup boiling water
1 cup chilled whipping cream

Reserve a few strawberries for garnish. Mash remaining strawberries; stir in sugar and kirsch. Sprinkle gelatin on cold water to soften; stir in boiling water until gelatin is dissolved. Stir gelatin mixture into strawberries. Refrigerate, stirring occasionally, until mixture mounds slightly when dropped from a spoon, about 45 minutes.

Beat whipping cream in chilled bowl until stiff. Fold whipped cream into strawberry mixture. Pour into 6-cup mold or 8 dessert dishes. Refrigerate until firm, about 4 hours; unmold. Garnish with reserved strawberries and, if desired, whipped cream.

8 servings

PER SERVING: Calories 200; Protein 2 g; Carbohydrate 26 g; Fat 10 g; Cholesterol 35 mg; Sodium 15 mg

PERSIAN APPLE DESSERT

Rose water or orange flower water mark this light fruit dessert as Middle Eastern. Both of these subtle flavorings can be found at pharmacies as well as in gourmet and specialty shops.

3 medium apples, pared and cut up
2 to 3 tablespoons sugar
2 tablespoons lemon juice
1 tablespoon rose or orange flower water (optional)
Dash of salt

Place half the apples and the remaining ingredients in blender container. Cover and blend until coarsely chopped, 20 to 30 seconds. Add remaining apples; blend until coarsely chopped.

3 servings

PER SERVING: Calories 130; Protein 0 g; Carbohydrate 30 g; Fat 1 g; Cholesterol 0 mg; Sodium 90 mg

BANANAS BAKED WITH CREAM CHEESE

BANANES CÉLESTE (bah-nahn seh-lehst)

This rich banana dessert, with a hint of rum, comes from Martinique. Served bubbling hot, it needs no embellishment.

3 tablespoons margarine or butter
6 ripe but firm medium bananas, peeled and cut lengthwise into halves
1 package (8 ounces) cream cheese, softened
¼ cup packed brown sugar
¼ cup whipping cream
2 tablespoons dark rum
¼ teaspoon ground cinnamon

Heat margarine in 10-inch skillet over medium heat until melted. Cook bananas in margarine, a few at a time, until brown on both sides; gently remove.

Place cream cheese, brown sugar, whipping cream, rum and cinnamon in blender container. Cover and blend on high speed, stopping blender occasionally to scrape sides, until smooth, about 1 minute.

Arrange half of the bananas in ungreased square baking dish, 8 × 8 × 2 inches. Spread half of cream cheese mixture over bananas; top with remaining bananas and cream cheese mixture. Bake uncovered in 325° oven until corners are bubbly, 20 to 25 minutes.

6 servings

PER SERVING: Calories 370; Protein 4 g; Carbohydrate 37 g; Fat 23 g; Cholesterol 50 mg; Sodium 190 mg

BANANA-COCONUT BAKE

AKWADU (ah-kwah-doo)

Coconut, lemon and orange distinguish this banana dessert from Ghana. It takes only eight minutes in the oven, perfect for satisfying a spur-of-the-moment craving.

5 medium bananas
1 tablespoon margarine or butter
1/3 cup orange juice
1 tablespoon lemon juice
3 tablespoons packed brown sugar
2/3 cup shredded coconut

Cut bananas crosswise into halves; cut each half lengthwise into halves and arrange in greased 9-inch pie plate. Dot with margarine; drizzle with orange and lemon juices. Sprinkle with

brown sugar and coconut. Bake in 375° oven until coconut is golden, 8 to 10 minutes.

5 or 6 servings

PER SERVING: Calories 240; Protein 1 g; Carbohydrate 43 g; Fat 7 g; Cholesterol 0 mg; Sodium 65 mg

CARAMEL BANANAS WITH RUM

This is an Australian adult version of the banana split. The sauce is a luxurious combination of rum and caramel, one to keep in mind for topping ice cream another day.

2/3 cup packed brown sugar
2 tablespoons whipping cream
1 tablespoon margarine or butter
3 tablespoons rum
4 medium bananas
1/2 cup chilled whipping cream
1 tablespoon packed brown sugar
1/4 cup sliced almonds

Cook and stir 2/3 cup brown sugar, 2 tablespoons whipping cream and the margarine over low heat until sugar is dissolved and mixture is smooth. Remove from heat; stir in rum. Cover and refrigerate at least 1 hour.

Cut bananas crosswise into halves; cut each half lengthwise into halves. Arrange in serving dishes; top with refrigerated caramel sauce. Beat 1/2 cup whipping cream and 1 tablespoon brown sugar in chilled bowl until stiff. Spoon over bananas and sauce; garnish with almonds.

4 to 6 servings

PER SERVING: Calories 465; Protein 3 g; Carbohydrate 68 g; Fat 18 g; Cholesterol 40 mg; Sodium 65 mg

CHINESE GLAZED FRUIT

The Chinese are not known for their love of desserts, but these elegant tidbits are as unusual as they are delicious. Pieces of fresh fruit are dipped into batter and fried, then turned in a syrup.

¾ cup cold water
⅓ cup all-purpose flour
¼ cup cornstarch
¾ teaspoon baking powder
½ teaspoon salt
Peanut or vegetable oil
2 medium apples, pared and cut into eighths
2 firm medium bananas, cut diagonally into ½-inch slices
2 cups sugar
1 cup water
½ cup light corn syrup
¼ cup white or black sesame seed
Iced water

Beat ¾ cup water, the flour, cornstarch, baking powder and salt with hand beater until smooth. Heat oil (1 to 1½ inches) to 360°. Stir apples into batter until coated. Remove 1 piece at a time with slotted spoon, letting excess batter drip into bowl. Fry 6 to 8 pieces at a time, turning occasionally, until golden brown, about 5 minutes; drain. Repeat with bananas.

Thoroughly mix sugar, 1 cup water and the corn syrup in heavy 3-quart saucepan. Heat to boiling, without stirring, over high heat. Cook, without stirring, over high heat to 300° on candy thermometer or until small amount of mixture dropped into very cold water separates into threads that are hard and brittle (mixture will be light golden brown). Decrease heat to very low; stir in sesame seed.

Generously oil large flat serving plate. Stir 1 piece of fruit at a time into syrup until evenly coated. Immediately remove from syrup and place on oiled plate. Do not let pieces touch. At the table, dip each piece of fruit into iced water to harden coating.

6 servings

PER SERVING: Calories 570; Protein 2 g; Carbohydrate 114 g; Fat 12 g; Cholesterol 0 mg; Sodium 260 mg

DANISH BERRY PUDDING
RØDGRØD (rohl-grohl)

Similar to Russian *Kissel* (page 317), this simple pudding is thickened with cornstarch and only lightly sweetened. The combination of raspberries and strawberries (frozen and easy to find year-round) ensures a richly flavored result.

1 package (10 ounces) frozen raspberries, thawed
1 package (10 ounces) frozen strawberries, thawed
¼ cup cornstarch
2 tablespoons sugar
½ cup cold water
1 tablespoon lemon juice
2 tablespoons slivered almonds

Purée berries in blender or press through sieve. Mix cornstarch and sugar in 1½-quart saucepan. Gradually stir in water; add purée. Heat to boiling, stirring constantly. Boil and stir 1 minute. Remove from heat; stir in lemon juice. Pour into dessert dishes or serving bowl. Cover and refrigerate at least 2 hours. Sprinkle with almonds; serve with half-and-half if desired.

6 servings

PER SERVING: Calories 150; Protein 1 g; Carbohydrate 34 g; Fat 1 g; Cholesterol 0 mg; Sodium 5 mg

RUSSIAN APRICOT PUDDING
KISSEL (<u>kiss</u>-uhl)

The Russians make *Kissel* with other fruits as well, notably cranberries. Enjoy it warm, or chill it and serve with cream.

2 cups water
1 cup dried apricot halves (6 ounces)
¼ cup sugar
3 tablespoons cornstarch
Dash of salt

Heat water and apricots to boiling; reduce heat. Cover and simmer until tender, about 20 minutes. Place apricots and ½ cup cooking liquid in blender container; cover and purée until uniform consistency. Press purée through sieve.

Mix sugar, cornstarch and salt in 1½-quart saucepan; gradually stir in apricot purée and remaining cooking liquid. Heat to boiling over medium heat, stirring constantly. Boil and stir 1 minute.

Pour into dessert dishes. Serve with half-and-half or sweetened whipped cream if desired.

4 servings

PER SERVING: Calories 155; Protein 1 g; Carbohydrate 38 g; Fat 0 g; Cholesterol 0 mg; Sodium 70 mg

Almonds

Green almonds, soft and unripe, have a slightly fuzzy inner skin; in parts of the world where almond trees abound, green almonds are enjoyed like any fruit, the sweet pulp squeezed out of its fuzzy jacket. Native to western Asia and the Mediterranean basin, almonds are used in savory and sweet dishes alike.

CANADIAN BLUEBERRY CRISP

Bright, juicy blueberries bubble beneath a sweet, oatmeal-crunchy crust in this dessert, a favorite with our neighbors to the north.

4 cups blueberries*
2 tablespoons lemon juice
⅓ cup packed brown sugar
2 teaspoons cornstarch
⅔ cup quick-cooking oats
½ cup all-purpose flour
⅓ cup packed brown sugar
Dash of salt
⅓ cup margarine or butter
Vanilla ice cream (optional)

Toss blueberries with lemon juice in ungreased 1½-quart casserole. Mix ⅓ cup brown sugar and the cornstarch; stir into blueberries. Mix oats, flour, ⅓ cup brown sugar and the salt; cut in margarine with fork. Sprinkle over blueberries. Bake uncovered in 350° oven until topping is light brown and blueberries are bubbly, about 40 minutes. Serve warm with ice cream.

5 or 6 servings

*1 package (16 ounces) frozen unsweetened blueberries can be substituted for the fresh blueberries.

PER SERVING: Calories 385; Protein 4 g; Carbohydrate 63 g; Fat 13 g; Cholesterol 0 mg; Sodium 220 mg

SLICED ORANGES IN SYRUP

Sprinkling fresh fruit with a little sugar seems to bring out its juicy nature; sugar syrup does that, too. This orange dessert is a model of simplicity and may be prepared ahead of time. Although sliced Oranges in Syrup is probably of Greek extraction, today it is popular across the Middle East.

3 seedless oranges
½ cup water
⅓ cup sugar

Cut thin slivers of peel from 1 orange with vegetable parer or sharp knife, being careful not to cut into white membrane. Cover peel with boiling water; let stand 5 minutes. Drain. Heat orange peel, water and sugar to boiling; simmer uncovered until slightly thickened, 10 to 15 minutes. Cool.

Pare oranges, cutting deep enough to remove all white membrane. Cut into slices. Pour syrup over slices; cover and refrigerate. Garnish with sprig of mint if desired.

4 servings

PER SERVING: Calories 115; Protein 1 g; Carbohydrate 28 g; Fat 0 g; Cholesterol 0 mg; Sodium 0 mg

Orange Flower Water

Like rose water, this flavoring is a clear distillation from fresh blossoms. It is most often used in Middle Eastern cooking but has made occasional inroads into Western kitchens. Orange blossoms are the traditional bridal flower; white, small and delicate, they symbolize purity. In Mexico they make little wedding cakes that are flavored with orange flower water.

SLICED ORANGES WITH DATES

In Morocco the love of oranges is surpassed only by the love of dates. This fresh-tasting dessert is made with only four ingredients, each of which, taken by itself, is ordinary enough. Together, they create an exotic fantasy.

4 large oranges, pared and sliced
⅓ cup pitted dates, cut into fourths
2 tablespoons toasted chopped almonds
1 to 2 tablespoons orange flower water

Arrange orange slices on serving platter. Sprinkle with dates and almonds. Drizzle with orange flower water. Cover and refrigerate at least 4 hours. Garnish with fresh mint leaves if desired.

4 to 6 servings

PER SERVING: Calories 160; Protein 3 g; Carbohydrate 33 g; Fat 2 g; Cholesterol 0 mg; Sodium 0 mg

DUTCH APRICOT COMPOTE
GEDROOGDE ABRIKOZEN
(Khehd-rokh-de ah-bree-goh-zehn)

Many times of the year, the fresh fruits we want are not to be had for love or money. Here is a luscious version of stewed dried apricots, fragrant with white wine.

1 package (8 ounces) dried apricots, cut into halves
1½ cups medium white wine
½ cup water
½ cup sugar
¾ cup whipped cream
2 tablespoons toasted slivered almonds

Heat apricots, wine, water and sugar to boiling in 2-quart saucepan; reduce heat. Cover and simmer until apricots are tender, about 30 minutes. Cover and refrigerate at least 24 hours. Top each serving with whipped cream; sprinkle with almonds.

6 servings

PER SERVING: Calories 240; Protein 2 g; Carbohydrate 42 g; Fat 3 g; Cholesterol 0 mg; Sodium 10 mg

DRIED FRUIT COMPOTE

KHOSHAF (<u>hoh</u>-shef)

Dried Fruit Compote is a versatile preparation from the Middle East, with a dash of fresh lemon juice to keep the flavors bright. Serve it warm over ice cream, if you like.

1 package (8 ounces) mixed dried fruit
¾ cup dried figs
3 cups water
½ cup raisins
2 tablespoons honey
2 teaspoons lemon juice

Cut dried fruit and figs into bite-size pieces. Heat dried fruit, figs, water and raisins to boiling; reduce heat. Cover and simmer until tender, about 20 minutes. Stir in honey and lemon juice. Top with sweetened whipped cream and sliced almonds if desired.

8 servings

PER SERVING: Calories 170; Protein 1 g; Carbohydrate 42 g; Fat 0 g; Cholesterol 0 mg; Sodium 10 mg

FRENCH BAKED CHERRY DESSERT

CLAFOUTI (klah-foo-<u>tee</u>)

In France, *Clafouti* may be made with a variety of fruits. This dessert could not be easier: simply whip up the batter, pour it over the fruit and bake. Serve leftover *Clafouti* cold, with cream.

3 eggs
1 cup milk
½ cup all-purpose flour
¼ cup granulated sugar
1 teaspoon vanilla
2 cups pitted dark sweet cherries
Powdered sugar

Heat oven to 350°. Beat eggs, milk, flour, granulated sugar and the vanilla with hand beater until smooth. Spread cherries in greased oblong baking dish, 10 × 6 × 1 ½ inches, or square baking dish, 8 × 8 × 2 inches. Pour batter over cherries. Bake uncovered until puffed and golden brown, 45 to 60 minutes. Sprinkle with powdered sugar. Serve warm.

6 servings

PER SERVING: Calories 175; Protein 6 g; Carbohydrate 29 g; Fat 4 g; Cholesterol 110 mg; Sodium 50 mg

Cream

Heavy cream can be whipped because it contains a generous amount of butterfat. Whipping cream should have 35 percent butterfat. Ultrapasteurized cream does not whip as quickly (or as well) as pasteurized cream. Cream whips more quickly if the bowl and beaters have been chilled; this is especially helpful in hot weather. Do not overbeat cream or butter will result.

MANGO CREAM

This Indian dessert combines the mouth watering flavor of ripe mangoes with silky whipped cream. Serve it in small bowls and pass thin cookies.

1 ripe mango, pared and cut into pieces
1 cup chilled whipping cream
2 tablespoons sugar
¼ cup toasted sliced or slivered almonds

Place mango in blender container. Cover and blend until smooth, about 10 seconds. Beat whipping cream and sugar in chilled bowl until stiff. Fold mango into whipped cream a few times for swirled effect. Sprinkle with almonds.

6 servings

PER SERVING: Calories 190; Protein 2 g; Carbohydrate 12 g; Fat 15 g; Cholesterol 45 mg; Sodium 15 mg

FRESH PINEAPPLE COMPOTE

Pineapple made its way to Great Britain and the Continent several hundred years ago, and for that reason fresh pineapple compotes are hardly strange to us. This Cambodian version, though, includes a newcomer to the Western world: litchis. Their crisp, sweet flesh is unlike that of any other fruit.

1 can (11 ounces) litchis
2 teaspoons lime juice
2 cups cut-up fresh pineapple
1 medium orange, pared and sectioned

Drain litchis, reserving ½ cup syrup. Mix reserved syrup and lime juice. Cut litchis into halves; toss with pineapple and orange sections. Pour syrup mixture over fruit; cover and refrigerate.

4 to 6 servings

PER SERVING: Calories 130; Protein 1 g; Carbohydrate 29 g; Fat 1 g; Cholesterol 0 mg; Sodium 5 mg

FINNISH CRANBERRY WHIP
VATKATTU MARJAPUURO
(vaht-kah-too mahr-yah-poor-oh)

This sweet-tart pudding is a sensational shade of pink. Use fresh cranberries to make this quickly assembled dessert.

2 cups cranberries (6 ounces)
1½ cups water
1 cup sugar
1 cup water
Dash of salt
⅓ cup farina

Heat cranberries in 1½ cups water to boiling; reduce heat. Simmer uncovered until berries pop, about 8 minutes. Press cranberries through sieve to remove skins. Return juice to saucepan.

Add sugar, 1 cup water and the salt; heat to boiling. Add farina gradually, stirring constantly. Cook, stirring occasionally, until thickened, 3 to 5 minutes. Pour into small mixer bowl. Beat on high speed until pudding becomes fluffy and light pink, 3 to 5 minutes.

4 to 6 servings

PER SERVING: Calories 270; Protein 1 g; Carbohydrate 67 g; Fat 0 g; Cholesterol 0 mg; Sodium 70 mg

Clockwise from top: Carrot Pudding (page 329), Sweet Golden Yogurt (page 332) and Mango Cream

PEARS WITH NUT STUFFING

The Hungarians know a thing or two about rich, hot desserts. Poached pears are filled with a brandy and nut mixture and brought to the table with melting-sweet sour cream. Use firm, ripe pears.

⅓ cup sugar
⅓ cup water
1 tablespoon lemon juice
4 pears, cut into halves
⅓ cup finely chopped nuts
2 tablespoons sugar
1 tablespoon brandy
1 tablespoon dairy sour cream
¼ teaspoon vanilla
½ cup dairy sour cream
1 tablespoon sugar

Mix ⅓ cup sugar, the water and lemon juice in ungreased square pan, 8 × 8 × 2 inches, until sugar is dissolved. Arrange pears in pan, turning to coat with sugar mixture. Cover and bake in 325° oven until pears are almost tender when pierced with fork, 25 minutes.

Place 1 pear half, cut side up, in each of 8 serving dishes. Mix nuts, 2 tablespoons sugar, the brandy, 1 tablespoon sour cream and the vanilla; fill centers of pear halves with nut mixture. Mix ½ cup sour cream and 1 tablespoon sugar. Top each pear half with dollop of sour cream mixture.

8 servings

PER SERVING: Calories 175; Protein 1 g; Carbohydrate 27 g; Fat 7 g; Cholesterol 10 mg; Sodium 10 mg

PINEAPPLE WITH PORT

ANANAS AO PORTO (ah-nah-nahj aoh pohr-toh)

This fresh dessert is popular in Portugal. If desired, use Madeira instead of port.

4 slices fresh pineapple, each ½ inch thick
2 to 3 teaspoons sugar (see Note)
¼ cup ruby port or Madeira

Place each slice pineapple on dessert plate; sprinkle with sugar. Sprinkle 1 tablespoon of the port over each slice pineapple. Cover and refrigerate at least 4 hours. Garnish with fresh mint leaves it desired.

4 servings

PER SERVING: Calories 70; Protein 0 g; Carbohydrate 14 g; Fat 0 g; Cholesterol 0 mg; Sodium 5 mg

NOTE: If pineapple is sweet, omit sugar.

RHUBARB PUDDING

RABARBRAGRØT (rrah-barr-brra-groot)

Ruby-tinged and acidic, rhubarb pokes up out of the thawing soil in early spring. The Norwegians are fond of this slightly chunky, stewed fruit pudding.

1¾ cups water
¾ cup sugar
1½ pounds fresh rhubarb, cut into ½-inch pieces (4 cups)
¼ cup cold water
3 tablespoons cornstarch
½ teaspoon vanilla
1 cup chilled whipping cream
2 tablespoons sugar

Heat 1¾ cups water and ¾ cup sugar to boiling, stirring occasionally. Add rhubarb. Simmer uncovered until rhubarb is tender, about 10 minutes.

Mix ¼ cup water and the cornstarch; stir into rhubarb. Heat to boiling, stirring constantly. Boil and stir 1 minute. Stir in vanilla. Pour into serving bowl or dessert dishes. Cover and refrigerate.

Beat whipping cream and 2 tablespoons sugar in chilled bowl until stiff. Pipe through decorators' tube or spoon onto pudding.

6 servings

PER SERVING: Calories 270; Protein 1 g; Carbohydrate 39 g; Fat 12 g; Cholesterol 45 mg; Sodium 20 mg

Carambola

Known also as star fruit, Chinese star fruit and the five-angled fruit, *carambola* was introduced to American markets on a widespread basis only in the last ten years. This fruit runs about three to six inches long and would be oval if not for the five deep channels that extend the length of it. The waxy skin is a rich yellow. When star fruit is sliced into cross sections, each piece has the shape of a five-pointed star. This tropical fruit is native to Asia. It has a sweet-sour flavor and does not need to be peeled or seeded.

TROPICAL FRUIT WITH CHOCOLATE SAUCE

On the island of Curaçao, they make and enjoy a light-bodied, orange-flavored liqueur. Fresh fruit allowed to macerate (soak or marinate) in sweet liqueur becomes even more succulent. Select the tropical fruits you love best for this simple—but sophisticated—dessert.

Chocolate Sauce (below)
3 to 4 cups assorted fresh tropical fruit, cut up (see Note)
2 to 3 tablespoons orange-flavored liqueur or rum

Prepare Chocolate sauce. Toss fruit and liqueur. Cover and refrigerate, stirring once or twice, at least 1 hour. Spoon fruit into dessert dishes; drizzle with Chocolate Sauce.

6 to 8 servings

PER SERVING: Calories 310; Protein 3 g; Carbohydrate 48 g; Fat 12 g; Cholesterol 5 mg; Sodium 40 mg

CHOCOLATE SAUCE

1 package (6 ounces) semisweet chocolate chips
½ cup evaporated milk
½ cup sugar
2 teaspoons margarine or butter
1 tablespoon orange-flavored liqueur or rum

Heat chocolate, milk and sugar to boiling over medium heat, stirring constantly; remove from heat. Stir in margarine and liqueur. Let stand 1 hour. Cover and refrigerate any remaining sauce.

NOTE: Suggested fruits are banana, pineapple, strawberries, papaya, mango and carambola.

Following pages: Fresh Fruit with French Cream, *left* (page 326), and Tropical Fruit with Chocolate Sauce

COCONUT-RAISIN PUDDING

DULCE DE COCO (<u>dool</u>-say deh <u>koh</u>-koh)

From Brazil comes this sweet pudding thick with coconut, touched with rum. This is a time for the sensational crunch of fresh coconut only.

3 cups shredded fresh coconut
1 cup sugar
2 cups milk
Dash of salt
3 eggs, beaten
½ cup raisins
3 tablespoons rum

Heat coconut, sugar, milk and salt to boiling in 3-quart saucepan over medium heat, stirring frequently. Stir at least half of the hot mixture gradually into eggs. Blend into hot mixture in saucepan. Cook over low heat, stirring constantly, until mixture is thickened, 5 to 8 minutes. Remove from heat; stir in raisins and rum. Serve warm or cold.

6 servings

PER SERVING: Calories 495; Protein 7 g; Carbohydrate 70 g; Fat 21 g; Cholesterol 115 mg; Sodium 240 mg

FRESH FRUIT WITH FRENCH CREAM

French crème fraîche is something like sour cream but less acid or "soured" tasting. The sauce below is our quick version.

⅔ cup whipping cream
⅓ cup dairy sour cream
2 to 3 cups assorted fresh fruit (see Note)
Ground nutmeg or sugar

Gradually stir whipping cream into dairy sour cream. Cover and refrigerate no longer than 48 hours. Serve over fruit. Sprinkle with nutmeg.

4 to 6 servings

PER SERVING: Calories 195; Protein 2 g; Carbohydrate 11 g; Fat 16 g; Cholesterol 55 mg; Sodium 25 mg

NOTE: Suggested fruits are blueberries, raspberries, strawberries, sliced peaches or cubed pineapple.

PERUVIAN CARAMEL SAUCE WITH FRUIT

NATILLAS PIURANAS (nah-<u>tee</u>-yahs pee-yur-<u>ah</u>-nahs)

Goat's milk is a traditional ingredient in this sauce, but the concentrated flavor of evaporated milk does nicely Long, careful cooking ensures that this sauce has the fullest caramel flavor possible. It is particularly luscious over a mixture of sliced bananas and peaches.

1 can (12 ounces) evaporated milk
2 cups milk
½ teaspoon baking soda
1½ cups packed dark brown sugar
¼ cup water
3 to 4 cups assorted fresh fruit

Heat evaporated milk, milk and baking soda to boiling; remove from heat.

Heat brown sugar and water in Dutch oven over low heat, stirring constantly, until sugar is dissolved. Add milk mixture. Cook uncovered over medium-low heat, stirring frequently, until mixture is very thick and golden brown, about 1 hour. Pour into serving bowl. Cover and refrigerate at least 4 hours. Serve with fruit.

7 or 8 servings

PER SERVING: Calories 320; Protein 6 g; Carbohydrate 63 g; Fat 5 g; Cholesterol 20 mg; Sodium 160 mg

CREAMY CUSTARD SAUCE WITH FRUIT

CRÈME ANGLAISE AUX FRUITS
(krem ahn-glaze oh frwee)

It would not be an exaggeration to say that *Crème Anglaise* is one of the most important sauces in all of French cooking. It is the base for luscious ice creams, bombes and bavarians, the foundation of many molds and custards, and by itself is delicious spooned over plain cakes, pastries and fruit.

3 egg yolks, slightly beaten
3 to 4 tablespoons sugar
Dash of salt
1 cup milk
½ teaspoon vanilla
2 to 3 cups assorted fresh fruit (see Note)

Mix egg yolks, sugar and salt in heavy 2-quart saucepan. Stir in milk gradually. Cook over low heat, stirring constantly, until mixture coats a metal spoon, 15 to 20 minutes. (Do not boil; custard sauce will thicken slightly as it cools.)

Remove sauce from heat; stir in vanilla. Place saucepan in cold water until sauce is cool. Cover and refrigerate at least 2 hours but no longer than 24 hours. Serve over fruit.

4 to 6 servings

PER SERVING: Calories 145; Protein 4 g; Carbohydrate 21 g; Fat 5 g; Cholesterol 170 mg; Sodium 110 mg

NOTE: Suggested fruit combinations are blueberries or raspberries and sliced peaches, strawberries and cubed pineapple.

ITALIAN WINE CUSTARD

ZABAGLIONE (dzah-bah l'yoh-neh)

This thin custard is meant to be eaten freshly made and warm. It is flavored with Marsala, Italy's distinctive sweet fortified wine. Zabaglione is a wonderful sauce for fresh berries, plain cake or fruit-filled crèpes.

4 egg yolks
1 egg
⅓ cup sugar
⅓ cup Marsala wine or sherry
Dash of salt

Beat egg yolks and egg in small mixer bowl on high speed until thick and lemon colored, about 3 minutes. Gradually beat in sugar, scraping bowl occasionally. Beat in wine and salt on low speed.

Pour mixture into top of double boiler.* Add enough hot water to bottom of double boiler so that top does not touch water. Cook over medium heat, stirring constantly, until slightly thickened, about 5 minutes. (Water in double boiler should simmer but not boil.) Remove from heat. Serve immediately.

4 to 6 servings

*A metal bowl placed over a saucepan of simmering water can be substituted for a double boiler.

PER SERVING: Calories 165; Protein 4 g; Carbohydrate 19 g; Fat 6 g; Cholesterol 270 mg; Sodium 90 mg

CARAMEL CUSTARD

FLAN (flahn)

It seems that most cuisines have their version of *flan*. In Mexico it is sometimes flavored with toasted coconut, and in France it is called *crème caramel*. Cooking the custard in a water bath maintains even, moist heat, which helps to cook the eggs gently without danger of curdling.

½ cup sugar
3 eggs, slightly beaten
1 can (12 ounces) evaporated milk (1⅔ cups)
⅓ cup sugar
2 teaspoons vanilla
⅛ teaspoon salt

Heat ½ cup sugar in heavy 1-quart saucepan over low heat, stirring constantly, until melted and golden brown. Divide syrup among four 6-ounce custard cups; rotate cups to coat bottoms. Allow syrup to harden in cups, about 5 minutes.

Mix remaining ingredients; pour into custard cups. Place cups in square pan, 9 × 9 × 2 inches, on oven rack. Pour very hot water into pan to within ½ inch of tops of cups. Bake in 350° oven until knife inserted halfway between center and edge comes out clean, 40 to 50 minutes. Immediately remove from water. Unmold and serve warm, or refrigerate and unmold at serving time.

4 servings

PER SERVING: Calories 330; Protein 12 g; Carbohydrate 52 g; Fat 8 g; Cholesterol 175 mg; Sodium 230 mg

SPICED BRANDY CUSTARD: Stir 2 tablespoons brandy, ¼ teaspoon ground cinnamon and ⅛ teaspoon ground nutmeg into eggs.

DANISH RICE PUDDING

This make-ahead molded pudding is regally sauced with a vibrant red currant and raspberry mixture. The dessert looks richer than it really is—not a single egg—and would be a sweet finale to even a filling meal.

½ cup sugar
½ cup water
2 envelopes unflavored gelatin
½ teaspoon salt
2 cups milk
1½ cups cooked rice
2 teaspoons vanilla
1 cup chilled whipping cream
Raspberry-Currant Sauce (below)

Heat sugar, water, gelatin and salt in 2-quart saucepan, stirring constantly, until gelatin is dissolved, about 1 minute. Stir in milk, rice and vanilla. Place saucepan in a bowl of iced water, stirring occasionally, until mixture mounds slightly when dropped from a spoon, about 15 minutes.

Beat whipping cream in chilled bowl until stiff. Fold whipped cream into rice mixture. Pour into ungreased 1½ quart mold. Cover and refrigerate until firm, about 3 hours. Unmold and serve with Raspberry-Currant Sauce.

8 servings

PER SERVING: Calories 315; Protein 5 g; Carbohydrate 49 g; Fat 11 g; Cholesterol 40 mg; Sodium 330 mg

RASPBERRY-CURRANT SAUCE

1 package (10 ounces) frozen raspberries, thawed (with syrup)
½ cup currant jelly
1 tablespoon cold water
1½ teaspoons cornstarch

Heat raspberries and jelly to boiling. Mix water and cornstarch; stir into raspberry mixture. Heat to boiling, stirring constantly. Boil and stir 1 minute. Cool. Press through a sieve to remove seeds if desired.

CARROT PUDDING

GAJAR HALVA (gah-jer hul-vuh)

With gentle cooking, the natural sweetness of carrots comes shining through. Cardamom is a spice the Indians use to enhance sweetness, though it is not sweet in itself. This rich pudding should be served in rather small portions. A bit of vanilla ice cream would add an American touch.

6 medium carrots (about 1 pound), finely shredded
2 cups half-and-half
½ cup packed brown sugar
½ cup golden raisins
¼ cup margarine or butter
½ teaspoon ground cardamom
¼ teaspoon salt
¼ cup unsalted pistachios or slivered almonds

Heat carrots and half-and-half to boiling in 2-quart saucepan; reduce heat. Simmer uncovered, stirring frequently, until half-and-half is absorbed, about 1 hour.

Stir in brown sugar, raisins, margarine, cardamom and salt. Cook over low heat, stirring constantly, until brown sugar is dissolved and mixture is desired consistency, about 15 minutes. Garnish with pistachios.

6 servings

PER SERVING: Calories 355; Protein 4 g; Carbohydrate 40 g; Fat 20 g; Cholesterol 30 mg; Sodium 270 mg

NOODLE AND RAISIN PUDDING

LUKSHEN KUGEL (lookh-shehn koo-guhl)

This comforting dessert from eastern Europe is just right when something substantial—not fluffy—is longed for.

1 package (8 ounces) wide egg noodles
2 eggs, slightly beaten
1 cup dairy sour cream
1 cup small-curd cottage cheese
½ cup golden raisins
½ cup sugar
½ teaspoon salt
¼ teaspoon ground cinnamon
⅛ teaspoon ground nutmeg

Cook noodles as directed on package; drain. Mix remaining ingredients; toss with noodles. Pour into greased 2-quart casserole. Bake uncovered in 350° oven until golden brown, 40 to 50 minutes.

6 to 8 servings

PER SERVING: Calories 370; Protein 12 g; Carbohydrate 54 g; Fat 12 g; Cholesterol 135 mg; Sodium 520 mg

Pistachios

These small, elongated nuts are a stunning parrot green. They are grown in Iran, Afghanistan and Turkey, and, contrary to popular belief, their hard shells are beige; the magenta shells that turn our fingers red have been dyed. The Eastern world tends to use pistachios for savory as well as sweet preparations. Like other oil-rich nuts, pistachios are safely kept in the freezer, a measure that keeps them from turning rancid quickly.

FRIED MILK

LECHE FRITA (lay-chay <u>free</u>-tah)

These little Spanish squares are dipped into crumbs, then gently fried. A crisp, golden coating hides a creamy custard interior.

½ cup sugar
½ cup cornstarch
¼ teaspoon ground nutmeg
3 cups milk
1 tablespoon margarine or butter
¼ teaspoon grated lemon peel
2 eggs, well beaten
¾ cup dry bread crumbs
Vegetable oil

Mix sugar, cornstarch and nutmeg in 3-quart saucepan; gradually stir in milk. Heat to boiling over medium heat, stirring constantly; boil and stir 1 minute. Remove from heat; stir in margarine and lemon peel. Spread evenly in ungreased square baking dish, 8 × 8 × 2 inches. Refrigerate uncovered until firm, at least 3 hours.

Cut custard into 2-inch squares with wet knife. Dip custard squares into eggs; coat with bread crumbs. Heat oil (1 to 1½ inches) to 360°. Fry 2 to 3 squares at a time until light brown, 1 to 2 minutes; drain. Sprinkle with powdered sugar if desired.

8 servings

PER SERVING: Calories 255; Protein 6 g; Carbohydrate 31 g; Fat 12 g; Cholesterol 60 mg; Sodium 150 mg

Candied Walnuts with Cream, *top* (page 356), and Fried Milk

PINEAPPLE MERINGUE BREAD PUDDING

KUEH PROL NANAS (<u>koo</u>-en prol <u>nah</u>-nes)

Indonesian flavor is here defined by cinnamon, coconut milk and pineapple. This is an easy dessert; the meringue is added for the last ten minutes of baking.

3 cups ½-inch cubes French bread
1 can (15¼ ounces) crushed pineapple, drained (reserve syrup)
3 eggs, separated
⅓ cup packed brown sugar
½ teaspoon grated lemon peel
½ teaspoon ground cinnamon
½ teaspoon salt
1 cup Coconut Milk (page 72)
¼ teaspoon cream of tartar
¼ cup sugar

Place bread cubes in greased oblong baking dish, 10 × 6 × 1½ inches, or square baking dish, 8 × 8 × 2 inches. Spread pineapple on top. Beat egg yolks slightly; stir in brown sugar, lemon peel, cinnamon, salt and the reserved syrup. Slowly stir in Coconut Milk. Pour over bread cubes and pineapple. Bake uncovered in 350° oven until knife inserted halfway between center and edge comes out clean, 30 to 40 minutes.

Remove from oven. Beat egg whites and cream of tartar on medium speed until foamy. Beat in ¼ cup sugar, 1 tablespoon at a time; continue beating until stiff and glossy. Do not overbeat. Spread over pudding. Bake until delicate golden brown, 8 to 10 minutes. Let stand 5 minutes.

8 servings

PER SERVING: Calories 210; Protein 4 g; Carbohydrate 30 g; Fat 8 g; Cholesterol 80 mg; Sodium 240 mg

ENGLISH PLUM PUDDING

The forerunners of this pudding were mainstays of the medieval diet: savory, steamed puddings. This yuletide dessert is fragrant with spices and moist with dried fruits. Don't be put off by the suet; it is the fat that cushions beef kidneys, easy to find in most supermarkets, where it will be obligingly ground for you.

½ cup all-purpose flour
½ teaspoon ground cinnamon
⅛ teaspoon ground nutmeg
⅛ teaspoon ground cloves
½ teaspoon baking soda
½ teaspoon salt
1 cup raisins
½ cup currants
¼ cup cut-up candied fruit peel
¼ cup cut-up candied cherries
¼ cup chopped walnuts
¾ cup soft bread crumbs
1 cup ground suet (4 ounces)
½ cup packed brown sugar
2 eggs, beaten
1 tablespoon brandy
¼ cup brandy (optional)
Hard Sauce (right)

Mix flour, spices, baking soda and salt. Stir in fruit, walnuts and bread crumbs. Mix suet, brown sugar, eggs and 1 tablespoon brandy; stir into flour mixture. Pour into well-greased 4-cup mold; cover with aluminum foil.

Place mold on rack in Dutch oven; pour boiling water into Dutch oven to rack level. Cover and boil over low heat until wooden pick inserted in center comes out clean, about 3 hours. (Add boiling water if necessary.)

Remove mold from Dutch oven; unmold. Heat ¼ cup brandy until warm; ignite and pour over pudding. Serve with Hard Sauce.

8 servings

PER SERVING: Calories 665; Protein 5 g; Carbohydrate 73 g; Fat 39 g; Cholesterol 115 mg; Sodium 450 mg

HARD SAUCE

½ cup margarine or butter, softened
1 cup powdered sugar
2 tablespoons brandy

Beat margarine, powdered sugar and brandy until smooth.

SWEET GOLDEN YOGURT
SHRIKHAND (shree-khahnd)

Indian cooks make frequent and ingenious use of yogurt. Here it makes an appearance as a dessert, festively tinted with exotic saffron. A costly spice, saffron threads come from the stamens of crocus flowers; fortunately, little saffron is needed to make its presence known.

1 carton (18 ounces) plain yogurt
½ cup sugar
1 teaspoon rose water (optional)
½ teaspoon ground cardamom
Dash of ground nutmeg
Few grains or threads of saffron powder
4 teaspoons finely chopped green pistachios

Mix all ingredients except pistachios. Cover and refrigerate at least 2 hours. Stir; spoon into dessert dishes. Sprinkle with pistachios.

4 servings

PER SERVING: Calories 195; Protein 7 g; Carbohydrate 35 g; Fat 3 g; Cholesterol 10 mg; Sodium 90 mg

SEMOLINA PUDDING

MA'MOUNIA (mah-moo-<u>nay</u>-ah)

Semolina Pudding is a Syrian counterpart to our nursery rice pudding. It is studded with raisins and almonds and makes a very persuasive hot breakfast dish.

2 cups water
¾ cup sugar
¼ cup margarine or butter
¾ cup semolina (couscous)*
½ cup raisins
¼ cup slivered almonds
¼ teaspoon salt
Ground cinnamon

Heat water and sugar to boiling; reduce heat. Simmer uncovered 10 minutes; remove from heat and reserve. Heat margarine in 1½-quart saucepan until melted; add semolina. Cook over low heat, stirring constantly, 5 minutes.

Stir in reserved sugar syrup, raisins, almonds and salt. Heat to boiling. Cook, stirring constantly, until thickened, 5 to 8 minutes. Pour into serving dishes; sprinkle with cinnamon. Serve warm or cold with sweetened whipped cream if desired.

4 to 6 servings

*⅓ cup farina can be substituted for the ¾ cup semolina.

PER SERVING: Calories 485; Protein 6 g; Carbohydrate 81 g; Fat 15 g; Cholesterol 0 mg; Sodium 280 mg

LITTLE SALZBURGER SOUFFLÉS

SALZBURGER NOCKERLN (<u>zalts</u>-boor-ger <u>nawk</u>-airl'n)

This airy sweet is named for the charming city of Salzburg, but it is enjoyed throughout Austria and Germany. The soufflés are golden brown and touched with lemon, a light dessert. Set them adrift in a pool of custard (the Creamy Custard Sauce on page 327 would be a nice choice), or serve them with crushed fresh berries.

4 eggs, separated
¼ teaspoon cream of tartar
Dash of salt
⅓ cup sugar
2 tablespoons all-purpose flour
2 teaspoons finely shredded lemon peel

Heat oven to 350°. Butter oblong baking dish, 11 × 7 × 1½ inches. Beat egg whites, cream of tartar and salt in large mixer bowl until foamy. Gradually beat in sugar, 1 tablespoon at a time; continue beating until stiff and glossy. Do not underbeat.

Beat egg yolks in small mixer bowl until thick and lemon colored, about 3 minutes. Beat in flour and lemon peel. Carefully fold egg yolk mixture into meringue.

Spoon meringue mixture into 6 separate mounds in baking dish. Bake until golden, 18 to 20 minutes. Serve immediately. (Separate mounds by gently pushing them apart with backs of two forks.) Serve with sweetened sliced strawberries if desired.

6 servings

PER SERVING: Calories 100; Protein 4 g; Carbohydrate 14 g; Fat 3 g; Cholesterol 140 mg; Sodium 95 mg

ENGLISH BERRY TRIFLE

The English are great enthusiasts of puddings, to the point of building them from other desserts. They add ladyfingers, sprinkled with their favorite sherry, to a soft custard and then cover the whole with whipped cream and almonds.

½ cup sugar
3 tablespoons cornstarch
¼ teaspoon salt
3 cups milk
3 egg yolks, beaten
3 tablespoons margarine or butter
2 teaspoons vanilla
1 teaspoon almond extract
1 package (3 ounces) ladyfingers
2 tablespoons sherry
2 cups sliced strawberries or raspberries or both
1 cup chilled whipping cream
2 tablespoons sugar
2 tablespoons toasted slivered almonds

Mix ½ cup sugar, the cornstarch and salt in 3-quart saucepan; gradually stir in milk. Heat to boiling over medium heat, stirring constantly; boil and stir 1 minute. Stir at least half of the hot mixture gradually into egg yolks. Stir back into hot mixture in saucepan. Boil and stir 1 minute. Remove from heat; stir in margarine, vanilla and almond extract. Cover and refrigerate at least 3 hours.

Split ladyfingers lengthwise into halves. Layer half of the ladyfingers, cut sides up, in 2-quart glass serving bowl. Sprinkle with 1 tablespoon of the sherry. Layer half of the strawberries and half of the cold egg yolk mixture over ladyfingers; repeat. Cover and refrigerate at least 4 hours but no longer than 8 hours.

English Berry Trifle

Beat whipping cream and 2 tablespoons sugar in chilled bowl until stiff; spread over dessert. Sprinkle with almonds.

8 to 10 servings

PER SERVING: Calories 330; Protein 6 g; Carbohydrate 34 g; Fat 19 g; Cholesterol 140 mg; Sodium 200 mg

ALMOND CUSTARD WITH LITCHIS

HSING-JEN-TOU-FU (shee-ong-ren-dough-foo)

This is a perfectly stunning dessert: diamonds of delicate almond custard nestled on a bed of sweet, crunchy litchis. This would be an elegant finish to a Chinese banquet.

¾ cup water
¼ cup sugar
1 envelope unflavored gelatin
1 cup milk
1 teaspoon almond extract
2 cans (11 ounces each) litchis (with syrup)

Heat water, sugar and gelatin to boiling, stirring occasionally, until sugar and gelatin are dissolved. Remove from heat. Stir in milk and almond extract. Pour into loaf pan, 9 × 5 × 3 inches. Cover and refrigerate until firm, at least 4 hours.

Cut gelatin custard into 1-inch diamonds or squares. Place litchis in serving bowl; arrange custard around fruit.

4 to 6 servings

PER SERVING: Calories 225; Protein 4 g; Carbohydrate 48 g; Fat 2 g; Cholesterol 5 mg; Sodium 35 mg

SWEET RICE WITH CINNAMON

ROZ MAFOOAR (rohz m'foo-err)

Powdered sugar disappears beautifully into grains of white rice to sweeten this Moroccan dish. Cinnamon adds a warm touch.

1⅓ cups regular rice
2⅔ cups water
½ teaspoon salt
¼ cup margarine or butter
¼ cup powdered sugar
Ground cinnamon

Heat rice, water and salt to boiling in 3-quart saucepan, stirring once or twice; reduce heat. Cover and simmer 14 minutes. (Do not lift cover or stir.) Remove from heat. Fluff rice lightly with fork; cover and let steam 5 to 10 minutes. Stir in margarine and powdered sugar. Sprinkle with cinnamon; serve warm.

6 servings

PER SERVING: Calories 150; Protein 1 g; Carbohydrate 18 g; Fat 8 g; Cholesterol 0 mg; Sodium 440 mg

Cheesecake Pastry (below)
1½ pounds ricotta cheese, well drained
½ cup granulated sugar
3 tablespoons all-purpose flour
3 eggs
1 teaspoon grated orange peel
1 teaspoon vanilla
¼ teaspoon salt
2 tablespoons golden raisins
2 tablespoons finely cut-up candied citron
2 tablespoons chopped blanched almonds
2 tablespoons powdered sugar
½ teaspoon ground cinnamon

Prepare Cheesecake Pastry. Beat ricotta cheese, granulated sugar, flour, eggs, orange peel, vanilla and salt in large mixer bowl on high speed until smooth and creamy, about 4 minutes. Stir in raisins, citron and almonds. Pour into pastry-lined pan. Bake in 350° oven until center is set and top is golden brown, 1¼ to 1½ hours. Cool. Refrigerate 12 to 24 hours. Remove outer rim of pan. Mix powdered sugar and cinnamon; sprinkle over cheesecake. Serve with green grapes if desired.

12 to 16 servings

PER SERVING: Calories 245; Protein 9 g; Carbohydrate 25 g; Fat 12 g; Cholesterol 70 mg; Sodium 220 mg

ITALIAN RICOTTA CHEESECAKE

CROSTATA DI RICOTTA (kroh-stah-tah dee ree-koht-tah)

Ricotta lends a sophisticated note to cheesecake, Italian style. Unlike American versions, European cheese-based cakes often incorporate dried fruits and zest into their fillings. Prepare this cake ahead of time, as it must be chilled for at least twelve hours.

CHEESECAKE PASTRY

¾ cup all-purpose flour
⅓ cup margarine or butter, softened
2 tablespoons sugar
⅛ teaspoon salt

Mix all ingredients until blended; press evenly in bottom of ungreased 9-inch springform pan. Bake in 475° oven 5 minutes.

CHEESE AND HONEY PIE

Cheesecakes may have their origin in the kitchens of ancient Greece, and honey is a Greek favorite. The sesame seed for the crust is toasted first, enhancing its nutty flavor.

Sesame Seed Pastry (below)
2 packages (8 ounces each) cream cheese, softened
2 eggs
½ cup sugar
½ cup honey
½ cup whipping cream
1 teaspoon grated lemon peel
¼ teaspoon ground nutmeg

Prepare Sesame Seed Pastry. Beat cream cheese in large mixer bowl on medium speed until creamy. Add remaining ingredients; beat until light and fluffy. Pour into baked pie shell. Bake in 350° oven until firm, 40 to 50 minutes. Refrigerate until serving time.

10 to 12 servings

PER SERVING: Calories 415; Protein 6 g; Carbohydrate 37 g; Fat 27 g; Cholesterol 105 mg; Sodium 280 mg

SESAME SEED PASTRY

1 cup all-purpose flour
⅓ cup margarine or butter, softened
1 tablespoon sugar
1 tablespoon toasted sesame seed
¼ teaspoon salt

Mix all ingredients until blended; press firmly and evenly against bottom and side of 9-inch pie plate. Bake in 475° oven 5 minutes.

ORANGE-ALMOND CAKE
TORTA DE ALMENDRA (<u>tohr</u>-tah deh ahl-<u>mehn</u>-drah)

Spanish heritage is evident in this Mexican cake, which is a simple nut-decorated torte in classic European fashion. Fresh fruit would be nice with this orange-scented cake.

1¼ cups all-purpose flour or 1½ cups cake flour
1 cup sugar
1½ teaspoons baking powder
½ teaspoon salt
¾ cup milk
⅓ cup shortening
1 egg
2 teaspoons grated orange peel
¼ cup sliced almonds
1 tablespoon sugar
2 tablespoons orange-flavored liqueur

Heat oven to 350°. Grease and flour round layer pan, 9 × 1½ inches, or square pan, 8 × 8 × 2 or 9 × 9 × 2 inches. Beat all ingredients except almonds, 1 tablespoon sugar and the liqueur in large mixer bowl on low speed, scraping bowl constantly, 30 seconds. Beat on high speed, scraping bowl occasionally, 3 minutes. Pour into pan; sprinkle with almonds.

Bake until wooden pick inserted in center comes out clean, round pan 40 minutes, square pans 40 to 45 minutes. Sprinkle with 1 tablespoon sugar; drizzle with liqueur. Cool 10 to 15 minutes. Remove from pan; cool completely.

8 servings

PER SERVING: Calories 290; Protein 4 g; Carbohydrate 44 g; Fat 11 g; Cholesterol 30 mg; Sodium 220 mg

GERMAN PLUM CAKE

ZWETSCHGENKUCHEN (ts'vetch-g'n-koo-kh'n)

The end of summer, when purple plums are at the peak of perfection, is the time to make this classic German dessert. A dash of cinnamon coaxes all the natural sweetness from these yellow-fleshed fruits. The pie is a lovely color from the skins of the plums—no peeling necessary.

Pastry (below)
2 pounds purple or red plums, halved and pitted (about 5 cups)
¾ cup sugar
2 tablespoons all-purpose flour
1 teaspoon ground cinnamon
¼ cup slivered almonds

Prepare pastry. Place plum halves, cut sides down and overlapping slightly, in pastry-lined pan. Mix sugar, flour and cinnamon; sprinkle over plums. Sprinkle with almonds. Bake in 375° oven until pastry is golden brown and plums are bubbly, 35 to 45 minutes.

6 servings

PER SERVING: Calories 570; Protein 8 g; Carbohydrate 89 g; Fat 20 g; Cholesterol 35 mg; Sodium 430 mg

PASTRY

½ cup margarine or butter
2 cups all-purpose flour
¼ cup sugar
1 teaspoon baking powder
½ teaspoon salt
½ teaspoon grated lemon peel
¼ teaspoon ground mace
1 egg, beaten
2 tablespoons cold water

Cut margarine into flour, sugar, baking powder, salt, lemon peel and mace until mixture resembles fine crumbs. Mix egg and water; stir into flour mixture. Gather pastry into a ball; knead just until smooth, 5 or 6 times. Press evenly on bottom and side of ungreased round layer pan, 9 × 1½ inches.

ISLAND RUM CAKE

BOLO DI ROM (boh-loh dee rohm)

Island rum is stirred right into the batter to make this cake from Curaçao, and cornmeal gives it a nice "crumb." Take this cake along on picnics; it travels well.

1¼ cups all-purpose flour
1 cup sugar
⅓ cup yellow cornmeal
⅓ cup shortening
⅓ cup dark rum
⅓ cup water
2 teaspoons baking powder
1 teaspoon grated orange peel
¼ teaspoon salt
1 egg
Powdered sugar

Heat oven to 350°. Grease and flour square pan, 9 × 9 × 2 inches. Beat all ingredients except powdered sugar in large mixer bowl on low speed, scraping bowl frequently, 30 seconds. Beat on medium speed 2 minutes, scraping bowl frequently. Pour into pan; spread evenly. Bake until crust is light golden brown and wooden pick inserted in center comes out clean, 30 to 35 minutes. Cool; sprinkle with powdered sugar.

9 servings

PER SERVING: Calories 250; Protein 3 g; Carbohydrate 41 g; Fat 8 g; Cholesterol 25 mg; Sodium 150 mg

CARIBBEAN PINEAPPLE PIE

Serve this fresh pineapple pie with a thick, pineapple-scented cream, rich and easily made.

6 cups cut-up fresh pineapple (about 2 medium)
1 cup sugar
2 tablespoons rum
Pastry (right)
½ cup sugar
½ cup all-purpose flour
¼ teaspoon ground cinnamon
⅛ teaspoon ground nutmeg
1 tablespoon margarine or butter
1 package (8 ounces) cream cheese, softened

Place pineapple in large glass or plastic bowl. Stir in 1 cup sugar and the rum. Cover and refrigerate at least 4 hours.

Prepare Pastry; gather into ball. Divide into halves; shape each half into flattened round on lightly floured cloth-covered board. Roll 1 round 2 inches larger than inverted pie plate, 9 × 1¼ inches, with floured stockinet-covered rolling pin. Fold pastry into fourths; unfold and ease into plate, pressing against bottom and side.

Drain pineapple, reserving liquid. Spoon pineapple into pastry-lined pie plate. Mix ½ cup sugar, the flour, cinnamon and nutmeg in 1-quart saucepan. Stir in ½ cup of the reserved liquid (reserve remaining liquid). Heat to boiling, stirring constantly. Boil and stir 1 minute. Remove from heat; stir in margarine. Pour over pineapple. Trim overhanging edge of pastry 1 inch from rim of plate.

Roll other round of pastry; cut circle into ½-inch strips. Place 6 strips across filling. Weave a cross-strip through center by first folding back every other strip going the other way. Continue weaving lattice, folding back alternate strips each time cross-strip is added. Fold trimmed edge of lower crust over ends of strips; seal and flute. Cover edge with 3-inch strip of aluminum foil to prevent excessive browning; remove foil during last 15 minutes of baking. Bake in 425° oven until crust is brown and filling is bubbly, 35 to 45 minutes.

Gradually beat ¼ cup plus 2 tablespoons reserved pineapple liquid into cream cheese until smooth and creamy. Serve with pie.

8 servings

PER SERVING: Calories 645; Protein 6 g; Carbohydrate 83 g; Fat 32 g; Cholesterol 30 mg; Sodium 370 mg

PASTRY

2 cups all-purpose flour
1 teaspoon salt
⅔ cup plus 2 tablespoons shortening or ⅔ cup lard
4 to 5 tablespoons cold water

Mix flour and salt; cut in shortening until particles are size of small peas. Sprinkle in water, 1 tablespoon at a time, tossing with fork until all flour is moistened and pastry almost cleans side of bowl (1 to 2 teaspoons water can be added if necessary).

SICILIAN CHEESE AND CHOCOLATE CAKE

CASSATA ALLA SICILIANA
(kahs-sah-tah ah-lah see-chee-l'yah-nah)

This luscious, cream-filled layer cake is in the best tradition of Sicilian pastry chefs, renowned for their way with sweets. The Italians often mix ricotta with morsels of chocolate and chopped candied fruit as a filling for baked goods.

Sponge Cake (below)
1 carton (about 16 ounces) dry ricotta cheese
¼ cup sugar
2 tablespoons milk
2 tablespoons orange-flavored liqueur
¼ teaspoon salt
⅓ cup semisweet chocolate chips, chopped
⅓ cup finely chopped mixed candied fruit
Chocolate Mocha Frosting (right)

Prepare Sponge Cake. Beat ricotta cheese, sugar, milk, liqueur and salt in small mixer bowl until smooth, 2 to 3 minutes. Stir in chocolate chips and candied fruit. Cut cake into 4 rectangles, 10½ × 3¾ inches. Alternate layers of cake and ricotta filling, beginning and ending with cake. Frost with Chocolate Mocha Frosting.

12 to 14 servings

PER SERVING: Calories 405; Protein 7 g; Carbohydrate 65 g; Fat 13 g; Cholesterol 65 mg; Sodium 260 mg

SPONGE CAKE

3 eggs
1 cup granulated sugar
⅓ cup water
1 teaspoon vanilla
¾ cup all-purpose flour or 1 cup cake flour
1 teaspoon baking powder
¼ teaspoon salt
Powdered sugar

Heat oven to 375°. Line jelly roll pan, 15½ × 10½ × 1 inch, with aluminum foil or waxed paper; grease generously. Beat eggs in small mixer bowl on high speed until thick and lemon colored, about 5 minutes. Pour eggs into large mixer bowl. Beat in granulated sugar gradually. Beat in water and vanilla on low speed. Add flour, baking powder and salt gradually, beating just until batter is smooth. Pour into pan.

Bake until wooden pick inserted in center comes out clean, 12 to 15 minutes. Immediately loosen cake from edges of pan; invert on towel sprinkled generously with powdered sugar. Carefully remove foil. Trim off stiff edges if necessary. Cool on wire rack at least 30 minutes.

CHOCOLATE MOCHA FROSTING

2½ cups powdered sugar
⅓ cup margarine or butter, softened
2 squares (1 ounce each) unsweetened chocolate, melted and cooled
2 teaspoons instant coffee
3 tablespoons hot water

Beat powdered sugar, margarine and chocolate in small mixer bowl on low speed. Dissolve instant coffee in water. Add coffee gradually; beat until smooth and creamy. If necessary, stir in additional water, a few drops at a time.

Caribbean Pineapple Pie (page 339)

FRENCH RING CAKE

SAVARIN (sah-vah-<u>rang</u>)

Much like a *baba* except for its shape, French Ring Cake is soaked with a liqueur-flavored syrup. The French serve it with fresh fruit.

1 package active dry yeast
½ cup warm water (105 to 115°)
¾ cup margarine or butter, softened
4 eggs, beaten
2 tablespoons sugar
½ teaspoon salt
2 cups all-purpose flour
Savarin Syrup (right)
½ cup apricot preserves
2 tablespoons sugar

Dissolve yeast in warm water in 3-quart bowl. Stir in margarine, eggs, 2 tablespoons sugar, the salt and 1 cup of the flour. Beat until smooth. Stir in remaining flour until smooth. Beat 25 strokes. Spread batter evenly in well-greased 6½-cup metal ring mold or tube pan, 10 × 4 inches. Cover; let rise in warm place until almost double, 50 to 60 minutes.

Heat oven to 375°. Bake until golden brown, 25 to 30 minutes. (If top is browning too quickly, cover loosely with aluminum foil.) Cool in mold 10 minutes. Remove from mold; cool slightly on wire rack.

Prepare Savarin Syrup. Place cake on serving plate. Slowly drizzle syrup on cake until all syrup is absorbed (see Note). Press apricot preserves through strainer. Heat preserves and 2 tablespoons sugar to boiling, stirring constantly; reduce heat. Simmer uncovered until slightly thickened, 1 to 2 minutes. Cool 10 minutes. Spread apricot glaze over cake. Cake can be served with fresh berries or peaches and sweetened whipped cream if desired.

12 to 14 servings

PER SERVING: Calories 315; Protein 4 g; Carbohydrate 46 g; Fat 13 g; Cholesterol 70 mg; Sodium 250 mg

SAVARIN SYRUP

1 cup sugar
1 cup water
¼ cup brandy, rum or orange-flavored liqueur

Heat sugar and water to boiling; reduce heat. Simmer uncovered 2 minutes; cool to lukewarm. Stir in brandy.

BABA AU RHUM: Stir ½ cup raisins into batter. Spread in well-greased 8- or 9-cup metal mold or 9-cup bundt cake pan. Bake until golden brown, about 30 minutes. Use rum in the syrup and omit apricot glaze if desired.

NOTE: A fine skewer can be used to make holes in the French Ring Cake or Baba au Rhum before drizzling with syrup to facilitate absorption of syrup.

CHOCOLATE-CINNAMON CAKE ROLL

Mexican cooks are fond of pairing chocolate with cinnamon; in fact, some brands of Mexican chocolate are flavored with cinnamon.

3 eggs
1 cup sugar
⅓ cup water
1 teaspoon coffee-flavored liqueur
¾ cup all-purpose flour or 1 cup cake flour
¼ cup cocoa
1 teaspoon baking powder
¼ teaspoon salt
Cocoa
2 tablespoons coffee-flavored liqueur
Cinnamon Whipped Cream (page 343)

Chocolate-Cinnamon Cake Roll

Heat oven to 375°. Line jelly roll pan, 15½ × 10½ × 1 inch, with aluminum foil or waxed paper; grease generously. Beat eggs in small mixer bowl on high speed until thick and lemon colored, about 5 minutes; pour into large mixer bowl. Gradually beat in sugar. Beat in water and 1 teaspoon liqueur on low speed. Gradually add flour, ¼ cup cocoa, the baking powder and salt, beating just until batter is smooth. Pour into pan.

Bake until wooden pick inserted in center comes out clean, 12 to 15 minutes. Immediately loosen cake from edges of pan; invert on towel sprinkled generously with cocoa. Carefully remove foil. Trim off stiff edges of cake if necessary.

While hot, carefully roll cake and towel from narrow end. Cool on wire rack at least 30 minutes. Unroll cake; remove towel. Sprinkle 2 tablespoons liqueur over cake. Spread with Cinnamon Whipped Cream; roll up. Sprinkle with cocoa and powdered sugar if desired. Refrigerate until serving time.

10 servings

PER SERVING: Calories 235; Protein 4 g; Carbohydrate 34 g; Fat 9 g; Cholesterol 90 mg; Sodium 120 mg

CINNAMON WHIPPED CREAM

1 cup chilled whipping cream
3 tablespoons powdered sugar
1 tablespoon coffee-flavored liqueur
1 teaspoon ground cinnamon

Beat all ingredients in chilled bowl until stiff.

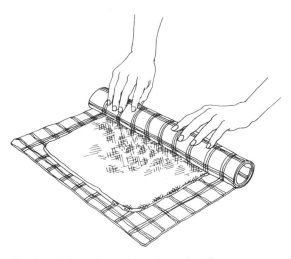

Gently roll hot cake and towel together from narrow end.

THOUSAND LEAVES TORTE

TUSENBLADSTÅRTA (thew-sen-blahds-<u>tawr</u>-tah)

The ideal dessert to conclude an evening of entertaining at home, this Swedish torte needs to chill for at least two hours before it is served. Thousand Leaves Torte is a dramatic and very unusual dessert: cinnamon pastry layered with a custard cream and applesauce.

Cinnamon Pastry (below)
6 tablespoons sugar
Custard-Cream Filling (right)
1 cup thick applesauce
1 teaspoon lemon juice
Sliced almonds (optional)

Prepare Cinnamon Pastry. Divide pastry into 6 equal parts. Roll each part into 7-inch circle on lightly floured cloth-covered board; place on ungreased cookie sheets. Heat oven to 425°. Prick circles with fork; sprinkle each with 1 tablespoon sugar. Bake until light golden brown, 12 to 15 minutes. Cool on wire racks.

Prepare Custard-Cream Filling. Mix applesauce and lemon juice. Stack circles, spreading alternately with ⅓ cup applesauce mixture and ½ cup Custard-Cream Filling. Spread top layer with remaining filling. Garnish with almonds. Refrigerate at least 2 hours before serving.

12 to 14 servings

PER SERVING: Calories 290; Protein 4 g; Carbohydrate 33 g; Fat 16 g; Cholesterol 30 mg; Sodium 380 mg

CINNAMON PASTRY

¾ cup margarine or butter
2 cups all-purpose flour
1 teaspoon salt
1 teaspoon ground cinnamon
3 to 4 tablespoons cold water

Cut margarine into flour, salt and cinnamon 6until particles are size of small peas. Sprinkle in water, 1 tablespoon at a time, tossing with fork until all flour is moistened and pastry almost cleans side of bowl (1 to 2 teaspoons water may be added if necessary). Gather pastry into a ball.

CUSTARD-CREAM FILLING

¼ cup sugar
1 tablespoon cornstarch
¼ teaspoon salt
1 cup milk
1 egg, slightly beaten
1 teaspoon vanilla
½ cup chilled whipping cream

Mix sugar, cornstarch and salt in 1-quart saucepan. Stir in milk gradually. Cook over medium heat, stirring constantly, until mixture thickens and boils. Boil and stir 1 minute. Stir at least half of the hot mixture gradually into egg. Stir back into hot mixture in saucepan. Boil and stir 1 minute. Remove from heat; stir in vanilla. Cover and cool slightly; refrigerate until completely cooled. Beat whipping cream in chilled bowl until stiff; fold into cooled mixture.

HONEY CAKE

LEKACH (lek-ahk)

This eastern European honey cake celebrates the holidays of Rosh Hashanah and Simhath Torah.

1 cup sugar
1 cup honey
½ cup vegetable oil
4 eggs
1 tablespoon finely shredded lemon peel
3 tablespoons lemon juice
2 tablespoons brandy
3½ cups all-purpose flour
1½ teaspoons baking powder
1 teaspoon baking soda
½ teaspoon salt
1 teaspoon ground cinnamon
½ teaspoon ground ginger
¼ teaspoon ground nutmeg
2 teaspoons instant coffee
⅔ cup cold water
¾ cup chopped nuts
½ cup raisins
Lemon Sugar (right)

Heat oven to 350°. Beat sugar, honey, oil, eggs, lemon peel and juice and brandy in large mixer bowl on medium speed 2 minutes. Mix flour, baking powder, baking soda, salt, cinnamon, ginger, nutmeg and instant coffee; stir into sugar mixture alternately with water. Beat on high speed, scraping bowl occasionally, 2 minutes. Fold in ½ cup of the nuts and the raisins.

Pour into greased tube pan, 10 × 4 inches, or 12-cup fluted tube pan. Bake until wooden pick inserted in center comes out clean, about 1 hour 10 minutes. Cool in pan 15 minutes; remove from pan. Prick top of cake carefully with fork; drizzle with Lemon Sugar. Sprinkle with remaining nuts.

12 to 14 servings

PER SERVING: Calories 540; Protein 7 g; Carbohydrate 92 g; Fat 16 g; Cholesterol 70 mg; Sodium 230 mg

LEMON SUGAR

1 cup sugar
⅓ cup lemon juice

Mix sugar and lemon juice.

SPANISH CRULLERS

CHURROS (choo-rohs)

These sugar-sprinkled fried cakes are great favorites in Mexico as well as Spain. *Churros* is the name of a sort of shaggy-coated sheep, and these rough-coated crullers do look a bit shaggy themselves.

Vegetable oil
1 cup water
½ cup margarine or butter
¼ teaspoon salt
1 cup all-purpose flour
3 eggs
¼ cup sugar
¼ teaspoon ground cinnamon

Heat oil (1 to 1½ inches) to 360°. Heat water, margarine and salt to rolling boil in 3-quart saucepan; stir in flour. Stir vigorously over low heat until mixture forms a ball, about 1 minute; remove from heat. Beat in eggs all at once; continue beating until smooth.

Spoon mixture into decorators' tube with large star tip. Squeeze 4-inch strips of dough into hot oil. Fry 3 or 4 strips at a time until golden brown, turning once, about 2 minutes on each side; drain. Mix sugar and cinnamon; roll crullers in sugar mixture.

About 24 crullers

PER CRULLER: Calories 90; Protein 1 g; Carbohydrate 6 g; Fat 7 g; Cholesterol 25 mg; Sodium 75 mg

MEXICAN HONEY PUFFS

SOPAIPILLAS (soh-py-<u>pee</u>-yahs)

The puffs are named for the little pillows they resemble. Serve them warm, with Honey Butter or Cinnamon Sugar, as a sweet treat.

1 tablespoon shortening
2 cups all-purpose flour
1 teaspoon baking powder
½ teaspoon salt
⅔ to ¾ cup cold water
Vegetable oil
Honey Butter or Cinnamon Sugar (right)

Cut shortening into flour, baking powder and salt until mixture resembles fine crumbs. Gradually add enough water to make a stiff dough, tossing with fork until all flour is moistened and dough almost cleans side of bowl. Gather dough into a ball; divide into halves and shape into 2 flattened rounds. Cover half to prevent drying.

Heat oil (1½ to 2 inches) to 360°. Roll 1 half of dough ⅛ to ¼ inch thick. Cut into rectangles, 3 × 2 inches, or 3-inch diamonds.

Fry 3 to 4 rectangles at a time, turning once, until puffed and golden brown, 1 to 2 minutes on each side; drain. Repeat with remaining dough.

Dip puffs into Honey Butter or sprinkle with Cinnamon Sugar.

About 20 puffs

PER PUFF: Calories 105; Protein 1 g; Carbohydrate 14 g; Fat 5 g; Cholesterol 0 mg; Sodium 90 mg

HONEY BUTTER

⅓ cup honey
2 tablespoons margarine or butter

Heat honey and margarine until hot.

CINNAMON SUGAR

3 tablespoons sugar
¼ teaspoon ground cinnamon

Mix sugar and cinnamon.

DO-AHEAD TIP: Puffs can be reheated uncovered in 350° oven about 8 minutes.

DUTCH FRIED PUFFS

OLIE BOLLEN (oh-lee boh-len)

In the Netherlands, chopped apples or other fruit are sometimes stirred into the batter for these round fried cakes.

Vegetable oil
¾ cup milk
½ cup sugar
¼ cup vegetable oil
2 eggs
3 teaspoons baking powder
½ teaspoon salt
½ teaspoon ground mace
2½ cups all-purpose flour
½ cup currants or raisins (optional)
¼ cup sugar
½ teaspoon ground cinnamon

Heat oil (2 to 3 inches) to 375°. Beat milk, ½ cup sugar, ¼ cup oil, the eggs, baking powder, salt, mace and 1 cup of the flour in large mixer bowl on low speed, scraping bowl constantly, 30 seconds. Beat on medium speed, scraping bowl occasionally, 2 minutes. Stir in remaining flour and the currants.

Drop batter by teaspoonfuls into hot oil. Turn puffs as they rise to the surface. Fry until golden brown, 2 to 2½ minutes on each side; drain. Mix ¼ cup sugar and the cinnamon. Roll puffs in sugar mixture.

About 30 puffs

PER PUFF: Calories 90; Protein 1 g; Carbohydrate 13 g; Fat 4 g; Cholesterol 15 mg; Sodium 80 mg

DEEP-FRIED WONTON COOKIES

TEEM GOK (teem gawk)

Chinese wonton skins are instant pastry. These cookies are crisp and brown, with a moist coconut and fruit filling.

1½ cups chopped prunes*
1 cup chopped dried apricots
1½ cups packed brown sugar
1½ cups flaked coconut
1 cup chopped almonds
24 wonton skins
Vegetable oil

Mix prunes, apricots, brown sugar, coconut and almonds. Place about 2 teaspoons mixture in center of each wonton skin. Moisten edges with water. Fold each skin in half to form triangle; press edges firmly to seal. Cover to prevent drying.

Heat oil (1 to 1½ inches) to 360°. Fry 3 to 4 wontons at a time, turning occasionally, until golden brown, about 1 minute on each side; drain. Cool thoroughly and store in airtight container. Serve with ice cream or sherbet if desired.

About 24 cookies

*1½ cups chopped dried apples can be substituted for the prunes.

PER COOKIE: Calories 230; Protein 3 g; Carbohydrate 37 g; Fat 8 g; Cholesterol 5 mg; Sodium 90 mg

GREEK CRESCENT COOKIES

KOURAMBIETHES (kur-em-bee-<u>eth</u>-ehs)

These crisp cookies are flavored with ouzo, the Greek anise-flavored liqueur. An anisette or any other anise- or licorice-flavored liqueur may be substituted.

1 cup margarine or butter, softened
½ cup powdered sugar
1 egg yolk
2 teaspoons ouzo or brandy
½ teaspoon almond extract
2 cups all-purpose flour
Powdered sugar

Heat oven to 350°. Mix margarine, ½ cup powdered sugar, the egg yolk, ouzo and almond extract; stir in flour. Shape dough by teaspoonfuls into crescent shapes. Place about 1 inch apart on ungreased cookie sheet. Bake until light brown on bottom, 12 to 15 minutes. Sprinkle with powdered sugar while hot. Cool on wire racks.

About 48 cookies

PER COOKIE: Calories 60; Protein 0 g; Carbohydrate 6 g; Fat 4 g; Cholesterol 5 mg; Sodium 45 mg

Dutch Fried Puffs, *left* (page 347), and Dutch Apricot Compote (page 318)

BRANDY SNAPS

These lacy cookies are British teatime favorites. Don't fill the cookies until just before serving so that they stay nicely crisp.

½ cup margarine or butter
½ cup dark corn syrup
⅓ cup packed brown sugar
2 teaspoons brandy
¾ cup all-purpose flour
½ teaspoon ground ginger
1 cup chilled whipping cream
2 tablespoons powdered sugar
1 tablespoon brandy

Heat oven to 350°. Heat margarine, corn syrup and brown sugar to boiling in 1½-quart saucepan, stirring frequently; remove from heat. Stir in 2 teaspoons brandy. Mix flour and ginger; gradually stir into syrup mixture.

Drop dough by teaspoonfuls about 5 inches apart onto lightly greased cookie sheets. Bake until cookies spread into 3- or 4-inch rounds and are golden brown, 6 to 8 minutes.

Cool cookies 1 to 3 minutes before removing from cookie sheets. Working quickly, roll each cookie around greased handle of wooden spoon; slip from spoon and place on wire racks. If cookies become too crisp to roll, return to oven to soften about 1 minute.

Beat whipping cream and powdered sugar in chilled bowl until stiff; fold in 1 tablespoon brandy. Using decorators' tube with plain or star tip, pipe whipped cream into each end of cookies.

About 30 cookies

PER COOKIE: Calories 95; Protein 0 g; Carbohydrate 10 g; Fat 6 g; Cholesterol 10 mg; Sodium 45 mg

NOTE: Store unfilled cookies in airtight container.

Ingredients for Garden Apple Ice Cream

Garden Apple Ice Cream

GARDEN APPLE ICE CREAM

Here is a lovely and sentimental English dessert. A touch of rose water adds the essence of warm-weather blossoms. Serve this ice cream with thin wafer cookies.

3 egg yolks, beaten
½ cup sugar
½ cup milk
¼ teaspoon salt
2 cups chilled whipping cream
¾ cup frozen apple juice concentrate, thawed
  (6 ounces)
½ to 1 teaspoon rose water
3 to 4 drops red food color (optional)

Mix egg yolks, sugar, milk and salt in 2-quart saucepan. Cook over medium heat, stirring constantly, just until bubbles appear around edge. Pour into chilled bowl; cover and refrigerate until room temperature, 1 to 2 hours.

Stir remaining ingredients into milk mixture. Pour into freezer can; put dasher in place. Cover and adjust crank. Place can in freezer tub. Fill freezer tub ⅓ full of ice; add remaining ice alternately with layers of rock salt (6 parts ice to 1 part rock salt). Turn crank until it turns with difficulty. Drain water from freezer tub. Remove lid; take out dasher. Pack mixture down; replace lid. Repack in ice and salt. Let stand several hours to ripen.

8 servings

PER SERVING: Calories 300; Protein 3 g; Carbohydrate 25 g; Fat 21 g; Cholesterol 150 mg; Sodium 100 mg

Rose Water

It is the influence of India and the Middle East that has made rose water known throughout the culinary world. This clear liquid, distilled from fresh rose petals, is a flavoring that can be subtle and romantic when used judiciously, soapy when added with a heavy hand. Rose essence, a more concentrated form of rose flavoring, should be added more sparingly to dishes than rose water.

BISCUIT TORTONI

Cherries, rum, toasted almonds and crushed macaroons flavor this Italian ice-cream classic.

1½ cups chilled whipping cream
⅓ cup sugar
1 cup almond macaroon or vanilla wafer crumbs (about 24 cookies)
½ cup chopped toasted almonds
¼ cup maraschino cherries, drained and chopped
2 tablespoons rum or dry sherry
1 teaspoon vanilla

Beat whipping cream and sugar in chilled bowl until stiff. Reserve ¼ cup macaroon crumbs; fold remaining ingredients into whipped cream. Divide among 12 small dessert dishes or paper-lined medium muffin cups, 2½ × 1¼ inches. Sprinkle with reserved crumbs. Freeze until firm, about 4 hours.

12 servings

PER SERVING: Calories 190; Protein 2 g; Carbohydrate 14 g; Fat 14 g; Cholesterol 35 mg; Sodium 35 mg

GINGERED PEAR SORBET

The French love their sorbets, made without the smallest touch of cream. Ginger brings up the refreshing flavor of ripe pears for an elegant change of pace. Decorate each serving of sorbet with a dash of ground ginger, a fresh mint sprig or a sprinkling of finely chopped crystallized ginger.

1 can (29 ounces) pear halves, drained (reserve syrup)
¼ cup sugar
2 tablespoons lemon juice
1 to 1½ teaspoons finely chopped crystallized ginger or ⅛ teaspoon ground ginger

Heat 1 cup of the reserved syrup and the sugar to boiling, stirring constantly; remove from heat. Cool. Place pears, half at a time, in blender container; cover and purée until smooth. Mix syrup, purée, lemon juice and ginger; pour into metal ice cube tray with the dividers removed, or loaf pan, 9 × 5 × 3 inches. Freeze until partially frozen, 1 to 1½ hours.

Pour into blender; blend on medium speed until smooth and fluffy. Return to ice cube tray. Freeze until firm, about 3 hours. Let stand at room temperature about 10 minutes before serving.

6 servings

PER SERVING: Calories 140; Protein 0 g; Carbohydrate 35 g; Fat 0 g; Cholesterol 0 mg; Sodium 10 mg

LEMON ICE
GRANITA DI LIMONE (grah-<u>nee</u>-tah dee lee-<u>moh</u>-nay)

Finely shredded lemon peel adds intense citrus impact to this traditional Italian ice. Remember to use only the colored portion of the peel, avoiding the bitter white pith. Lemon Ice would be welcome refreshment on a hot summer's night.

2 cups water
1 cup sugar
1 tablespoon finely shredded lemon peel
1 cup lemon juice

Heat water and sugar to boiling; reduce heat. Simmer uncovered 5 minutes. Remove from heat; stir in lemon peel and juice. Cool to room temperature. Pour into loaf pan, 9 × 5 × 3 inches. Freeze 3 to 4 hours, stirring every 30 minutes.

Serve in chilled dessert dishes. (If ice is not to be served immediately, cut into ½-inch chunks; place in bowl. Cover and freeze until serving time.)

8 to 10 servings

PER SERVING: Calories 110; Protein 0 g; Carbohydrate 27 g; Fat 0 g; Cholesterol 0 mg; Sodium 10 mg

MERINGUE-TOPPED APPLES
ÄPFEL MIT MERINGUE (<u>ahp</u>-f'l mit meh-ring)

This Swiss classic is best made with tart apples, which will contrast nicely with the sweet meringue and, as a rule, don't seem to become as mushy when cooked. The French influence here is seen in the use of Calvados, a dry fruit brandy made from Normandy-grown apples.

4 tart cooking apples, pared and cut into thin slices
3 tablespoons margarine or butter, melted
2 tablespoons sugar
¼ cup raisins or currants
1 tablespoon Calvados or applejack
3 egg whites
¼ teaspoon cream of tartar
¼ cup sugar

Arrange apples in greased square baking dish, 8 × 8 × 2 inches. Pour margarine over apples; sprinkle with 2 tablespoons sugar, the raisins and Calvados. Cover and cook in 350° oven until apples are tender, about 30 minutes.

Beat egg whites and cream of tartar on medium speed until foamy. Beat in ¼ cup sugar, 1 tablespoon at a time; continue beating on high speed until stiff and glossy. Spread over apples. Bake until meringue is golden brown, 12 to 15 minutes.

6 to 8 servings

PER SERVING: Calories 215; Protein 2 g; Carbohydrate 38 g; Fat 6 g; Cholesterol 0 mg; Sodium 110 mg

PORTUGUESE POACHED MERINGUE

PUDIM MOLOKOV (poo-<u>deem</u> mo-lo-<u>kov</u>)

This gently cooked meringue ring is served with a sweet-tart, sunset-colored apricot sauce.

Apricot Sauce (right)
Sugar
10 egg whites
½ teaspoon cream of tartar
1 cup sugar

Prepare Apricot Sauce. Grease 12-cup bundt cake pan; sprinkle with sugar. Heat oven to 350°. Beat egg whites and cream of tartar in large mixer bowl until foamy. Beat in sugar, 1 tablespoon at a time; continue beating until soft peaks form. Pour into pan; cut gently through batter with metal spatula.

Place pan in shallow roasting pan on oven rack. Pour very hot water (1 inch) into roasting pan. Bake until top is golden brown and meringue is set, about 45 minutes.

Immediately loosen meringue from edges of pan; invert on heatproof serving plate. Cool 30 minutes; refrigerate uncovered no longer than 24 hours. Cut meringue into wedges; serve with Apricot Sauce.

18 servings

PER SERVING: Calories 80 ; Protein 2 g; Carbohydrate 18 g; Fat 0 g; Cholesterol 0 mg; Sodium 35 mg

Portuguese Poached Meringue

APRICOT SAUCE

1 package (6 ounces) dried apricots (about 1 cup)
2 cups water
2 to 3 tablespoons sugar to taste
½ teaspoon ground cinnamon
1 teaspoon lemon juice

Heat apricots, water, sugar and cinnamon to boiling; reduce heat. Cover and simmer until apricots are tender, about 15 minutes.

Place apricot mixture and lemon juice in blender container. Cover and blend on medium-high speed, stopping blender occasionally to scrape sides, until smooth, about 15 seconds. Stir in 1 to 2 tablespoons water, if necessary, until of desired consistency. Refrigerate until chilled, about 3 hours.

WHISKEY FOG

The whiskies and the heavy mists of the British Isles are legendary. This cloudlike sweet is layered with gently flavored cream and crisp macaroon crumbs.

2 cups chilled whipping cream
2 tablespoons sugar
2 tablespoons Irish whiskey or Scotch whisky
½ teaspoon vanilla
¾ cup coarsely crushed crisp macaroons

Beat whipping cream, sugar, whiskey and vanilla in chilled bowl until stiff. Fold in macaroons. Spoon into dessert dishes. Sprinkle with additional crushed macaroons if desired.

8 servings

PER SERVING: Calories 270; Protein 2 g; Carbohydrate 16 g; Fat 22 g; Cholesterol 65 mg; Sodium 100 mg

FROSTED MERINGUE WITH KIWIFRUIT

PAVLOVA (pahv-loh-vah)

This Australian dessert celebrates the brilliance of ballerina Anna Pavlova; it was created especially to welcome her during her tour.

3 egg whites
¼ teaspoon cream of tartar
½ teaspoon vanilla
¾ cup sugar
1 cup chilled whipping cream
2 tablespoons sugar
3 kiwifruit*, peeled and sliced

Heat oven to 225°. Line bottom of round layer pan, 8 or 9 × 1½ inches, with brown paper. Beat egg whites and cream of tartar until foamy; add vanilla. Beat in ¾ cup sugar, 1 tablespoon at a time; continue beating until stiff and glossy. Spread in pan. Bake 1½ hours. Turn off oven; leave meringue in oven with door closed 1 hour. Finish cooling meringue at room temperature.

Loosen edge of meringue with knife; hit pan sharply on table to remove meringue. Invert onto plate (Meringue will be crumbly on bottom and around edge.) Remove paper. Beat whipping cream and 2 tablespoons sugar in chilled bowl until stiff. Frost side and top of meringue, building up edge slightly. Arrange kiwifruit slices on top. Cut into wedges to serve.

8 servings

*1½ to 2 cups fresh strawberries, cut into halves, raspberries, blueberries, or a combination of these can be substituted for the kiwifruit.

PER SERVING: Calories 195; Protein 2 g; Carbohydrate 27 g; Fat 9 g; Cholesterol 35 mg; Sodium 40 mg

CANDIED WALNUTS WITH CREAM

NUECES CARAMELIZADAS CON NATA
(nway-sehs kah-rah-meh-lee-zah-dahs kohn nah-tah)

Clouds of whipped cream sprinkled with a walnut praline create one version of paradise, Andalucia style. It would be difficult to improve on this simple Spanish dessert.

1 cup walnut pieces
⅓ cup sugar
1 cup chilled whipping cream
1 tablespoon sugar
1 teaspoon vanilla

Cook walnuts and ⅓ cup sugar in 10-inch skillet over low heat, stirring constantly, until sugar is melted and walnuts are coated. Immediately pour mixture onto aluminum foil-covered cookie sheet; carefully spread in single layer. Cool; break apart. Store at room temperature.

Beat remaining ingredients in chilled bowl until stiff. Spoon whipped cream into 6 goblets or dessert dishes. Sprinkle with sugar-coated nuts.

6 servings

PER SERVING: Calories 310; Protein 3 g; Carbohydrate 18 g; Fat 25 g; Cholesterol 45 mg; Sodium 15 mg

RUSSIAN EASTER DESSERT

PASHKA (pahsh-kah)

Russian Orthodox Christians created this dessert of sweetened cheese in celebration of Easter. It is packed into a mold and left in the refrigerator to drain off the whey. The result is a smooth, creamy dessert, studded with chopped almonds and candied fruit, that can be beautifully decorated when unmolded.

3 egg yolks, slightly beaten
1 cup whipping cream
¾ cup sugar
⅛ teaspoon salt
1 teaspoon vanilla
6 cups small-curd creamed cottage cheese
¼ cup margarine or butter, softened
½ cup chopped mixed candied fruit
¼ cup finely chopped blanched almonds

Mix egg yolks and whipping cream in heavy 2-quart saucepan. Stir in sugar and salt. Cook over low heat, stirring constantly, until mixture just coats a metal spoon, 12 to 15 minutes. Remove from heat; stir in vanilla. Place saucepan in cold water until custard is cool. (If custard curdles, beat with hand beater until smooth.)

Place 3 cups of the cottage cheese and 2 tablespoons of the margarine in blender container. Cover and blend on medium speed, stopping blender occasionally to scrape sides, until smooth. Repeat with remaining cottage cheese and margarine. Stir custard into cheese mixture until smooth. Stir in candied fruit and almonds.

Line a 2-quart non-clay flower pot (with opening in bottom) with double layer dampened cheesecloth. Pour cheese mixture into pot; fold ends of cheesecloth over top. Place pot in shallow pan; place weights on top. Refrigerate 12 to 24 hours, pouring off any liquid that accumulates in pan.

To serve, unmold onto serving plate; remove cheesecloth. Garnish as desired with additional candied fruit and blanched almonds. Refrigerate any remaining dessert.

12 to 14 servings

PER SERVING: Calories 300; Protein 15 g; Carbohydrate 22 g; Fat 22 g; Cholesterol 90 mg; Sodium 520 mg

CARDAMOM FUDGE

SHEER PAYRA (sheer pay-rah)

Here is a rich Afghan candy, one brought out to celebrate festive occasions. The exotic flavor of cardamom is enhanced by crunchy walnuts and pistachios.

2 cups sugar
⅔ cup milk
¼ teaspoon salt
2 tablespoons light corn syrup
2 tablespoons margarine or butter
½ teaspoon ground cardamom
¼ cup chopped walnuts
¼ cup chopped pistachios

Cook sugar, milk, salt and corn syrup in 2-quart saucepan over medium heat, stirring constantly, until sugar is dissolved. Cook, stirring occasionally, to 240° on candy thermometer or until small amount of mixture dropped into very cold water forms a soft ball that flattens when removed from water; remove from heat.

Add margarine. Cool mixture to 120° without stirring. (Bottom of pan will be lukewarm.) Add cardamom; beat vigorously and continuously until candy is thick and no longer glossy, 5 to 10 minutes. (Mixture will hold its shape when dropped from spoon.) Quickly stir in nuts. Spread mixture in buttered loaf pan, 9 × 5 × 3 inches; let stand until firm. Cut into 1-inch squares.

32 candies

PER CANDY: Calories 75; Protein 0 g; Carbohydrate 14 g; Fat 2 g; Cholesterol 0 mg; Sodium 30 mg

CHOCOLATE MARZIPAN SLICES

MANDULÁS SZALÁMI (mahn-doo-lash sah-lah-mee)

This Hungarian version of Europe's favorite marzipan is flavored with chocolate throughout.

2 tubes (3½ ounces each) almond paste
2 squares (1 ounce each) semisweet chocolate, melted and cooled
¼ cup chopped almonds
Powdered sugar

Mix almond paste, chocolate and almonds thoroughly. Knead on surface sprinkled with 1 to 2 tablespoons powdered sugar until of uniform color and consistency. Shape into roll, about 6 inches long; roll in powdered sugar.

Wrap in plastic wrap; refrigerate at least 12 hours. Cut roll into ¼-inch slices.

About 2 dozen candies

PER CANDY: Calories 70; Protein 1 g; Carbohydrate 7 g; Fat 4 g; Cholesterol 0 mg; Sodium 5 mg

INTERNATIONAL FOOD TERMS
AND INGREDIENTS

Annatto seed: This rust-colored seed comes from the tropical annatto tree. The seeds are sometimes ground and added to foods to give a bright, yellow color. Alternatively, they may be cooked in fat, then discarded once they have lent their color. Caribbean and southwestern cooking make occasional use of annatto seed.

Antipasto: Literally, the food that is served before the pasta. This is an Italian contribution, a cold or hot appetizer. The most widely popular version of *antipasto* is cold and has come to include meats, vegetables both pickled and fresh and some sort of fish.

Aromatic bitters: This mixture, usually in an alcoholic base, is flavored with bitter roots and aromatic herbs. It is used as a seasoning in mixed drinks, stewed dishes and, somewhat archaically, as a tonic.

Aspic: This is a savory jelly that is solid at room temperature or when chilled. As a liquid, it is spooned over meat, fish or poultry for an elegant glaze that becomes firm with refrigeration. Years ago, aspic was made from broth that was strong enough to "set up" or gel; that is, the broth contained enough gelatin from the bones used to make it that it became solid. Today it is common to add commercial gelatin to a broth—or other liquid—when making an aspic. Most, though not all, aspics are clear; there are tomato and other vegetable aspics.

Baba: This French cake, leavened with yeast, is soaked in a sugar syrup flavored with rum, kirsch or other liqueur after baking. Most *babas* contain raisins or other dried fruits. The open texture of the cake helps it to absorb the syrup.

Basmati rice: A very narrow and long Indian rice, basmati is a prized grain. It has a distinctive, pungent fragrance and gentle, faintly nutty flavor. It grows well in the Himalayan foothills.

Béchamel: This is the classic French white sauce, made by adding milk to a cooked paste of equal amounts butter and flour.

Bok choy: This variety of Chinese cabbage has long stalks and tender, flavorful leaves.

Bombe: A bombe is a French molded dessert. It is made by lining the mold with one flavor of ice cream and freezing that until it is firm. Then, another flavor is used to line the first, and so on, using as many kinds of ice cream as desired.

Borscht: There are many variations on the theme of *borscht*, but what they have in common is the inclusion of beets. There are hot borschts, cold borschts, sweet and sour borschts, beefy borschts. One classic favorite is made with beef broth and served hot. A delicious garnish for almost any borscht is a dollop of sour cream and freshly snipped dill weed.

BOUQUET GARNI: Another French culinary invention, the bouquet garni is a bundle of herbs added to a stew while it cooks and is removed, intact, before serving. The classic combination of herbs includes parsley, thyme and bay leaf. The herbs may be tied together with thread or string, wrapped in cheesecloth or enclosed in a tea ball.

BRIOCHE: This French yeast bread, made with generous quantities of eggs and butter, has a delicate, feathery texture.

CALVADOS: This apple brandy, which ranges in color from pale gold to brown, is named for the French town, in the Normandy region, where it is supposed first to have been distilled. Applejack is a reasonable American substitution.

CALZONE: A savory turnover, calzone is an Italian pastry that resembles a pizza folded in half. The fillings may include cheese, ham, sausage, onions, capers and olives.

CHAYOTE: This smooth, pale green squash is shaped something like a pear. Chayote is a relative of melons and gourds, and it frequently appears under other names: mirliton, christophine and vegetable pear.

CHILI: Chilies are members of the *Capsicum* family of peppers native to South America. The many varieties of peppers vary in strength, from mild to extremely hot. Chilies are not related to the black pepper (*Piper nigrum*) from India.

CHUTNEY: Chutneys are sweet-sour, richly spiced vegetable or fruit relishes of East Indian origin. Chutney is a condiment traditionally served with curries.

CANNELLINI: These white Italian beans are similar to white kidney beans.

CAPER: Capers are the brined flower buds of a shrub that grows around the Mediterranean. Capers enliven sauces and are especially delicious with many fish and veal dishes.

CARDAMOM: Cardamom seeds can be purchased still in their little pods. These dried green, brown or white aromatic pods come from an East Indian plant and are extremely fragrant. Cardamom is used in curries and sauces and adds a mysterious and warm flavor to tea, coffee, pastries and sweets. When cardamom pods, whole or slightly crushed, are added, they are fished out and discarded before the food is served.

CELLOPHANE NOODLES (BEAN THREADS): These Southeast Asian noodles are made from mung beans. They are dramatically translucent and especially nice when added to clear soups.

CHORIZO: A spicy, garlic-flavored pork sausage, chorizo is commonly used in Spanish and Mexican cooking.

CILANTRO: The pungent, citric leaves of fresh coriander are widely used in Oriental, Middle Eastern, Indian, Mexican and Portuguese cooking. The leaves are similar in appearance to flat-leaf parsley, but they are more rounded.

COQUILLE: This is the French word for "shell." It has come to mean the shell-shaped individual baking dishes called for in some seafood recipes, but true scallop shells—uncracked and well cleaned—may be used for serving, too.

COUSCOUS: Ground durum wheat (semolina) that has been moistened and then rolled in flour is couscous. Couscous is also the name of a stew, served primarily in Morocco, Algeria and Tunisia, that is accompanied by a side dish of steamed couscous grains.

CURRY: Curry powder is really an elaborate blend of spices associated with Indian cooking. The name *curry* comes from the name of one ingredient in particular, the cari leaf. Originally the spice mixture had another purpose in addition to seasoning food: it was thought to have medicinal or antiseptic qualities. Most commercial curry powders include turmeric, chili, ginger and clove.

DAL: This is a general, all-embracing term for all plain Indian legume preparations.

DEMITASSE: In French, a "half cup." Espresso, very strong coffee always drunk black, is served in these small cups.

DOLMA: The Greeks stuff cabbage and grape leaves and even some scooped-out vegetables. *Dolma* refers to the stuffed presentation.

DRIED SHRIMP: These small dried shellfish have an intensely fishy flavor. They are used whole or ground in Oriental, Latin American and African cooking.

EN BROCHETTE: The French call foods that are threaded on skewers before cooking *en brochette.*

FARINA: This is a cereal made from the flour or meal of whole wheat, barley, potato flour or other whole grains.

FAVA BEANS: These are also known as dried broad beans. They vary in size and have approximately the same shape as lima beans. These brown beans require a lengthy soak; often three to four hours is recommended.

FENNEL: This is an anise-flavored, bulbous vegetable with feathery fronds sprouting from its top. Rather common in the United States today, it is of Mediterranean origin.

FENUGREEK: Used frequently in Greek and Egyptian cooking, fenugreek seed tastes somewhat bitter.

FETA CHEESE: This is a Greek cheese usually made of goat's milk. It is distinguished by its strong, salty flavor and crumbly consistency. Often it is sold in brine, to keep it moist.

FISH SAUCE: Made from salted fish, this brown sauce is a seasoning to use sparingly. Sometimes sold as *nuac nam*, it is used throughout Southeast Asia, particularly in Thailand and Vietnam, to add a seafood flavor to a variety of dishes. It is related to the ancient Roman seasoning *garum*, the liquid skimmed from a vat of fermenting fish.

FIVE SPICE POWDER: A great Chinese favorite, this powder is a fragrant and pungent blend of spices, most often used in meat and poultry dishes. Five spice powder is best used sparingly. It is made up of equal measures of ground cinnamon, clove, anise and Szechuan or black pepper.

FLAT-LEAF PARSLEY: There is debate over which variety of parsley—curly or flat-leaf—has stronger flavor. Flat-leaf parsley comes to us from the Middle East.

FRITTATA: This is an Italian omelet, generally containing as much in the way of vegetables as eggs.

FROMAGE: "Cheese," in French.

GARAM MASALA: Indian cooks prepare their own highly individual ground spice mixtures, but *garam masala* may be purchased as a commercial spice blend, too. It usually contains cardamom, cinnamon, clove and black pepper and may go on to include any number of additional spices. See also page 40.

GHEE: The Indians clarify their butter so that it will not burn over high heat. (The French are known for this also.) Clarified butter is nothing more than butter that is gently heated so that the white milk solids separate from the clear, yellow liquid. The solids are discarded.

GNOCCHI: Made from potato or any number of flours, gnocchi are Italian dumplings.

GOULASH: In Hungary, thick vegetable stews with beef or veal featuring the pungent and comforting flavor of paprika are called *goulash*.

GROUNDNUT: This is simply the old-fashioned name for a peanut, making reference to the fact that the nuts are harvested from the soil.

HOISIN SAUCE: This is a sweet brown sauce used in Oriental cooking.

HON DASHI: This stock is used in Japanese cooking. It is flavored with seaweed and dried bonito, a tuna-like fish that has been brined.

HORS D' OEUVRE: The French counterpart to the Italian *antipasto, hors d' oeuvre* means "aside from the main event" and refers to an appetizer.

JUNIPER BERRY: The purple fruit of an evergreen that grows wild, juniper berries start out green and then ripen to violet. Juniper bushes are common in the American wilds as well as along the southern Alpine slopes and in Scandinavia. The berries perfume gin, sauerkraut and game dishes.

KASSERI CHEESE: This is a hard, white sheep's milk cheese from Greece. The flavor is mild and salty; the texture is smooth, even and slightly dry.

KEFALOTIRI CHEESE: Here is another hard, Greek sheep's milk cheese. It is much like Kasseri cheese, but it is sharper in flavor.

KOFTA: This dish is favored in the Middle East, North Africa and Asia. Highly seasoned minced lamb, veal or beef is molded into bite-size pieces and grilled, often on skewers, like a kabob.

KULICH: This is a sweet Russian bread traditionally baked at Eastertide.

LEFSE: A potato-based fried flatbread, *lefse* is popular in Norway.

LEGUME: A vegetable bearing its seed in pods is a legume. Beans, peas and lentils are examples of legumes.

LEMON GRASS: This is a tall, woody-stemmed, gray-green grass that resembles an onion but that has an astonishing lemony flavor. It is an essential ingredient in many Thai dishes and can be found dried and, increasingly, fresh.

LITCHI: For years most of the litchis (or "litchi nuts," as they were frequently known) to be found in the United States were imported from China. Now litchis are beginning to take root in the United States. Litchis are sweet, juicy, white-fleshed tropical fruits that are canned in heavy syrup. They can, however, be found fresh and no amount of imagination can accurately predict the pleasure of biting into a fresh litchi—right through the crisp brown shell—for the first time.

MARZIPAN: This European confection is made from almond paste, powdered sugar and, sometimes, kirsch (a clear brandy made from cherries). As a candy, it is often tinted and shaped to form diminutive fruits, vegetables and animals. In pastry making, marzipan may be rolled out and used between layers of cake or other pastry.

MIRIN: A sweet Japanese cooking wine, it is often used in dipping sauces and glazes.

MOCHA: Meaning "coffee-flavored," *mocha* has come to also describe the combination of chocolate and coffee.

MUSHROOM:

Black Chinese mushrooms: These are meaty mushrooms characterized by smoky flavor and chewy texture. Black Chinese mushrooms are dried and must be soaked in hot water until soft before they can be used. The hard stems are discarded.

Cloud ears: Known also as *wood ears, tree ears* and *mo er* mushrooms, cloud ears have an irregular shape and are bought dried. They are a type of tree fungus, popularly used in Oriental cooking. Cloud ears tend to absorb the flavor of the liquid in which they are cooked, adding a whiff of their own aroma. As with Black Chinese mushrooms, the stems are not eaten.

Oyster mushrooms: Mild Oriental mushrooms with oval, gray caps and white stems, oyster mushrooms are available fresh, dried and canned.

Porcini: These mushrooms are called *porcini* by the Italians, *cèpes* by the French. Fresh, they have a hearty, chewy quality; dried, their woodsy flavor becomes even more intense.

NOPALITOS: The broad, flat leaves of the *nopal*, or prickly pear cactus, are called *nopalitos* by the Mexicans. The thorns are removed and the flesh is boiled until tender. *Nopalitos* are a nice, somewhat crisp addition to salads.

ORANGE FLOWER WATER: This is the liquid distilled from fresh orange blossoms. It is used as a flavoring principally in Middle Eastern countries, but France and Mexico in particular make use of it in baking sweets. It has a delicate, floral flavor. See also page 318.

OXTAIL: The tail of a beef cow or steer is known as an oxtail. The British are renowned for their oxtail preparations. Oxtails make an excellent base for soups and stews because they have a naturally high gelatin content.

OYSTER SAUCE: This rich Oriental sauce is strong, so a little goes a long way. The principal ingredients are soy sauce and oysters.

PILAF: When rice or other grains are cooked and stirred briefly in fat and then cooked in broth,

the result is a pilaf. Pilafs (also known as *pilaus*) are not necessarily side dishes. The addition of meat, fish or poultry can make for a substantial dish.

PINE NUT: These small, creamy, tear-shaped kernels are the seeds of the stone pine cone. They have a sweet flavor and oily consistency and are commonly used in sauces, salads, vegetable dishes and as a garnish for cakes and cookies.

PIROZHKI: These savory Russian pastries are often filled with cabbage or meat.

PLANTAIN: Relative of the banana, the plantain is larger and not fully ripe until its peel is quite thoroughly black. Plantains are higher in starch and lower in sugar than bananas, too. Latin countries commonly use the plantain as a starchy vegetable.

POLENTA: The Italians call their cornmeal mush *polenta*. It is delicious with butter, salt and pepper, or with cheese stirred in while the *polenta* is hot.

PRALINE: Caramelized sugar and almonds together are *praline*. Praline is usually crushed and stirred into creams or sprinkled between pastry layers and over desserts as a garnish. In the American South, pralines are a classic plantation candy more frequently made with pecans than almonds.

PUFF PASTRY: The *pâte feuillettée* of the French bakes into incomparably flaky layers. It is made by folding butter over and over again between layers of dough. It is the process of alternately folding and turning butter in the dough that produces flaky layers that puff when baked. Commercial puff pastry can be bought, frozen, in many supermarkets.

PULSE: Pulses are the protein-rich seeds of legume plants, including peas, lentils, beans and chick-peas. When they are combined with whole grains, pulses provide complete protein that otherwise is available only in meat and fish.

PURI: This puffy, deep-fried bread is an Indian favorite.

ROSE WATER: Middle Eastern taste is particularly partial to this gentle flavor. Rose water is distilled from fresh, unblemished rose petals. It is available in specialty stores and pharmacies. See also page 350.

SAKE: A clear, intensely alcoholic Japanese rice wine.

SALSA: This is the general name for sauces used in Mexican-based cooking. *Salsa* usually refers to a sauce made from fresh tomatoes, onions, hot chili peppers and garlic.

SAVARIN: The French savarin is essentially a *baba* that is baked in a special savarin mold (usually a ring mold).

SEMOLINA: This coarsely ground durum wheat is a basic grain in many foreign kitchens. Couscous is made from semolina.

SOBA: A Japanese buckwheat noodle, *soba* is often used in soups.

SPÄTZLE: In Germany, a dumpling mixture is forced through a large-mesh sieve or colander into boiling liquid to make free-form *spätzle*. The Pennsylvania Dutch of the Middle Atlantic states are known for their way with *spätzle*. *Spätzle* are sometimes cooked right in the broth they'll be served in.

STILTON CHEESE: This British blue-veined cheese is moist and crumbly. It is a superb cheese for eating all by itself.

STOUT: Ale brewed from roasted malt and hops is known as stout. It has a darker color, higher alcoholic content and stronger flavor than beer.

TAHINI: Sesame seed is ground to a thick, richly flavored paste known as *tahini*.

TAMALE: In Mexico, meat or fish may be combined with a moist cornmeal mixture that is wrapped in cornhusks to form neat little packages. The cornhusk packages—tamales—are then steamed or boiled.

TAMARIND: This sweet and sour, acidic fruit is native to India. Its fibrous brown pods must be soaked in water before the tamarind pulp can be coaxed from the pods. Tamarind is used in curries, chutneys and as a flavoring in drinks.

TERRINE: *Terrine* is the French name for a ceramic loaf pan in which vegetable, fish, poultry or meat pâtés are cooked. A pâté cooked in such a pan is known as a terrine, too.

TOFU: Soy bean curd, cholesterol-free, is a mainstay in some forms of Oriental cooking.

TORTILLA: These unleavened flatbread rounds of Mexico are made with cornmeal or flour.

VINDALOO: Of Portuguese-Indian heritage, vindaloos are dishes with a fiery reputation. Usually vindaloo features meat that has been marinated either in wine or vinegar, with garlic and other spices.

WASABI: Wasabi is a Japanese condiment, available both as powder and paste. With its intense punch, it is similar to horseradish.

YELLOW BEAN PASTE: Used in oriental cooking, yellow bean paste is commonly found in Oriental markets; sometimes it is referred to as *bean sauce*. Yellow bean paste consists of soy beans, salt, flour and sugar. It is used to enrich dishes with its mild bean flavor.

REGIONAL INDEX

GENERAL INDEX

Betty Crocker

80 POINTS

SAVE these Betty
Crocker Points and redeem
them for big savings on hundreds of kitchen, home, gift and
children's items! For catalog, send 50¢
with your name and address to: General
Mills, P.O. Box 5389, Mpls., MN 55460.
Redeemable with cash in USA before May 1999.
Void where prohibited, taxed or regulated. **S**

CUT OUT AND SAVE